Fighter Command
1936–1968

Fighter Command
1936–1968

AN OPERATIONAL AND HISTORICAL RECORD

KEN DELVE

Pen & Sword
AVIATION

First published in Great Britain in 2007 by
PEN & SWORD AVIATION
an imprint of
Pen & Sword Books Ltd
47 Church Street
Barnsley
South Yorkshire
S70 2AS

Copyright © Ken Delve, 2007

ISBN 1 84415 613 9

Typeset by Concept, Huddersfield, West Yorkshire
Printed and bound in Great Britain by
CPI UK

Pen & Sword Books Ltd incorporates the Imprints of
Pen & Sword Aviation, Pen & Sword Maritime, Pen & Sword Military,
Wharncliffe Local History, Pen & Sword Select,
Pen & Sword Military Classics and Leo Cooper.

For a complete list of Pen & Sword titles please contact
PEN & SWORD BOOKS LIMITED
47 Church Street, Barnsley, South Yorkshire, S70 2AS, England.
E-mail: enquiries@pen-and-sword.co.uk
Website: www.pen-and-sword.co.uk

Contents

Fighter Command Badge

'In front of a Portcullis a sword erect' (elements of the Badge were subsequently used by Strike Command). The sword is indicative of the Command's offensive operations and the Portcullis symbolises its defensive role; this duality it also shown in the motto of 'Offence Defence'. The Badge was approved by in March 1945.

CHAPTER ONE

Development, Roles and History

For a few short months in late 1940, Fighter Command of the Royal Air Force was pitted against the might of the German *Luftwaffe* in a struggle that would help determine the course of the Second World War. The Battle of Britain will always remain the Command's 'Finest Hour' but it comprised only a few months of a war that lasted nearly six years – and Fighter Command was involved in active operations for much of that time.

As with all history the benefits of hindsight and access to previously classified documentary sources has to be balanced by the researcher's removal in time and context from the period under study. To truly understand decisions, policies, actions and attitudes is all but impossible. This book covers the entire period of Fighter Command from its origin in 1936 to its demise – into Strike Command – in 1968. Whilst all periods of the Command are covered it is inevitable that the major focus is on the period of World War Two. The book has been divided into five main sections: an Introduction and Overview, which sets the framework for the development of Fighter Command and includes both policy and politics; an Operations chapter, which focuses on the combat operations of the Command; a brief look at each of the operational Groups; an overview of aircrew training; and, finally, an Aircraft chapter, looking in chronological sequence at all operational aircraft types. The annexes provide a variety of historical data.

The chapters frequently quote extracts from the Operational Record Books (ORB) of various squadrons; these have been selected as typical of the type of missions being flown. It would be impossible in a book of this sort to research every squadron record for Fighter Command and there are similar accounts, and perhaps better ones, in many of the other ORBs – if a reader believes 'his' squadron has been ignored I can assure him that that was not the intent!

Origins and doctrine

Fighter Command was formed on 14 July 1936, under the command of Air Marshal Sir Hugh Dowding, as part of a general reorganisation of the RAF, and headquartered at Bentley Priory, Middlesex. This reorganisation saw the Metropolitan Air Force split into three operational Commands (Fighter, Bomber and Training). At the time of its formation Fighter Command's equipment comprised a variety of biplane fighters, the most modern of which was the Gloster Gladiator. As the first RAF fighter with eight machine-guns and an enclosed cockpit, the Gladiator represented a major advance on previous types and despite its obvious limitations was able to distinguish itself during the Battle of Britain.

Since the early 1930s two key issues had plagued RAF planners – the percentage of bomber to fighters in the overall strength of the RAF and the types of weapons they should carry. There had been a glimmer of hope in the early 1920s, a period of doldrums for the RAF when its very existence as an independent service was under

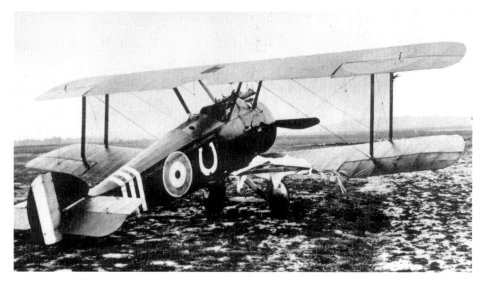

Fighter doctrine and tactics were developed in the latter part of World War One, with aircraft such as the Sopwith Camel.

question and its main 'strength' was in remote parts of the Empire such as Mesopotamia. In April 1923 the Steel-Bartholomew Committee on the Air Defence of Great Britain led to Government approval in June of a plan for a Home Defence air strength of 52 squadrons, to include 17 fighter squadrons 'with as little delay as possible'. As a percentage of the total strength the fighter element was poor – but this was the period when air strategists were convinced that bombers were the way to win wars. In December

Map of the 1923 Air Defence Plan.

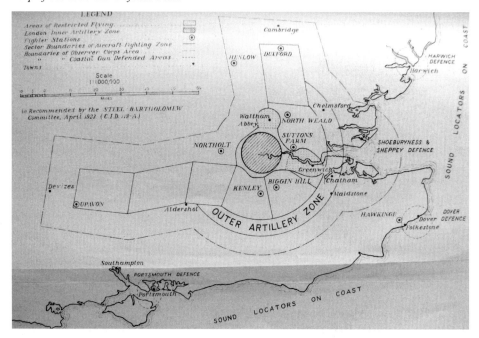

The Siskin was one of the inter-war agile but poorly-armed fighters equipping the RAF's fighter force.

1925 the Government's interpretation of 'as soon as possible' changed to 'by 1935–1936. Air Marshal Sir John Salmond had taken over as Air-Officer-Commanding Air Defence of Great Britain in January that year and he had firm views on air defence, which in his view – and his experience from World War One – included searchlights and anti-aircraft guns. In this study of Fighter Command only occasional reference is made to the other elements that made up the UK's air defence network, primarily because they were independent Commands. It is worth noting that the 'active defence' planned for the UK, and to be in place by 1939, comprised 2,232 heavy anti-aircraft guns, 4,700 searchlights

When the Gladiator entered service it was a major improvement on the previous biplanes but was still far from being a modern fighter, although it remained in front-line service with the RAF in the early part of the war.

and 50 squadrons of fighter aircraft. However, on the outbreak of war there were only 695 heavy and 253 light anti-aircraft guns and 2,700 searchlights.

In December 1929 and again in May 1933 the Government slipped the programme back, the latter revision taking it to 1939–1940. This reluctance did not change until 1934, a year after Hitler had come to power in Germany and there was a realisation that peace in Europe was by no means a certainty. The next few years saw a change of attitude and a series of Expansion Plans, albeit still dominated by strategic bombing.

The 'bomber first' mentality that had dominated the Expansion Plans of the early 1930s did not change until Scheme M, which was approved in November 1938 (after the Munich Crisis), with an effective date for completion of March 1942. This scheme envisaged 163 squadrons to be based in the UK, of which 64 were to be fighter squadrons (14 of these being Auxiliary Air Force), each with an establishment of 16 aircraft. The table below presents the details for the Plans put forward between 1934 and 1938.

RAF Expansion Schemes, 1934–1938					
Scheme	Approved	Effective	Squadrons	Fighter squadrons	UE fighter squadron
A	18 Jul 1934	31 Mar 1939	84	28+5	12
C	21 May 1935	31 Mar 1937	123	35+5	12
F	25 Feb 1936	31 Mar 1939	124	30+5	14
H	14 Jan 1937	31 Mar 1939	145	34+9	14
J	22 Dec 1937	Summer 1941	154	38+9	14
K	14 Mar 1938	31 Mar 1941	145	38+9	14
L	27 Apr 1938	31 Mar 1940	141	38+9	16
M	7 Nov 1938	31 Mar 1942	163	50+14	16

Note: Approved – Date the scheme was approved by the Cabinet; Effective – Date at which the scheme should be complete; Squadrons – Total home-based squadrons; Fighter squadrons – Regular squadrons + auxiliary squadrons; UE fighter squadron – Aircraft establishment.

This was of course only a paper air force; the desire to have 64 squadrons, each with 16 aircraft – and with the requisite pilots, ground staff, equipment and airfields – had to be transferred into reality. That meant taking short cuts with the aircraft types, 'form a squadron with whatever was to hand and re-equip it later' and pressure to find pilots, and train them in the minimum period of time. Both of these aspects would cause the Command problems.

Role of the Fighter

The concept of the fighter aircraft had been born in World War One, when manoeuvrability was one of the key performance criteria; for the Royal Flying Corps/ Royal Air Force, the experience with monoplanes had been an unhappy one and the war ended with small, single-seat highly-agile biplanes, armed with two 0.303 in guns, as the standard day fighter. The situation did not change over the next 20 years and the RAF's fighter squadrons continued to fly a range of delightful little fighters that by the late 1920s had all but lost touch with the realities of a future air war – but the RAF's doctrine, tactics and training had also not changed. It was not until the early 1930s that a more realistic specification for a future fighter was issued. However, Specification F10/35 still encapsulated the 1930's fighter doctrine; the following extracts illustrate the major points.

Specification F10/35. Requirements for Single-Engine Single-Seater Day and Night Fighter

General. The Air Staff require a single-engine single-seater day and night fighter which can fulfil the following conditions:

    a. Have a speed in excess of the contemporary bomber of at least 40 mph at 15,000 ft.

    b. Have a number of forward firing machine guns that can produce the maximum hitting power possible in the short space of time available for one attack.

Performance.

    a. Speed. The maximum possible and not less than 310 mph at 15,000 ft at maximum power with the highest possible between 5,000 and 15,000 ft.

    b. Climb. The best possible to 20,000 ft but secondary to speed and hitting power.

    c. Service ceiling. Not less than 30,000 ft is desirable.

    d. Endurance. ¼ hour at maximum power at sea level, plus one hour at maximum power at which engine can be run continuously at 15,000 ft. This should provide ½ hour at maximum power at which engine can be run continuously (for climb, etc), plus one hour at the most economical speed at 15,000 ft (for patrol), plus ¼ hour at maximum power at 15,000 ft (for attack).

Armament. Not less than 6 guns, but 8 guns are desirable. These should be located outside the airscrew disc. Reloading in the air is not required and the guns should be fired by electrical or means other than Bowden wire. It is contemplated that some or all of these guns should be mounted to permit a degree of elevation and traverse with some form of control from the pilot's seat.

Ammunition. 300 rounds per gun if 8 guns are provided and 400 rounds per gun if only 6 guns are installed.

View.

    a. The upper hemisphere must be so far as possible unobstructed to the view of the pilot to facilitate search and attack. A good view for formation flying is required.

    b. A field of view of about 10 degrees downwards from the horizontal line of sight over the nose is required for locating the target.

Handling.

    a. A high degree of manoeuvrability at high speeds is not required but good control at low speeds is essential.

    b. The aircraft must be a steady firing platform.

It is interesting to look at how the fighter requirement had changed during the 1930s as this explains the development of both the aircraft's capabilities and the tactical doctrine. During the 1930s the basic concepts were still those that had been developed in the latter years of World War One; with no significant combat experience in the 1920s and in the absence of conflict (and funding) no appreciable development of technology or tactics this was not really surprising. The main fighter specification that eventually led to the new generation of fighters was F7/30 for a 'Single-Seater Day and Night Fighter.' This Specification was dated October 1931 and the General Requirements paragraph included statements such as 'a satisfactory fighting view is essential and designers should consider the advantages offered in this respect by the low-wing monoplane or pusher.' The main requirements for the aircraft are:

    a. Highest possible rate of climb.
    b. Highest possible speed at 15,000 ft.
    c. Fighting view.
    d. Capability of easy and rapid production in quantity.
    e. Ease of maintenance.

This was a lengthy document and amongst the key provisions was that the 'aircraft must have a high degree of manoeuvrability.' By the time of F10/35 this requirement had been toned down as being 'not required'. The aircraft was to have provision for four 0.303 in Vickers guns and a total of 2,000 rounds of ammunition, with a minimum supply of 400 rounds per gun, as well as being able to carry four 20 lb bombs. It stated that two of the guns were to be in the cockpit, with interrupter gear if required, and the other two in cockpit or wing. There was no requirement for an enclosed cockpit and the pilot's view was a prime concern: 'the pilot's view is to conform as closely as possible to that obtainable in 'pusher' aircraft.' Virtually all of these requirements could be said to apply to an aircraft that suited the latter part of World War One, such as the Sopwith Camel

or Bristol Fighter but with (slightly) improved performance. If the manufacturers had followed these requirements to the letter then the Spitfire and Hurricane might never have been born.

In terms of overall air doctrine the emphasis was on the bomber – the 'war-winning' weapon that will always get through no matter what the defenders try and do, but it was not until the mid 1930s that a fighter specification addressed the problem of shooting down these 'war winners'. Whilst the basic provisions of F7/30 could be said to describe an agile, manoeuvrable fighter, those of F5/34 (dated 16 November 1934) tipped the balance to what is best described as a bomber destroyer. The introduction to this specification stated that: 'the speed excess of a modern fighter over that of a contemporary bomber has so reduced the chance of repeated attacks by the same fighters(s) that it becomes essential to obtain decisive results in the short space of time offered for one attack only. This

Not only the aircraft but also the tactics remained out-of-date into the 1930s; Hawker Demons of 23 Squadron; the Squadron did not re-equip from Demons until December 1938.

Hurricane prototype K5083 flew in November 1935 – the modern age had arrived and 600 had already been ordered 'off the drawing board'.

specification is issued to govern the production of a day fighter in which speed in overtaking the enemy at 15,000 ft, combined with rapid climb to this height, is of primary importance. In conjunction with this performance the maximum hitting power must be aimed at, and 8 machine guns are considered advisable.' No mention here of manoeuvrability; what is needed is to catch the enemy (bomber) and hit him hard in a single attack. All of this was encapsulated in F10/35 but with the added provisions under 'Handling' that emphasised the requirement for the fighter to be 'a steady gun platform' in which a 'high degree of manoeuvrability at high speeds is not required.' Of course, the British were not alone in this fighter theory and in Germany the Bf 110 came from a similar bomber-destroyer requirement. The latter proved a disaster in day fighting and if the RAF's new day fighter had been of a similar ilk then the Battle of Britain would have been short-lived – and lost. Rather than entering the annals as one of the great fighters, a Spitfire to this requirement would have followed the Defiant into the records as a glorious failure (as a day fighter).

From its first flight on 6 November 1935 the Hawker Hurricane showed every indication of being a winner; true it did not have the agility, and some would argue beauty, of the older biplanes but it *looked* the part of a modern fighter – and it had eight guns. An order for 600 was promptly placed and two years later the first Hurricanes entered squadron service, going to 111 Squadron at Northolt to replace Gauntlets; by summer 1939 the number of squadrons had increased to 12 and the Hurricane was the most significant fighter in the Order of Battle. By that time it had been joined by the Supermarine Spitfire, which had first flown five months after the Hurricane but had been slightly slower in production development, the first machines not joining 19 Squadron at Duxford until August 1938. The Spitfire too was an immediate hit with those who saw it and certainly with those who flew it; true, both types had teething troubles and both were lacking what would soon be considered as essential operational equipment, but they were nevertheless an indication of massive progress.

Two other aircraft types entered service with the Command in response to doctrine that called for a 'turret fighter', as a bomber-destroyer, and long-range fighter. It must be remembered too that at this time the threat was perceived as bombers from Germany – bombers that would have to fly such a distance that single-seat fighter escort was not an option. The Boulton Paul Defiant was the turret fighter with its four Brownings in a rear;

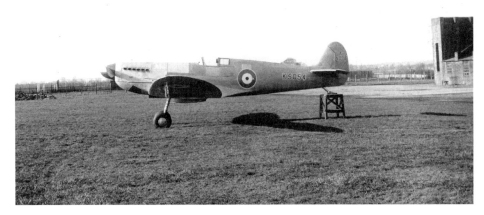

The Spitfire prototype flew in early 1936 but did not enter squadron service until August 1938 – only a year before the war.

the prototype flew in August 1937 and the type entered service with 264 Squadron in December 1939, by which time the concept was already being questioned. The Bristol Blenheim was the long-range fighter and startled the RAF when it flew in 1936, as this private venture for a bomber had far better performance than any of the fighters in service. Fighter Command was duly impressed and an order for 150 Blenheim fighters was placed, the main role being long-range bomber-destroyer, for which a forward-firing four-gun armament pack was added. Hawkinge-based 25 Squadron was first to equip with the Blenheim 1F day fighter, December 1938.

Despite the arrival of new aircraft, the basic tactics remained unchanged and in 1938 doctrine was still based on a limited number of well-rehearsed – but unproven – Fighter Command Attacks, which seemed to be based on the premise that the target, a lumbering

Blenheim of 600 Squadron at Manston mid 1940; the Blenheim entered service with Fighter Command as a long-range fighter – in which role it would have been a disaster.

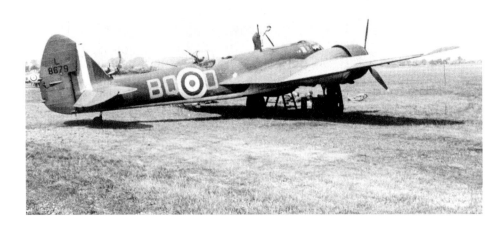

bomber, would fly straight and level while the fighters queued up to attack it! The three main attacks, as directed in 1938, were:

> No. 1 Attack was a succession of single aircraft attacking a single bomber from astern, with Sections stepped down in line astern behind the target. The Section Leader opens fire at 400 yards and maintains his fire on the target at this range until he decides to break away, with the procedure then followed by his Number 2 and Number 3.
> No. 2 Attack was pretty much the same except that the Sections were not stepped down but fanned out to rear and flanks of the bomber.
> No. 3 Attack was an attack by a vic Section of 3 against a vic of three bombers, with the normal plan being for two Sections abreast to engage two groups of bombers, one Section breaking left after completing the attack and the other breaking right.

There were numerous other set attacks for single-engine and turret fighters but these three encapsulate a number of the major problems the fighters were to encounter when the shooting war started. Firstly, the determination that 400 yards was the optimum range to open fire and that the fighter should maintain this range until out of ammunition (or shot down). Whilst there was some variation on this directive, they still involved an error of appreciation of the *real* optimum harmonisation and engagement range. Secondly, the rigid nature of the tactics was totally unsuited to the fluid nature of 'modern' air combat. These lessons were soon to be learnt.

War almost came in autumn 1938 with the so-called Munich Crisis; if it had done so then it would have found Fighter Command in a parlous state in terms of aircraft and its Control and Reporting (C&R) organisation. The Command needed the extra year that came following Prime Minister Neville Chamberlain's meeting with Adolf Hitler and the

Catterick March 1940, Blenheim 219 Squadron; although the Blenheims saw some service as day fighters it was in the night role that they became an important element of Fighter Command.

now infamous 'peace in our time' agreement. During that year more modern fighters entered service and their pilots gained experience, the C&R organisation grew in size and experience and the airfield building programme started in earnest.

Control and Reporting – and integrated defence

There is one line in the 1965 'Battle of Britain' film where Dowding is asked if he is 'trusting in radar and praying to God', to which he replied that he was 'trusting in God and praying for radar'. It is a well-established part of the Battle of Britain story that radar was the secret weapon that saved the day. How true is this?

The early 1930's British Air Defence Plan was based upon that employed during the First World War and comprised an Aircraft Fighting Zone 15 miles wide and 150 miles long, from Duxford and around London to Devizes in Wiltshire. This was divided into

ten sections, each 15 miles wide and with one or more dedicated day fighter squadrons, with associated searchlights and anti-aircraft guns. There was an additional ring of searchlights and guns around London. The Aircraft Zone was positioned 35 miles from the coast, a distance based upon the time it would take the fighter to climb to 14,000 ft. Initial detection of raiders depended upon visual sighting by the Observer Corps, plus a limited number of 'acoustic mirror devices'. Each HQ received information from the observation units and displayed raids on a plotting table, thus allowing the overall picture of the air situation to be seen by the controller. However, it was not until new radios, such as the TR.9, were introduced in 1932 that reasonable ground-to-air radio communication, as opposed to W/T, was possible; even then the effective range was only 35 miles.

The weak link remained that of detection – it was a big sky so how did you find the enemy? If the enemy could not be accurately located, it was almost impossible to effect an interception. This was borne out in the July 1934 annual air exercise, when at least half of the day bomber formations reached their targets without being intercepted by fighters. If the fighters could not find bomber formations in good weather by day, what chance would they have at night? Not that this was of any concern at the time.

The radar stations around the coast were a vital element in Fighter Command's Control and Reporting network.

At the first meeting of the Committee for Scientific Survey of Air Defence, in January 1935, the problems highlighted by the previous year's exercise were discussed, as were the prospects of any scientific break-through that might provide an answer. The Committee members consulted Robert Watson-Watt, head of the radio research branch of the National Physical Laboratory, as to the feasibility of using radio waves. A month later he presented his thoughts on how to use such radio waves to detect aircraft, the principle being to 'bounce' the waves off the aircraft and pick up the echo. Within a matter of weeks an experiment had been arranged using the BBC's transmitter at Daventry. The idea was for an aircraft to fly through the centre of the transmitting beam while Watson-Watt and his colleagues attempted to detect its presence on a cathode-ray oscillograph. It worked as planned, the passage of the aircraft causing a blip on the equipment. All that was needed now was high-level support for development of the technique, and that came from Air Marshal Hugh Dowding, the Air Member for Research and Development.

The radio research station at Orfordness became the experimental site for the development of RDF (the name was not changed to radar until 1941), and throughout the summer a number of trials were conducted. Tracking ranges of 40 miles were soon being achieved, and it was obvious that here was the solution to the problem; all that was needed was time to develop and introduce the equipment, and integrate it into the Fighter Command system. In September 1935 the Air Defence Sub-Committee acquired Treasury funding for a chain of RDF stations along the east coast; a remarkable achievement so early in the development of the technique. The next three years saw a number of technical developments of the equipment, many individuals making invaluable contributions to the work, so that by mid-1938 the completed stations were functioning reasonably well

Since the initial proving of the RDF principle in 1936, progress had been fairly rapid, although many problems still remained. By mid-1937 three stations were in operation, at Bawdsey, Canewdon and Dover, along with an experimental filter station at Bawdsey. The development of the last of these added a new dimension to the system by providing, as the term implied, a filtering of the mass of information from the various sources so that the controllers could be provided with a simpler, more accurate air picture on which to base their operations. The earlier problem of track discrimination had virtually been solved, but height prediction remained a significant problem. The system's first major test came in the 1938 Home Defence exercises, and in general terms it appeared to work well, some 75% of attempted interceptions (day and night) proving successful. New RDF stations (codenamed Chain Home – CH, and Chain Home Low – CHL) were constructed in a plan to create unbroken coverage around the east and southern coasts of Britain. At the same time an extensive programme for the construction of Command, Group and Sector operations rooms was under way.

The enemy could now be located by day or night; radar made no real distinction between the two. Defending fighters could be positioned so that by day they could acquire the bombers visually, but what about the night situation? Would the fighter be able to pick up its targets? Among his early proposals, Watson-Watt had included thoughts on an airborne version of RDF to prevent reliance on searchlights or good visibility. However, because priority was given to the ground stations, little work was carried out on developing equipment small enough to be carried by aircraft. June 1937 saw an experiment whereby the 'fighter' had a receiver that could pick up the trans-missions (and echoes) of the CH stations. The principle appeared to work, but it was not a satisfactory solution and was abandoned. Not until late that year was Airborne

Fighter Ops room with WAAF plotters; whilst the fighters were the 'sharp end', it was the whole Control and Reporting system that made the air defence effective.

Intercept (AI) equipment developed, using the technique of lobe switching to determine the azimuth of the target. Although this worked, there were still problems to be overcome, mostly concerning the receiver part of the system, and it was mid-1939 before a successful airborne installation was under trial.

By September 1939 twenty CH (Chain Home) stations were operational with detection ranges in excess of 100 miles. The additional system of CHL (Chain Home Low) was also well underway.

A post-war Fighter Command report summarised the importance of the non-aircraft elements: 'how valuable this system was to be, was proved in the Battle of Britain, for without its help the courage and determination of the pilots and the devotion and hard work of the ground staff would have been to little avail. This system of radar allied with the reports by sight and sound of the Royal (from 1941) Observer Corps developed rapidly through the war.'

It is also important to realise that radar was only one of the elements that made up the integrated defence network, which comprised a Reporting, control and command chain, balloon barrages, searchlights and anti-aircraft guns. It was the combination of warning systems, including the Observer Corps and ground intelligence, as well as radar, analysed by Filter Rooms and then acted upon by Sector Controllers that made the system successful and reasonably robust against attack. Another key factor was integration of command, with Dowding controlling the Observer Corps, Balloon Command (from its formation in November 1938) and units of Anti-Aircraft Command.

The London Balloon Barrage was established in 1937 and within a year had four Balloon Centres and ten Balloon Squadrons under the command of No. 30 (Balloon

Barrage) Group within Fighter Command. With extension of the balloon barrage concept to other cities and important installations, three further Groups were formed and brought under the control of Balloon Command. By the outbreak of war there were 624 balloons flying over the UK. The main aims of the balloon barrage were:

1. Strengthen public morale.
2. Make attacking aircraft fly too high for accurate bombing and prevent a long run in to the target.

The London Balloon Barrage was established in 1937 and the system was rapidly extended to other key cities, ports and industrial installations; the Barrage Balloons, many of which were 'manned' by WAAFs were another important part of the air defence network.

This total had increased by September 1940 and balloon barrages were flying over most key cities and installations. Shooting down runaway balloons became a routine task for Fighter Command.

The elements of an integrated but still unproven system of high-performance fighters with RDF direction and ground control were in place. The ultimate test was not long in coming.

Outbreak of War

In the last week of August 1939 the Auxiliary Air Force squadrons had been embodied into the RAF – in other words they were called up to full-time service – and the role these VR (Volunteer Reserve) pilots were to play in the first years of the war was of great importance. Fighter Command statistics for 4 September 1939 show 39 squadrons of fighters, comprising:

30 single-engine squadrons with 570 aircraft and 659 pilots
7 twin-engine squadrons with 131 aircraft and 107 crews
2 squadrons with Gauntlet/Hind.

The aircraft numbers relate to serviceable aircraft and not establishment and the pilot figures relate to 'available' pilots; what is interesting, especially in the light of subsequent events, is the pilot/crew to aircraft ratio. With only 89 'spare' pilots for the single-engine fighters the Command was ill-equipped to cope with expansion or losses, and with more aircraft than crews for the twin-engined types the position was even more desperate.

The Auxiliary Air Force supplied a cadre of trained and motivated pilots who provided a major boost to the RAF's front-line capability. On 13 August 1939, the Spitfires of 611 Squadron arrived at Duxford for their annual training camp and it

On 13 August 1939, the Spitfires of 611 Squadron arrived at Duxford for their annual training camp and it was here, their designated war station, that they received notification on 26 August of their call-up.

was here, their designated war station, that they received notification, on 26 August of their call-up. The Squadron had 13 Spitfires available from a notional establishment of 21 aircraft (16 IE [Initial Establishment] plus five CR [Command Reserve] aircraft); pilot establishment was eleven officers and ten airmen, with two officers and 140 airmen making up the groundcrew component. Despite being a well-established station, Duxford was short of accommodation and the airmen of 611 Squadron had to live in tents, although in October they moved into newly-completed brick H-type barrack blocks.

At this time, Fighter Command had three operational groups – No. 11 Group (HQ Uxbridge) covering the South of England and the South Midlands, No. 12 Group (HQ Hucknall) covering the North Midlands, NW England and North Wales, and No. 13 Group (HQ Newcastle-upon-Tyne) covering NE England, Scotland and the Orkney and Shetland Islands. The defensive organisation was oriented to counter the perceived threat posed by long-range bombers from Germany, which would not be escorted by single-engine fighters as these did not have the range.

Squadron equipment remained a focus of concern during the first months of the war. Although the focus was on getting as many Hurricanes and Spitfires into service as quickly as possible it was still policy to form squadrons with whatever equipment was available; for example, 263 Squadron formed at Filton in October 1939 with the Gloster Gladiator, a type with which they were to achieve a measure of fame in spring 1940 over Norway. The Squadron diarist was one of those who recorded useful snippets for later historians:

14 November 1939: 'The Squadron re-equipped with Browning 303 on all aircraft; these are a great asset to the unit.'

25 November 1939: 'Owing to the outstanding success and capabilities of the Squadron they have been ordered to take-over the air safety of the western part of England. They are the only squadron detailed for this area, which speaks very highly of its standard considering that it was formed seven weeks ago and 18 of the pilots were straight from Flying Training Schools.' Is this sarcasm or genuine pride?

22 January 1940: Summary of a report on gun harmonisation and air firing: 'The experiments conducted have shown conclusively that guns installed in Gladiator aircraft have not the spread of bullets that have been previously calculated, and it is estimated that gun spread is approximately one foot per 100 yards up to a range of 300 yards. It is understood that experiments were conducted by the Air Fighting Development Unit in determining bullet spread by means of photographing tracer ammunition. It is suggested for consideration that the trajectory of tracer ammunition is not so accurate as ball ammunition.'

The interesting points from these extracts are the fact that the Gladiator was still a front-line fighter – and that its armament was still not operationally fit – and that the Command was stretched thin and only able to provide a single squadron of biplane fighters to cover a large geographic area. The situation would only slowly improve over the next few months – imagine how it would have been if the war had started with the Munich Crisis in late 1938.

Spitfire K9987 of 66 Squadron, the Squadron had re-equipped with Spits in October 1938 at Duxford.

In February 1940 a memo was issued stating the 'decision to rearm nine fighter squadrons from Blenheims, in the following order of priority: with Hurricanes (601, 229, 245, 145 squadrons), with Spitfires (64, 222, 92, 234 squadrons) and with Defiants (141 squadron). This is to be complete as near to 31 March 1940 as possible.' (SOM 109/40 dated 13 Feb 1940).

France and Dunkirk
Under the terms of the alliance with the French an expeditionary force was despatched to France, and this included an air element; the Fighter Command contribution being six Hurricane squadrons, although this was later raised to ten. On 7 July 1939 Dowding wrote to the Air Ministry complaining at this massive reduction in his fighter force, with ten squadrons equalling a sizeable chunk of his force. War came on 3 September 1939 and the Command duly sent the first four Hurricane squadrons (1, 73, 85, and 87) to France. In France there was little to do except carry on training, patrol up and down the border and take in a spot of French culture, as well as attempt to co-operate with their Allies. The first success came on 2 November but for Dowding the downside was the call for two more squadrons that same month, although the Gladiator-equipped 607 and 615 squadrons were sent, both moving to Merville on 15 November – and both eventually re-equipping in France with Hurricanes (spring 1940).

The so-called 'Phoney War' that lasted for six months ended with the German invasion of Denmark and Norway in April 1940, the rapid success of which was followed by the Blitzkrieg attack on France via the Low Countries on 10 May 1940. Fighter Command's involvement in the Scandinavian campaign had been the commitment of two squadrons, 46 and 263 to the Narvik region of Norway; the heroics of Gladiator operations from frozen lakes and the tragic loss of pilots with the sinking of HMS *Glorious* are covered in the Operations chapter.

From the perspective of the Fighter Command story the French experience is of more interest as it revealed both the good and the bad about aircraft, pilots and tactics.

Hurricane of 73 Squadron being rearmed in France; the dispatch of Hurricane squadrons to France was a mixed blessing – it provided vital operational experience but it also cost a large number of aircraft.

In the meantime, with the beginning of the campaign against Holland, Belgium and France on the 10 May 1940, the *Luftwaffe* became involved in a new series of attacks. The objects of these attacks, based on previous battle experience were:

1. The destruction of the enemy's Air Forces and their sources of supply.
2. Indirect and direct support of the Army.
3. Attacks on enemy harbours and shipping.

These tasks were entrusted to *Luftflotten* 2 and 3. Out of a strength of 5,142 aircraft, the Luftwaffe had 3,824 serviceable aircraft available at that time. (Out of an average of 3,824 serviceable aircraft there were 591 reconnaissance aircraft, 1,120 bombers, 342 Stukas, 42 ground attack aircraft, 248 T.E. fighters, 1,016 S.E. fighters, 401 transport aircraft and 154 seaplanes). Compared with this, the Allies (including the Belgian and Dutch-Air Forces) had 6,000 aircraft, of which 3,000 were at continental bases. Right at the outset of the campaign the full weight of the German air offensive simultaneously hammered the ground organisations of the Netherlands, Belgium and Northern France. The Dutch and Belgian Air Forces were destroyed and the Franco-British Air Forces were hard hit and forced to use bases in the rear.

(Survey by 8th *Abteilung* September 1944)

In addition to the units operating from France, the Command sent daily reinforcements that went out and returned to their home base at dusk. Typical of this effort was that by 253 Squadron, which had only been declared operational on 27 April. The six aircraft of 'B Flight' went to France on 16 May, with 'A Flight' and a Flight from 111 Squadron forming a composite squadron the following day at Kenley. Their brief was to move to Poix, patrol from there and return to Kenly at dusk. Over the next two

Hurricane L1831 of 87 Squadron; the Squadron moved to France the day after the declaration of war and remained there until 22 May 1940 when the remnants arrived at Debden.

days the Squadron lost six aircraft, although all four pilots 'lost' on 18 May subsequently returned. On 16 May Dowding had sent a letter to the Under Secretary of State for Air expressing in unequivocal terms the dangers posed to the defence of the UK by the drain of fighters to France. This letter has been seen as one of the most significant in RAF history as it – may – have influenced Churchill, who saw it, to moderate his response to the endless calls for more aircraft from the French. The letter is shown in full at Annex A.

Engagements with fighters and bombers, attempts to support Allied bombers, the effective German flak, all provided a series of lessons for commanders and pilots. Some of the pre-war breed stuck rigidly to the rules and tactics that had been drummed into them, others started to recognise that they were being outclassed, out-gunned and out-numbered. Furthermore, it was discovered that the standard harmonisation on the guns of 400 yards was no good against the fighters and that 250 yards 'achieved far more lethal results'. But every lesson learned cost a few more aircraft and pilots, some caught on quicker than others, those that didn't usually were not around for very long.

The Hurricanes certainly gave a good account of themselves and the *Luftwaffe* crews grew to respect the tenacity and skill of their latest opponents. Many of the RAF pilots involved believed that a few more squadrons would make all the difference and why didn't 'they' send across more of the chaps – even a few Spitfires. This, however, was total anathema to Dowding who, by the middle of May, was fighting against a French request for ten more squadrons . . . 'the Hurricane tap is now full on and you will not be able to resist the pressure to send Hurricanes to France until I have been bled white . . .' he said. The period from 16 to 26 May saw ever more Fighter Command squadrons being dragged into the conflict in France, but on a rotational basis of up to three squadrons a day – a useful way to broaden the experience level, but unfortunately each squadron seemed to have to learn the lessons for itself and so the same mistakes and losses occurred.

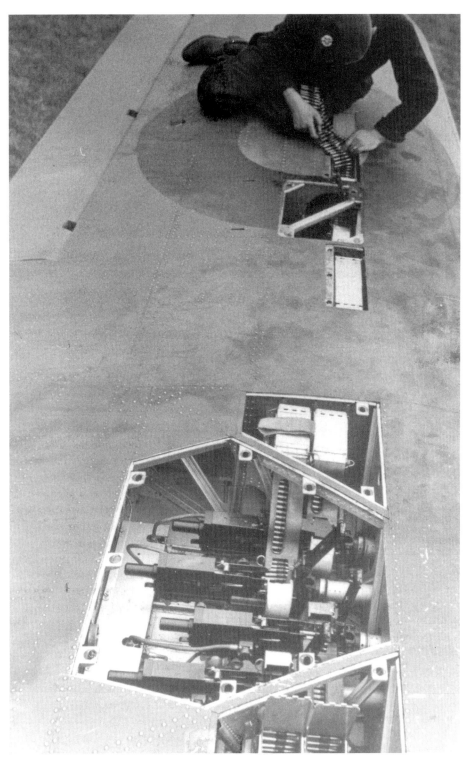

Armourer working on the Brownings in a Hurricane wing; standard armament of the Hurricane and Spitfire was eight 0.303in Colt Browning machine-guns, four in each wing.

Squadrons had begun to move back to the UK as early as the 19 May but not until the French request for an Armistice on 17 June did the last ones leave. In the meantime the 'Battle' of Dunkirk had been fought – over a period of nine days the evacuation of Allied troops had been carried out in the face of intense air attack. Despite popular belief amongst the troops waiting on the beaches, the RAF were present and trying to hold off the waves of attacking German bombers. With an average of 300 sorties a day from the UK it was a great strain on Fighter Command and yet another source of concern for Dowding as just over 100 Spitfires and Hurricanes were lost – along with another slice of experienced pre-war trained pilots. The net result of the campaign in France was loss of almost 1,000 aircraft, roughly half of which were fighters; it is now generally agreed that the period 10 May to 3 June (the end of Dunkirk) cost 432 fighters, plus the losses over Dunkirk.

On 4 June Dowding sent a short message to squadrons that had been involved in the fighting over France:

My Dear Fighter Boys. I don't send out many congratulatory letters and signals, but I feel that I must take this occasion, when the intensive fighting in Northern France is for the time being over, to tell you how proud I am of you and the way in which you have fought since the 'Blitzkrieg' started. I wish I could have spent my time visiting you and hearing your accounts of the fighting, but I have occupied myself in working for you in other ways. I want you to know that my thoughts are always with you, and that it is you and your fighting spirit which will crack the morale of the German Air Force, and preserve our Country through the trials which yet lie ahead. Good luck to you.

The RAF fighters could have taken some comfort from a later German assessment: 'Of all the enemy air forces operating in 1940, the British Air Force was the most formidable in battle. Encounters of German units with British Spitfire and Hurricane formations during the Western campaign, and above all along the Channel at the time of the British retreat to Dunkirk, had been the hardest so far. In supporting the BEF, and also their French Ally in France, the British had brought only parts of their Royal Air Force into operation.' (Lecture by *Hptm.* Otto Bechtle at Belin-Gatow, dated 2 February 1944, hereafter simply listed as Bechtle). How much of this was a true realisation of the new enemy and how much was a look-back from 1944 is of course debatable.

The German occupation of Norway, the Low Countries and France gave Fighter Command an increased frontage to defend as the *Luftwaffe* now had additional bases over a wider geographic area. Consequently the Command's existing organisation had to be modified to provide additional cover for the North-East and South-West of England to 're-dispose and strengthen the country's defences as a matter of paramount importance.' The AHB summary of this critical period continued 'the Fighter Command organisation was extended with the intention of protecting the West and South-West of England, and the number of squadrons in the Command was increased as quickly as aircraft, pilots and ground facilities became available. Greater efforts were made to hurry the moment when No. 14 Group in the North of Scotland could assume an operational role, the area of No. 10 Group was extended as quickly as possible to include Cornwall and No. 9 Group was formed to cover the West.'

No. 10 Group had been formed on 31 May 1940, becoming effective on 13 July. The Group HQ was at Rudloe Manor, Wiltshire and most accommodation was in tents pending the construction of huts.

Northolt's camouflaged hangars with a Hurricane of 253 Squadron, spring 1940; the Squadron only received its Hurricanes in February.

No. 9 Group formed on 9 August at Barton hall, Preston, when it became apparent that the geographic area assigned to No. 12 Group was too unwieldy, but did not assume operational control until 1 December.

The final operational Group to form was No. 14 Group, which was announced in June 1940 to form at Inverness by 1 August, although it was actually 25 August before

Hornchurch August 1940, Defiant of 264 Squadron; the Defiant was the RAF's 'turret-fighter', a concept intended as a bomber-destroyer when no fighter opposition was expected.

the HQ was in place at Drummossie Hotel, Inverness. On 1 September the Group took operational control of Castletown and Skeabrae as well as the Sector Station at Wick and Sector HQ at Dyce.

'But the organisation necessary for the exploitation of fighter defences takes time to prepare. Meanwhile, all defensive operations were carried out by the four fighter groups already established.' The need for additional airfields – not to mention aircraft and pilots – put a severe strain on the already limited resources.

Squadron strength, 28 May 1940

	Operational sqns			Non-operational sqns			Total		
	Sqns	*IE*	*Strength*	*Sqns*	*IE*	*Strength*	*Sqns*	*IE*	*Strength*
Spitfire	19	304	351	3	48	45	22	352	396
Hurricane	19	306	315	6	96	59	25	400	334
Gladiator	1	16	13	–	–	–	1	16	13
Defiant	1	16	21	1	16	16	2	32	37
Blenheim	6	96	119	2	32	35	8	154	154
Totals	46	738	819	12	192	155	58	954	934

Aircraft strength in UK

	IE	Strength
Op sqns	656	647
Non-op sqns	192	132
Total	848	779

Pilot strength UK

Pilot establishment UK	1,268
Pilot strength UK	932

Note: Establishment based on 25 pilots per squadron and 16 aircraft per squadron.

On 16 June 1940 Fighter Command strength was 549 aircraft immediately available for operations, which comprised 260 Spitfires, 182 Hurricanes, 88 Blenheims and 19 Defiants. This was a significant decrease from the 730 that had been serviceable and available on 28 May and was an indication of the losses suffered in the France/Dunkirk operations. A new type, the Westland Whirlwind, entered service with the Command in early July but it was many months before the type was operational. The forthcoming daylight air battles for control of the skies over the Channel and Southern England would primarily be fought by the Hurricane and Spitfire squadrons in the No. 11 Group area, and as Wellington said after the Battle of Waterloo in 1815 it was 'a close run thing'. When the German switched their bomber effort to night bombing the RAF faced a second major challenge. The last six months of 1940 were amongst the most dramatic in history. In the words of that overused statement – 'the Battle of France is over, the Battle of Britain is about to begin.'

The Battle of Britain
In July 1940 the Germans estimated that Fighter Command strength stood at 50 squadrons equipped with 900 fighters, of which 675 were serviceable – 40% of these being Spitfires and the rest Hurricanes. This intelligence assessment was remarkably accurate, as on 10 July the Command's statistics were 54 squadrons equipped with 864 aircraft, of which 656 were serviceable, a good recovery from the low point of the previous month.

The percentages of types was in error as Spitfires made up 35% of the total, Hurricanes 50% and the remainder comprised Blenheims and Defiants, both types having been ignored in the German assessment. The importance of the German figures is their use by the Germans to assess the strength of Fighter Command in the light of *Luftwaffe* claims after each day's combat. By combining this with an assessment of British fighter production capacity the planners could arrive at an operational availability figure and thus work out the combat effectiveness of Fighter Command. However, as we shall see, it did not work quite as simply as that!

The Initial Establishment (IE) of a fighter squadron at this period was 16 aircraft; this was the establishment to which the squadron was entitled and at which it was supposed to be maintained. However, the reality was often different and actual strength, rather than establishment, could vary from 12 to 20, whilst the number of serviceable aircraft was even more variable. It is interesting to note that of the 54 Fighter Command squadrons, 43 were equipped with Hurricanes (25) or Spitfires (18) in early July, which would give a notional IE of 688 aircraft. However, standard tactics involved a 12-aircraft formation, so in theory only 516 of this 688 would be airborne for a full-strength show.

An organisational memo dated 11 July outlined a temporary increase in unit establishments: 'add four Hurricanes to IE of 30 squadrons and four Spitfires to six squadrons. Additional pilots will not be provided as the aircraft in question are to be regarded as an emergency force. This is a temporary measure and aircraft will be withdrawn and formed into squadrons later' (SOM 655/40).

The dates for the Battle of Britain are usually accepted as 10 July to 31 October 1940, and during these 15 weeks the course of the war took a major turn, with the Germans postponing their plans to invade the British Isles. As the Battle intensified a few hundred RAF fighters operating from 20 or so airfields in SE England were pitted against an air armada that had previously been unbeaten. The morale of the *Luftwaffe*, boosted by easy victories over Poland and France, was high, some might even say

Pilots of 603 Squadron at rest; most personal accounts of the Battle of Britain talk of long periods of doing nothing – sleeping, playing cards, writing a diary and generally enjoying the hot summer of 1940.

verging on arrogance – certainly most of the German pilots believed that the RAF would soon be destroyed.

On 16 July Hitler issued Directive No. 16, Operation Sealion, the invasion of England which came with the proviso that 'the British Air Force must be eliminated to such an extent that it will be incapable of putting up any sustained opposition to the invading troops.' After almost a year of war, the RAF was a very different organisation to that of September 1939, more fighter squadrons with modern aircraft (Spitfires and Hurricanes), but its control system, using radar and Sector HQs, had yet to be put to the test.

The Battle of Britain is usually split into four phases:

I   – Early July to 12 August, attacks on coastal shipping and installations, plus limited attacks on radar stations and airfields.
II – 13 August to 6 September, attacks on airfields and associated installations.
III – 7 September to late September, initial attacks on London.
IV – Late September to 31 October, daylight fighter sweeps and fighter-bomber raids, increased weight of night bombing on London.

At this stage, the tactical advantage lay very much with the Germans as the *Luftwaffe* could choose the time, place and size of any attack. It was able, on paper, to mass overwhelming force at any one point whilst maintaining a threat to other areas that would prevent any attempt by the RAF to concentrate its forces. The German bomber force was capable of reaching over the entire UK land area and surrounding waters, a massive geographic area for the defenders to cover. It was, of course, realised by both sides that the decisive conflict would have to take place in SE England but the ability to stretch and weaken the British fighter force was a significant tactical card to play. The fact that the *Luftwaffe* failed to take full advantage of this was, as we shall see, one of the main factors in the failure of the German air campaign.

Spitfire R6597 of 152 Squadron 1940; during the Battle of Britain the Squadron claimed 61 victories for the loss of 20 Spitfires.

The relative strength of the two air forces at the outbreak of the Battle has been a source of debate. An RAF estimate of GAF strength gave the following breakdown:

Long-range bombers	1,200
Dive-bombers	280+
Single-engine fighters	760
Twin-engine fighters	220
Long-range reconnaissance	50
Short-range reconnaissance	90

In addition to these numbers for France and the Low Countries, were 190 aircraft in Norway (130 long-range bombers, 30 twin-engine fighters and 30 long-range reconnaissance types). Together this gave a total of 2,790 combat aircraft and it was estimated that the bomber force had 69% serviceability whilst the fighter force had an impressive 95% serviceability. German records (from VI *Abteilung*) show that the estimates were reasonably accurate in terms of the total but that the breakdown was in error:

Bombers	981
Stukas	336
Single-engine fighters	839
Twin-engine fighters	282

These figures are for serviceable aircraft.

With its superiority of numbers, tactical disposition and greater experience:

The Command hoped that it would not require more than four days to smash the enemy fighter defences in Southern England. Once this goal was reached, the offensive was to be extended northwards, sector by sector across the line King's Lynn to Leicester until all England was covered by day attack. At the beginning of the daylight attack, the principle of giving bomber formations the minimum necessary fighter escort so as to leave the majority of fighters free to pursue their real task of destroying the enemy in open combat was generally accepted.

(Bechtle)

On 8 July 1940 the first major air battle took place when Fighter Command scrambled five squadrons to intercept a large enemy force attacking a convoy; the fight eventually involved over 100 aircraft. Convoy attacks of this type, varying in intensity and sometimes limited to small numbers of unescorted raiders using cloud cover, was the pattern of the Battle for the first few weeks. Most activity centred on shipping off Dover. During July the average number of defensive sorties was 5–600 a day, the highest rate occurring on 28 July when 794 sorties were flown, during which the RAF claimed ten aircraft for the loss of five of their own. Day-fighter strength grew during July, enabling the Command to field 49 Hurricane and Spitfire squadrons by early August – the number of Spitfire units remained at 18 but an additional four Hurricane units were now in the line.

August 1940

August 13th 1940 saw the opening of the air offensive against England, carried out by *Luftflotten* 2, 3 and 5 from bases in France, Belgium, Holland and Norway. The *Luftwaffe* had, at that date 4,632 aircraft, of which 3,306 were serviceable.

(Of an average of 3306 serviceable aircraft there were 390 reconnaissance, 981 bombers, 336 Stukas, 34 ground attack, 282 T.E. fighters, 839 S.E. fighters, 288 transport aircraft, and 156 seaplanes). The strength of the British air defences had remained unimpaired by the campaign in the West. The RAF had over 675 fighters, 860 bombers and 402 reconnaissance aircraft available in July 1940.

(8th *Abteilung* survey)

There was great variation in the RAF's daily sortie rates for August, from as few as 288 to a high of 974. The latter took place on 15 August as part of the *Luftwaffe's* concerted attacks on the RAF's airfields under the so-called *Adler Tag* (Eagle Day). This new strategy to destroy Fighter Command's combat potential consisted of a series of attacks on radar installations and fighter airfields and was launched on 12 August. The first raids were on Hawkinge, Manston and Lympne, the latter being hit twice with the result that by the end of the second attack, the airfield was pockmarked with craters and there was barely a clear space on which to land. Hawkinge was hit at around 1700, with Ju 88s destroying two hangars, workshops and other buildings, as well as leaving the airfield surface badly damaged. Overnight the craters were filled, the unexploded bombs dealt with and the airfield was declared operational again within 24-hours. It was a similar story at Manston, with 65 Squadron's Spitfires taking off as the bombs fell. This pattern of airfield attacks continued to the end of the first week of September but, with a few notable exceptions, there appears to have been little in the way of overall co-ordination of the strategy.

That same day Goering held a conference at Karinhall in which he made a number of points concerning the development of the Battle: 'The fighter escort defences of our Stuka formations must be readjusted, as the enemy is concentrating his fighters against our Stuka operations. It appears necessary to allocate 3 fighter *Gruppen* to each Stuka

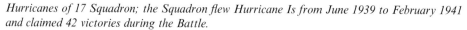

Hurricanes of 17 Squadron; the Squadron flew Hurricane Is from June 1939 to February 1941 and claimed 42 victories during the Battle.

Spitfire I of 72 Squadron; the Squadron operated from Biggin Hill and Croydon during the Battle of Britain.

Gruppe, one of these fighter *Gruppen* remains with the Stukas, and dives with them to the attack; the second flies ahead over the target at medium altitude and engages the fighter defences; the third protects the whole attack from above. It will also be necessary to escort Stukas returning from the attack over the Channel. . . . I have repeatedly given orders that twin-engined fighters are only to be employed where the range of other fighters is inadequate, of where it is for the purpose of assisting our single-engined aircraft to break off combat. Our stocks of twin-engined fighters are not great, and we must use them as economically as possible. . . . It is doubtful whether there is any point in continuing the attacks on radar sites, in view of the fact that not one of those attacked has so far been put out of operation.'

In order to protect the vital airfields, Fighter Command had to use valuable assets on standing patrols and within a matter of weeks the damage to the airfields and associated facilities, plus fighter losses and the general strain of constant operational flying, were having an effect. It was at this point that the Battle of Britain was most finely balanced. However, the *Luftwaffe* was also having difficulties, morale was suffering and every aircraft lost over England also meant the loss of trained aircrew.

Hpt Bechtle's 1944 lecture continued: 'in the first few days of the air war it became apparent that the numerous dogged British fighter pilots who were supplemented by formations of volunteers from nations conquered by Germany made operations by bombers and Stukas so difficult that it was necessary to have an escort of two or even three times the strength of the formation which was being escorted.'

During the critical period of 12–19 August the German Official War Communiqués claimed that 624 RAF aircraft had been destroyed and admitted to a loss of 174 aircraft.

At a conference on 19 August Goering stated:

To sum up: we have reached the decisive period of the air war against England.
The vital task is to turn all means at our disposal to the defeat of the enemy Air
Force. Our first aim is the destruction of the enemy's fighters. If they no longer
take to the air, we shall attack them on the ground, or force them into battle by
directing bomber attacks against targets within range of our fighters. At the same

Fighter combat; close, fire and get-away – keeping an eye out for the Hun sneaking up.

time, and on a growing scale, we must continue our activities against the ground organisation of the enemy bomber units. Surprise attacks on the aircraft industry must be made day and night. Once the enemy Air Force has been annihilated, our attacks will be directed as ordered against other vital targets.

Amongst the individual points he had made were:

Until further notice, the main task of Luftflotten *2 and 3 will be to inflict the utmost damage possible on the enemy fighter forces. With this are to be combined attacks on the ground organisation of the enemy bombers, conducted however in such a manner as to avoid all unnecessary losses. I will return later to the question of operations against the enemy aircraft industry.*

As long as the enemy fighter defences retain their present strength, attacks on aircraft factories must be carried out under the cover of weather conditions permitting surprise raids by solitary aircraft. Such operations demand the most meticulous preparations, but can achieve very satisfactory results. The cloudy conditions likely to prevail over England in the next few days must be exploited for such attacks. We must succeed in seriously disrupting the material supplies of the enemy Air Force, by the destruction of the relatively small number of aircraft engine and aluminium plants.

These attacks on the enemy aircraft industry are of particular importance, and should also be carried out by night. Should it however not be possible to locate an industrial target because of poor visibility or bad weather conditions, some other worthwhile target must be attacked. It would appear desirable for the purpose of night operations to allocate to units particular areas, which they will come to know well during each successive raid. Within this area a list of target priorities should be drawn up, so that each sortie will produce some valuable result and flights will not be wasted due to failure of the aircraft to find one particular target. There can no longer be any restriction on the choice of targets. To myself I reserve only the right to order attacks on London or Liverpool.

Bf 109 wreck; Southern England was littered with the remains of German aircraft, all of which were guarded and then removed for investigation and recovery of anything useful.

On 20 August 1940, Goering ordered his units to 'continue the fight against the British Air Force until further notice with the aim of weakening British fighter strength. The enemy is to be forced by ceaseless attacks to bring his fighter formations into operation.' This undoubtedly correct tactic was, unfortunately for the Germans, not followed through and whilst airfield attacks continued into early September, the bombing of London on 24/25 August and the British retaliatory raid on Berlin, changed the nature of the Battle, with Hitler declaring that he would destroy the British capital. For the next few weeks, London was to be the focus of numerous large-scale German attacks, and the Battle took on a new significance.

Statistics for the last week of August 1940 (from the Fighter Command Diary) show the intense nature of the Battle at this period:

Losses, 25 August–1 August 1940

Date	German losses	RAF losses	RAF pilots saved
25 Aug	55	13	4
26 Aug	47	15	11
27 Aug	5	0	0
28 Aug	28	14	7
29 Aug	11	9	7
30 Aug	62	25	15
31 Aug	88	37	25
Totals	296	113	69

The column that shows RAF pilots saved is also very significant as the two factors in maintaining operational capability were aircraft and pilots; as we shall see, the former was never a problem, whilst the latter reached breaking point.

September 1940

The Battle reached its climax in September, with the *Luftwaffe* seeming to be on the verge of victory – at least by their accounting of RAF losses – and the RAF struggling in the early part of the month to maintain the fighting strength of its squadrons. The rotation of squadrons between the main area of the Battle and quieter zones helped, as did throwing in pilots when they were not truly combat ready (see below for comments of pilot shortage). New squadrons continued to form, but not all were thrown into the Battle. When the *Luftwaffe* launched its surge of offensive ops in the middle of the month it expected low levels of resistance; instead it was met by a determined RAF that had actually recovered somewhat from the hammering of the previous weeks. On 15 September, which is now marked as Battle of Britain Day, Fighter Command had 17 squadrons airborne to meet the midday attack. This day's operations are covered in detail in the Operations Chapter.

The first 'Eagle' squadron (71 Squadron) formed at Church Fenton on 19 September: 'pilots will be American citizens commissioned or enlisted in the RAFVR. The ground personnel will be RAF. Establishment will be 16 Brewster Buffalos' (SOM 875/40). The choice of equipment must have come as shock for the keen volunteers from America but, fortunately, Fighter Command's dalliance with this unsuitable fighter was short-lived and the Americans were flying Hurricane Is by November.

The German tactic of draining the strength of Fighter Command were beginning to pay off, although this does not appear to have been recognised by the German air planners and a decision was taken to switch the focus of the attack.

The battle against the British Air Force was continued on the lines of this directive without a decision being obtained. Recognising this fact, the German High Command decided in September to switch the main weight of the air offensive to London, the heart of the enemy power. Incomparably greater success than hitherto could be anticipated from this policy. For while the main objective of wearing down the British fighter forces was not abandoned, economic war from the air could be embarked upon with full fury, and the morale of the civilian population subjected at the same time to a heavy strain.

The few daylight attacks by strong bomber formations (200–300 bombers of all types were over the target every time) achieved good results against dock and supply installations along the Thames. Major conflagrations caused extensive devastation. These attacks were continued until the 27th September. Losses suffered by formations led thereafter to a reduction of the forces engaged on any single daylight attack to one Ju.88 Gruppe, and from the beginning of October to the use of fighter-bomber formations only (Me 109's each carrying one Sc.250 (250 Kg) bomb. The individual bomber Gruppe as well as the fighter-bomber formations with a strength of up to 120 aircraft, was escorted in its outward and return flights by 2–3 fighter Geschwader. When the weather situation did not permit attacks by regular formations in the prescribed form, use was made of cloud-cover for nuisance raids by single aircraft. The month of October saw the continuation of the war of attrition against

London and the final shifting of the main weight of attack from daylight to night raids. In September, these had been carried on simultaneously with daylight attacks.

(Bechtle)

The night campaign is covered later.

Aircraft and Pilots

Great play has been made by some historians of wastage rates and supply of fighters and whilst it is true that during the height of the Battle, the situation did deteriorate, it never became critical. The weekly situation in respect of wastage rates along with output from manufacturers and, a significant element in the equation, Cat 2 aircraft repaired and returned to service, were highlighted in an RAF analysis. In RAF records Cat 2 means repairable but not at unit level and Cat 3 is a write-off.

The low point occurs in the first week of September when the wastage rate was 270 aircraft, 112 of which were Spitfires, against an ASU (Aircraft Storage Unit) stock of 86 Hurricanes and 39 Spitfires. A 1945 Air Historical Branch (AHB) study summarised the position: 'wastage in aircraft during the fighting in July and early August was more than offset by output. Less than 300 aircraft were lost in the period 20 July to 10 August whereas just over 500 were produced or repaired. But as soon as heavy fighting began, wastage leapt ahead of output and remained practically twice as high until the second

56 Squadron pilots at North Weald September 1939; the Squadron lost 22 aircraft in combat and pilot turn-over to casualties and postings were average.

week in September. It is apparent that the two weeks from 25 August to 7 September constituted the crisis of the battle as far as aircraft supply was concerned. There is only one inference to be drawn; that despite the great labours of all those concerned with the supply and production of aircraft, a disastrous situation would shortly have been reached if the Germans had maintained the scale of their attacks.'

Strength and serviceability, 10 July–25 September			
Date	Squadrons	Total IE	Serviceable
10 Jul	54	864	656
15 Jul	52	956	655
20 Jul	50	920	605
25 Jul	53	976	631
30 Jul	54	996	662
5 Aug	56	1,036	719
10 Aug	56	1,036	709
15 Aug	54	996	670
20 Aug	57	1,060	711
25 Aug	59	1,096	721
30 Aug	57	1,060	710
5 Sep	58	944	710
10 Sep	60	960	668
15 Sep	61	976	652
20 Sep	60	960	698
25 Sep	61	–	665

One thing that is immediately apparent from the figures in this table is the consistent level of serviceable aircraft – never less than 600 and often just over 700 aircraft, despite the intensity of the conflict at various times during this period.

On 6 October Churchill asked the Secretary of State for Air for 'figures of total losses of Hurricanes and Spitfires during the months of August and September.' The following day he received this reply:

	August 1940			September 1940		
Reason for loss	Hurricane	Spitfire	Total	Hurricane	Spitfire	Total
Enemy Action	238	143	381	228	134	362
Accidents	15	11	26	15	8	23
Total	253	154	407	243	142	385

It is usually accepted that Fighter Command's weak link was its supply of pilots. Despite the fact that it was fighting over home territory and therefore pilots who were shot-down could return to the front line, there is much truth in this assertion. The AHB summary concluded: 'During August 304 pilots had become casualties; during the fortnight 25 August to 7 September 125 pilots were killed and 133 wounded. This casualty rate, plus the small number of pilots posted to instructional work, represented wastage of some 400 pilots a month. Output from OTUs in August, however, was 260 pilots – the Command, in short, was wasting away.'

With an establishment of 24 pilots per squadron, the Command should have had 1,200 pilots on strength at the end of August but it was 201 short of this. Added to which a further 160 were classified as non-operational, the majority ... 'because they had not reached a sufficiently high standard of training. There was, therefore, an average deficiency of six or seven operational pilots in each squadron.' It was this deficiency, plus the difficulty of replacing tired squadrons by complete and rested squadrons – a policy that had been employed earlier in the battle – that led Dowding to introduce his Stabilisation Scheme. Under this squadrons were categorised A, B or C:

> A class squadrons – No. 11 Group plus the Duxford and Middle Wallop sectors.
> B class squadrons – mainly No. 10 and No. 12 Groups.
> C class squadrons – mainly No. 13 Group.

The idea was to keep the A class squadrons at 19–20 operational pilots by drawing on the C class squadrons. The B class units, and there were only five of these when the scheme was introduced, were potential replacements for any A class unit that had to be withdrawn from the battle. 'The implication [of this scheme] is that pilot casualties so far exceeded output during this critical fortnight that almost half of the squadrons in Fighter Command had to be reduced to a semi-operational state in order to devote their best energies to producing pilots for the squadrons that were actively engaging the enemy. Insofar as the battle was largely confined to south-east England, the scheme was practicable and prudent. But it starkly reveals how dangerous was the pilot position' (AHB). For the period 10 July to 31 October the Command lost an average of four pilots a day Killed In Action (KIA), with an average of 28.9 per week.

Conclusion

The last of the massed daylight raids took place on 30 September and was given a very rough handling by a Fighter Command that was now much stronger than it had been at any point in the Battle. From then until the end of the accepted Battle period (31 October) the main *Luftwaffe* effort comprised small formations or lone aircraft (the latter often fighter-bombers) – undertaking as many as 1,000 sorties a day. Whilst the damage they inflicted was small they represented a major problem for the defending fighters and the Command had to resort to standing patrols. The end date for the Battle is somewhat arbitrary as these types of raid continued well into 1941.

The following statistics on German losses were given in answer to a Parliamentary question on 14 May 1947:

Luftwaffe losses			
Period	*RAF estimate*	*German estimate*	*Admitted*
19 Jul–7 Aug	188	192	63
8 Aug–23 Aug	755	403	213
24 Aug–6 Sep	643	378	243
7 Sep–30 Sep	846	435	243
1 Oct–31 Oct	260	325	134
Totals	2,692	1,733	896

Note: Columns show: RAF claims; From German records; and admitted by Germans at the time in communiqués.

66 Squadron pilots; throughout the Battle the main problem for Fighter Command was shortage of pilots.

The RAF post-war record of the Battle admitted losses of 915 aircraft (Spitfires, Hurricanes and Blenheims) in aerial combat, plus losses of other types such as Defiants. This total was broken down as:

Hurricanes	564
Spitfires	339
Blenheims	12

A further 42 aircraft of these three types were admitted as destroyed on the ground by enemy action.

Just fewer than 3,000 pilots, from 14 nationalities, fought on the RAF side in the Battle, and of these some 507 were killed. The RAF claimed to have shot down 2,692 German aircraft, although post-war research has reduced this figure to 1,733. The *Luftwaffe* claimed to have shot down 3,058 RAF aircraft, but subsequent analysis has reduced this to 915. 'The Few', as Churchill described them, had won a stunning victory. The airfields of southern England and the aircraft that flew from them had replaced the wooden walls of the Royal Navy as Britain's main line of defence. Many in the *Luftwaffe* were not convinced that they had been beaten: 'The struggle for mastery of the air, when discontinued by Germany, had not been fought through to a conclusion.' (*Hpt* Bechtle). In 1953 Adolf Galland wrote an appraisal of the Battle of Britain for the RAF's Air Historical Branch, extracts from this, and commentary on those extracts, is at Annex C.

Dowding – Architect of Victory

The eldest of four children, Hugh Dowding was raised in the strict atmosphere of St Ninians's School, Moffat, which his father had founded in 1879. In 1895 he went on to Winchester School and after his four years there, entered the Royal Military Academy at Woolwich, destined for the Royal Engineers.

The course at Woolwich had been halved to 12 months because of the pressure of the South African War and when Dowding graduated he was posted to the Garrison Artillery and assigned to Gibraltar. In the

Hugh Dowding was quite rightly called the Architect of Victory in respect of the Battle of Britain, mainly because of his pre-war role in Research and Development and his determination to resist political pressure.

following year, 1901, the Company moved to Colombo where the social life was somewhat improved – but to Dowding, the prospects seemed equally limited and so he applied for a transfer to the more active Mountain Artillery. His request was granted and he went to No. 7 Mountain Artillery Battery at Rawalpindi. He spent the next six years in India, transferring to a Native Battery where he was in his element with an independent command, often working in remote areas with infantry units.

In January 1912 he entered Staff College and it was at this point that his interest in aviation really began. One task he led involved the use of six aircraft in support of his ground forces, and it became obvious to him that few people in the Army knew how to employ aircraft. Dowding considered it important to understand this new element and so decided to learn to fly.

He arranged his lessons at the Vickers Flying School at Brooklands so that he could be back for college classes at 10 am. After only one hour and 40 minutes of flying he was given his licence! Dowding followed this with a three-month course at the Central Flying School after which he received his wings. Returning to the Mountain Artillery, he applied for a Royal Flying Corps (RFC) Reserve post. In 1914 he went back to the Garrison Artillery with a posting to coastal defence on the Isle of Wight, but only hours after the outbreak of war, Dowding was called up as an RFC Reserve pilot.

His first appointment was as Commandant of the Dover assembly point for squadrons en route to France. Within a matter of weeks, however, he went to Farnborough to join the newly-forming 7 Squadron. He was eager to get to France and so pestered for a posting to an active squadron. His wish was granted – but not quite as he desired – with a posting as an Observer to 6 Squadron at Ostend. This did not last long as heavy losses and a series of rapid moves led to a pilot shortage and he was soon back in the front seat. By the end of the year he had moved to 9 Squadron, a specialist 'wireless' unit. Because of his experience he was posted back to Farnborough to create a wireless experimental establishment.

By the summer of 1915 he was back on the Continent as Commanding Officer of 16 Squadron. He was now aged 33 and a Major, but his career to date had not been particularly remarkable. To improve squadron training and morale he introduced a bombing contest on the airfield. This was brought to a hasty conclusion when the one and only bomb ended up in a canal next to the airfield! During his time as CO, the Squadron operated in the support roles of bomber, recce and artillery observation.

Dowding was promoted to Lieutenant Colonel and returned to Farnborough to work up a unit with Sopwith One-and-a-half Strutters, before taking command of 9th Wing, a unit attached to the Commander-in-Chief for reconnaissance duties. In June 1916 Dowding arrived at Trenchard's HQ at Fienvillers for the Battle of the Somme. During this bloody battle his units carried out not only their recce duties but also played a part in trying to achieve local air superiority over parts of the battlefield.

Another promotion and back to England once more, this time to the Southern Training Brigade at Salisbury. In spring 1918 Dowding heard that he had not been listed to join the small post-war permanent Royal Air Force and was to return to the artillery. Fortunately, his CO, a Vice-Admiral, disputed this decision and, with the added support of Trenchard, it was revoked. Dowding went to Kenley as Group Commander.

Over the next ten years he had a number of staff and organisational posts in the UK and Middle East, eventually becoming Air Member for Supply and Research – the post in which he first made his stamp on the forthcoming conflict. It was his job to shape the future RAF. He energetically threw his weight behind a number of projects during the critical period of the 1930s, when there was still considerable opposition to any expenditure on rearmament. Among his interests were the use of materials other than wood for aircraft construction, the development of a land-based design of the Schneider racing aircraft, and the development of radar. On balance this was perhaps his most critical period, as without a strong stance being taken in the 1930s it is certain that the RAF would have entered the Battle of Britain in a very poor state.

In 1936 he took the post for which he is best known – head of Fighter Command. His new HQ opened at Bentley Priory on 14 July 1936, and his theoretical Command consisted of 30 squadrons along with 600 guns, searchlights, and barrage balloons. He increased this to a planned 53 squadrons, but had to fight for every scrap of equipment. Dowding's previous range of duties fitted him well for these mammoth tasks and slowly but surely his air defence system took shape. At the time of the Munich Crisis in September 1938 there was still considerable disorder, the RAF was certainly not ready for war; 12 months later Fighter Command was very much a 'going concern'.

Upon the outbreak of war he had 39 squadrons fit for duty and fought hard to preserve the bulk of these for the defence of the UK, despite pressure to send squadrons to other Commands and, more especially, to France. The Hurricane fighter squadrons that deployed to France suffered heavy losses although they also achieved a great deal, not least by gaining valuable experience that could be passed on to others and which led to changes in tactics and equipment. However, as Dowding rightly saw, the Battle for France was being lost and to have continued to put fighter squadrons across the Channel, especially his precious Spitfire units, would have courted disaster in the next round of the conflict. His foresight in preparing Fighter Command for the Battle was in large measure responsible for its success, although the dogmatic determined way in which he dealt with those who opposed his views, especially Churchill, undoubtedly led to his eventual downfall. Perhaps the only criticism that can be levelled at his conduct of the Battle of Britain is the failure to make the Group Commanders of No. 11 and No. 12 Group work together, the conflict between Park and Leigh-Mallory could have had dire consequences.

After four years of running Fighter Command, Dowding was moved out in November 1940. The Battle of Britain had been won and he was exhausted, but many have seen this move as a shameful political act motivated by Churchill. Given a number of 'special' assignments but no real job, Dowding resigned in 1942. His place as a great air commander cannot be denied.

Big Wings?
One of the most acrimonious debates of the war was that which took place between AOC No. 11 Group, AVM Keith Park, and his counterpart in No. 12 Group, AVM Trafford Leigh-Mallory. However, before briefly discussing that debate it is worth outlining No. 11 Group's tactics as stated by Park to Hugh Dowding:

The general plan adopted was to engage the enemy high-fighter screen with pairs of Spitfire squadrons from Hornchurch and Biggin Hill half-way between London and the coast, and so enable Hurricane squadrons from London Sectors to attack bomber formations and their close escort before they reached the line of fighter aerodromes East and South of London. The remaining squadrons from London Sectors which could not be despatched in time to intercept the first wave of the attack by climbing in pairs, formed a third and inner screen by patrolling along the lines of aerodromes East and South of London. The fighter squadrons from Debden, Tangmere and sometimes Northolt, were employed in wings of three or in pairs to form a screen South-East of London to intercept a third wave of the attack coming inland, also to mop up retreating formations of the earlier waves. The Spitfire squadrons were re-disposed so as to concentrate three squadrons at both Hornchurch and Biggin Hill. The primary role of these squadrons was to engage and drive back the enemy high-fighter screen, and so protect the Hurricane squadrons, whose task was to attack close escorts, and then the bomber formations, all of which flew at much lower altitude.

The nature of the problem centred on the support given by adjacent Groups to the hard-pressed No. 11 Group. This came into particularly sharp focus in August when the *Luftwaffe* offensive was at its most intense and when the Group's airfields were being attacked. Numerous documents issued by No. 11 Group during this period show Keith Park's ire at what he perceived to be a lack of co-operation from his counterpart in No. 12 Group, whereas No. 10 Group, on the other hand, received nothing but praise. Typical of these is the 'No. 11 Group Instructions to Controllers' dated August 27, 1940: 'Thanks to the friendly co-operation afforded by No. 10 Group, they are always prepared to detail two to four squadrons to engage from the West mass attacks approaching the Portsmouth area. The AOC No. 10 Group has agreed that once his squadrons have been detailed to intercept a group of raids coming into Tangmere Sector, his controllers will not withdraw or divert them to some other task without firstly consulting us.'

'Up to date, No. 12 Group, on the other hand, have not shown the same desire to co-operate by despatching their squadrons to the places requested. The result of this attitude has been that on two occasions recently when 12 Group offered assistance and were requested by us to patrol our aerodromes, their squadrons did not, in fact, patrol over our aerodromes. On both these occasions our aerodromes were heavily bombed, because our own patrols were not strong enough to turn all the enemy back before they reached their objective.'

Park and his supporters considered that whilst the 'Big Wing' of three of more squadrons put up by No. 12 Group might look impressive, its failure to arrive in time made it worse than useless.

In an effort to clarify its own position, Fighter Command issued an instruction, dated 24 October, concerning the 'reinforcement of No. 11 Group by No. 12 Group': 'As a result of recent discussions the following principles are laid down. No. 11 Group must always give No. 12 Group the maximum possible notice of probable intention to call on him [AOC No. 12 Group] for assistance. It will be seldom that No. 11 Group can diagnose from preliminary symptoms that the first attack will be on a scale so large as to necessitate assistance being called from No. 12 Group. It may, however, often happen that the first raid has been met in strength by No. 11 Group and the assistance of No. 12 Group is required when it is seen that further raids are building up over the Straits of Dover.'

'In any case No. 11 Group must remember 12 Group's requirements with regard to warning, and, even if it is doubtful whether assistance will be required, warning should be given to enable 12 Group to bring units to readiness and stand-by. No. 12 Group should not send less reinforcement than the amount asked for if it is in a position to meet the requirements, but he may send more at his discretion.'

The tone of this is very much supportive of the stance taken by Leigh-Mallory, and it is perhaps equally indicative of where Dowding stood on the matter that Keith Park was replaced as AOC No. 11 Group in December 1940 – by Trafford Leigh-Mallory. In his August 1941 report to the Air Ministry, Dowding stated: 'I am personally in favour of using fighter formations in the greatest strength of which circumstances permit.' However, he qualified this in respect of the Battle of Britain by adding: 'I think that, if the policy of big formations had been attempted at this time by No. 11, Group, many more bombers would have reached their objectives without opposition.'

Sholto Douglas replaced Dowding in November and made it clear where his support lay and by doing so dictated the Command's policy for 1941: 'I have never been very much in favour of the idea of trying to interpose fighter squadrons between enemy bombers and their objective. The best, if not the only, way of achieving air superiority is to shoot down a large proportion of enemy bombers every time they come over ... I would rather shoot down 50 of the enemy bombers after they have reached their objective than shoot down only 10 before they have done so.' Sentiments that would not have pleased many citizens of British cities and would perhaps have caused them to have a different view of the 'heroic Few'. This is one debate that will continue to rage as long as historians examine the Battle of Britain!

However, as we shall see below, by early 1941 Big Wings were policy within No. 11 Group.

Night Attacks

As noted above in the statement by Hpt Bechtle, the main weight of *Luftwaffe* attacks, with London as the main target, had shifted to night by October, which gave the RAF a whole new set of problems.

At the first meeting of the Night Interception Committee, 14 March 1940, Air Marshal Peirse had stated that: 'defence against night attacks was one of the biggest problems we had to face. Even if the enemy began by raiding in large numbers by day, our good defences would force him to adopt night bombing.' Recognition of the threat and the capability to do anything about it were two very different things. Fighter Command had realised in the late 1930s that night interception would be required and in November 1938 Air Fighting Committee Report No. 57 addressed this issue: 'A few recent experiments carried out at night have indicated that it should be possible to navigate fighters by means of D/F intercept techniques to within about 4 miles of an enemy – providing sufficient information regarding track and height of the enemy is available. The accuracy of interception by D/F at night will be such that fighters will usually be unable to sight the target unless the latter is illuminated by some means or unless further detection aids are provided.'

The report went on to look at the options for such detection aids:

> Use of AI – it is suggested that at least one aircraft in the fighter formation should have AI equipment in order to determine whether this apparatus would enable the aircraft to make visual contact with a target which is not illuminated.
> Searchlights – on a clear night, the intersection of searchlight beams should be sufficient indication of the position of the target. Experiments should be made to determine, under various conditions of visibility and at various altitudes, the range at which the intersection of searchlight beams is visible and the range at

Blenheim of 23 Squadron at Wittering, January 1940; this was the first squadron for L6730, which went on to serve with No.54 Operational Training Unit and 256 Squadron before finishing its career with No.12 Pilots Advanced Flying Unit.

which a target illuminated by searchlight beams is visible. Owing to the limited number of fighter units which can be operated by D/F techniques, it would seem desirable for fighters to fly in formation at night; therefore, aircraft will need to be equipped with station-keeping lights and IFF [identification friend or foe].

The trials did not take place until the following spring and summer. The first series were flown between 12 April and 4 May, with a 38 Squadron Wellington as the target and a 111 Squadron Hurricane as the fighter, the bomber being finished in the latest night camouflage scheme of matt black. After a number of sorties the general conclusion was that: 'the range at which pilots can see an unlit bomber whose position has been indicated, depends upon the experience of the pilot concerned. The upper limit appears to be about 600 yards astern and below, and 3,000 ft directly below. Aircraft engine exhaust can be seen up to one mile away. The average range for detecting searchlight intersection is 15–25 miles and 8–15 miles to distinguish an aircraft being held by searchlights.'

So far, so good. The second phase was conducted between 8 May and 7 July, the same aircraft being involved:

It is likely even under good conditions that searchlights will only help the fighter by 'flick-overs', to close with and attack a bomber in the dark. If, however, the lights continue to hold the bomber or make a series of 'flick-overs' without dropping behind it while the fighter closes until he can see the bomber itself, it is practically certain that the fighter will be able to deliver an attack. The approach to and attack on both a lit and unlit target should be made from behind and below, fire probably being opened at a maximum of 200 yards. Fighter patrols should be placed at least 10 miles behind the front line of searchlights in order to avoid confusion and to allow the fighter to go forward to intercept when a pick-up has been made. Use of the aircraft landing light as a searchlight did not prove successful.

During the trials 143 attempted interceptions were set up, of which 43 resulted in visual pick-up and 'combats'. An experimental AI set was fitted to a Fairey Battle in May 1939 and trials with a Harrow as a target proved the concept of the system, despite it being difficult to use and subject to equipment failure. Air and ground-based radar was indeed the solution to the night war and the progress of the RAF in this respect over the next few years was truly remarkable – for which much credit must be given to the behind-the-scenes 'boffins' and the RAF technicians who battled to keep the sets serviceable.

The Chain Home stations (radar) were of course effective both day and night but vectoring an aircraft close enough to pick-up a single raider at night was different to putting a fighter in a position to pick-up a formation of enemy aircraft by day. The principles were the same, as indeed were the Filter Rooms and all the other elements of the system; what was needed was more practice and appropriate night-fighters, ideally with airborne radar (AI) – both were lacking in mid 1940.

Experiments and trials continued into 1940, with a number of the Command's Blenheim squadrons now involved and despite the comment that the 'Mark I equipment is of no operational value and is being used for training' progress was generally forward. With the formation of the Night Interception Unit (soon renamed Fighter Interception Unit) at Tangmere in March 1940 the Command had a unit equipped with six AI Blenheims and a remit to make it work. By the time AI Mk IIIB was introduced in May 1940, with a maximum range of 9,000 ft and minimum range of 600 ft – along with greater reliability – a practical set had at last arrived. AI MK IV was under trial the following month and was even better, with a min range of 400 ft and better anti-clutter, although it was not in full production until September.

Meanwhile, the first night attack took place on 18/19 June, the German crews of KG.4 having been told that the RAF had no night-fighters; the main targets were the airfields of Honington and Mildenhall, with a diversionary raid on Southend. However, the RAF did have fighters ready, a mix of Blenheims and Spitfires and the night was to end with the loss of six German bombers and four RAF aircraft. A summary of this first night battle is included in the Operations chapter. Both sides appear to have forgotten this episode as attention turned to the day sphere and the Battle of Britain and it was August before matters became serious, statistics for the month showed 828 sorties by Fighter Command on 26 nights, with claims for four enemy aircraft destroyed (only three were eventually credited); a further 20 aircraft fell to other causes, mainly the anti-aircraft guns. The fighters were active, the targets were there – but there was a distinct lack of success.

The first phase of the night blitz on London lasted from 7/8 September to 13/14 November and the C-in-C of Fighter Command was worried that the Germans would be 'able to bomb this country with sufficient accuracy for his purposes without even emerging from clouds. The most depressing fact which has emerged from the past weeks is that the Germans can fly and bomb with considerable accuracy in weather in which our fighters cannot leave the ground. Their navigation is doubtless due to the excellence of their radio aids.' In part it was also due to the German use of KG.100 as a specialist and 'pathfinder' force. The radio aids, *Knickebein* beams, were a problem but the British knew of their existence and a counter-measure was being developed to jam the radio aids; this unit, No. 80 Wing was operational in autumn.

With the AI Mk IV production underway and a commitment to install these sets in Beaufighters (when the aircraft were available) the future looked promising but in the meantime the Blenheims soldiered on and overall strength was increased by moving three Defiant squadrons (73, 85 and 151) and three Hurricane squadrons to the night role,

Charmy Down, 87 Squadron pose with black-painted Hurricane; the Squadron became specialists in the night role.

although the latter did not take place until October. That same month Dowding wrote 'our task will not be finished until we can locate, pursue, and shoot down the enemy in cloud by day and night, and AI must become like a gun sight.' The first true GCI station, at Durrington, became operational in October and added a vital link in the chain of engaging enemy aircraft at night (and by day).

The second phase of the German night offensive saw a broadening to include other targets, which further stretched the defences. 'From the middle of November the massed night attacks were extended to the industrial cities and ports of the midlands. The central feature of the prosecution of the war remained the attack on London, however, attacks by day being continued as already described. The tactics of air war by night developed during the ensuing winter months. Only those details of tactics, which differ from those, now applied will be mentioned here. Concentration of attack in one place and at one time was not necessary because of the weak defences. The individual units proceeded to the targets along separate courses. To increase the strain on the morale of the population the duration of the attack was prolonged as much as possible. Only the weather rendered it necessary to concentrate the attack. On the other hand attacking those parts of the target area where the most important economic and industrial targets were allocated to units in each attack. To facilitate locating of targets and the individual objectives within the target areas themselves, the major attacks were carried out by moonlight. London, offering a large target area, was attacked chiefly during moonless nights. ... The month of November saw 23 major GAF attacks on vital British centres. In each attack 100–600 tons of bombs were dropped on these targets. During the period of 1–15th November 1940, 1,800 bombers dropped 1,900 tons of H.E.'s and 17,500 incendiary bombs on London alone. Of the towns attacked, Coventry, a centre of the British aircraft industry, must be mentioned. During the night of 14/15th November, 454 aircraft raided this town, dropping 600 tons if H.E. and incendiary bombs. Coventry has become a by-word wherever operational air-war is discussed as a result of the extensive damage caused by this raid.'

The attack on Coventry on the night of 14/15 November was indeed particularly effective – and worrying to the RAF. It was estimated that over 300 enemy aircraft took part and although the RAF flew 110 night patrols there were no combats. This attack is examined in more detail in the Operations chapter. When Air Marshal Sholto Douglas took-over as C-in-C or Fighter Command in late November one of his first concerns was to address the problem of night defence. His report of 8 December also stated that: 'I am convinced that the main obstacle to frequent intercepts by night is the lack of accurate tracking inland from the coast, and most important of all, lack of accurate information with regard to the height of the enemy bomber.'

He summed up the requirements for a good night fighter, stating that:

1. There should be at least 20 night squadrons equipped with AI. They would then provide a semi-circle of night-fighters from Newcastle to Devonshire, with a squadron each in the Birmingham and Coventry area.
2. There should be night flying airfields with AI homing beacons, Lorenz blind landing and other facilities.
3. There should be at least one large regional control airfield with a proper flying control staff to ensure the safety of night flying aircraft.
4. Special training using the AI by day with crews wearing dark glasses should be carried out. Later practices by night could commence.
5. Crews selected for night fighting should be specially tested for vision.

All of these points were addressed over the next few months; the training element led to the formation of a special night-fighter Operational Training, with No. 54 OTU duly formed at the end of December. The selection of crews was also put in hand and many a pilot found himself destined for night-fighters because his vision was assessed as better than normal. It would be some while, however before any of these measures became effective.

The first success for an AI Beaufighter came on 19/20 November, falling to John Cunningham of 604 Squadron; there were still only 47 Beaufighters in the Order of Battle and re-equipment has only started in October. However, the night war was starting to turn in favour of the defenders.

Loss Rates and Tour Lengths

In March 1941 the Air Council issued a letter that laid down a general rule that 'so far as the general war situation permitted, personnel should be relieved from operational flying after a maximum of 200 hours in one tour of operational flying.' This decision had been made after a great deal of debate, which the AHB report summarised: 'The difficulties in establishing such a datum line were considerable because whatever factors were used, the question of degree of stress arose. For example 100 hours operational flying in one Group of Fighter Command could easily be considered equal to 200 or more of similar flying in another Group of the same Command. It was evident that the datum line when established should not be so low as to cause a rapid turnover, leading to a shortage of experienced pilots, not should it be so high as to be impossible of attainment by the average pilot. At the same time it was plain that action could be taken immediately by moving fighter pilots to quieter sectors or other pilots to operational training units.'

The 1941 letter also stated that provision had to be made for 'early withdrawal of those of less robust constitution and for extension of the operational tour for fighter pilots from areas where enemy fighter opposition was weak or absent.' In November 1941 the 200 hours was confirmed but it was made clear that defensive sorties only ranked as 50% value when calculating the 200 hours. This remained the case to March 1943 when it was further stated that only half the flying hours spent on convoy protection and interception patrols beyond the range of enemy short-range fighter cover would count towards the 200 hours.

The tour length for night fighter pilots, including Intruders, was set at 100 hours or a maximum of 18 months; the tour for Intruder squadrons was changed in December 1943 to give a First Tour of 35 sorties and a Second Tour of 20 sorties, which could be increased to 30 sorties at the discretion of the AOC.

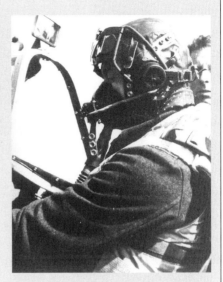

In March 1941 the Air Council issued a letter that laid down a general rule that 'so far as the general war situation permitted, personnel should be relieved from operational flying after a maximum of 200 hours in one tour of operational flying.'

The RAF's statisticians collected data on losses and came up with predicted survival rates for each operational role; survival was an unfortunate choice of term and 'chance of completing a tour' would have been a better option! For the Fighter-Command roles, all with 200-hours as the length of Operational Tour, the percentage chances of survival were:

Role	After one tour (%)	After two tours (%)
Day Fighter	27½	7½
AI Night Fighter	51	26
Twin-engine Intruder	13	1½
Single-engine Intruder	2	n/a

Notes:
1. Twin-engine intruder includes Fighter-Bomber and Bomber-Recce.
2. Single-engine Intruder includes Fighter-Bomber and Fighter-Recce.

The losses suggested by this survival statistic included prisoners of war and it was estimated that 20% of fighter pilots that were casualties became PoWs. A quick look at the table would suggest that AI night-fighters were the place to be! This RAF table is dated January 1943 and would therefore be a reasonable reflection of what was happening, although the single-engine intruder figures look a little suspicious. Out of interest the highest survival rate prediction was for the Catalina flying-boat with 55½% in a tour of 800 hours.

It was clear from all the facts at the Air Ministry's disposal that the chances of completing two tours were not good in most classes of squadron. On the other hand it was difficult to see where Squadron and Flight Commanders were to come from if the second tour was vetoed. This was a crucial factor as the squadrons needed experienced pilots in these key posts – and they could only come from those with operational experience. One suggestion was for a second tour of half the standard length, but only for selected personnel in the same roles, although this restriction was not placed on AI night-fighter squadrons.

1941 – Consolidation and new strategies

Whilst defending the skies over Britain remained the primary task for Fighter Command throughout the war, it was not long before thoughts turned to ways of taking the war to the enemy. Under various code-names such as *Mosquito*, *Circus*, *Ramrod*, *Rodeo* and *Rhubarb* (see Annex P for definitions of code-names) the Command waged an increasingly offensive war. As we shall see, in its early months it was not without its critics. Whilst the most interesting aspects of the Command's work were increasingly connected with offensive operations, the defensive element still occupied the majority of effort throughout 1941 and into early 1942; for example, in July the Command flew 6,200 offensive and 9,924 defensive sorties. It is also interesting that 6,475 of the defensive sorties were connected with protection of coastal shipping.

Before looking at the offensive aspect, we will review the defensive role and a number of general problems faced by the Command. One of these was the question of pilot experience, a problem neatly summed-up by the AHB narrative. 'It was estimated that nearly half the operational pilots in the squadrons on August 1st, 1940 were seasoned men, most of whom had fought successfully in May and June. Between that date and March 31st, 1941 the Command lost, as a result of combats, accidents and

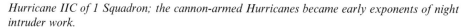

Hurricane IIC of 1 Squadron; the cannon-armed Hurricanes became early exponents of night intruder work.

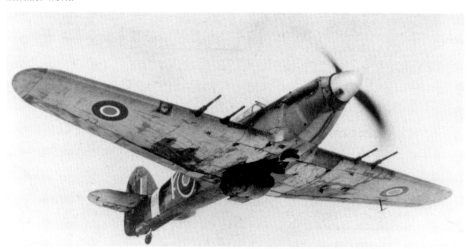

postings, some 1,300 pilots, or roughly equivalent to its entire strength. Although some of the casualties were newcomers, so that a back-bone of veterans remained, these casualties included many of the most experienced pilots in the Command. Replacements were drawn almost entirely from men who had been hurried through the OTUs in the autumn and whose operational training had been hampered by winter weather. It was hardly to be doubted that this handicap would outweigh the extra experience gained since August of the few veterans who had gone right through the fighting and were still in the Command.'

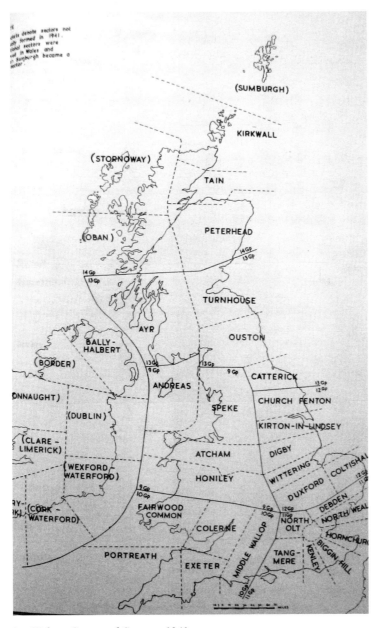

Map showing Fighter Command Sectors, 1941

Sholto Douglas was requesting an 'immediate' force of 80 day and 20 night squadrons as the 'crisis would come in spring and summer (1941) and that thereafter it would be unnecessary to increase the size of the fighter force and might even be possible to reduce it in order to build-up other Commands.' However, 1941 was a time when everyone wanted more – and immediately, and the emphasis was being firmly placed on Bomber Command. The Air Staff approved an increase to 81 squadrons, to be effective as near to April 1941 as possible; by February the Command's strength was 76 squadrons, with a further five in process of formation, not all of which were in place by the 1 April date. In fact the C-in-C had 77½ squadrons for the coming 'battle' and not the 100 he wanted. The Command was also continuing to reorganise, which included a new Sector for No. 9 Group, based on Valley and effective from 1 April. A summary also stated that 'the Hebrides, Western Highlands and the Minches remained outside the shelter of the Fighter Command umbrella, which now extended its protection to every other part of the UK.'

The C-in-C had also imposed a restructuring based on his belief in the Wing concept – he was a supporter of Leigh-Mallory's point of view, and Leigh-Mallory was now AOC of No. 11 Group. The intention was for Spitfire Wings in the Hornchurch and Tangmere Sectors, a Hurricane Wing in the Kenley Sector and another North of London, and mixed Wings in Duxford, Middle Wallop and Wittering Sectors. Approval was also given for appointment of a Wing Commander at 15 of the principal stations to act as Wing Leader. These would prove a crucial role and the RAF employed some superb leaders in this role, many of whom had been junior pilots in the Battle of Britain.

A memo was issued by No. 11 Group on 17 February 1941 detailing the 'employment and training of Wings and Circuses' and it is worth quoting extracts from this as it encapsulates the defensive plan for 1941.

> During the air battle in the autumn of 1940, the enemy employed mass formations of bombers and fighters with the object of destroying our fighter defence, and inflicting damage at vital points. It is probable that an even heavier scale of attack may have to be countered in the spring of 1941. To meet these large enemy formations it is inadequate to dispatch small formations of fighters that are unlikely to succeed in stopping the enemy bombers. It is therefore necessary to meet this type of attack with large formations, which are capable of providing protection against the enemy fighter screen for those fighters whose role it is to break up the enemy bomber formations and destroy the bombers. It has been decided to organise Wings throughout No. 11 Group, which will be composed of two or three squadrons. These Wings will, on occasion, operate in Circuses, which will be composed of two or more Wings.
>
> The object of employing Wings and Circuses in defence is to engage powerful enemy formations with sufficient large numbers to:
>
> a. Stop the enemy bombers reaching their objectives.
> b. Break up the enemy bomber formations.
> c. Annihilate the enemy when the breaking up process has been achieved.
> d. Have sufficient aircraft to provide protection against enemy escorting fighters.
>
> The object of employing Wings and Circuses in offensive operations is to provide the necessary number of fighters, working in co-operation and giving mutual support, to establish air superiority over the enemy in his own country.

April also brought a change of tactical structure in the squadrons, with official adoption of a Section of two aircraft as the smallest tactical unit; three such Sections made up each Flight and two Flights made up a Squadron. There had been a long and drawn-out debate on such tactical matters, with some preferring this more flexible tactic whilst others maintained that the existing tactic was perfectly good, although there was general agreement – as well as the Command directive. However, 'adoption of the three-squadron Wing as a tactical unit was very different. It would be hard to think of a tactical measure in the whole field of air defence whose utility was more widely debated or which caused livelier controversy' (AHB Narrative).

In late June the Air Ministry agreed to a further increase in Fighter Command strength to 94 day and 30 night squadrons – to be achieved by the end of the year. Progress on expansion was steady both in terms of numbers of units and equipment; as the table below shows, the number of Spitfire squadrons had grown significantly between April and July, and this was now the dominant type in the Command.

Summary of squadrons, April and July 1941

	8 April 1941			1 July 1941		
	Operational	*Non-op*	*Total*	*Operational*	*Non-op*	*Total*
Hurricane I	26½	½	27	11	1	12
Hurricane II	12	–	12	18	–	18
Spitfire I	4	2	6	5½	6½	12
Spitfire II	18	–	18	20	1	21
Spitfire V	1	–	1	7	–	7
Defiant	7	–	7	7	4	11
Tomahawk	1	–	1	–	–	–
Blenheim	–	1	1	–	–	–
Beaufighter	4	–	4	6	–	6
Blen/Beau	1	–	1	–	1	1
Blen/Havoc	1	–	1	2	–	2
Whirlwind	1	–	1	1	1	2
Havoc	1	–	1	3	–	3
Boston	1	–	1	–	–	–
Total	78½	3½	82	80½	14½	93

Notes for July ORBAT:
+ Havoc only.
Squadrons 96, 151, 255 and 256 also have four Hurricanes (N) and 92 Squadron has an additional two Spitfires (N) (N=standing for Night).

The July figures are also interesting for the number of non-operational squadrons, the bulk of which were newly-formed squadrons with Spitfires or Defiants. It was also significant that the Spitfire V was starting to appear in larger numbers, with seven operational squadrons by July. This new variant of the Spitfire gave the RAF pilots the edge over the majority of 109 variants – but that balance was to change later in the year when the Germans introduced a fighter that was to cause the RAF major problems; the Fw 190 entered service in late summer and by the end of the year it was clear that the RAF's fighters were being out-classed. The Fw 190A was being operated by JG26 and had the edge over the Spitfire V in a number of crucial performance areas.

Pilots of 66 Squadron at Perranporth in 1941 – as with many squadron pictures there is, of course, a dog! The Squadron was at Perranporth from April 1941 to the end of the year.

The Air Ministry's interrogators took every opportunity to record the views of captured German aircrew and from time to time the results of such interrogations were circulated. One such document was Tactical Bulletin No. 1 issued in July 1941; this outlined the view of a Bf 109F pilot in respect of its comparative performance in respect of the Spitfire. 'This pilot believes the Me109F is superior in every respect – except that the new Spitfire (the Mark V) might, when handled by an equally good pilot, be superior to the 109F in steep turns at high speed. This difference, however, can be more than counter-balanced if the German pilot is better.'

The report also included other related comments. 'The outstanding disadvantage of the Me109 is that the wings are not as stable as they might be. At least two German pilots have been killed within the last three weeks by tearing the wings off their 109s when trying to follow Spitfires in a snaking dive. After a fast dive pilots have to pull out fairly gradually. The new arrangement of guns in the nose of the 109F enables pilots to fire very accurately whilst in a turn and to open fire at a greater range. This pilot, however, usually opens fire at 100 yards, closing to 50 yards.'

One of the key tactical lessons from the Battle of Britain was that the fighters with height advantage at the start of a combat were well-placed; this was expressed by a senior pilot at Hornchurch in July 1941: 'diving attacks are always the most effective as the element of surprise is achieved' – but he also stated that the ability to get higher should not be at the expense of other performance elements. '... but turning radius and acceleration are equally important. At all heights a Spitfire can turn inside an Me 109, but the 109 appears to have quicker initial acceleration in a dive and also in climbing. ... Reserve of power and manoeuvrability are the foremost requirements for efficient

Clipped-wing Spitfire V; the Mark V was seen as an interim measure but served in large numbers. 'At present the Spitfire V has insufficient reserves of power to stay in combat with the ME 109 at 35,000ft. The latter definitely has greater speed at that height on the level, climb or dive.'

fighting at great heights. The superiority in this respect of the Me 109, particularly the Me 109F, must, to a large extent, be due to its light weight. At present the Spitfire V has insufficient reserves of power to stay in combat with the Me 109 at 35,000 ft. The latter definitely has greater speed at that height on the level, climb or dive.'

It appeared, therefore, that the Spitfire V was on a par with or even slightly better than its main opponent, the Bf 109E and 109F, with pilot experience and tactics of more importance than aircraft performance. The Spitfire V was not the only 'new boy' with the Command in 1941; the Bell Airacobra and Tomahawk, and the latest Hawker offering, the Typhoon, became operational during the year. The Airacobra went to 601 Squadron but despite some operational flying was a quickly rejected, whilst the highly promising *Tiffie* suffered development problems but eventually went to 56 Squadron as the Typhoon IA in September 1941. It was not the happiest of introductions as problems with the Sabre engine and various other snags limited the initial employment of the type.

By the end of the year the plan for 94 day and 30 night squadrons had not been achieved. There were only 75 day squadrons and of the night units only 23 were true night-fighter units, along with 10 Turbinlite Flights and two night-intruder squadrons.

Defensive Operations 1941
The main daylight war over England had almost come to an end by early 1941. The *Luftwaffe* fighter-bomber and fighter sweeps had more or less ended in mid December and did not resume until mid February, and even then on a relatively small scale. Between February and the end of March the main day enemy activity was fighter-bomber attacks on airfields in the No. 11 Group area, such as Hawkinge, Lympne and Manston. From 1 April to 29 May the RAF recorded 283 day and night attacks on airfields, raids that were referred to as 'pirate raids' and that were hard to counter.

The AHB narrative neatly summarises the problems these caused: 'the favourite objectives for such raids were airfields and aircraft factories and, during the winter of 1941, a number of successful enemy low-level, daylight attacks were carried out. These showed evidence of careful planning and were normally carried out by aircraft operating either singly or in pairs. They were, moreover, difficult to intercept and, although special

Spitfire formation of 81 Squadron; the Squadron acquired Spitfire Vs at the end of 1941 and operated the type to October 1942 when they departed for North Africa.

measures were taken to deal with single raiders – such as the use of AI fighters by day when the weather was bad – the problems remained unsolved at the end of the year.'

Fighter Command had its 'Big Wing' tactic ready to counter any resumption of large-scale daylight activity – but it never came. There were a number of fighter sweeps between February and May but they were small-scale and 'gave Fighter Command no chance of using the large wing formations . . . and the problems of interception was thus, as with the long-range bombers, unsolved in July, when both the low-level attacks and fighter sweeps were discontinued'. The main reasons for the virtual ending of such offensive action in mid 1941 were the reorganisation of German air power for the invasion of Russia and the increasing pressure of the Allied daylight air offensive. Indeed, a plan to rotate elements of JG2 and JG26 to Russia had to be cancelled as the Allied offensive grew in magnitude. The initiative had firmly passed to the RAF (and soon the joint RAF-USAAF offensive) in terms of daylight operations, although there was still a hard fight ahead. The main combat activity over the UK in 1941 was by night.

Night Defence

The problems of night defence had started to become increasingly apparent in the latter months of 1940 – and there was little immediate improvement in the early months of 1941. Fighter Command ORS Report No. 235 summarised the 'trend of air defence at night'. The following extracts of the report highlight its main points:

> 1.1. Fighters had practically no success in intercepting enemy bombers by night from October 1940 until February 1941 inclusive.

1.2. The month of March saw the beginning of effective operations by the GCI system, and the use of 'Fighter Nights' over target areas. The success of fighters rose month by month; 24 enemy aircraft were destroyed in March, 52 in April, and 102 in May. In particular, on the night of 10/11th May, over 8% of the enemy aircraft employed on an attack on London were destroyed by fighters. The total losses of the enemy were nearly 10%.

1.3. During the period March, April, May 1941, about 40% of fighter success was obtained with GCI/AI technique. Since then the enemy has made only slight, dispersed raids, ideally suited to the GCI/AI technique, and the percentage has risen considerably, so that at the present time AI machines carry out practically all the night interceptions of these dispersed raids.

1.4. The present limitation of the GCI/AI technique lies in the difficulty of obtaining visual contact in the final stages of the chase. A significant difference exists between the moonlit and moonless hours of the night. With existing skill of the average GCI station and average AI squadron, it can be conservatively estimated that during moonlit hours of the night one attempt in 8 will go to combat; and that during moonless hours of the night one attempt in 20 will go to combat. These attempts can be made by present GCI stations at the rate of 4 to 5 per hour if sufficient night fighters are available. The combats will result in 3 out of every 4 enemy aircraft being destroyed or probably destroyed.

1.5. An improvement in the efficiency of the GCI/AI technique has occurred, that may be attributed mainly to increased skill of the flying personnel.

1.6. A noticeable component of the rising success of night fighters is a much greater lethality of combats by Beaufighters, which is not likely to have been caused by the prolongation of twilight in he Summer.

The report made a number of interesting points, especially those relating to the capacity of the system – the number of targets that could be handled by the GCI system and the availability of fighters – and the increased lethality brought about by improved skills and the introduction of the Beaufighter. The GCI network was rapidly expanding; by January 1941 six sites were operational (Avebury, Durrington, Orby, Sopley, Walding Field and Willesborough) and in the first six months it was estimated that 100 German aircraft fell to intercepts controlled in this way.

The report also 'speculated' on a number of other techniques; it proposed that AI fighters should be allowed to free-lance rather than always being closely controlled by GCI, and it commented on Long Aerial Mines and airborne searchlights.

3.3. Long Aerial Mines. They should not be regarded as a competitor to GCI/AI or free-lance AI, but as a supplement. They will be useful in the case of very high density raids. They should be used on long-duration aircraft in order that they may be used to overcome weather limitations that affect normal fighters. The sketchy evidence available at the moment is quite insufficient to either damn or to praise LAMs.

3.4. Searchlight aircraft. A much better ratio of combats to attempts would be obtained if illumination of the target from the air can be obtained after closing in on AI. This assumes, of course, that the enemy is unable to adopt successful countermeasures, and that the 'formation flying' needed does not affect the overall efficiency by a greater amount than the searchlight improves it.

Beaufighter of 255 Squadron at Honiley; the AI-equipped Beaufighter was the first truly-effective night-fighter in the Command; 255 Squadron operated Beaufighters from July 1941, moving to Honiley in June 1942.

LAMs were to have little future – but the searchlight idea was persevered with.

There was a steady increase in the number of night squadrons in late 1940–early 1941, albeit many of these were initially equipped with Defiants; for example, 255 Squadron, which formed at Kirton-in-Lindsey in November 1940 and became operational the first week in January.

Fighter Command was better equipped to cope with the threat, having six AI-equipped squadrons, five with Beaufighters. The more capable AI Mk. V and improved training also helped to make the defences more efficient. However, there was still a shortage of aircraft and coverage of the UK was patchy, with gaps in coverage.

The third phase of the German night offensive ran from the middle of February to the middle of May and was essentially an offensive on British ports, with 36 of the 61 attacks being on port towns in the South-West. British cities were still on the target list: 'The heaviest night attack on London was made in April, with a total of 711 aircraft over the target (the operation consisted of a double attack) dropping a bomb load of 1,026 tons of H.E. and 150 tons of incendiary bombs. Also worthy of mention are the two heavy attacks on Glasgow in May 1941.' (Bechtle)

'On 12th May, the day the great enemy night assault came to an end, the C-in-C, Fighter Command told the Night Air Defence Committee that "AI with GCI was the most profitable means of night interception, notwithstanding the successes obtained by Cats Eye fighters". He demanded acceleration in the provision of Beaufighters. On 11th June he wrote "the expansion of the Night Fighter force is now in sight, and we expect the supply of GCI sets to come forward at a quicker rate in the future."' Indeed, four more squadrons were formed in June (125, 409, 410, 456), although all initially had Defiants.

The Germans had reduced their scale of effort in the summer as part of a re-organisation of air assets from West to East for the invasion of Russia rather than in response to any increase in the effectiveness of the British defences. However, the latter had been recognised and the *Luftwaffe* began to adopt various tactics to confuse the defenders, such as low approach and erratic courses. The decreasing scale of losses was noted by Fighter Command and in a report of 19 November was put down to 'vigorous evasive action had become a routine measure with enemy pilots when approaching our coasts, and they flew low over the sea in the knowledge that by doing so they could not be "seen" by our radar.' It was not only the GCI radars and Chain Home that had problems of seeing low-level targets, as the AI radars were invariably ineffective below 5,000 ft because of ground returns masking the target. It was intended to bring the Chain Home Low stations into play to provide better cover and it was hoped that new tactics with AI Mk. IV would improved performance down to at least 3,000 ft – and new radars under development would be even better.

By the end of the year the Command had flown 11,980 night defence sorties, with 4,967 being by AI-equipped aircraft. The fighters had claimed 258 enemy aircraft out of the estimated 25,334 aircraft that had flown over the UK in this period, with a further 131 falling to anti-aircraft guns and 44 to 'other' causes. The busiest period had been March to June, both in terms of sorties and successes. The Fighter Night operations were constantly under review as they seemed to produce few results but occupied squadrons that could have been used for other purposes. A summary for the period January to May 1941 showed 17 Fighter Nights and claims for 41 aircraft, the most successful night being 10/11 May when the target was London and 12 aircraft were claimed. The latter appeared to prove the belief that 'close protective patrols by Cat's Eye fighters was only profitable in good moonlight and in clear weather. . . . This form of patrol was only profitable in highly concentrated areas of enemy activity.'

Defiant crews of 264 Squadron; after its disastrous daylight career (despite early promise), the Defiant was used by a significant number of squadrons for night-fighter ops, with 264 Squadron performing this role to July 1942.

The performance of the anti-aircraft guns had steadily improved, and the figure of 20,000 rounds to down an aircraft (September 1940) had fallen to 2,963 rounds by February 1941. The guns had also been redistributed following the increase in attacks on targets other than London; by May 1941 AA Command was fielding 1,691 Heavy and 940 Light Guns, supported by 4,532 searchlights. Whenever Fighter Night operations were underway – the bright moonlight when day fighters were employed – the guns were restricted to burst heights 2,000 ft below the lowest level at which the fighters would be operating.

Night-fighter strength was increased with the decision to form specialist Flights to operate modified AI-equipped Havocs, the modification being the addition of a high-power searchlight (The Helmore searchlight). Each of these Fighter Flights was to have an establishment of 8 + 1 Turbinlite Havocs in what on paper looked like the brilliantly simple idea of taking a searchlight into the air to help turn night into day. In essence the system was simple, a Turbinlite Havoc would work as a pair with a single-seat fighter and both would initially be vectored to the target by a ground controller. Once the Havoc AI operator had acquired the target he would home it, position the fighter and when the time was right, turn on the searchlight to allow the fighter to make his attack.

No. 93 Squadron carried out initial development work, having virtually given-up its previous work with the LAM, but it was the formation of No. 1451 (Fighter) Flight at Hunsdon in May 1941 that really got the project underway. The Flight was tasked with training four other Turbinlite Flights and it was one of these, No. 1452 Flight that developed the standard tactic. On 6 November the CO, Sqn Ldr J E Marshall, submitted a progress report in which he detailed this tactic: 'In this attack, the parasite, when given the word, dives forward so as to lose about 500 ft. The AI operator keeps the Turbinlite pilot directed on to the target, and gives the pilot the word to illuminate when he can see by his tubes that the parasite is approximately 300 yards behind the target. The parasite then sees the target illuminated slightly above him and is able to make a well-timed and effective attack.' A follow-up report stated: 'success in the scheme depends among other things on each member of the crew taking the correct action at the appropriate moment. As orders are passed from one to another, and as the conditions of the intercept will

Turbinlite team – Havoc and Hurricane; one of the less successful attempts at boosting the night defences of Fighter Command.

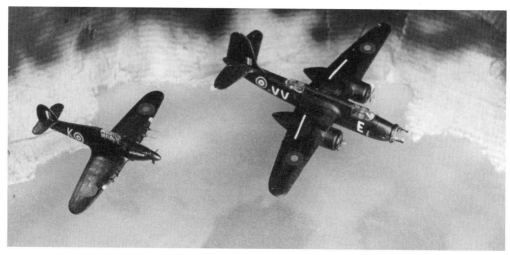

seldom be identical on two nights, it is clear that a complete understanding must exist between each member of the team. The satellite pilot should always work with the same Turbinlite pilot ... it is particularly easy in the first few seconds to miss an illuminated target.' The original concept was for the Flight to work with single-seat squadrons, although Marshall was convinced that the fighter needed to be part of the Turbinlite unit. All ten Flights had formed by the end of the year (see table) and all were engaged with intensive training to try and make the system work; it was 1942 before they were truly part of the night-defence Order of Battle.

Turbinlite Flights		
Flight no.	Formed	Airfield
1451 Flt	22 May 1941	Hunsdon
1452 Flt	7 Jul 1941	West Malling
1453 Flt	10 Jul 1941	Wittering
1454 Flt	27 Jun 1941	Colerne
1455 Flt	7 Jul 1941	Tangmere
1456 Flt	24 Nov 1941	Honiley
1456 Flt	15 Sep 1941	Colerne
1458 Flt	6 Dec 1941	Middle Wallop
1459 Flt	20 Sep 1941	Hunsdon
1460 Flt	15 Dec 1941	Acklington

Shipping Protection

After July 1941 the main German daylight offensive was against shipping, with roughly two-thirds of the total effort dedicated to this. Before we look at the situation in late 1941 it is worth reviewing the overall role to date of Fighter Command in the protection of shipping.

In the early months of the war the Command had been mounting an average of 1,000 sorties a month in defence of shipping; this had risen to 2,000 sorties by early 1940 and over 3,000 sorties by July. The basic policy was one of providing fighter cover rather than standing escort; the policy was dictated by lack of aircraft but there were occasions when standing escort was made available. The early battles over the Channel, that were precursors to the Battle of Britain, have been covered above. In November 1940 the *Luftwaffe* once more mounted heavy attacks on shipping, with the Ju 87s also making a renewed appearance. On 6 March 1941 Fighter Command received a new Directive stating that the primary task was now defence of the Clyde, Mersey and Bristol Channel areas and was told to make 'such changes in deployment of his resources as was necessary.'

The German view was that the year had been pretty successful: 'Attacks on shipping targets were carried out making full use of the element of surprise in daytime, at dawn and dusk or during nights of good visibility according to weather conditions. Bombing attacks were made at low-level or in a shallow dive with bombs of 250 kg or 500 kg. The successes achieved in 1941 with small losses to ourselves were good. As an example the results for the month of November may be given: these were sunk – 82,100 gross register tons, probably sunk – 49,000 tons, and damaged – 66,000 tons' (Bechtle). This must relate to the early part of the year, before Fighter Command had increased its efforts to counter the threat; in March 18% (2,103 sorties) of the Command's defensive sorties were on shipping protection and the enemy sank 21 ships within 40 miles of coast during daylight and a further two at night. The following month – after the Directive had taken effect – the effort was 49% (7,876 sorties) and the losses were down to ten ships. Sholto Douglas sent a memo to the Chief of the Air Staff: 'you will be pleased to hear that for once the Navy is pleased with Fighter Command.' In July they would have been even more pleased as only one ship was sunk in the area covered by Fighter Command.

There is one specific convoy protection activity that deserves separate mention – the **Merchant Ship Fighter Unit** (MSFU). Debate had been underway for some time concerning a ship-borne fighter, as the lack of aircraft carriers meant that it was not possible to provide this expensive type of air cover. The Chief of Air Staff submitted the following note to the March Chiefs of Staff Committee: 'I am convinced that neither shore-based aircraft in the numbers that we can hope to provide in the next six to nine months nor gun armament can secure our shipping in the Atlantic against the scale and type of long-range air attack that we must now expect ... the only method of protection likely to be effective is the ship-borne high performance fighter operating from specially converted ships which must accompany every convoy in the danger area. I urge that these ships ... should be given the highest possible priority.' The outcome of this was the MSFU, which formed in May 1941 as a No. 9 Group unit under the command of Wg Cdr E S Moulton-Barrett. In essence this called for a single-seat fighter to be mounted on a catapult rail such that it could be launched 'at an appropriate moment' to engage the enemy – and then ditch, the pilot being picked up out of the water. The Hurricane was the chosen type, for both its sturdiness and availability, and in May sixty aircraft were converted; the overall plan called for 200 aircraft, 50 of which would be stored in Dartmouth, Nova Scotia (the other end of the Atlantic convoy route) for use on the return trip.

Plt Off H J Davidson made a trial launch from the SS *Empire Rainbow* on 31 May, which was almost a disaster when his wing-tip touched the water. Further trials proved the basic concept and the first operational aircraft were at sea in early June aboard the SS *Empire Rainbow* (Plt Off Davidson) and SS *Empire Moon* (Fg Off A R M Campbell). On 1 November, some 6550 miles West of Achill Head, Fg Off G W Varley launched from SS *Empire Foam* to intercept an Fw 200 Kondor. However, the enemy aircraft managed to hide in the cloud and Varley was unable to intercept. After a 2-hour patrol at 3,000 ft, in which the *Kondor* stayed away, he ditched and was picked-up, after four

Fighters at sea on merchant ships; an emergency measure to counter German long range aircraft.

minutes in the water, by a destroyer. The fact that the enemy was not engaged was less important than the fact that it had been chased away from the convoy. The Navy was also engaged in similar activity with the Catapult Armed Merchantmen (CAM) but this is outside of our story of Fighter Command. The first success for the MSFU did not come until 25 May 1942 when Fg Off John Kendal shot down a Ju 88 inside the Arctic Circle, but in poor weather he baled out too low and was killed – the only fatal casualty for the MSFU in action, although aircraft and personnel were lost when their ships were sunk. A number of combats were flown over the ensuing 15 months until the disbandment of the Unit on 7 September 1943, the final successful combats having taken place on 28 July.

But we have now moved ahead of the Fighter Command story. Whilst the Germans had been reasonably pleased with the results in 1941, the changes made by the defenders soon altered this view: 'the position changed surprisingly at the beginning of the year 1942. A/A defence aboard the vessels and protection of the convoys by fighter aircraft had been strengthened considerably; for instance, K.G.2 lost during 5 weeks (February– March 1942) 13 crews after scoring only slight successes.' (Bechtle)

Offensive Operations 1941

On 8 December 1940 a Fighter Command Order for 'Sector Offensive Sweeps' was issued; these were to made by three squadrons in the afternoons and flown above 20,000 ft, the intention being to: 'harass the Germans by daily "tip and run" operations, to make them feel flying over Northern France or Belgium is unsafe, and so force them to some system of readiness in order to protect themselves.' This was not the only type of offensive operation and was not actually the first flown; the first acknowledged offensive mission was flown on 20 December, when two Spitfires of 66 Squadron attacked Le Touquet airfield, a '*Mosquito*' (a code-name that was changed to '*Rhubarb*' on 17 January 1941). The No. 11 Group order for these operations stated: 'On suitable days a selected Flight in one Sector is to be "Released" for Mosquito raids. Each Sector is allotted in rotation one day per week on which they are, when the weather is suitable, to Release a Flight for this purpose. Should it be impossible due to weather or any other reason for a Flight to operate on their selected day, their opportunity to do so will be lost for that week and the next named Sector will take over on the day following in accordance with he roster.

'Mosquito raids are only to be undertaken when the weather is suitable, that is when cloud cover is available to enable our fighters to fly in or above clouds, dart out from clouds to attack hostile aircraft and return immediately into the clouds. These raids are not to be made when the clouds base is below 2,000 ft. If conditions are found to be unsuitable on approaching the French coast, the task is to be abandoned and aircraft are to return to base.

'The Squadron Commander of the Squadron which is to carry out a raid is to decide on the number of aircraft to be employed and on the detailed method of carrying out the operation. Only experienced pilots are to be detailed. They are not to take unnecessary risks and they are to be told that the object of these raids is to inflict the maximum casualties on the enemy without loss to themselves.'

The order also gave the rotation of Sectors, starting with North Weald for 22 December, the first official day of *Mosquito* and then rotating through Tangmere, Hornchurch, Northolt, Debden, Biggin Hill, Kenley and back to North Weald.

In the period from 22 December 1940 to June 1941 the Command ordered 149 such missions, of which 45 were not completed, usually because of bad weather. Fighters engaged in 18 combats, claiming seven victories, and also attacked 116 ground targets. This was a reasonable result for a loss of eight aircraft.

The code-name *Circus* has caused some confusion as it was applied to fighter and bomber operation as well as a large-scale fighter sweep. These *Circus* operations, during which a bomber force would attack targets in France, aimed to 'raise and engage that portion of the *Luftwaffe* fighter strength based on the Western Front' (Fighter Command operational memo). The tactic was amplified in the operational order of 24 December, which stated that the intent of these missions was to 'take offensive action which will harass the enemy, force him to adopt a defensive preparedness and enable our patrols to meet him in the air with the tactical advantages of height and surprise.' It continued, 'normally not less than six fighter squadrons will be employed with or without the co-operation of a small bomber force. Periodically, to carry out offensive sweeps over occupied territory with large fighter forces, the fighters operating on occasions in company with one of more bomber squadrons.' It also stated that should no enemy aircraft be encountered then the Hurricane Wing 'may, on occasions, come down low to attack targets on the ground.' Interestingly, the same freedom of action was not permitted to the Spitfire Wings.

The first of the fighter sweeps was flown on 9 January, with 1 Squadron and 615 Squadron patrolling at 21,000 ft from Cap Griz Nez to near Calais, and three squadrons (65, 145, 615) patrolling at 22,000 ft from Boulogne to St Omer. Neither formation saw any enemy aircraft. There was a general belief that the *Luftwaffe* might prove reluctant to engage the fighter sweeps, which was why the bomber option had been included.

The first of the *Circus* missions with bombers was flown on 10 January 1941, with Bomber Command Blenheims to 'harass the enemy on the ground by bombing the Foret de Guisne, to destroy enemy aircraft in the air or, should insufficient or no enemy aircraft be seen, to ground strafe St Inglevert aerodrome, with particular attention to aircraft grounded and petrol tankers.'

The second such mission was flown on 5 February the target being the airfield at St Omer/Longuenesse, but it was no more successful in provoking the desired reaction. A few days later the Command reaffirmed the aim of these missions as being to 'bomb selected targets, and to take advantage of the enemy reaction to shoot-down his fighters under conditions favourable to our own fighters.' A Bomber Command analysis

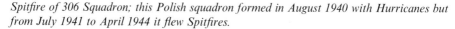

Spitfire of 306 Squadron; this Polish squadron formed in August 1940 with Hurricanes but from July 1941 to April 1944 it flew Spitfires.

showed that although bomber losses were low for this type of mission, at around 3%, the associated Fighter Command statistics were not so good. In 9,486 sorties Fighter Command claimed 118 enemy aircraft – but for a loss of 166. This should not really have come as any great surprise, as in essence the tactic was little different from that employed, without success, by the *Luftwaffe* over Britain in 1940.

A review of offensive ops to mid February suggested that all was not well; Sholto Douglas stated that, 'our idea was to fly over the other side and leap on the enemy from a great height in superior numbers; instead of which it looks as though we ourselves are being leapt on.' The main fighter opponents were JG2, with bases to the South of the Seine, and JG26, with bases in the Pas de Calais, both were equipped with the latest Bf 109 variants and both continued to display skill and aggressiveness.

As early as March the suggestion was being mooted that the fighters should carry small incendiary bombs in makeshift containers fitted to the flare tubes as a way of adding to the 'offensive firepower'. This was rejected as not being worth the effort, but the concept of giving the fighters a bomb-load was by no means forgotten. Around the same time, approval was being sought for clearance to attack moving trains, which were still forbidden targets. This was rejected and it was not until October that such clearance was finally given for attacks on moving Goods trains; train-busting (*Chatanoogas* to the Americans) became a major task for the roving fighters, especially in 1944.

In the first six months of *Mosquito/Rhubarb* the Command flew 336 such sorties, 45 of which were abortive, mainly because of weather. The most frequent target types attacked were ships, airfields, gun and searchlight posts, and road transport, with 110 attacks on these types of target. The fighters made claims for seven enemy aircraft shot-down and the Command lost eight pilots. The number of *Rhubarb* sorties more than doubled in the second half of the year, with 886 sorties, October being the busiest month (246). The number of target types increased and 297 targets were attacked, with trains and the railway system top of the list (74), for the loss of 19 pilots. Claims were made for 14 enemy aircraft.

On 8 October 1941 Fighter Command took over responsibility for Channel Stop from No. 2 Group of Bomber Command; these anti-shipping operations were designed

The Battle of Britain had cost the RAF 448 pilots, offensive ops in 1941 cost it 462 pilots, over half of these occurring during the Circus *operations. Fighter Command claimed the destruction of 731 enemy aircraft. Spitfire BL479 of 316 Squadron.*

to prevent German military and merchant shipping using the Channel. Two squadrons, 402 and 607 with Hurricane bombers were allotted to this task, supported by other units of No. 11 Group.

The Battle of Britain had cost the RAF 448 pilots, offensive ops in 1941 cost it 462 pilots, over half of these occurring during the *Circus* operations. Fighter Command claimed the destruction of 731 enemy aircraft (540 of these during *Circus* ops) but post-war research in German records suggested the real total was only 135. As examples of the discrepancy, on 21 June the RAF claimed 27 victories, whereas German records show only seven, and on the following day the difference was even more marked – 31 claims against two actually lost. This is not to say that the RAF pilots were attempting to inflate their claims; the RAF had a very rigorous process for determining such things, but it was obviously going wrong somewhere, even allowing for some errors in the German records. However, this is not to say that the offensive campaign was ineffective; indeed it was proving very effective both materially and for morale. The material effect was felt with shipping, evidenced by a reduction in coastal shipping activity and the allocation of greater resources for protection, industrial production, and military capability. Amongst the latter was a direct effect on the combat capability of the two main fighter units, JG2 and JG26, as combat capability involved more than just losses. At the height of the year's offensive, August, the two units had only 97 serviceable aircraft out of an establishment of 248 aircraft. The fact that this was at least in part due to the RAF offensive was proven by the way the units recovered after the scale of the offensive was reduced from mid August; by the end of September both were almost back to full strength.

Night Offensive
On 21 December 1940 the first night intruder mission was flown, Blenheims of 23 Squadron operating over enemy airfields. This was the start of a campaign that would eventually see Fighter Command notch-up over 11,000 such sorties and make claims for over 500 enemy aircraft destroyed. For most of 1941 it was almost a lone war by 23 Squadron, who flew 488 of the 559 Intruder sorties in the year. The Squadron acquired Havocs in March to replace the Blenheims and increase the offensive capability and flew the first mission with the new aircraft in April. The scale of the offensive increased with the employment of single-seat fighters; the Hurricanes of 87 Squadron flew their first mission on 14/15 March, two aircraft 'visiting' the Caen/Carpiquet where they found 20 aircraft on the ground but due to poor weather only managed to claim one. Defiants joined in on 7/8 April with 141 Squadron flying their first Intruder. Other squadrons also took part during the year.

In November 1941 the Fighter Command ORS produced a report into the 'relative effectiveness on intrusive efforts' with the conclusion drawn from statistics for January to June and June to October. The figures were:

Jan–Jun, 180 sorties with 29½ enemy aircraft destroyed.
Jun–Oct, 263 sorties with 11½ enemy aircraft destroyed.

This may not at first sight look impressive but the report quite rightly pointed out that destruction of aircraft was not the main role of this type of mission, but rather it was the overall effect caused by the attacks on the airfields: '... the bombing of aerodromes is not, however, the chief mission of Intruders, they carry a very small bomb-load, and the bombs they drop cause much greater morale than material damage; the bombing of our aerodromes by German intruders substantiates this.' However, it also said that the 'only reliable measure of the utility of Intruders is the number of enemy aircraft they claim to

The most unusual of Fighter Command's offensive operations was the deployment of two Hurricane squadrons as No.151 (Fighter) Wing to Murmansk, Russia in August 1941.

destroy.' With this it was pointed out that results were not always observed and that 'whatever the actual damage, the morale effect must be considerable, and some German aircraft may have become casualties by having to land on unfamiliar aerodromes after their home base had been attacked.' (ORS Report No. 267 dated 8 November 1941). By the end of the year the total number of sorties had risen to 575, with 502 of those being flown by 23 Squadron, still the only dedicated night intruder squadron; the remainder were flown by Defiants and Hurricanes.

Russian Interlude

The most unusual of Fighter Command's offensive operations was the deployment of two Hurricane squadrons as No. 151 (Fighter) Wing to Murmansk, Russia in August 1941. The Wing was part of Force *Benedict* and formed at Leconfield on 26 July, comprising 81 and 134 squadrons, both with Hurricane IIBs. Moving to Hendon in August the Wing sailed for Russia on HMS *Argus,* landing at Archangel on 30 August and moving to their main base at Vaenga on 7 September.

The first missions were flown a few days later and brought immediate success, three Bf 109s and an HS 126 having been claimed by the end of the day for the loss of one Hurricane. The detachment rapidly added to its score, which soon stood at 15 claimed for one loss. Whilst operational sorties, including escort to Russian bombers, were an important part of the task, equally important was the training of Russian personnel in the erection, maintenance and operation of Hurricanes, as Churchill had agreed to ship 240 crated Hurricanes to Russia. By the time the Wing departed the Russians had three Hurricane squadrons assembled and ready for action.

Operations for the RAF terminated in mid November and the RAF personnel returned to the UK, handing the remaining aircraft to the Russians. On their return to the UK both squadrons re-equipped with Spitfires. Sgt 'Wag' Haw was the top scorer with the detachment, and as such was one of four recipients of the Order of Lenin, the highest Soviet decoration.

1942 – Losing the edge

Circus operations remained a key element of the Command's work during 1942, but it is worth noting a special operation that took place in August that year. On the 19th a raid on Dieppe was supported by the largest array of RAF squadrons yet employed on a single operation, some 68 squadrons being airborne. For many units it was their most hectic time since the Battle of Britain, with up to three sorties being flown during the day. The air battles over and around Dieppe were by far the largest yet experienced, and losses on both sides were roughly equal. Whilst the general pattern of operations remained the same, the RAF's losses on offensive daylight ops increased, one of the main reasons being the increased numbers of Fw 190s with JG26. The Focke-Wulf was better all-round than the Spitfire V, with the exception of turning circle, but German tactics meant that dog-fighting turns were increasingly rare; the aircraft also had a greater ceiling and combats now tended to start at higher levels.

The problems had been foreseen by Fighter Command in early 1941: in a memo dated 20 April 1941 the C-in-C Fighter Commander (Air Marshal Sir W Sholto Douglas) expressed his views in answer to the debates on future Spitfire production. 'It is agreed that we are heading for specialisation in fighters and this is inevitable. Specialisation must be between the pressurised and unpressurised fighter. In other words, the dividing line must come on the limit of altitude which can be tolerated by the human body unassisted by artificial pressure. Let us put this line at 35,000 ft. Below this there can be no specialisation and our aim must be to provide all aircraft (unpressurised) with a performance to make them reasonable for fighting machines up to 35,000 ft. Another class of fighter for employment up to, say, 25,000 ft, would place quite intolerable

Fighter Command Group boundaries and radar cover, 1942.

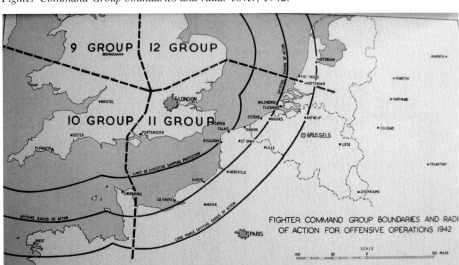

FIGHTER COMMAND GROUP BOUNDARIES AND RADII
OF ACTION FOR OFFENSIVE OPERATIONS 1942

operational limitations on fighter operations and could not be accepted as policy. Although the Mk II has merged into the Mk V we must anticipate it being outclassed by 1942 when nothing below a maximum speed of 400 mph will be of much use to us.' Spitfires were the heart of Fighter Command and so the development of the type into specialisations – later designated by LF and HF for Low-Flying and High-Flying characteristics – was the direction the Command took, although 1942 was a year of problems and not solutions.

In July 1942 the AFDU was able to evaluate 'a Spitfire from an operational squadron' against an Fw 190 that had landed at Pembrey 'in error' the previous month. Acquiring an intact operational enemy fighter straight from a war sortie was a fantastic opportunity – but it soon confirmed the superiority of the Fw 190 that Allied pilots had already discovered. The report concluded that: 'The manoeuvrability of the Fw 190 is better than that of the Spitfire VB except in turning circles, when the Spitfire can quite easily out-turn it. The Fw 190 has better acceleration under all conditions of flight and this must obviously be most useful during combat.

'When the Fw 190 was in a turn and was attacked by the Spitfire, the superior rate of roll enabled it to flick into a diving turn in the opposite direction. The pilot of the Spitfire found great difficulty in following this manoeuvre and even when prepared for it, was seldom able to allow the correct deflection. A dive from this manoeuvre enabled the Fw 190 to draw away from the Spitfire which was then forced to break off the attack.

'Several flights were carried out to ascertain the best evasive manoeuvres to adopt if "bounced". It was found that if the Spitfire was cruising at low speed and was "bounced" by the Fw 190, it was easily caught even if the Fw 190 was sighted when well out of range, and the Spitfire was then forced to take avoiding action by using its superiority in turning

Fw 190 'in service' with the RAF: 'Several flights were carried out to ascertain the best evasive manoeuvres to adopt if "bounced". It was found that if the Spitfire was cruising at low speed and was "bounced" by the FW 190, it was easily caught even if the FW 190 was sighted when well out of range, and the Spitfire was then forced to take avoiding action by using its superiority in turning circles.'

circles. If on the other hand the Spitfire was flying at maximum continuous cruising and was "bounced" under the same conditions, it had a reasonable chance of avoiding being caught by opening the throttle and going into a shallow dive, providing the Fw 190 was seen in time.

'If the Spitfire VB is "bounced" it is thought unwise to evade by diving steeply, as the Fw 190 will have little difficulty in catching up owing to its superiority in the dive.

'The above trials have shown that the Spitfire VB must cruise at high speed when in an area where enemy fighters can be expected. It will then, in addition to lessening the chances of being successfully "bounced", have a better chance of catching the Fw 190, particularly if it has the advantage of surprise.'

Defensive Operations 1942

On the defensive front there were three main elements to counter: reconnaissance, shipping attacks and night attacks. The Command flew a total of 49,793 interception sorties in the year, of which just over 14,000 were by night; the busiest month was August, with just under total 6,400 sorties.

The basic day tactics had not changed for either side, and the reality was that the *Luftwaffe* was little more than a nuisance and could perform no real strategic task over land other than reconnaissance, although the hit-and-run fighter-bombers did occupy a great deal of Fighter Command resources, especially when standing patrols had to be instituted. There was still the odd surprise, such as a large(ish) attack by Fw 190s and JU 88s on Canterbury and coastal areas in the evening of 31 October, with some 60–70 aircraft involved. Jamming of the British radar caught the defenders unprepared and the attack was, by German standards for 1942, a success. The defending fighters claimed six destroyed, five of these to 91 Squadron, with a further five falling to the gun and balloon belt.

The Spitfire VI was a specialized version (pressure cabin and a few other mods) designed to counter the high-flying reconnaissance aircraft.

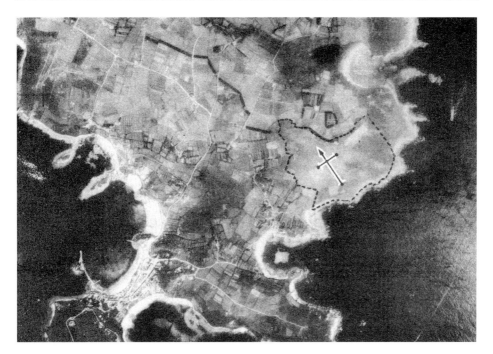

Landing Ground at St Mary's, Isles of Scilly – one of the most remote of the Command's operational airfields.

The high-flying recce Ju 86Ps were almost impossible to counter and a specialist version of the Spitfire, the Mark VI, entered service in April 1942 (with 616 Squadron). The entire squadron had re-equipped by early June and the comment made by the AFDU pilots on cockpit over-heating was supported by 616, who recorded that 'the major problem was that of excessive heating below 20,000 ft with the pilots gently frying and being unable to do anything about it. As an interim solution a ban was placed on operational flying below 20,000 ft' (616 Squadron ORB). The improved Mark VII entered service in September. The bread-and-butter routine became patrols at 20,000 ft to 25,000 ft to prevent hit-and-run raids; this produced little result other than a signal complementing 'the efficient patrols kept up by the Squadron which deterred any enemy aircraft from reaching the SW coast.' Modified Spitfire IXs were also used in the attempt to get at the high-fliers, but the greater significance of the Mark IX was that it redressed the balance with the Fw 190. The first aircraft went to 64 Squadron in June but it was some months before it was available in significant numbers, and for most of 1942 the Spitfire V was the most numerous type with Fighter Command.

Night Defence

A fundamental change in the conduct of air war took place from April 1942 when reprisals were called for as an answer to enemy terror attacks against the Reich which began at that time. Reprisal action opened with massed attacks on the cities of Exeter and Bath. For this all bomber units of Luftflotte *3 were called upon. Even training crews of the fourth* Gruppen *were unexpectedly ordered to take part. In the course of further raids, the latter, which were still operating with aircraft like the Do 17a and He 111, sustained painful losses. Thus within a short time the training programme, the importance of which was constantly increasing, lost valuable training personnel instructors. Following the tactics so successfully employed by the enemy against Lubeck and Rostock, concentrated raids of short duration were carried out for the first time to minimise defensive action. Outward flights were made along a single approximately common course in stepped up formation. Incendiaries and flares were used to light up the target as before. The raid on Bath had a really annihilating effect. During the night of the 25/26th April, only 4 aircraft out of a total of 151 (each aircraft making two flights) were lost (duration of raids 30 min each). In the period following, reprisal raids were carried out on the lines of the Bath one while the moon was full. Amongst others, for instance Sunderland, Newcastle, York, Norwich, Bradford, Canterbury and Weston-Super-Mare were bombed by an operational force of 40–70 aircraft. The enemy defence, becoming increasingly effective with its single and twin-engined night fighters, made it necessary to reduce still further the duration of the raids (to 10–20 minutes by the end of 1942), and each aircraft had in particularly dangerous zones to take continuous evasive action sudden changes of course and height smartly executed). The Ju 88 and Do 217 squadrons engaged exclusively in shallow dive-bombing.*

(Bechtle)

Despite the propaganda tone in much of the above, it was true that the offensive caught the defenders unawares. Minor and ineffective raids in late March and early April were followed by the first of the major attacks, with Exeter being hit on 23 April and again the following night, although accuracy was poor. The consecutive attacks on Bath (25 and 26 April) involved more bombers and were more accurate; with 246 bombers on the two nights dropping over 300 tons of bombs and losing only five aircraft to the defences. Annex R details the other urban areas attacked during this 1943 phase of attacks.

The night-fighter force had reached a stable level by mid 1942, with an average of 25 squadrons, the majority of which were AI-equipped twin-engined squadrons, primarily with Beaufighters but with the first Mosquito units also operational. The *Mossie* had entered the night-fighter role in January with 157 Squadron at Castle Camps, with 223 Squadron next to receive the type. The first operational sorties were flown on 27/28 April and whilst the Beaufighter proved to be a reliable and effective night-fighter, the Mosquito, especially with the centimetric radar (from early 1943) was a true exponent of the art. At the beginning of the year the Order of Battle still included six Defiant squadrons, but by the latter part of the year all had re-equipped. Better aircraft, the improved AI Mk. VII from spring 1942, better training and a more effective GCI network and controllers all combined to make the night defences increasingly potent.

The Turbinlite Flights were all operational by early 1942, which in theory boosted the night defence capability, and indeed all were upgraded to squadron status – as 530 to 539 squadrons – in September 1942. However, their operational record was poor, with plenty of flying accidents but very few successes and in January 1943 they were all disbanded. Fighter Command flew over 16,000 night sorties in 1942, including intruder operations, and claims were made for the destruction of 182 enemy aircraft (43 of those by intruder ops), with a further 43 'Probables' and 137 'Damaged'. The Command lost 40 aircraft destroyed in night ops over the UK. The Fighter Command Diary summarised the night operations for 1942: 'the year was largely one of consolidation

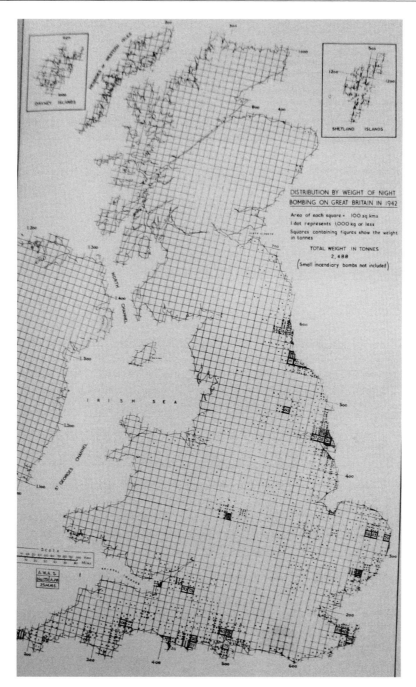

Map of the German night offensive 1942 showing distribution of bomb tonnage. Note that most targets were close to the coast.

and unremitting patrol work. If there were no spectacular achievements, Fighter Command's success must be measured not by the number of aircraft shot down but by the relatively few occasions on which British towns and industries were troubled by night air attack.'

Offensive Operations

At the end of January the Command had 55 squadrons available for offensive operations, all but two of which had Spitfire VBs; most were now organised into Wings but there were questions as to the standards of training of some of the Wings. With the exception of the Kenley and Northolt Wings, which were considered well trained, and the Biggin Hill Wing, which was 'adequate', the others were rated by the C-in-C as 'hardly fit for serious operations.' This was quite a damning statement and in part reflected problems of experience and morale, and during the year a number of Wing Leaders would be lost, including Bob Stanford Tuck and Victor Beamish.

During the first three months of the year the main offensive operations were *Rhubarbs*, with 46 being flown, and *Rodeos*, 17 flown. The RAF was seriously embarrassed on 12 February when the Germans executed the 'Channel Dash' when three major combat vessels (*Gneisenau, Prinz Eugen* and *Scharnhorst*) moved through the English Channel in daylight. Bombers, torpedo-bombers, fighter-bombers and fighter escort all went hunting and in most cases failed to find the ships; those that did find the ships failed to do any serious damage. In strategic terms it meant little as the German Navy had by this time adopted a defensive strategy but it was a morale victory for the Germans.

On 17 March Fighter Command informed Nos 10, 11 and 12 Groups that *Circus* operations would recommence, but it was stressed that fighter losses had to be avoided and that targets must be carefully chosen. The targets must take account of the radius of action of the fighters, an average of 150 miles, as experience had shown that losses increased close to the limit of range. A total of 58 targets were listed by the Air Ministry. The attacks started on 24 March, the targets being the Comines Power Station and the

The Norwegian 331 Squadron at Catterick; the Squadron formed here in summer 1941.

marshalling yards at Abbeville. German single-engined fighter strength in the West was around 350 aircraft, with a further 80 or so with Reserve Training Units; this relates to units able to oppose Allied operations over France and the Low Countries.

For *Rhubarbs* it was decided that, as previously, the priority targets should be transportation, including rail, road and river/canal traffic. The No. 1 priority was the destruction of locomotives and interference with fuel distribution. Electricity switching and transformer stations were listed as secondary objectives.

> The situation in the middle of 1942 was one of stalemate. Fighter Command had the advantage of numbers but the balance was redressed in favour of the enemy by the superiority of the Fw 190. Until the Typhoon and the Spitfire IX could take part in operations, Fighter Command was faced with two alternatives. It could either maintain the offensive at the level of the previous few months and accept the possibility of comparatively heavy losses as the price of holding the enemy fighter force, or it could reduce the scale of the offensive, engaging in combat only when its formations possessed some tactical advantage. In either case it was unlikely that the chief aim of the offensive – to destroy German fighters – would be effectively realised.
>
> (AHB Narrative).

However, a major air battle – the first since the Battle of Britain – was soon to be fought.

Dieppe August 1942

The 'raid' on Dieppe was made by a Combined Arms task force dominated by the Canadians and centred on the 2nd Canadian Army; it had strictly limited aims and was intended to demonstrate the Allies ability to land in Europe, conduct a quick operation and then withdraw, with air power playing a vital role in protecting and supporting the attack.

The brunt of the air combat was borne by the Spitfire squadrons of Fighter Command, some 48 of which were available for use, including four equipped with the new Spitfire IX. Whilst fighter cover prevented any substantial *Luftwaffe* interference with the operation, and certainly kept the enemy clear of the vulnerable shipping, in the air combats it was the *Luftwaffe* that ended the day with the higher score, the RAF losing 106 aircraft to all causes and the Germans losing 48. The RAF flew some 3,000 sorties in the space of 16 hours on 19 August 1942. In response, the *Luftwaffe* flew just under 1,000 sorties. The lessons of Dieppe were to prove invaluable nearly two years later on D-Day but for the Canadians they had been costly lessons.

Night Offensive

The night intruder offensive increased in scale as more squadrons were tasked with this activity, especially in the optimum period of April to August. Whilst much of the effort remained targeted against airfields in the first half of the year, the emphasis switched from June to marshalling yards and trains. The first Mosquito sortie (by 23 Squadron) was flown on the night of 5/6 July, but numbers of *Mossies* remained limited. By the middle of September the Intruder force comprised three dedicated squadrons: 23 Squadron (Mosquito) and 418 and 605 squadrons, both with Bostons. Added to this were the single-seat squadrons allocated by the Command when considered appropriate; this force was increased in December with the decision to employ the Typhoons of 609

Squadron for part-time intruder work. During the week of the full moon, two aircraft were at readiness at Manston for operations in the area Walcheren-Lille-Arras-Amiens. The chief task of these aircraft was to attack enemy aircraft and airfields but railways were given as alternative targets. If a train was damaged and halted, the pilots were to return and report the position to No. 137 Squadron. Subject to the Controller's approval, this Squadron would then send a Whirlibomber to attack the stationary train with bombs.

'Thus by the end of the year the night offensive, although small in comparison with daylight operations, was becoming a carefully planned, economic way of using at least a part of the night fighter force' (AHB Narrative). During December Fighter Command received a number of Monica sets, which picked up German radar transmissions, and Gee sets, a radio aid to navigation. The Command was also looking forward to a significant increase in the number of Mosquitoes with which to extent the night offensive.

A total of 1,508 night intruder sorties were flown in 1942, during which 299 enemy aircraft were seen and 48 claimed as destroyed, with losses of 38 of the intruders during the year, nine of those in June, which was also the month with the highest number of sorties (336). The AHB narrative summarised the overall effect of the Intruder campaign at this stage of the war: 'the effects of intruder activity on the German Air Force are not precisely known but prisoner of war reports showed that such activity caused the diversion of returning bombers either to waiting areas or alternative airfields, the adoption of special landing procedures and the use of illuminated decoys and dummy airfields. Enemy crews were therefore forced to operate with restricted facilities and at a higher than normal nervous tension. It is probable that the enemy accident rate was increased.' This was an example of offensive defence – reducing the enemy bomber capability – but the Intruders were primarily aimed at night fighter airfields in support of Bomber Command and the same comments would apply to these airfields, as well as the shock of having aircraft shot-down at the airfield.

1943 – Putting on the Pressure

The pace of offensive operations continued to increase throughout 1943, whilst the corresponding need for 'Home Defence', continued to decline, with little in the way of daytime threats but still a requirement for a robust night defence. This was also the year in which two major reorganisations of the Command took place, one in June and the other in November. Spitfire IXs became available in numbers later in the year, and with more aircraft and more experienced pilots and leaders, the Command was able to take the initiative and begin the fight for air superiority that would be vital for the invasion of Europe. Morale improved and there was a general feeling that the battle was being won. The tabular summary of squadrons for January 1943 shows the dominant role of the Spitfire with the day squadrons, although there were now eight Typhoon squadrons, and with the Beaufighter and Mosquito as the main night types. Total established strength was 1,268 aircraft and the Command had just over 1,000 available with crews. The Typhoon had done some good work in countering the hit-and-run raiders but by early 1943 it was generally agreed that it was not an ideal fighter but that its participation in offensive ground-attack ops had shown promise and it was in this role, especially when later equipped with Rocket-Projectiles (RPs) that the *Tiffie* made a name for itself with 2nd Tactical Air Force.

'Cocky' Dundas and pilots of 56 Squadron with Typhoon; the Squadron was the first to equip with the potentially effective – but initially troublesome – Hawker Typhoon.

War Room Summary of Fighter Command Strength, January 1943

Aircraft	Squadrons	Establishment	Available with crew
Hurricane	1 Flt	4	30
Spitfire	47 Sqns	752	633
Typhoon	8 Sqns	128	80
Whirlwind	2 Sqns	32	26
Beaufighter	12 Sqns	192	151
Mosquito	8 Sqns	128	84
Boston	2 Sqns	32	19
Boston/Havoc	?	?	20
Totals	79 Sqns, 1 Flt	1,268	1,063

The disbandment of Army Co-operation Command (ACC) and the formation of the Tactical Air Force (TAF) on 1 June 1943 were part of the restructuring of Allied air power in preparation for the invasion of Europe; both of these changes affected Fighter Command. When ACC disbanded its components were reassigned to Fighter Command and the TAF, with the exception of No. 72 Group which went to Technical Training Command.

The Tactical Air Force (redesignated 2nd TAF from 15 November) comprised Nos 2, 83 and 84 Groups but to make matters more complex it was initially placed in Fighter Command and was 'under the general direction of the Air Officer Commanding-in-Chief, Fighter Command.' No. 83 (Composite) Group had formed on 19 March in order to 'provide facilities for training ground units and squadrons to work together under field conditions, and to provide a means of working out the full requirements and

The Typhoon entered service as fighter but was never truly effective in this role; by the time teething troubles had been resolved it had started to take-on the ground-attack role at which it was to excel.

organisation of a Composite Formation' (AHB Narrative). The Group had been created out of the 'Z' Composite Group that had been brought together for Exercise Spartan in March and initially comprised four day-fighter squadrons, four Army Support squadrons and two Tactical Reconnaissance squadrons. The Group was commanded by Air Vice-Marshal W F Dickson and was initially non-operational, although it did become operational under Fighter Command for its early involvement in offensive ops. It was originally intended that No. 84 Group would form from the existing resources of No. 11 Group and be commanded by that Group's AOC; however, this plan was changed and when the Group formed in July it had its own AOC and was part of the Tactical Air Force, albeit still initially under Fighter Command. On 12 June Leigh Mallory issued his first directive to the TAF and stated that: 'until the preparatory operations for the assault across the Channel began, the TAF must play its part together with the rest of Fighter Command in the battle for supremacy over the Channel. For the time being he himself would control these offensive operations which were directed by the static fighter Group organisation (No. 11 Group). At the same time the Composite Group commanders would be given opportunities to exercise their formations in actual operations.' The result of all this was that all tactical aircraft in the South-East of England, with the exception of night fighters, ended up doing much of the same work – which can make it difficult to sort out units, missions and statistics for the different Command groupings within the overall organisation.

The formation on 15 November 1943 of the Allied Expeditionary Air Force under Air Marshal Sir Trafford Leigh-Mallory brought the next major change for Fighter Command, including its change of name. The instruction forming the AEAF stated that: 'Headquarters, Air Defence of Great Britain, is to form in Allied Expeditionary Air Force with effect from 15th November 1943, on which date are to be transferred to its control all such formations, stations and units in Fighter Command as have not at that

The Mark XII was the first of the Griffon engine variants and entered service in February 1943 with 41 Squadron.

date been transferred on Air Ministry instructions, to the 2nd Tactical Air Force or, as independent formation, to the Allied Expeditionary Air Force. The squadrons in ADGB and the 2nd TAF will be interchanged and readjusted, as necessary, under the instructions of the Air Commander-in-Chief.' Air Marshal R M Hill was appointed to command ADGB, with his HQ at Bentley Priory.

In November Air Marshal Hill was issued with a new directive by Leigh Mallory setting out his responsibilities:

1. To be responsible for the air defence of Great Britain and Northern Ireland.
2. To command the following formations: Nos 9, 10, 11, 12, 13 Fighter Groups, RAF Northern Ireland (operational control of fighters), No. 60 Signals Group, and No. 70 (Training) Group.
3. To control operational activities of AA Command, the Royal Observer Corps, Balloon Command and other static elements of air defence controlled operationally by Fighter Command.
4. To conduct defensive and offensive operations which involved the use of squadrons of both ADGB and TAF until further notice.
5. To develop air interception methods and apparatus for eventual use on ADGB and other theatres.

The primary role of ADGB was 'standing patrols over coastal areas and as far as 40–50 miles South of the Isle of Wight' (Fighter Command historical summary). This task was directly connected with the invasion preparations and was intended to deny reconnaissance to the enemy as well as prevent any attempt at offensive action.

The final change in the Command structure came on 17 December 1943 with the formation of No. 85 Group, which formed using six day and six night fighter squadrons from No. 11 Group. Its task was the defence of the 'base and lines of communication' of the Allied Expeditionary Force when established in France; however, until the Group moved overseas the operational control of its aircraft was assigned to the AOC of No. 11 Group.

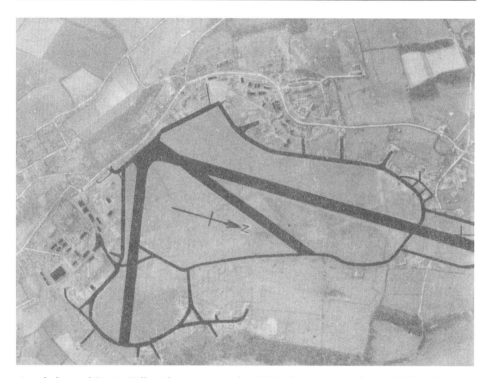

Aerial photo of Biggin Hill, with runway overlay, 1944; having been a key airfield in the Battle of Britain, by late 1941 Biggin Hill was on the offensive sending its Wing ranging over northern France.

Defensive Operations 1943

The expectation was that the established pattern of fighter-bomber hit-and-run raids would continue and that they would continue to be ineffective, other than on civilian morale, and would remain very difficult to counter. Fighter Command estimated that up to 200 fighters could be employed in this role, although the Joint Intelligence Committee believed that the scale of operation would be far less than this. They both agreed that the Germans would operate in the same area as previously and with the same range of targets. Likewise, shipping would remain a primary target for the Germans.

The RAF had resorted to the use of standing patrols to help counter these raids; this was never an ideal solution as it placed a strain on the defenders without providing an effective counter. The Typhoon squadrons were tasked with much of this work as the Typhoon was believed to be the best fighter aircraft for intercepting the low level raider, but it had not yet proved altogether successful in this role and was undergoing teething troubles with its Sabre engine. Five Typhoon squadrons – 1, 257, 266, 486 and 609 – were allocated to this role by maintaining standing patrols or keeping aircraft at immediate readiness. A number of Spitfire squadrons also held readiness – 122, 331, 332, 340, 4012 and 611 – whilst the Spitfire XIIs of 91 Squadron maintained readiness to deal with long-range bombers on day attacks, and for convoy protection.

The German conclusion for the year, as expressed by *Hpt* Bechtle in his lecture was that: 'The day-time nuisance raids were almost exclusively spread over the southern and south-eastern area of England, and from 1943 did not extend beyond the latitude of London into the Midlands. In this type of operation, consisting of bombing and strafing,

The Spitfire IX was produced in large numbers (around 5,665) and was vital in clawing back the combat advantage from the Fw 190.

bomber units suffered heavy losses. A great number of operations had to be abandoned because of weather conditions. Fighter-bomber attacks which had been carried out from spring 1942 until May 1943 on targets in South and South-East England and on shipping along these coasts had also proved too costly in relation to the results achieved. Therefore nuisance raids were carried out thereafter by night only by the two new high-speed bomber Gruppen, one being equipped with Fw 190s and the other with Me 410.'

Night Defence 1943

The German High Command was not impressed by progress of the night operations against the UK and in March 1943 a new staff organisation was created, *Angriffafuehrer* (England Attack Command) to control the bombing operations of *Fliegerkorps* IX. The total German night effort against overland targets in 1943 was 2,055 sorties, flown on 133 nights, in which 1,985 tons of bombs were dropped. The greatest weight of bombs had fallen in the London area. In the same period Bomber Command dropped 136,000 tons of bombs on Germany. RAF defenders still comprised a mix of AI-equipped and Cats Eye, although the latter only provided around 15% of the monthly effort and from June onwards this steadily decreased. RAF night-fighter claims for 1943 were 133 destroyed, 18 probables and 34 damaged, with the effectiveness of AI being shown by the fact that 131 of the 133 were by AI aircraft.

The AHB Narrative summary for the second half of 1943: 'After the raids on Hull and Grimsby in early July the character of the night bombing changed from one of occasional raids by heavy bombers to sporadic attacks by high-speed bombers such as the Fw 190 and Me 410; targets were found in southern and south-east England coastal towns rather than in the north-east. The British air defences were clearly more than a match for the enemy, for although the Do 217 was better equipped with defensive armament than other German bombers, it could not, because of the greater weight, easily evade night fighters once they had marked it down. The two features of enemy night attacks in the latter part of 1943 were attacks by intruder aircraft on airfields in the Midlands and East Anglia in retaliation for the increasingly powerful combined bomber

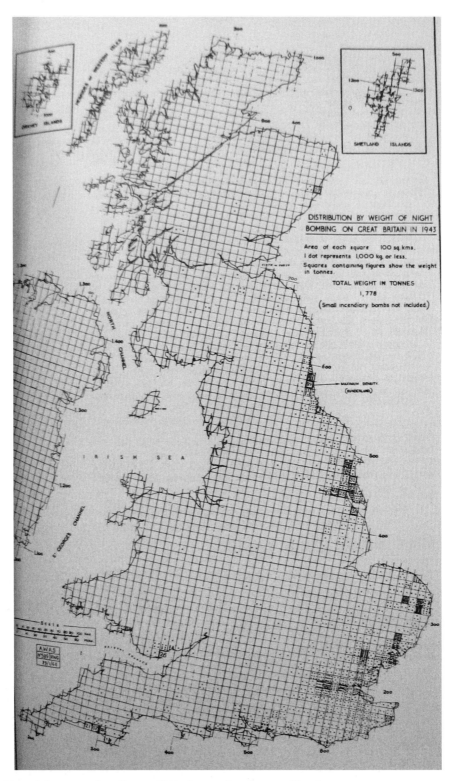

Map of German night offensive 1943 showing distribution of bomb tonnage.

'Fighter leadership consists not in scoring personal victories but in the achievement of success with the whole Wing. My job would be to lead and to fight.' Offensive sweeps by the Spitfire IXs of Fighter Command would play a major role in securing air superiority.

offensive and, secondly, renewed attacks on London by fighter-bombers in the autumn, accompanied by the dropping of "duppel" [the German equivalent of "window"]. From July to December 1943 the enemy flew some 818 long-range bomber, 165 fighter-bomber and seven reconnaissance sorties overland – a total of 990. The RAF claimed the destruction of 66½ and the guns another 20½.' On a major raid, Bomber Command would be putting nearly 800 bombers over a single target in one night.

Offensive Operations 1943

The majority of offensive sorties were escort for bomber formations, the majority of these being the American daylight bombers, with Fighter Command providing cover in the immediate area of the UK and to the enemy coast. The range and combat duration of the RAF's fighters were increasingly cause for concern and was one of the major

Typhoons of 609 Squadron at Manston, 1943; by summer 1943 the Command was spending virtually all of its day effort on offensive missions, albeit at a rising cost in aircraft and pilots.

limitations of the Spitfire – it was a great aircraft but there was not room for more internal fuel and the only alternative was drop-tanks. The fighters eventually used two main drop-tanks, the 45-gallon and the 90-gallon, the concept being to use that fuel first and then drop the tanks when combat had to be joined. The idea was sound but the tanks were problematical. At a time when USAAF P-51 Mustangs were starting truly long-range escorts, including Berlin, the RAF's fighters were looking distinctly short-legged. One possible solution was, of course, to equip with Mustangs; this option was eventually taken-up but for now the priority for P-51s was with the USAAF.

Typical of the new Fighter Command formations charged with this work was No. 127 Wing, which formed at Kenley in May 1943, with an initial strength of two Canadian squadrons (403 and 416) equipped with Spitfire IXs. Wg Cdr 'Johnnie' Johnson was one of the most effective Wing Leaders and later wrote: 'fighter leadership consists not in scoring personal victories but in the achievement of success with the whole Wing. My job would be to lead and to fight.'

Night Offensive Operations

The pattern of night offensive ops followed that of 1942 with Intruder, Ranger, Rhubarb and Mahmoud sorties targeting airfields and transportation, especially rail facilities. There was an increase in the use of the Mosquito and more squadrons being tasked, although not permanently allocated to the night role; for example, in May a total of 395 sorties were flown by 17 squadrons; of this total 225 were Intruders, 166 Rangers and four Rhubarbs.

A new type of operation commenced on the night of 15/16 June when five Beaufighter *Serrate* ops were flown as part of the war against German night-fighters. The equipment was initially fitted to the Beaufighters of 141 Squadron and intensive trails were flown at Drem from May 1943. The equipment was able to detect enemy AI transmissions at up to 100 miles and it was to play an increasing role in the anti-fighter war, especially with No. 100 Group (Special Duties) Group from late 1943.

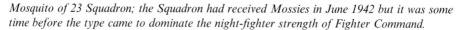

Mosquito of 23 Squadron; the Squadron had received Mossies in June 1942 but it was some time before the type came to dominate the night-fighter strength of Fighter Command.

A Bf 110 was claimed on that first night and despite a high percentage (23%) of technical failures with equipment, the system was considered to be effective. Fighter Command ORS report No. 494 examined the results of *Serrate* operations in the period to 6/7 September; on the 233 ops flown, 1,180 contacts were established of which 108 were converted to AI pick-up; there were a total of 49 attempts at intercept, with 33 going to visual, which resulted in 20 combats and claims for 13 enemy aircraft destroyed. The poor performance of the Beaufighter was considered to be one of the main reasons for the low(ish) conversion rate: '... the classical curve of pursuit method of homing on to a Serrate contact irrespective of its range has had to be modified. The crews suggest that no intercept should be attempted on Serrate contacts more than 4–5 miles away, unless they are head on.' It was also commented that 'the Serrate equipment is so sensitive in recording changes in azimuth and elevation of the target that the crews prefer to use it if possible for the whole of the interception, using AI as little as possible for occasionally checking the range.' The solution was to put the equipment in the Mosquito, which took place in late 1943.

The Command flew 3,278 night offensive sorties in 1943, losing 60 aircraft and making claims for 72 enemy destroyed, although it must be remembered that for many sorties destruction of enemy aircraft was not the primary aim. The busiest, and most successful, month was August with 551 sorties claiming 12 aircraft. This month included the first Mahmoud sortie (22/23 August); this type of mission was defined as: 'operations by night fighters against enemy night-fighters outside the radius of Bomber Command operations or on nights when Bomber Command was not operating.' By the end of the year 119 Mahmoud sorties had been flown.

1944–1945 – Invasion of Europe and the end of the war

The command and control of squadrons, which had started to become confused with the creation of ADGB and the TAF continued to be confusing in the first half of 1944. It is often difficult in the records to discern who a particular unit was 'owned' by, especially as aircraft types and roles often appear identical. So, we have ADGB squadrons operating against ground targets in France and we have AEAF squadrons flying defensive ops in the UK! No. 85 (Base) Group, an AEAF organisation, still had all its squadrons under the operational control of ADGB in the first half of 1944; this including Nos 141, 142, 147, 148, 149 and 150 Wings. As we did for the latter part of 1943, the operations by fighter and fighter-bomber units are treated as a single organisation unless a defined difference can be made. At the start of January, ADGB's day squadrons comprised ten 'long-range' Spitfires, nine Spitfire VB, two Spitfire VII, two Spitfire IXF, two Spitfire XII, ten Typhoon and three Mustang FR. In 2nd TAF's fighter element there were 15 Spitfire, nine Mustang and six Typhoon squadrons. Although ADGB flew 3,700 offensive sorties in January this was exceeded by the growing, and dedicated, fighter/fighter-bomber strength of the TAF, who flew 5,430 such missions. By March the ADGB contribution was down to 1,456 sorties – but even so this was still a significant figure and showed that the Command was not entirely defensive. Many of the statistical summaries for this period include ADGB and 2nd TAF without splitting into the respective Commands; for example, in the period January to May 1944 the combined statistics for offensive operations was a loss of 299 aircraft, with only four pilots saved, and claims for 291 German aircraft destroyed. USAAF fighters claimed a further 1,226 for the loss of 463 of their own. However, German records suggest a total loss of only 338 in air combat but with a significant number of aircraft being destroyed on the ground, for example, 124 in May alone. Interestingly, the Germans also had 407 non-operational losses in the same period, which is a reflection on the lower quality of pilots and training and the overall impact of the Allied assault on airfields.

The latest, and in some opinions the best, Spitfire variant entered service in 1944. In January 1944 Spitfire Mk. XIV RB141 was delivered to the Air Fighting Development Unit at Duxford for tactical trials, although in the same month it was also issued to the first operational unit, 610 Squadron at Exeter. The general conclusions from the AFDU were that: 'the Spitfire XIV is superior to the Spitfire IX in all respects. It has the best all-round performance of any present-day fighter, apart from range.' One of the trials was flown against a Bf 109G. 'The Spitfire XIV is 40 mph faster at all heights except near 16,000 ft where it is only 10 mph faster. Climbing at full throttle it draws away from the Me 109G quite easily. The Spitfire XIV easily out-turns the Me 109G in either direction; it is superior to it in every respect.' The Fw 190 was more or a problem; the trials involved flight against a 190 with a BMW 801D engine and concluded that: 'In defence, the Spitfire XIV should use its remarkable maximum climb and turning circle against any enemy aircraft. In the attack it can afford to "mix it" but should beware the quick roll and dive. If this manoeuvre is used by an Fw 190 and the spitfire XIV follows, it will probably not be able to close the range until the Fw 190 has pulled out of its dive.'

Whilst escort and sweep remained a major task for the fighter squadrons, especially the Spitfires, there was an increasing call for ground-attack, a role performed by the Typhoons and Hurricane IVs. The Spitfires too began to take-on more of this role,

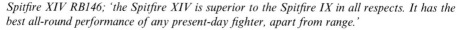

Spitfire XIV RB146; 'the Spitfire XIV is superior to the Spitfire IX in all respects. It has the best all-round performance of any present-day fighter, apart from range.'

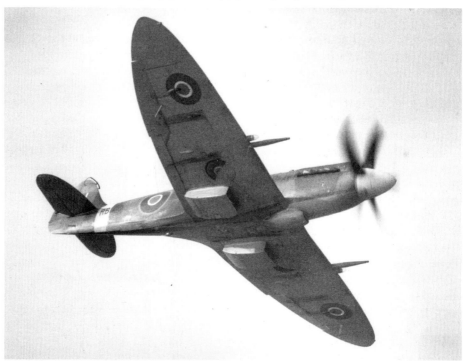

initially with strafe but then as fighter-bombers with the addition of under-fuselage and under-wing bombs – much to the disgust of some fighter pilots!

A memo from General Arnold (Commander USAAF) to ACM Portal (British Chief of Air Staff) queried the Spitfire's combat range and the British 'reluctance' to make best use of their substantial fighter force:

> Overlord *hangs directly on the success of our combined aerial offensive and I am sure that our failure to decisively cripple both sources of German air power and the GAF itself is causing you and me concern. I am afraid that we are not sufficiently alert to changes in the overall course of the air war. In particular I refer to the fact that we are not employing our forces in adequate numbers against the* GAF *in being, as well as his facilities and sources. On my part I am pressing Eaker to get a much higher proportion of his forces off the ground and put them where they will hurt the enemy.*

One of his main points was the lack of fighter support for the daylight bombers:

> *as presently employed it would appear that your thousands of fighters are not making use of their full capabilities. Our transition from the defensive to the offensive should surely carry with it the application of your large fighter force offensively. Is it not true that we have a staggering air superiority over the Germans and we are not using it?*

Arnold also made the point that the P-47's basic design had a shorter range than that of the Spitfire but when fitted with long-range tanks it was working well as an escort. The implication was that the American daylight offensive could be far more effective and less costly if the RAF's fighters were used as escorts and employed in an offensive way. The RAF response was that attempts were being made to improve the range of the Spitfire but that an external tank only gave an extra 50 miles and besides, 'our fighter force has been designed to obtain air superiority over northern France, for which it is eminently suitable.'

Between 1 April and 5 June ADGB flew 18,639 sorties in support of the *Overlord* plan, claiming 111 victories for the loss of 46 fighters. The total Allied air effort in this period was 195,255 sorties with 2,655 claims and 1,987 losses – which puts the ADGB effort into perspective! The June 1944 Order of Battle for ADGB, including No. 85 Group, comprised 54 squadrons, as shown in the table.

By 10 June fighters were operating from airfields in France and increasingly from that date the offensive was mounted from the Continent, as were defensive sorties over the area occupied by the Allies. Over the next few months the direct role of ADGB

ADGB Aircraft Strength, June 1944		
Type	No. of squadrons	Establishment
Hurricane IIB	1 Flt	4+2
Spitfire LF.V	13	16+2
Spitfire VII	3	16+2
Spitfire IX	4	16+2
Spitfire LF.IX	4	16+2
Spitfire HF.IX	2	16+2
Spitfire XII	1	16+2
Spitfire XIV	3	16+2
Tempest V	2	16+2
Mustang III	1	16+2
Typhoon	2	16+2
Typhoon	1 Flt	6+0
Hurricane IIC	1	16+2
Beaufighter	2	16+2
Mosquito XII/XIII	9	16+2
Mosquito XVII	4	16+2
Mosquito VI (Intruder)	2	16+2

Notes
1. Established for two Mosquito XXX squadrons (219 and 456) but not yet re-equipped.
2. Not including three Seafire squadrons of Fleet Air Arm under operational control.

continued to decline and its focus became much more a defensive one. By November, and the loss of No. 85 Group, the number of squadrons had decreased to 46½, which still included five squadrons on loan from 2nd Tactical Air Force.

Defensive Operations 1944

With the invasion of Europe all fighter assets were committed to support the invasion; for ADGB the role was two-fold – defending the home base and supporting the offensive. Ensuring that the Germans were kept in the dark about Allied dispositions the fighter force worked hard at keeping enemy recce aircraft at bay, as well as making sure that no bombers could attack the crowded marshalling and embarkation areas. The offensive over Europe was so intense that the Germans had little opportunity to consider offensive action of their own, with the exception of some night activity.

Night Defence 1944

A large part of the German night effort was against airfields and followed the pattern of the night intruder raids flown by the RAF, with strafing and bombing of airfields and the attempt to shoot-down aircraft in the circuit. These attacks were usually by loan Me 410s or Ju 88s and between January and May 82 aircraft made attacks on airfields, with a further 33 attacks on dummy airfields; April was the busiest month when 35 attacks were recorded and the RAF had 13 aircraft destroyed. Attacks were still being made on cities, with London receiving about one-third of the total tonnage, and the overall scale of effort was higher than in 1943; indeed the 1943 total had been exceeded by April.

The first of the new attacks on London took place on 21/22 January with two waves of bombers, totalling 447 aircraft. A second major raid was mounted on 29/30 January, with 285 aircraft. Both caused damage but losses were high at 57 aircraft (7.5% of the attack forces). Nuisance raids had been carried out on London on six other nights in

Map of German night offensive 1944 showing distribution of bomb tonnage.

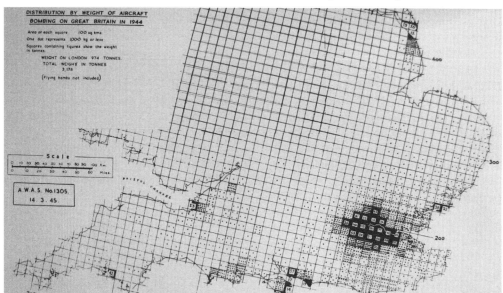

January. The City was attacked on seven nights in February, by a total of 1,200 bombers with German records stating for the attack of 3/4 February 'enemy night fighter defences were particularly strong.' Although London remained the focus of attention in March, attacks were also made on Hull and Bristol

The RAF's night-fighter force was now very effective and was almost entirely Mosquito, with nine squadrons of Mosquito XII/XIII and four of Mosquito XVII, with the final two Beaufighter squadrons in the process or re-equipping. In addition the Command fielded two intruder squadrons with the Mosquito VI. Between January and June the Command flew 2,312 sorties and made claims for 145½ aircraft destroyed, plus 21 probables and 30 damaged. A further 70 bombers were shot-down by anti-aircraft fire. German records more or less agree with this total of just over 200 losses. The RAF lost only three night-fighters in this period.

The final night raid on the UK took place on 27/28 June, the targets being the USAAF airfields at Bungay and Seething. This did not mean that Britain was safe from night attack; the Germans opened a second blitz – day and night – using the V-1 flying bomb.

Second Blitz

At 0418 in the morning on 13 June 1944, the peace at Swanscombe, near Gravesend, Kent, was shattered by a fierce explosion. The first of Hitler's new 'terror' weapons had landed on English soil. Within an hour, three more of these V-1 flying bombs had come to earth – one crashing into a railway bridge at Grove Road, Bethnal Green, in London, and causing six deaths and a substantial amount of damage.

Intelligence reports had been building since 1943 and it was evident that the weapon would eventually reach operational status, and that London would be on the receiving end. Thus, in December 1943 a series of studies were undertaken to determine the most effective air defence structure to protect the capital. It was very much a return to the early days of air defence, with a plan for three zones; fighter aircraft, anti-aircraft guns and balloons.

However, the problem could not have arisen at a worse time, as the planning staffs were devoting time and resources to building the invasion force, and were reluctant to commit any additional aircraft and guns to the defensive scheme.

The revised Diver plan of February 1944 called for eight day-fighter squadrons, plus a number of night-fighter units, but for a lower total of anti-aircraft guns. In the 24-hour period from 2230 on 15 June to 16 June 1944, British records show 151 reported launches, with 144 V-1s crossing the English coast. Of those, 73 reached the London area. The defences notched up only a modest score, seven falling to the fighters, 14 to the guns and one shared, whilst a further eleven were shot down by the guns of the Inner Artillery Zone. The Hawker Tempests of No. 150 Wing at Newchurch had been at readiness for defensive patrol since dawn on 15 June.

Early the following day the Wing Leader, Wing Commander Roland Beamont, and his No. 2 were airborne on such a patrol when they sighted a V-1. Giving chase, the fighters were eventually able to carry out an attack, and Beamont scored his first flying bomb 'kill', the missile crashing near Faversham.

Overall, however, it was an inauspicious start. Too many bombs had reached the London area, but there was no simple solution to the problem. The V-1, spanning a little over 17 ft 6 in, made a very small target, and it flew fast (300–400 mph) and low. One first had to find this small target; then came the challenge of actually shooting it down. The official RAF account of the campaign summarised the speed problem: 'as for the fighters, the short time in which interception had to be made, demanded that they should be quickly and accurately directed on to the course of the bomb.'

By the third week in June the defences had started to settle down with guns and balloons in place and with eight single-seat fighter squadrons and four Mosquito squadrons deployed on anti-*Diver* patrols. It was also planned to increase the gun belts to include 376 heavy and 540 light guns and for an increase in balloons from 480 to 1,000.

The initial aim for the fighters was to intercept the flying bombs over the sea, but there were numerous difficulties with this. The technique was one of 'close control' where the fighter was vectored to its target by one of the radar stations involved in this role – Fairlight, Swingate and Beachy Head. However, even on a good day the best pick-up was a maximum of 50 miles from the coast, which gave the controller and fighter a maximum of six minutes to complete the interception. Overland the technique was different because of the problems of radar tracking of the target; here the technique was 'running commentary' with the position and course of the bomb being broadcast to all fighters working that frequency, it was then up to the fighter to work out his own intercept. The tracking information came from radar and from visual reports, mainly by the ROC.

Mustangs joined in the defence following a request from ADGB to 2nd TAF, with initially one Flight of 316 Squadron being transferred to this role on 1 July. This proved successful and a few days later an entire Mustang Wing was allocated, flying their first sorties on 12 July. The day fighter defences had now increased to 13 squadrons: four Mustang, three Spitfire XIV, three Tempest, two Spitfire IX and one Spitfire XII. It was important to dedicate aircraft to this role rather than mix roles as they were stripped of unnecessary equipment and external fittings and even had camouflage paint removed so that they could be polished – all in an attempt to gain a bit more speed. Engines were also tweaked and 150 Octane fuel used. The net result was an average improvement of 15–30 mph.

Tempests of 501 Squadron joined the fray in August, having re-equipped with the type in late July around a core of experienced pilots from the FIU; the first sorties were flown on 5 August and a week later the Squadron was re-designated as a Night Operational Squadron – an even trickier role. However, it was one in which they achieved notable success (see 'Operations' chapter).

The first phase of the flying-bomb campaign ended on 1 September 1944, with the Allied capture of those V-1 launching sites within range of London. By mid August the ADGB effort was at its height, with 15 day-fighter and 10 night-fighter squadrons tasked with the anti-*Diver* campaign. Although the campaign never resumed with the same intensity, from September 4 to 14 January 1945, the city was subjected to attack by V-1s launched from He 111 'mother' aircraft of I/KG.53, from over the North Sea. Defensive patrols remained in force, but there was even less warning of attack, so the ideal solution was to destroy the parent aircraft before they launched their weapons. A Wellington was fitted with ASV VI to act as an airborne radar and fighter control station, entering service in January.

In the overall campaign the Germans launched some 9,252 flying bombs, of which just under 5,900 crossed the English coast and 2,563 of those reached the London area. Around 4,000 flying-bombs were destroyed by the defences, the Fighter Command summary claiming that 1,847 were destroyed by its fighters, with 1,866 falling to Anti-Aircraft Command's guns, 232 to balloons and a mere 12 to naval gunfire.

Meteor of 616 Squadron; the RAF entered the jet age in July 1944 with 616 Squadron acquiring Meteor Is.

The V-2 ballistic missile was a weapon that was impossible to stop once it had been launched – so no air defence system was possible and the only effective counter was to destroy the production, storage and launch facilities. The Allies expended a huge effort on this type of site for all the V-weapons; ADGB/Fighter Command's part comprised 4,300 sorties (and 1,000 tons of bombs) hunting for the sites – with a rocket that was about to be launched being the prime (but rare) target. These *Big Ben* missions were flown by most Allied fighters and fighter-bomber types.

Offensive Operations 1944
Throughout 1943 and early 1944 much of the Allied air effort had been dedicated to preparing the way for the invasion of German-occupied Europe. By spring 1944 the intensity of operations was increasing as the date for D-Day, 6 June 1944, approached. The directive issued to the fighter forces stated:

> The intention of the British and American fighter forces is to attain and maintain an air situation which will assure freedom of action for our forces without effective intervention by the German Air Force, and to render maximum air protection to the land and naval forces in the common object of assaulting, securing and developing the bridgehead.

A veritable air armada of P-51 Mustangs, P-47 Thunderbolts, P-38 Lightnings and various marks of Spitfire was ranged ready for battle as RAF units of Air Defence of Great Britain (ADGB) and the 2nd Tactical Air Force joined with the American VIIIth and 9th Fighter Commands. The overall plan was for the American units to provide the bulk of the escort and high-cover patrols, while the low cover, especially over the beaches, was provided by RAF Spitfires. The entire invasion area was to be given a layered screen of fighters – the first squadrons to be in position by 0425 on the morning of 6 June 1944.

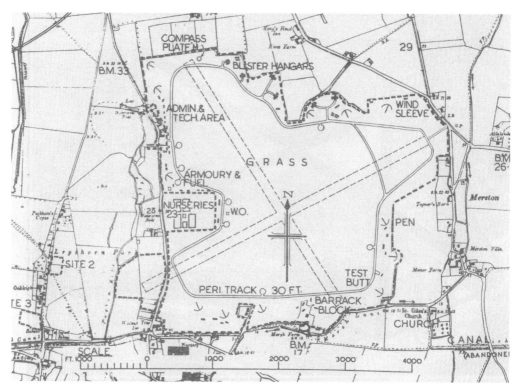

A large number of Advanced Landing Grounds were constructed in southern England for the air build-up for the invasion of Europe; Merston, 1944.

The Allied fighter Order of Battle included the RAF providing 55 squadrons of Spitfires, plus a number of Mustang and Mosquito units, out of an overall fighter strength of 2,000 aircraft. It was considered that the overcrowded airfields in England would make ideal targets for German tip-and-run fighter-bombers, so each airfield was required to maintain a fighter flight on stand-by. The direct involvement of ADGB on D-Day comprised 91 Spitfires as part of the beachhead cover and a further 40 Spitfires on a sweep over airfields in Brittany and attacking any transport they found.

In June ADGB and its associated formations flew 8,474 offensive day sorties, an increase of 1,000 on the previous month. This included 25 *Circus* and 21 *Ramrod* operations, with airfields, lines of communication and power stations being the main target types. The RAF claimed the destruction of 61 aircraft during these offensive ops, for the loss of 36 pilots. It was also noted that the 'enemy had retaliated with such vigour that fewer aircraft were destroyed than in the previous month and losses were heavier'.

In the period immediately after the D-Day landings, the ground forces were in danger of being bogged down, and in the absence of heavy weapons they had to rely on air power as 'flying artillery'. The Spitfire squadrons carried out a good deal of this type of work, and after a while became quite proficient. The 20 mm cannon proved to be a remarkably good air-to-ground weapon against all manner of 'soft skinned' vehicles, although it was unable to cause any serious damage to the average German tank.

The night offensive throughout the year was still primarily aimed at supporting the operations of Bomber Command by disrupting night-fighter operations (intruder work) and engaging enemy night-fighters with RAF fighters, with *Serrate* playing an increased

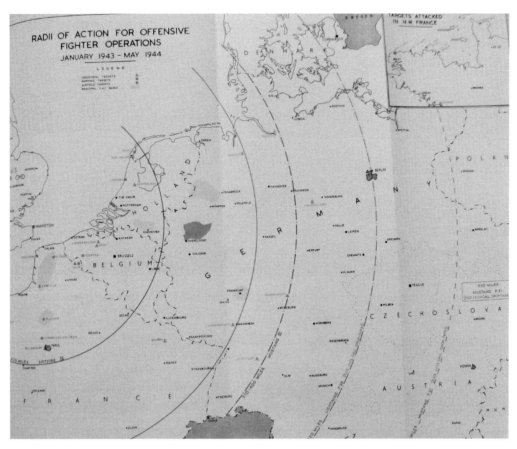

Map showing radius of Action for fighter offensive operations January 1943 to May 1944.

role. Although the formation of No. 100 Group in December 1943 provided a dedicated force for this work, ADGB units were still important and in February 1944 Air Marshal Harris stated that an increased effort was required to disrupt the main nigh-fighter bases such as Gilze-Rijen, Leeuwarden and Venlo. By early July he was demanding a force of 100 night-fighters and the redoubling of attacks on airfields. The reply from the Chief of the Air Staff was that the UK's night defences could not be weakened; however, Leigh-Mallory was informed that provided he did not neglect the air defence of the UK his squadrons were to give full support to the bomber offensive.

The majority of the night offensive effort in the early part of 1944 was against airfields, with the introduction (or more accurately renaming) of the patrolling of night fighter airfields as *Flower* ops. From January the Mosquito VIs of No. 2 Group joined in the *Flower* ops and between January and May a total of 623 *Flowers* had been flown, 233 of these in May. However, May also brought an increase in attacks on transportation, including trains, barges, shipping and MT. Within the overall Allied strategy the invasion was of primary importance in summer 1944 and both day and night missions were tasked with this in mind, the bulk of the night sorties being Intruders. It was not until November that direct support of night bomber operations was resumed, much of the Bomber Support role becoming the responsibility of a number of specialist Mosquito squadrons with No. 100 Group of Bomber Command.

August 1944–May 1945

With the Allies ashore and established, further Command changes took place in the RAF with ADGB reverting to its Fighter Command title on 15 October 1944, still under Air Marshal Sir Roderic Hill. The Command had been given a new Directive on 22 September that recognised the changed threat to the UK, recognising that there was no significant threat West of a line from the Humber to Southampton. Fighter defences supported by full radar and Royal Observer Corps covers were to be maintained East of the line Cape Wrath-Falkirk-Leyburn-Tamworth-Brackley-Gloucester-Bournemouth, including the Shetlands and Glasgow-Clyde area. Reduced defences were to remain to the West of this line but those in Northern Ireland and in the Portree-Oban area could be withdrawn.

This led to the disbandment of No. 9 Group, which lost its operational commitments on 4 August and the rest of its duties on 18 September. It also saw No. 10 Group become semi-operational, leading to disbandment in May 1945. A number of Sector HQs were also closed. At the end of December the Command fielded 31 day and nine night squadrons. The former included 11 units with the Mustang III whilst the latter included a Tempest unit that specialised in night ops against flying bombs.

From autumn 1944 to the end of the Second World War the Command had four main roles:

1. Offensive operations against rockets and flying-bombs; this primarily involved fighter-bomber attacks and armed reconnaissance against launch sites, storage sites and communications.
2. Defensive operations against attacks on bomber airfields and minelaying off East coast.
3. Long-range fighter to escort Bomber Command day operations.
4. Night-fighter squadrons for offensive ops in support of Bomber Command night operations.

The final few months of the war saw Fighter Command strength drastically reduced from its high point in January 1943 of over 100 squadrons. In January 1945 it had 41 squadrons fielding a total establishment of 634 aircraft, which now included a large number of Mustang IIIs (234 aircraft). This arrival of Mustangs was not always well received, in December 1943 Mustangs had arrived to re-equip 65 Squadron: 'Men stood open mouthed with disbelief. This simply couldn't be true. Mustangs! P-51s! American junk! To exchange our beloved *Spits* for such rubbish! Had the bloody Air Ministry brass gone off their rockers? This was intolerable! How low could they sink? That evening the pilots gave vent to their anger in a drunken brawl, resulting in fairly expensive repairs having to be carried out to the Mess.' (Tony Jonsson in *Dancing in the Skies*, Grub Street 1994)

The last throw of the dice as far as German intruder operations over England was concerned came on 3/4 March 1945 – Operation *Gisella* had been planned for some time and was intended as a mass attack on Bomber Command by following the bombers home and hitting them over England and at their airfields. Over 140 Ju 88s took part and the first bomber shot down was probably a 214 Squadron Fortress, which crashed at Woodbridge in Suffolk. The operation lasted less than three hours and the RAF lost at least 24 bombers, but the defences were quickly in action and eight of the attackers were shot down, with three others flying into the ground and others being written-off to various causes.

Day Fighter Operations

Fighter Command remained heavily involved in air operations in the latter part of 1944, initially still under the control of HQ AEAF; this included support of the airborne assault on *Market-Garden* in September. However, when Bomber Command was released to return to its offensive campaign, by day and night, the Command provided escort for the former and 'bomber support' for the latter. The first of the daylight attacks took place on 27 August when 243 bombers attacked the Rheinpreussen synthetic oil refinery at Meerbeck, near Homberg. This was the first daylight attack on Germany since August 1941 and it was escorted by nine squadrons of Spitfire IXs – all of whom, had nothing to do; the lone Bf 110 that was seen very sensibly made off in the opposite direction! Despite intense flak over the target no bombers were lost. This type of long-range escort became a routine part of the Command's work and up to 14 Mustang and five Spitfire squadrons were eventually dedicated to this role. The Mustang was increasingly being used by Fighter Command for this role and by September there were seven squadrons of Mustang IIIs, the four original squadrons, 129, 306, 315, 316 had been joined by 19, 65 and 122 squadrons which had transferred from the 2nd TAF. Actually it had been an exchange deal in which Fighter Command also acquired four Spitfire IX squadrons, having given up five Tempest and two Spitfire XIV squadrons. The number of Mustang units continued to increase as squadrons exchanged their beloved Spitfires for the American fighter, such that by the end of April 1945 the Command included 16 Mustang squadrons.

Although the Mustangs had a better combat radius than the Spitfires they were still restricted as they had no fuselage overload tanks. 'The radius of action of these Mustangs, after allowing 15 minutes at a fuel consumption of 60 gallons per hour for manoeuvring under combat conditions and a 10% fuel reserve, was not more 450 miles' (AHB Summary). It was decided to fit extra tanks to the Mustangs and Spitfires despite fears

Spitfire LFXVI RW396 in polished aluminium finish.

that this would affect combat performance, but the ideal solution according to Fighter Command was to have usable airfields for refuelling on the Continent. These restrictions do not appear to have concerned the USAAF to the same degree and their Mustangs were regular visitors to the Berlin area. When airfields such as Ursel, Belgium, became available the Command's Spitfires were able to provide escort 100 miles East of the Ruhr.

In February 1943 the Air Fighting Development Unit flew comparative trials between a Spitfire IX and Mustang X. The Manoeuvrability section had this to say: 'The aircraft were compared at varying heights for their powers of manoeuvrability and it was found throughout that the Mustang, as was expected, did not have so good a turning circle as the Spitfire. By the time they were at 30,000 feet the Mustang's controls were found to be rather mushy, while the Spitfire's were still very crisp and even in turns during which 15 degrees of flap were used on the Mustang, the Spitfire had no difficulty in out-turning it. In rate of roll, however, it found that while the Spitfire is superior in rolling quickly from one turn to another at speeds up to 300 mph, there is very little to chose between the two at 350 mph IAS and at 400 mph the Mustang is definitely superior, its controls remaining far lighter at high speeds than those of the Spitfire. When the Spitfire was flown with wings clipped, the rate of roll improved at 400 mph so as to be almost identical with the Mustang. The manoeuvrability of the Mustang, however, is severely limited by the lack of directional stability which necessitates very heavy forces on the rudder to keep the aircraft steady.' (AFDU Report No. 64, February 1943).

From mid October to the end of the year Fighter Command escorted 59 bomber raids, which amounted to 6,794 fighter sorties, the majority of which were recorded as arduous but boring. In the few combats that occurred claims were made for 15 enemy aircraft, for the loss of 20 RAF fighters to all causes. The escorts were largely successful and of the 124 bomber losses the vast majority were to flak. During one escort mission of 5 December the escorts reported over 100 German fighters – by far the largest number seen for a long time and an indication, although the Allies did not yet know it, of a reinforcement in preparation for the German offensive that was being planned (the Ardennes Offensive – the Battle of the Bulge).

From January 1945 to the end of the war Fighter Command flew a further 102 bomber escort missions (8,878 sorties) as well as 29 fighter sweeps over North-West Germany. The level of bomber ops increased in March with the Allied preparations for the crossing of the Rhine and the fighters were kept busy – or at least they flew long sorties but usually with little to do except watch the bombing.

The table shows Fighter Command strength had increased from 36 squadrons and 713 aircraft in 1939 to a high point of nearly 2,000 aircraft and 101 squadrons in 1943.

The statistics in the latter part of this table are misleading at first glance and suggest a massive and sudden decline after early 1943 but in reality this was primarily a re-allocation of squadrons following the formation of the Allied Expeditionary Air Force, with Fighter Command becoming ADGB and many of its units being transferred to the new tactical formations. This trend continued into early 1945 with the decreasing threat to the UK and the movement of more squadrons to the Continent.

Fighter Command strength, 1939–1945

Date	Squadrons	Strength	OTU strength
Jan 1939	36	713	–
Jan 1940	51	888	85
Jan 1941	73	1,362	210
Jan 1942	97+10 Flts	1,916	573
Jan 1943	101+1 Flt	1,852	643
Jan 1944	70+4 Flts	1,365	899
Jan 1945	41	815	637

1946–1968 – The Cold War

As with all major wars there was a disbandment process at the end of World War Two; indeed it had started in late 1944 as the war appeared to be almost won. By 1946 the run-down of RAF strength was in full swing and included saying farewell to many of the Allied squadrons that had formed such an important part of the combat capability; many of these went home, with their aircraft, to build a peace-time air force. There were also major changes in personnel as the RAF decided on its peacetime structure and who it would keep and who it would let go; some of those that stayed went down a number of ranks in order to remain in uniform. By mid 1946 the Command had reached a low point in strength with only around 500 operational aircraft. Late Mark Spitfires and Mustangs were the major types but the number of jets was also on the increase as it was already recognised that the future lay with the jet. The concept remained that of dedicated day and night fighters, with the Mosquito continuing to shoulder responsibility for the night role.

Fighter Command strength, 1945–1953				
	Operational Sqns		*Total with all units*	
Date	*UE*	*Strength*	*UE*	*Strength*
31 May 1945	929	1,032	–	–
27 Jun 1945	612	661	–	–
23 May 1946	496	496	–	–
31 Jan 1951	533	591	1,131	1,200
31 Jan 1953	603	605	1,328	1,339
31 Dec 1953	712	585	1,363	1,277

Notes
1. The 'all units' column includes operational, communications, training and miscellaneous. The stats for December 1953 include 712/585 operational, 51/82 communications, 521/523 training and 79/87 miscellaneous.
2. The stats for operational units 1951-1953 include squadrons of the RAuxAF, with an average of 160 UE and 158 strength of aircraft in these units; the remaining aircraft were with the regular squadrons.

The first post-war C-in-C, Air Marshal Sir James Robb (since May 1945), made it clear that all was not well and that his reduced force could not defend the UK, especially as there was increasing realisation that peace meant peace with the defeated Axis powers but looming confrontation with an old ally, Russia, not that this directly affected Fighter Command (yet) as the Russians were unable to reach the UK and the immediate problem lay in mainland Europe.

The Wing concept was still in use, with day-fighter Wings at Bentwaters (56, 74 and 245 squadrons) and Boxted (222, 234 and 263 squadrons), both with Meteor F.3s, whilst the Odiham Wing (54 and 72 squadrons) had Vampires. The Command's final piston type, the Hornet, had entered service in 1946 but saw limited service. Auxiliary squadrons began to re-equip with jets and the *Mossies* too gave way to night-fighter variants of the Meteor and Vampire as Fighter Command became an all-jet force. The Wing concept was modified to have two day and one night squadron, although this was not universally true, and the Control and Reporting system, including the arrangement of Sectors, was changed.

Pair of Hornets of 19 Squadron; the Hornet was the Command's final piston type but only saw limited service (Peter Green Collection).

By early 1951 the situation was stabilising in terms of organisation and equipment and strength had started to rise – and by then it had become clear that conflict was always a possibility.

Berlin Airlift

The RAF and USAAF had placed sizeable air forces in Germany at the end of the war and tensions continued to increase, culminating in the Russian closure of land access to Berlin. The Allies decided to support their part of the city by air and the Berlin Airlift was born, the first flights being made on 28 June 1948. Russian fighters buzzed the

Meteors of 616 Squadron with post-war RAW code; Meteors became the mainstay of the Command in the post-war period in both day and night versions.

transports and the tension was high; additional Allied fighters were deployed to the area and Fighter Command came to a higher state of alert. The Airlift lasted a year, ending in May 1949 but its end led to a stand-off across Eastern Europe with the formation of NATO and the Warsaw Pact. Henceforth, Fighter Command's main enemy was the Warsaw Pact and the threat from Soviet long-range bombers, with the added requirement to support NATO in other areas and the RAF in its world-wide commitments. The communist threat expanded in 1950 with the outbreak of the Korean War.

Korean War

The RAF's participation in the Korean War was limited, although a number of pilots flew with units such as the Meteor-equipped 77 Squadron of the RAAF, and with USAAF F-86 Sabre units. The real significance for Fighter Command was that Korea was the first true jet air-war and the performance of Western and Soviet types could be compared. The Meteor was found to be wanting whilst the F-86 Sabre gave a good showing – as did the Soviet types such as the MiG-15. The RAF had swept-wing fighters in development but the only immediate solution to a perceived capability gap was the acquisition of Sabres from the Americans.

'When the Korean War broke out, no fighter able to cope with the foreseeable threats was fully developed and the decision was taken to press ahead with the production of the Supermarine Swift, although in normal times this would not have been done without more thorough preliminary trails. Despite strenuous efforts to overcome its defects, the Swift proved in the end unacceptable to the Service except for certain specialised roles.' In November 1950 a development contract and production order for 100 Swifts was signed as 'the Swift represented the only possible way of getting an up-to-date fighter in service in the time available ... but then beset by problems.' This summary appeared in the 'Second Report from the Select Committee on Estimates (1956–1957) – the Supply of Military Aircraft'.

The prototype crashed after only 3-hours flying and the first production aircraft did not fly until August 1952. However, the programme was persevered with and there was no cancellation of orders until 1955.

The Russians joined the military atomic age in 1951 and the need to defend UK airspace against Russian bombers became even more important, and was to remain the rationale of Fighter Command for the rest of its existence. As the bombers would be unescorted the fighter task was back to where it was in the 1930s – a bomber destroyer with no need to dog-fight, although the lessons of the late 1930s and Korea were not wholly forgotten. Tactics were once more to find the enemy and get behind him to use guns to effect his destruction. Those guns were now of heavier calibre, with the 30 mm Aden cannon as the standard weapon.

Fighter Command had three swept-wing fighters enter service in 1954, the Swift only went to a single squadron and the Sabre to two others, although both types also served with units in Germany. Of greater significance was the arrival of the Hawker Hunter with 43 Squadron in July and although the early F.1s had their problems, it was not long before the first of the classic Hunters, the F.6, was in service. Nevertheless, this was still a day fighter with no radar and limited armament of four 20 mm cannon. A 1955 plan called for Fighter Command to have just over 900 aircraft, with 75% of those being day fighters, including the Auxiliary Air Force contribution of 160 aircraft. The threat was now very firmly identified as Russian long-range bombers, potentially armed with nuclear weapons and able to attack in bad weather and at night. There was an increasing

Meteors of 141 Squadron at Coltishall, 1953; Meteor NF.11s entered service with the Squadron in August 1951.

need, therefore, for a missile-armed all-weather fighter. In addition it was also generally agreed that fighters needed more speed, ideally supersonic (over Mach 1) and more range, requirements that did not really go hand-in-hand in this era before the advent of air-to-air refuelling.

All of these elements were under development in the early 1950s, although it would be the latter part of the decade before they entered service as operational aircraft.

Venom night-fighter at Waterbeach.

Javelin XA636 in company with Hunter XF440; the Javelin was the RAF's first true All-Weather fighter.

Problems and future plans

The 'Second Report from the Select Committee on Estimates (1956–1957) – the Supply of Military Aircraft' stated that in its deliberations it had taken evidence from a wide range of experts, including the aircraft industry and military. In his interview with the Committee on 6 March 1956, Captain F Hopkins, Director of the Naval Air Warfare Division stated that 'if we had much more money and greater resources we would prefer, in order to keep up to date, to introduce a new type of fighter, bomber and anti-submarine aircraft every two years. That would ensure that we always had pretty modern aircraft in service at any time. We obviously cannot afford to do that, and so we have to make each aircraft as it comes into service last much longer in the front-line and in the latter half of its life it is obsolescent.' Whilst this was a naval comment it equally applied to the RAF and it was an economic factor that was to affect Fighter Command throughout the 1950s and 1960s. Shortly before this interview the Command's latest fighter had entered service, with 46 Squadron at Odiham receiving its Javelin FAW.1s.

'Colonial Reinforcements'

In addition to its primary role of defending UK airspace, Fighter Command was also called on from time to time to contribute to reinforce other operational areas. This included involvement in the 1956 Suez conflict, with the Command deploying aircraft to Cyprus. However, the majority of such tasks, and they were fairly frequent were on a smaller scale. Typical of the minor involvements was that of 65 Squadron in 1958 when they flew their Hunter F.6s to Cyprus to cover the withdrawal of British airborne forces from Jordan. Indeed, because of the troubled nature of the Middle East, Cyprus became a regular detachment base. Later it was to become a routine destination for Fighter Command squadrons on Armament Practice Camp (APC) to take advantage of the good weather factor for intensive aerial gunnery practice.

Missile era

The Select Committee report made depressing reading as it dealt with the problems of developing fighter aircraft and the 'suggestion' that manned aircraft may have a limited future. Some elements have been referred to above but the real pointer to future thinking stated that 'as aircraft become more expensive, complicated and difficult to maintain

there would have to be fewer of them … moreover in modern warfare the stage was being reached when fighters would no longer provide any protection, at any rate in the UK, and the place of conventional air weapons might be taken by ballistic rockets.'

All of Fighter Command's re-equipment plans were thrown into confusion in the 1958 'Outline of Future Policy' statement by Defence Minister Duncan Sandys, which predicted a reduction in manned fighters in favour of surface-to-air missiles (SAMs). Decline of the operational fighter force had already set-in, with aircraft strength falling from 600 in 1956 to 326 in 1958; this decline accelerated over the next five years, reaching 272 in 1960 and a mere 140 in 1962.

The SAM entered service in December 1958 with 264 Squadron setting up the first

Surface-to-Air Missiles became a central part of air defence, with the main type in RAF service being Bloodhound.

Bloodhound site at North Coates, pointing out into the North Sea ready to engage Soviet bombers day and night. Over the next two years expansion of the missile cover was rapid and by autumn 1960 there were ten squadrons deployed. However, the promised supersonic interceptor also entered service in June 1960, with the Lightning F.1 going to 74 Squadron at Coltishall. The Javelin force declined in the early 1960s as the Lightning force expanded and Fighter Command's main operational strength for its last few years comprised Lightnings and Bloodhound SAMs.

The growing threat of the Warsaw Pact in the late 1950s led to reorganisation of NATO's air defences into a number of Air Defence Regions (ADRs), which included the UK ADR. Fighter Command now had a dual role of protecting the UK and protecting the UK ADR; however, the UK was seen as one of NATO's main air base locations for massive reinforcement from America and as such would become home to American fighters (and other aircraft) thus boosting the defence capability. Improvements in radar, the increased use of air-to-air refuelling to give the Lightnings a realistic chance of engaging the enemy out over the sea, and better AAMs all helped improved the overall capability as the very real threat of a Cold War turning into a nuclear war remained the prime concern. Fighter Command retained this posture to 1968 when a major reorganisation of the RAF took place and the old Command structure was scrapped in April that year, the four main operational commands being rolled-up into a new Strike Command. The first commander was the man who had undertaken the study and proposed the change, Air Marshal Sir Dennis Spotswood.

Having been in existence since 1936, Fighter Command had made its name during the few months in 1940 when it fought the Battle of Britain but that brief period carried with it a wealth of emotion and feeling. Strike Command could never evoke the same feelings as Fighter Command.

Lightnings of 56 Squadron at Wattisham, December 1963; the Lightning was the last new aircraft to enter service with Fighter Command prior to its disappearance into Strike Command in 1968.

CHAPTER TWO

Operations

Ten Little Fighter Boys

Ten little fighter boys
Taking off in line,
One was in coarse pitch,
Then there were nine.

Nine little fighter boys
Climbing through 'the gate'
One's petrol wasn't on,
Then there were eight.

Eight little fighter boys
Scrambling up to heaven
One 'weaver' didn't,
Then there were seven.

Seven little fighter boys
Up to all the tricks,
One had a hangover,
Then there were six.

Six little fighter boys
Milling over Hythe,
One's pressure wasn't up,
Then there were five.

Five little fighter boys
Over France's shores,
One flew reciprocal,
Then there were four.

Four little fighter boys
Joining in the spree,
One's sight wasn't on,
Then there were three.

Three little fighter boys
High up in the blue
One's rubber pipe was loose,
Then there were two.

Two little fighter boys
Homing out of sun,
Flew straight and level,
Then there was one.

One little fighter boy
Happy to be home,
Beat up dispersal,
Then there was none.

Ten little Spitfires nothing have
*   achieved,*
AOC at Group is very, very
*   peeved.*
'Fifty thousand smackers
Thrown down the drains
'Cos ten silly buggers
Didn't use their brains.

From its formation in 1936 Fighter Command expected that in the event of war it would be combating slow, poorly-armed and unescorted bombers over the UK in daylight. Its equipment and training were based on this threat premise. Four years later it was all to be very different. The outbreak of war in September 1939 put the Command on high alert with the expectation that German bombers would appear within hours of the declaration of war. German aircraft did appear over the UK but the first significant

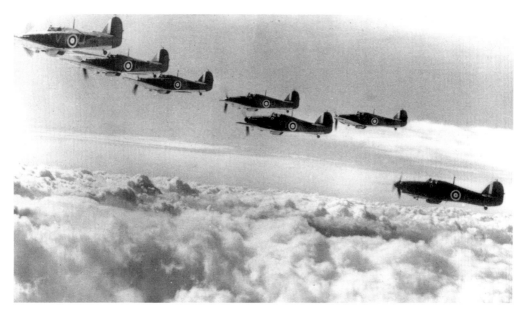

Formation of 85 Squadron Hurricanes out of Debden; the Squadron departed Debden for France on 9 September 1939 and by November had moved into Lille/Seclin, where it stayed until mid May – the Phoney War having ended in spectacular fashion with the German invasion on 10 May.

combat for the Command was from bases outside of the UK – on a small scale in Norway and a larger, and more worrying, scale in France. The deployment of Hurricane squadrons to France on the outbreak of war brought some contact with the enemy in the remaining months of the year but all fairly small-scale. For the sake of ease, the April 1940 Norwegian campaign is considered before the September 1939–June 1940 French campaign.

Norway

Two squadrons took part in operations from bases in Norway in late spring 1940. It was Fighter Command's oldest type, the Gladiator that first moved out to combat the enemy in Norway; the Gladiators of 263 Squadron left their base at Filton in late April and sailed to Norway aboard HMS *Glorious*. They were initially based at Lake Lesjeskog and Bardufoss but after a few days returned to the UK, only to come back again on 21 May aboard HMS *Furious*, along with a second carrier and a Hurricane squadron.

The Hurricane Is of 46 Squadron had been based at Digby since January 1940 with little to do other than train, and mount convoy patrols. On 9 May they moved to Abbotinsch to embark on HMS *Glorious*, three aircraft having been at Prestwick since 3 May for carrier-landing trials by Fleet Air Arm pilots. The carrier sailed on 14 May in company with HMS *Furious* (with 263 Squadron on their second venture to Norway). An advanced party was ashore at the Skaanland landing ground by 18 May and declared that it was not ready – so the carrier sailed back to the UK, only to set-off once more on 24 May and eventually disembark the 18 Hurricanes on 26 May. Two aircraft of the first two Flights were damaged on landing so the rest were diverted to Bardufoss. The first combat patrol was flown by a Flight of three Hurricanes from Skaanland but the orders were not to intercept unless their own airfield was threatened. A formation of He 111s

*Wreck of 263 Squadron Gladiator at Lake Leskajog; the Norwegian expedition by two of
Fighter Command's squadrons was short-lived.*

was spotted but as they were 'going the other way' no attempt was made to intercept. An
uneventful sortie was followed by another landing accident so the Squadron reunited at
Bardufoss on 27 May. The first patrol over Narvik, the main area of interest for the
British, was flown that evening, again with no action. However, the following day the
Hurricanes had their first success with Fg Off Lydall shooting-down a Ju88 and with two
four-engined flying-boats being strafed on Rombaksfjord. The following day brought six
more kills for the loss of three Hurricanes with two of their pilots. The day also brought
DFCs for Flt Lt Jameson and Plt Off Drummond.

The Gladiators of 263 Squadron had been flown aboard by FAA pilots on 12 May
and having sailed in the convoy of 14 May the Squadron was ashore at Bardufoss on
21 May. The main base was at Bardufoss but with a detachment at Bodo (where there is
memorial to the Squadron). On 22 May the Squadron mounted 54 sorties and reported
three combats, one of which ended with the loss of Plt Off Craig-Adams, although as an
He 111 was found near the crash the conclusion was made that the two aircraft had
collided in cloud. In its 13 days of operations the Squadron had flown 389 sorties, had 72
combats and claimed 26 enemy aircraft. One of the Gladiators still survives; N5641 has
been restored and is in the air museum at Bodo.

The British venture was all but over and the main task of the fighters in the first days
of June air cover of the evacuation of British forces. On 8 June both squadrons were
aboard HMS *Glorious* for the return to the UK; it was a nightmare as the Germans now
effectively controlled the sea and the carrier was sunk on 9 June, with 46 Squadron losing
ten aircraft, its Commanding Officer and seven pilots.

Battle of France
Under the terms of the Alliance with France, which along with the joint guarantee to
Poland had effectively brought Britain into the war, the British were to deploy forces
to fight in France. Settling in to their airfields and to the delights of local towns, the RAF
fighter pilots continued to train whilst providing patrols and, from time to time, escort

Hurricanes of 601 Squadron being refueled; the Squadron moved to France in February 1940 as part of the continued build-up (some would say, drain) of Fighter Command in France.

for Battles on recce flights. It was all very quiet and serene and as such became known as the 'Phoney War'. The first confirmed success for the RAF fighters in France came on 2 November 1939 when Flt Lt Robert Voase-Jeff of 87 Squadron downed an He 111.

No. 1 Squadron was based at Vassincourt from 9 October, as part of No. 67 Fighter Wing, and got their first victory early in November, as recorded by the author of 'Fighter Pilot – A personal record of the Battle of France'.

> *It was a beautiful sunny day, with no low clouds but quite a lot of Cirrus and Cirrostratus, and a bit of Altocumulus. I was on the aerodrome by my machine when we heard the noise of unfamiliar aircraft engines. After a lot of neck-craning and squinting we saw it – a Dornier 17 immediately above the aerodrome at about 20,000 ft, travelling west and just visible in the thinner clouds. Like all German aircraft of the* Luftwaffe *it was painted light-blue underneath, and was difficult to see. The French A.A. opened up but were nowhere near it. This was the first Hun we'd seen, and we were pretty excited. Sgt. S and I took off in pursuit, but of course had to watch our take-off and lost him. At 3,000 ft we saw him again, but lost him soon after. Up and up we clambered, turning gently from side to side and straining our eyes to find him. We never saw him again, and at 25,000 feet, with our sights alight and gun-buttons on 'Fire,' we cursed like hell and came down after some fifteen minutes' search.*
>
> *After lunch we went up to the aerodrome again. Not long afterwards a Hurricane dived across the field rocking its wings, turned, came back, and repeated the performance in an obviously excited manner. It turned out to be 'Boy', who had come to the Squadron in June. He had apparently just finished refuelling after a patrol over the aerodrome when the same Dornier went over. He took off immediately, without waiting for orders, pulled the 'plug' (boost-override), lost the Hun, clambered up to about 18,000 ft – and found him. He did*

Pilots of 1 Squadron pose outside of the Mess.

an ordinary straight astern attack, and fired one longish burst with his sights starting above the Dornier and moving slowly round the fuselage. The Hun caught fire immediately, went into a vertical spiral, and eventually made a large hole in the French country-side. It exploded on striking the ground, and there were no survivors.

24 November brought more action, with 1 Squadron claiming two Dorniers, with another three falling to 73 Squadron, and the two squadrons sharing a Heinkel 111.

Of our two Dorniers, one was intercepted by the 'Bull' and Hilly near Metz. They attacked alternately and continually from astern until the Hun went into a steep spiral and crashed in flames near the lines. I remember talking to the CO over the R/T and hearing him sing out: 'It's all right, we've got another one for the Squadron near...' 'Near where?' I asked, 'Say again,' and he repeated 'Homburg, as in hat!'

The Heinkel 111 was also brought down near Metz, and was intercepted by Blue Section. It was on fire, and losing height rapidly, when a bunch of French Moranes came rushing in, all so eager to have a bang that one of them knocked most of Sgt. C-'s tail off. He put up a very good show by getting the machine back to the aerodrome, though he had to land at 120 mph to keep control, overshooting and turning over. I saw him just after this little effort, and though he was laughing, he was trembling like a leaf and could hardly talk coherently. I saw his aircraft, too: one elevator and half the rudder were completely gone.

A section from 1 Squadron, led by 'Pussy', attacked the other Dornier about 20 miles north of the aerodrome. 'Pussy' led the attack from dead astern. By the time he had used all his ammunition the rear-gunner and navigator had escaped by parachute, one engine was on fire, and the Dormer was losing height and appeared to be more or less out of control. 'Pussy' then flew alongside the German to make sure the pilot was dead. He saw him slumped in his seat, his head lolling to one side. Suddenly, however, the Dornier throttled back, swerved on to 'Pussy's' tail, and put exactly 34 bullets through his aircraft. Hearing them rip through 'Pussy' ducked – thereby saving his life, for a bullet penetrated the locker behind his head, smashing the windscreen – and pushed his stick forward. Clouds of white smoke (which proved to be glycol) were pouring from his engine, which was stopped, and Pussy undid his straps and prepared to bale out. The 'smoke' stopped, however – presumably the glycol was all gone – and so he did his straps up again and forced-landed safely with his undercarriage retracted. Meanwhile, Killy and S, the Nos 2 and 3 of 'Pussy's' section, attacked, and with both engines on fire the German forced-landed more or less safely. Killy and S circled round and saw him wave as they passed low overhead. They then returned and landed.

The Dornier was found to have at least 500 bullet-holes in it – not enough, considering that three Hurricanes had had a go at it. Apparently the pilot had had to leave his seat to lock the gun with which he had shot 'Pussy' down. We all felt that this German had put up a damned good show, and as a tribute to the spirit that all pilots admire, we determined to have him to dine with us as our guest. The French authorities were very reluctant to part with him, but eventually he was allowed to come with Billy, whom we had sent to fetch him.

The main activity over the winter period was lone recce aircraft, usually at high level and providing little opportunity for engagement as by the time they were spotted they were unreachable. The enemy fighters seemed reluctant to cross the border but in mid April that changed and German fighter sweeps to Metz and Nancy ocurred, but at medium-high level and with no significant combat. Both sides appeared to be sizing each other up; what the Allies did not know was that there were only a few weeks to go before the *Blitzkrieg* commenced. On 10 May the Wing operations room reported 'plots all over the board'. It was a hectic day for the RAF fighters, with fighter patrols, escort to the

Hurricanes at dawn, Vassincourt. 'He took off immediately, without waiting for orders, pulled the 'plug' (boost-override), lost the Hun, clambered up to about 18,000ft - and found him. He did an ordinary straight astern attack, and fired one longish burst with his sights starting above the Dormer and moving slowly round the fuselage.'

AASF – and being on the receiving end of German bombs. The 109s were out in strength and this was the first time the Hurricanes came up against their opposite numbers in major battles. The 110s were also in action and proving no match for the Hurricanes, as recounted by a pilot of 1 Squadron:

> We went in fast in a tight bunch, each of us picking an adversary and manoeuvring to get on his tail. I selected the rear one of two in line-astern who were turning tightly to the left. He broke away from his No. 1 when he had done a half-circle and steepened his turn, but I easily turned inside him, holding my fire until I was within 50 yards and then firing a shortish burst at three-quarters deflection. To my surprise a whole lot of bits flew off him – bits of engine cowling and bits of his glass-house, and as I passed just over the top of him, still in my left-hand turn, I watched fascinated as he went into a spin, smoke pouring from him. I remember saying, 'My God, how ghastly!' as his tail suddenly swivelled sideways and came right off, while flames poured over the fuselage. Then I saw, with relief, a little white parachute open beside it.
>
> Good! I looked quickly around me. Scarcely half a minute had passed, yet as I looked I saw four other Huns going down – another with the tail off, a second in a spin, a third vertically in flames, and a fourth going up at 45 degrees in a left-hand stall-turn, with a little Hurricane on its tail and firing into its side, from which came a series of flashes and long, shooting, red flames. I shall never forget it. All the 110s at my level seemed to be hotly engaged, or about to be, so I looked around and above. Yes – those sods up there would be causing trouble soon! Three cunning lads were away from the fight, climbing all-out in line-astern to get over us and then pounce on the unwary. I had bags of ammunition left, so I immediately started clambering after them, with my 'plug' (boost-override) pulled. They were in a slight right-hand turn, and as I climbed I looked around. There were three others over on the right coming towards me, but they were below. I reached the rear Hun of the three above and shot him down in flames in a couple of bursts. Then I dived at the three coming up from the right and fired a quick burst at the leader head-on.
>
> I turned, but he was still there; so were the other two from above. In a moment I was in the centre of what seemed a mass of 110s, although there were in fact only five of them. I knew I hadn't the speed in my wooden-blader to dive away and beat it, so I decided to fight them and make the best of it. Although I was more manoeuvrable at this height (6,000 ft), than the Huns, I found it impossible to get an astern shot in, because whenever I got one almost lined up, tracers would come shooting past from another on my tail. So all I could do was to keep twisting and turning, and when a Hun got behind me, do as tight a turn as possible, almost spinning, with full engine, and fly straight at him, firing a quick burst, and then pushing the stick forward and going underneath him. Then I would pull up in a steep climbing turn to meet the next comer.
>
> Naturally they couldn't all attack at once without colliding, but several times I was at the apex of a cone formed by the cannons and machine guns of three of them. They used a lot of diving down and then climbing up and taking a full deflection shot. Their shooting was wild, and this manoeuvre was easily dealt with by turning towards them and going over their heads, causing them to steepen their climb until they were stalled and had to fall away. But don't imagine for a moment that I was enjoying this performance. Far from it. My mouth was becoming drier

and drier, and I was getting more and more tired and desperate. Would they run out of ammunition? Would they push off? Would help come? I knew I couldn't hold out much longer.

After what seemed an age (actually it turned out to be fifteen minutes), I was flying down head-on at a Hun who was climbing towards me. We both fired – and then I thought I had left it too late and that we were going to collide. I pushed the stick forward violently and there was a stunning explosion right in front of me. For a moment my brain did not work. The aircraft seemed to be falling, all limp on the controls. Then, as black smoke poured out of the nose and enveloped the hood, and as a hot blast and a flicker of reflected flame came into the dark cockpit, I said to myself, 'Come on, out you get!' I pulled the pin out of my harness, wrenched open the hood, and hauled myself head first out to the right. The wind pressed me tightly against the side of the aircraft, my legs still inside, and I remember catching hold of the trailing edge of the wing and heaving myself out. As I came free and somersaulted, it felt as though I was being whirled round and round through the air on the end of a piece of string by a giant. Then, as I fumbled for and pulled the rip-cord, I was brought the right way up with a violent jerk that nearly knocked the breath from my body. My head was pressed forward by the back pad that had slipped up behind it, and I couldn't look up to see if my parachute was all right. There was no sensation of movement – just a slight wind as I swung gently to and fro and for all I knew the thing might be on fire or not open properly.

He landed safely and was soon back with the Squadron.

The German ground offensive rolled on and the RAF fighters kept pulling back; the Germans had massive air superiority – although on paper the French Air Force should have made more of a contribution – and the RAF's bombers were shot out of the sky by fighters and ground fire, whilst the Hurricanes managed to give a good account of themselves. Nevertheless, the overall campaign was a disaster and the Allies were pushed back to the sea – and the 'miracle' of Dunkirk.

Dunkirk

Contrary to a widely-held belief at the time, especially in Army circles, and one perpetuated ever since, the RAF *was* present over the beaches of Dunkirk and a number of major air battles took place, which, for the first time, involved significant numbers of Spitfires. Flt Lt Bob Stanford Tuck as one of those pilots striving to protect the air space over the beaches and it was on one such patrol that he scored his first victory. 'I kept closing in on him and at about 1,000 yards I had him square in my sights, then I decided not to fire but to close in. From about 500 yards I opened fire; nothing happened, although I could see my bullets striking home. Then suddenly there was a puff of blue smoke and a few pieces of metal came off the aircraft and flew towards me. The aircraft was on fire now and it rose steeply before flicking to the left; it spun and went down through the clouds. I followed it, which was against orders, and watched it crash into a field where it exploded.' As a Flight Commander on the Spitfire-equipped 92 Squadron, Bob Stanford Tuck was an excellent pilot and something of a marksman, the latter due largely to his having been taught at an early age how to shoot game birds. He claimed two more 109s a few days later and was soon made CO of 92 Squadron, following the loss of Roger Bushell.

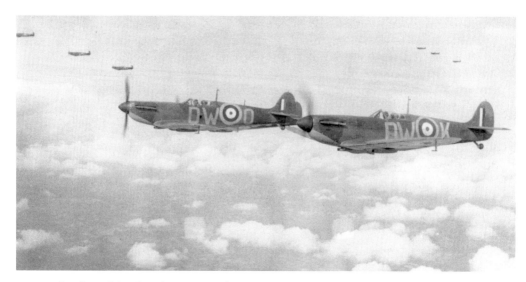

Spitfires of 610 Squadron on patrol.

David Crook was a pilot with 609 Squadron, which was also involved in flying protective sorties over the Dunkirk area: 'We shot a number of Huns down and lost four of our pilots. Desmond was also killed near Frinton-on-Sea; he lost his way back in bad weather and ran out of petrol, and was killed in trying to make a forced landing. I think there is no doubt that some of these losses were due to inexperience and lack of caution.

Pilots of 1 Squadron inspect a German machine-gun – collecting trophies was standard in the early part of war.

None of us had ever been in action before, and everybody's idea was to go all out for the first Hun that appeared. This policy does not pay when you are fighting a cunning and crafty foe, and the Germans frequently used to send over a decoy aircraft with a number of fighters hovering in the sun some thousands of feet above, who would come down like a ton of bricks on anybody attacking the decoy. This ruse almost certainly accounted for one pilot, Presser, and possibly one or two others – the last anybody saw of Presser was when he was diving down to attack a Junkers 88, and there were definitely some Messerschmitts above' (from 'Spitfire Pilot', Flt Lt David Crook DFC, Greenhill Books).

This neatly summarises one of the problems faced by the RAF pilots – they had no experience and were having to gain it 'on the job' and at no small cost. The important thing now was to learn the lessons and apply them; some of this hard-earned wisdom was transmitted through official and unofficial channels and brought-about various changes, not least to the harmonisation of guns to 250 yards rather than 400 yards. Other lessons of the 'Hun in the sun' and a host of others were applied by those with experience, passed on by Flight Commanders – and eventually at training schools – but many a new pilot in the forthcoming Battle of Britain still had to find out for himself; with luck the lesson came as a warning, without luck it was a parachute trip or a final crash.

The *real* battle was about to begin. The overall history of the Battle of Britain is in Chapter One, and the focus here is on combat accounts from that period.

Battle of Britain

Countless books and millions of words have been written on the Battle of Britain, including numerous memories of pilots. This part of the Operations chapter will therefore only give a few brief examples of combat action during this period.

It was a fine afternoon. We intercepted them over Brighton going out to sea. I did what my Flight Commander had said don't do (i.e. follow an Me 109 down – its partner would always be in the sun and would come after). Two 109s were in front of me. One started to go down. The other started to turn right, climbing into the sun. With quick glances at the one climbing, I got the one going down in my sight. I let go a long burst, trying hard to see if I had time before the other one came down. Blue-black smoke appeared. I then saw the other just coming out of the sun on me and, if he was firing, he went back claiming me, because I flicked the Spit over and pulled back, diving to sea level from 20,000 feet vertically.

So recounted a pilot of 41 Squadron on an encounter during a scramble in September 1940, it was typical scene and one that would be told to squadron intelligence officers by dozens of Fighter Command pilots as they returned to their bases on most days during the period known as the Battle of Britain.

On the afternoon of 8 July the British radar stations reported a build-up of enemy aircraft over France. A swarm of Do 17s with escorting Bf 110s and 109s attacked a convoy near Dover and Dover harbour. The Hurricanes of 32 Squadron tried to get through to the bombers but were swamped by the escorting fighters; 74 Squadron's Spitfires pitched into the melee and before long it had become every man for himself as the formations on both sides broke up and individual combats took place. 'Pilot Officer Cobden, leading Yellow Section (of 74 Squadron), followed Blue Section down. He picked out a straggling Do 17 and disabled its starboard engine. He then delivered a second attack on the bomber, but as he was breaking away was set upon by a group of Bf 109s and his Spitfire was riddled with their fire, engaging emergency boost he broke

The standard German bomber was the Heinkel III, a reasonably fast and well-armed aircraft but one that was very vulnerable to fighter attack as long as a critical component (engines or pilot for example) was hit.

away from his attackers in a steep climbing turn. It was a typical encounter ... into the fray, identify a target ... close, give it a burst or two ... but keep looking around and don't stay on a straight course for more than a few seconds. The need to keep the head moving continually was the main reason why most fighter pilots wore scarves, a way of "lubricating" the neck! Damage to the convoy was negligible and in this, the first "dogfight" involving over 100 aircraft, the RAF came out best.'

July had not been a good month for 609 Squadron and after a series of losses David Crook noted in his book: 'I think Buck's death was very largely due to inexperience and faulty tactics. We had not yet learnt that it did not pay to go out to sea to meet the enemy, but to let them come to us. Also we did not realise the importance that height

The Hurricane was the most numerous – and most successful – of the RAF fighters in the Battle but has always suffered from the better reputation of the Spitfire.

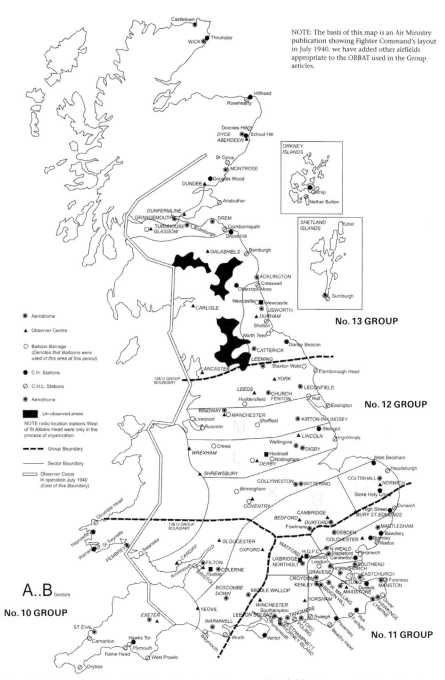

NOTE: The basis of this map is an Air Ministry
publication showing Fighter Command's layout
in July 1940. we have added other airfields
appropriate to the ORBAT used in the Group
articles.

The RAF in the Battle of Britain showing Sectors and airfields (Courtesy of FlyPast Magazine,
www.keypublishing.com).

meant. Afterwards we used to get as high as possible before going into action. This is
the whole secret of success in air fighting.' Buck was yet another pilot to end up in the
water; in this instance the pilot was not found but in many cases pilots drowned or
succumbed to their injuries as there was no rescue service in existence, other than naval

Pilots of 92 Squadron pose with trophy – part of the first Ju 88 the Squadron destroyed; quite a number of squadrons acquired German markings as their trophies.

launches. The Germans had a more efficient system with rescue rafts in fixed locations and dedicated pick-up aircraft. The RAF subsequently developed a very effective Air Sea Rescue service. The ability to recover pilots – from sea or land – was crucial to the survival of Fighter Command as lack of pilots was the real weakest point during the Battle of Britain.

On 7 August, convoy CW9 left Southend for Portsmouth but overnight it was attacked and scattered by E-boats. The following day the *Luftwaffe* employed some 300 aircraft in a major effort to destroy the scattered ships and bring the RAF to battle. The most notable engagement occurred when the Hurricanes of 145 Sqn pounced on a formation of Junkers Ju 87s, claiming to have shot down 21 – although later analysis reduced this to less than ten.

On 15 August, the day that Goering had determined for *Adler Tag* (Eagle Day) the *Luftwaffe* assumption was that the RAF was already on the ropes and that all its fighter strength had been concentrated in the South – leaving the Midlands and Northern England virtually undefended. The Staxton Wold radar station plotted a raid of 40+ aimed at the fighter stations of Church Fenton and Leconfield. A number of squadrons were scrambled; fourteen Spitfires of 616 Squadron scrambled and the Squadron was vectored to patrol over Flamborough and at 1315 hours, it intercepted a formation of around 50 Ju 88s of KG30. Squadron pilots reported that the enemy was flying in a very poor formation, with several stragglers. Flt Lt Denys Gillam, leading 'B Flight', was the first to spot the enemy, at 19,000 ft, and immediately led Blue Section into the attack. Plt Off Marples got in the first burst and as he broke away, Gillam took over; he kept up a continuous fire as the Ju 88 dived to 6,000 ft, jettisoning its bombs. Part of the tail broke away and the aircraft turned onto its back, enveloped in flames, before crashing

Hurricanes of 501 Squadron scramble from Gravesend on 15 August 1940 – Adler Tag
(Eagle Day) on which the Luftwaffe planned massive attacks on Fighter Command airfields.

into the sea. Meanwhile Marples, having pulled off from his first attack, immediately pursued another bomber, getting in two bursts before it entered cloud with one engine smoking. He then saw two other bombers north of Scarborough and gave chase, firing short bursts. One aircraft wheeled to port and dived to ground level, but Marples could only harass the bomber as it flew at 100 ft – he had run out of ammunition. Plt Off Murray (Blue 2) saw two Ju 88s flying through broken cloud at 10,000 ft; they were in close formation and one was smoking badly. He fired three long bursts and a second or two after the last burst, both bombers caught fire. He did not see them crash but it is most unlikely that they were able to make it back to Denmark. Plt Off Hugh Dundas, leading Green Section, saw Denys Gillam lead Blue Section into the attack and after Marples broke away, having severely damaged his second aircraft, he closed in and fired a three-second burst, setting both engines on fire. Plt Off Buck Casson (Green 2) had followed Dundas in, but being poorly placed he broke away to intercept a lone bomber heading out to sea at 5,000 ft. After two quarter attacks, the enemy dived to 1,000 ft – with the rear gunner keeping up a steady fire. Casson fired two more

'Buck' Casson of 616 Squadron; Plt Off Buck Casson (Green 2) had followed Dundas in, but being poorly placed he broke away to intercept a lone bomber heading out to sea at 5,000ft. After two quarter attacks, the enemy dived to 1,000ft – with the rear gunner keeping up a steady fire. Casson fired two more bursts and the aircraft dived to sea level, at which point Dundas re-appeared and, with Casson out of ammunition, took over the attack.

Spitfires of 616 Squadron at Leconfield from where they engaged the German formation on 15 August with great success.

bursts and the aircraft dived to sea level, at which point Dundas reappeared and, with Casson out of ammunition, took over the attack. By now, there was no return fire and the enemy bomber was last seen at very low level with smoke pouring from its port engine.

Red Section also attacked the main bomber force, with the CO, Sqn Ldr Robinson, damaging one bomber before he ran out of ammunition. Flt Lt Hellyer, accompanied by Plt Off Smith, dived astern a Ju 88, and fired all his ammunition into it; Smith then took over and fired a series of short bursts until the bomber suddenly dived steeply into the sea.

By now, the bombers were completely split up and a number of individual actions took place. Sgt Hopewell picked out a lone Ju 88 and hit it in both wings. The bomber took violent evasive action and turned inland; Hopewell continued to fire into the engines and pieces started to break off. Shortly afterwards the bomber crashed three miles NW of Bridlington. Sgt Westmoreland also attacked a lone bomber; firing two short bursts from 400 yards he set the port engine on fire, after which one of the crew baled out. Finally, Fg Off Moberley arrived on the scene after his late take-off. He had been listening on the radio and decided to head towards Flamborough, but before reaching the area he spotted a twin-engined aircraft low over the sea. He dived to 2,000 ft and identified a Ju 88 with smoke coming from one engine (probably the aircraft that had been attacked by Westmoreland). He made two or three attacks before the bomber's starboard engine stopped and the aircraft crashed into the sea. In just a few minutes, 616 Squadron claimed eight enemy bombers destroyed and six seriously damaged – for no loss.

Hugh 'Cocky' Dundas recorded the day in his excellent autobiography, *Flying Start*:

> *I set course and rammed the throttle 'through the gate', to get the maximum power output, permissible for only a limited period of time. Some of the others were ahead of me, some behind. We did not bother to wait for each other or try to form up into flights and section. We raced individually across the coast and out to sea. About 15 miles East of Bridlington I saw them, to the left front and slightly*

below – the thin, pencil shapes of German twin-engined bombers, flying in a loose, straggling, scattered formation toward the coast.

I switch on my reflector sight, setting the range for 250 yards, turned the gun button to the 'fire' position. Wheeling down in a diving turn, I curved towards the nearest bomber, judging my rate of turn and dive to bring me astern. A light winked from the rear-gunner's position and tracer bullets hosed lazily past. When I opened up with my eight Brownings the return fire stopped. The bomber turned and lost height. First a gush of black smoke, then a steady stream poured from its engine cowlings and it fell steeply towards the calm summer sea.

Turning to look for a second target I saw other Spitfires fastening on to the German planes on all sides. Beneath me a damaged bomber turned back out to sea and I decided to go in and finish it off. It was a foolish decision, made in the heat of the moment, for I should have looked for an undamaged plane still making for the coast. By the time I caught up with it and knocked it down I was several miles further out to sea. The sky was empty and I judged that my ammunition was nearly exhausted.

As the Squadron was soon to discover, it was a different war to that being fought in the South and 616 was to suffer a period of heavy losses.

For 249 Squadron 15 August was their first day in No. 10 Group, having moved to Middle Wallop the previous day from the quiet of Church Fenton. The morning of the 15th was one of settling in to their tented accommodation but at 1300 'A Flight' was brought to 'readiness' and 'B Flight' to '15 minutes', although nothing happened. It was not until 1715 that the Squadron was ordered up to patrol Warmwell at 15,000 ft. The ORB recorded that 'B Flight' attacked a formation of eleven Ju 88s and 50+ Me 110s! The Flight claimed the destruction of three Me 110s, whilst 'A Flight' reported nothing

Roland Beamont in cockpit of 87 Squadron Hurricane, August 1940.

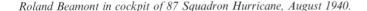

seen! Two further patrols were flown that day. The following day the Squadron was airborne at midday to patrol Ringwood to Poole; Red Section spotted a group of 109s and were ordered to investigate with the result that 'Red Section unfortunately bought it, being heavily attacked by fighters' (249 Squadron ORB). Two of the Hurricanes were shot down – Flt Lt Nicolson (Red 1) baling out OK but being shot-at by the Local Defence Volunteers as he came; Plt Off King got out of his Hurricane but his parachute had been damaged by a cannon shell and he was killed on impact with the ground as it did not slow him enough; Sqn Ldr King managed to make it back to base despite his aircraft having been hit numerous times.

The Intelligence Officer of 611 Squadron summarised the afternoon combat of 11 September thus:

> At 1530 hours 611 Squadron left G1 Duxford and went into position as second squadron of the wing formation which was ordered to patrol in a southerly direction towards the Thames estuary. At about 1550 when in the vicinity of SE London, 611 Squadron formed up in three sections of four aircraft in line astern. 100 plus enemy aircraft were seen coming north in the direction of our fighters. Our aircraft were then at 20,000 ft. The enemy formation consisted of Dornier 215s and a number of Heinkel 111s at 18,000 ft and a mass of Me 110s stepped up behind at 20,000 ft, with a large number of Me 109s stepped up behind at 24,000 ft. Our aircraft altered course, making a left turn, coming in to attack on the beam of the enemy formation. 611 Squadron attacked the Me 110s. Pilots report that from the moment of contact with the enemy it was impossible to keep formation, and a general melee ensued. F/Sgt Sadler, who was No. 4 of Yellow Section, got separated from his Section and attacked an Me 110, giving two long bursts closing from 500 yards to 100 yards, and using nearly all his ammunition. The fuselage was seen to catch fire and the EA was last seen losing height. P/O Lund, No. 4 of Blue Section, dived onto an Me 109 and fired a short burst on a deflection aim without visible effect. As another aircraft appeared in his mirror he climbed and saw five Me 110s. He selected the starboard aircraft and delivered an astern attack, closing to 100 yards. Black and white smoke was seen coming from the EA, which seemed to be losing height in relation to its formation. No evasive tactics were observed, and no enemy fire experienced. Sgt Burt saw a single Heinkel 111 following a formation of Dornier 215s. Our aircraft manoeuvred to attack the enemy from 3,000 ft above. Sgt Burt dived and opened fire at about 400 yards closing to 200 yards, giving a burst of about 5 seconds which apparently put the enemy rear gunner out of action, as enemy tracer fire ceased. Squadron landed at Duxford at approx. 1620 hours to refuel and rearm, and left for Digby where Squadron arrived at dusk. Sgt F E R Shepherd and his Spitfire P7298 are missing. Sgt S A Levenson force-landed near Kenley and is returning to Digby by train.

At this stage the fate of Fred Shepherd was unknown – he may, like Levenson, have been forced to land elsewhere or he may have been shot down but survived. Three days later the Squadron ORB recorded: 'We have now learnt that Sgt Shepherd died as a result of enemy action in the neighbourhood of Croydon but no further details are known'. Fred Shepherd had only joined the Squadron on 1 September and flown his first mission on 7 September; he only flew twice more before being killed in action.

15 September is the day now commemorated as Battle of Britain Day – so what was the significance of that date in 1940? The following extracts are taken from a later RAF account of the day's operations.

The Ju 87 Stuka formations proved vulnerable to the RAF fighters and were withdrawn from the battle.

'At dawn on Sunday the 15th the weather was fine and visibility was good; but as the morning wore on cloud steadily formed over SE England until by mid afternoon there was thick cloud (8/10 to 10/10 cover) at 4,000–6,000 ft.' The day started quietly other than a noticeable increase in German patrols over the Straits of Dover but this was soon to change. 'By 1100 hours it was obvious from the forces that were massing near Calais that a big attack was imminent; and a large force of British squadrons was sent into the air in the next 25 minutes. It was a further half hour, however, before the first of the enemy forces crossed the coast of Kent; and the success that our squadrons later enjoyed was not least due to the unusually long interval between the first warning of attack and the enemy's advance. The controller at No. 11 Group not only had sufficient time to couple ten squadrons into Wings of two squadrons, he was able to also bring in reinforcements from the adjacent Groups before the first German force crossed the coast. The squadrons ordered up at this stage were:

1035 72 Sqn, three aircraft from Biggin Hill to patrol Canterbury at 20,000 ft.
1103 72 Sqn (seven aircraft) and 92 Sqn (ten aircraft) from Biggin to patrol same area at 25,000 ft.
1115 229 Sqn and 303 Sqn from Northolt to patrol Biggin at 15,000 ft.
1115 253 Sqn and 501 Sqn from Kenley to patrol Maidstone at 15,000 ft.
1115 17 Sqn and 73 Sqn from Debden to patrol Chelmsford at 15,000 ft.
1120 504 Sqn from Hendon and 257 Sqn from Martlesham to patrol North Weald to Maidstone at 15,000 ft
1120 603 Sqn from Hornchurch to patrol Dover at 25,000 ft.
1120 609 Sqn from Middle Wallop to patrol Brooklands-Windsor at 15,000 ft.
1125 Duxford Wing (five squadrons – 19, 242, 302, 310, 611) to patrol Hornchurch at 25,000 ft.'

Fighter Command thus had 17 squadrons in the air covering the SE approaches to London. The bulk of the attacking force, in three columns, crossed the coast between Dover and Ramsgate between 1135 and 1140 and once inland spread out to

Pilots of 17 Squadron, Debden September 1940; on Battle of Britain day (15 September) the Squadron was airborne at 1115 to patrol Chelmsford at 15,000ft.

attack London. Patrolling the Canterbury area the Biggin Hill Spitfires were first into action, with 72 Squadron leading. The Combat Reports from the formation leaders stated:

72 Squadron. I was Tennis *Leader when ordered to patrol Canterbury angels 25 in company with 92 Sqn, 72 leading. I climbed to angels with the two squadrons. While I was on patrol I was ordered to attack fighters. The main bomber force with fighter escort was about 2,000 ft below with the fighters about 3,000 ft below. I ordered the Squadron into line astern and dived down on the fighters from out of the sun, as we dived I ordered the Squadron into echelon starboard, thus attacking as many fighters (Me 109s) as possible. The Me 109 which I attacked half rolled as I opened fire and before he could dive away he caught fire and exploded. I was then attacked by five other Me 109s. I did a steep turn to starboard and continued to turn until I out-turned one Me 109 which was on my tail. I gave him two short bursts and he burst into flames. I then spun down to get away from more Me 109s which dived down on me.*

I returned to base and was informed that enemy aircraft were over base at angels 14. I climbed up and saw a formation of Dorniers in front of me. I chased them and attacked the outside one on the starboard side. I gave him two short bursts from dead astern and his port engine stopped and he dropped out of the formation losing height. I attacked the Do 215 again and white vapour poured out from his starboard engine. Five or six friendly fighters then came up and started attacking him. He crashed into a wood and exploded. I returned to base and landed.

Spitfire of 72 Squadron; 'I was Tennis *Leader when ordered to patrol Canterbury angels 25 in company with 92 Sqn, 72 leading. I climbed to angels with the two squadrons. While I was on patrol I was ordered to attack fighters. The main bomber force with fighter escort was about 2,000ft below with the fighters about 3,000ft below.'*

At the time these first combats were taking place the next wave of RAF fighters was being scrambled, and between 1135 and 1142 the final six squadrons were airborne:

1135 46 Sqn and 249 Sqn from North Weald to proceed towards South London.
1140 1 (RCAF) Sqn from Northolt and 605 Sqn from Croydon to patrol over Kenley at 15,000 ft.
1140 41 Sqn from Hornchurch to patrol Gravesend at 20,000 ft.
1142 66 Sqn from Gravesend to intercept approaching enemy formation.

In the meantime, two other Wings had engaged as 229/303 squadrons and 253/501 squadrons attacked the enemy formations over Kent. These, along with engagements by 41 and 66 Squadrons, were in some respects preambles to the main events about to unfold nearer London.

Just after midday, the leader of the 257/504 Wing took his aircraft into combat against 'a square formation of 25 Do 172 and Do 215s in five lines of aircraft in line abreast, all at 18,000 ft, with escorting yellow-nosed Me 109s at 23,000 ft.' They were soon joined by two more No. 11 Group squadrons, 46 and 249, and seven Dorniers were subsequently claimed for the loss of two Hurricanes. The five squadrons of the Duxford Wing had also arrived on the scene but had to wait until the friendlies had cleared before they could engage the enemy. Whilst the three Hurricane squadrons engaged the bombers, the two Spitfire units went after the fighters and by the end of the combat the Duxford Wing had claimed 19 bombers and seven fighters.

The Air Ministry's News Service issued a press release on the evening of 15 September:

A Great Air Battle: Today was the most costly day for the German Air Force for nearly a month. During the day, between 350 and 400 enemy aircraft were launched in two waves against London and SE England. By 8pm it was known

Don Kingaby explains the controls of his 92 Squadron Spitfire; he was unique in being the only recipient of a Distinguished Flying Medal (DFM) and two Bars.

that 165 of these had been shot down, 161 by fighters and 4 by AA fire. The great majority of those that escaped were chivvied and harried at all stages of their journey. Thirty of our own fighters are lost or missing, but ten of the pilots are safe.

The press release continued with details of the two waves and 'combat reports' from Fighter Command pilots such as 'the whole formation was entirely broken up. They were flying west when we saw them. When we had finished, they were turning away fast towards home. As we broke off, a formation of Spitfires was just coming in to engage them.'

Fighter Command's Diary recorded a communiqué from the Prime Minister addressed to Fighter Command via the Secretary of State for Air: 'yesterday eclipses all previous records of the Fighter Command. Aided by squadrons of their Czech and Polish comrades, using only a small proportion of their total strength, and under cloud conditions of some difficulty, they cut to rags and tatters three separate waves of murderous assault upon the civil population of their native land, inflicting a certain loss of 125 bombers and 53 fighters upon the enemy, to say nothing of probable and damaged, while themselves sustaining only a loss of 12 pilots and 25 machines. These results exceed all expectations and give just and sober confidence in the approaching struggle.' Good solid Churchillian stuff!

The Germans claimed to have shot down 79 RAF aircraft for the loss of 43 of their own, a total somewhat at variance with the RAF's claims of 185 enemy destroyed for the loss of 25 of their own number. At the same time that these critical combats were taking place, the *Luftwaffe* had begun to increase its nightly raids.

'Battle of Britain Day' did not bring an end to the German daylight offensive and there were a number of significant raids in late September and early October. On

Fighter Command's only Victoria Cross winner – Flt Lt E J B Nicolson of 249 Squadron, awarded for his actions on 12 August 1940.

24 September the Hurricanes of 17 Squadron were airborne at 0830 to patrol their base, being joined by 73 Squadron: vectored towards 30+ bombers with fighter escort over the Thames, 17 Squadron 'acted as rear-guard to take on the fighters. Fg Off Bird-Wilson was shot-down and baled out; three other aircraft circled until they saw him picked-up by a boat. P/O Wissler was hit and injured but managed to crash-land at base. F/O Czernin claimed a probable on a 109 and P/O Pittman claimed a damaged 109.' Two of the named pilots had appeared in the ORB earlier that month with awards of DFCs, the citation of which read: Fg Off Harold Bird-Wilson 'has shot down six enemy aircraft and shared in the destruction of several others. He has shown fine fighting qualities and determination in his attacks'; Fg Off Count Manfred Czernin 'has displayed great keenness in his desire to engage the enemy, and has destroyed nine of their aircraft. In August 1940 he led his Section in a head-on attack on a large formation of enemy aircraft, destroying three of them.' A few days later, 27 September, the Squadron was in another pitched battle, again with 73 Squadron alongside. Airborne over base at 0905 they spotted 30–40 Me 110s over London at 18,000 ft in three large circles, revolving inside each other in opposite directions. The rear section of the Squadron was attacked by 109s and Sgt Bartlett landed at Debden with part of his tail fin shot away and the rudder controls unserviceable. The Squadron climbed to attack the Me 110s and Fg Off Czernin claimed a 110, as did Sgt Griffiths, who also claimed a probable, with Sgt Steward also claiming a 110. Plt Off Leary joined a Hurricane of another squadron and got behind two 110s, claiming one destroyed and one probable. Sgt Hogg got inside the 110s and flew in the opposite direction and claimed one shot down, which crashed at

Duxford, with Sgt Hogg landing at that airfield. When other Hurricanes and Spitfires joined in the enemy fled, with Manfred Czernin pursuing three 110s to the coast of France. The Squadron flew four further patrols that day, with a Bf 109 falling to Sgt Griffiths, and as an indication of the hectic pace for some pilots, Sgt Bartlett had flown on all four of the day's sorties.

October brought one of the most successful days for 602 Squadron out of Westhampnett, with four patrols flown on the 29th: 'one of them being perhaps the most successful the Squadron has yet fought, when at 27,000 ft the Squadron, led by F/L Mount, saw two formations of Me 109s, about 25 in each, approaching at 23,000 ft. With some advantage from the sun and the supreme asset of greater height, the Spitfires were able to inflict heavy casualties with 7 Me 109s being destroyed, 2 probably destroyed and 3 damaged. One of our own Spitfires was very slightly damaged' (602 Squadron ORB).

One of the most frequent comments made by fighter pilots involved in this, and indeed other, air battles, was the sudden change from a sky full of aircraft to being on your own. Bob 'Spud' Spurdle neatly expresses this in his autobiography 'The Blue Arena'

> *I rechecked that my gun's safety catch was off. The gun-sight graticule glowed clearly and I lowered my seat a notch. Malan [Sqn Ldr A G Malan, CO of 74 Squadron] curved to meet the Huns head on and all at once we were into them. Yellow spinners, stiff square-tipped wings with sparkles of light flickering. I tried to follow my leader around but, being fascinated by the enemy aircraft, somehow lost him. I couldn't find a single Jerry. Twisting and turning, I couldn't see a damned aircraft! Nothing! The sky was clean and bare. Far off, white contrails curved lazily this was and that. But I couldn't watch them. Where had everyone*

Gravesend 1940, pilots of 66 Squadron loiter in the crew-room.

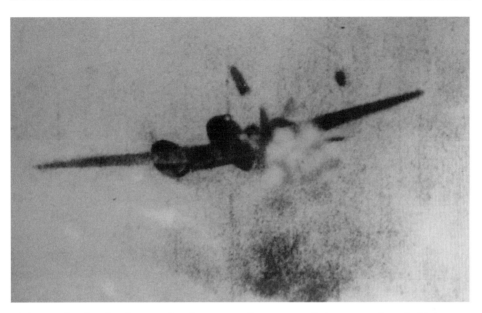

A German bomber breaks-up under the impact of concentrated close-range fire; the hitting power of the 0.303 Browning was often debated and the RAF eventually chose (later in the war) cannon as the main fighter armament.

> *gone? It was no use horsing around up here, twisting from side to side, looking up, back and around, frantic with disappointment. I dived for the deck – orders were to go straight back if separated and there was no fight in one's vicinity.*

On the way back he latched on to another Spitfire – Malan's – and compounded his error.

> *He looked at me and shook his fist. Automatically I lowered my undercarriage, Malan just turned away and slowly shook his head.*

The hand gesture normally means lower the undercarriage but in this case Malan was obviously just venting his feelings, as he did again back at Biggin Hill. 'Spud' Spurdle went on to have a fine combat career, ending up as CO of 80 Squadron and with a DFC and Bar. Some of the young men survived and learnt, but some did not.

Despite the occasional intense day, the general pattern from mid September was one of routine patrols and little action as the *Luftwaffe* recognised that it would have to re-think and re-group. As the daylight campaign began to wind down, the night campaign – the Blitz – was starting in earnest.

Night Blitz

The Germans had been taking advantage of the night skies from the start of the campaign and it was frustrating for the defenders, who still primarily had to rely on visual acquisition, often aided by searchlight activity. The patrols had mixed results:

> Several patrols went up during the night. The weather was generally unfavourable. Thick cloud hampered the searchlights, and although enemy aircraft were in the vicinity of our patrols, the Special Equipment failed to pick anything up
>
> (29 Squadron ORB for 9 August 1940).

On the night of 28/29 August Blenheim D of 600 Squadron was scrambled: 'I was told to get off as soon as possible and patrol base at Angels 17. For the next hour we received a good number of vectors and investigated innumerable searchlight concentrations. We were sent to patrol a line across which a lot of enemy aircraft were making their way to the Midlands. It was not long before I saw the exhaust flames of an aircraft close in front and above, so turned and went flat out after him, to find we could hardly climb any higher, and all the controls were pretty sloppy. So having staggered into a line astern at approx 400 yards, let go a good burst. The enemy aircraft turned and dived, proving too fast for us to catch. A bit later I saw exhaust flames below us and to starboard, so we dived on them and was getting really close when we were illuminated from behind. One searchlight coming in from the front, flicked over the aircraft in front before fastening on to us. It was sufficient to show that we were very close, so opened fire before the searchlight blinded us entirely. Exhausted the remainder of my ammunition and again saw enemy aircraft dive away too fast for me to catch.' The Blenheim landed at Hornchurch at 2320 with the crew uncertain as to if they had been successful.

In a speech on 9 September, Adolf Hitler said: 'We are giving our reply night after night. If the British declare that they will attack our cities heavily, then we will wipe out their cities.' The night blitz of London, and to a lesser extent other British cities, came as a major shock to the British people and became an abiding image of the war. This night campaign did not really get underway until autumn 1940 – but the first significant night raid on England had taken place on 18/19 June, the attackers being He 111s of KG.4. The bomber's targets were Mildenhall and Honington, two of Bomber Command's airfields, plus a diversionary raid towards Southend. Four RAF squadrons became involved in the night's activities – Blenheims of 23 and 29 Squadrons and Spitfires of 19 and 74 Squadrons. Two Heinkels on the Southend raid were first to fall on this clear night, both probably being shot-down by Flt Lt 'Sailor' Malan of 74 Squadron. His account of his second combat that night stated:

> *I gave it two five-second bursts and observed bullets entering all over the enemy aircraft. Enemy aircraft emitted heavy smoke and I observed one parachute open very close ... (aircraft) crashed in flames near Chelmsford.*

Malan had picked up the Heinkel because of searchlight activity in the area, spotting the bomber in a searchlight beam. Spitfires of 19 Squadron also had some success, one Heinkel falling to Flt Lt Clouston and Fg Off Petre being involved in the destruction of another. The latter incident involved a Heinkel, a Blenheim and a Spitfire – all of which were shot-down! The Heinkel was picked up by the 23 Squadron Blenheim of Sqn Ldr O'Brien. Just as the Blenheim opened fire so too did Petre's Spitfire. As the latter broke away to avoid the Blenheim it was shot-down by the German bomber, Petre baling out. The Blenheim too took avoiding action and lost control, with only the pilot surviving when the aircraft was abandoned. The bomber crew also had to bale out. Two 23 Squadron Blenheims took on another Heinkel, with the bomber and one Blenheim falling, whilst in the final combat of the night a 29 Squadron Blenheim damaged its target, which subsequently crash-landed on the beach near Calais, but then ended up in the Thames. An interesting night all round with lessons for both sides. There was little further night activity until August and it was not until the night attacks on London and other cities in the autumn that great concern was caused to politicians and air planners.

Having been withdrawn from the day battle, the Defiants were proving to be effective night fighters. In the early hours of 16 October Defiant N1621 of 264 Squadron was on patrol and shot down a Heinkel of KGr.126, which crashed near Hulton at 0200

Blenheim of 219 Squadron, 1940: the Squadron re-formed in October 1939 to operate Blenheims and became one of the Command's leading night-fighter squadrons.

with the loss of two of its crew. The pilot of the Defiant, Plt Off Desmond Hughes gave an account of the combat:

> ... *it was a bright moonlight night. Suddenly out of the corner of my eye I saw something move across the stars out to my left. If you are scanning the night sky it is normally completely still, so anything that moves attracts the eye. This just had to be another aircraft. I got Fred (Sgt Fred Gash) to swing his turret around and we both caught sight of a row of exhausts. It was a twin-engined aircraft. I slid alongside, below to the right of him, and slowly edged in 'under his armpit' while Fred kept his guns trained on the aircraft. Then we saw the distinctive wing and tail shape of a Heinkel – there was no mistaking it. I moved into a firing position, within about 50 yards of his wing tip and slightly below, so that Fred could align his guns for an upward shot. Obviously the German crew had not seen us, they continued straight ahead.*
>
> *Fred fired straight into the starboard engine. One round in six was tracer, but what told us we were hitting the Heinkel was the glitter of de Wilde rounds as they ignited on impact. Fred fired, realigned, and fired again. He got off two or three bursts. There was no return fire from the bomber; indeed, I doubt if any guns could have been brought to bear on our position on its beam. The engine burst into flames then the Heinkel rolled on its back, went down steeply and crashed onto a field near Brentwood.*

Whilst London was hit heaviest in terms of number of raids and bomb tonnage, the attack on Coventry on the night of 14/15 November was seen as important as it was the first use of massive air power against a small city with the intent being to cause widespread destruction; in essence virtually to obliterate the city. The weather was good and bright moonlight helped the bombers find the target, although the use of radio-directed pathfinders (KG.100) was also a factor. The attack started with a diversionary

Beaufighter of 25 Squadron at Wittering.

raid on London at 1915, with the attack on Coventry itself opening at 2020 and carrying on to 0610, by which time some 304 bombers had unloaded HE, incendiary and landmines over the city. The RAF had a dismal night, mounting 110 patrols but with no reports of combats other than an engagement near Swaffham, Norfolk when one bomber was claimed as damaged. The Fighter Command 'Form Y' summary for the night stated that ... 'enemy operations have been on a large scale and it is estimated that at least 350 E/A have operated, the majority of which flew at 12–15,000 ft. Coventry was the main target and was heavily bombed from 1900 hours.' It then listed the night fighter patrols, by Group:

> No. 9   Gp – nil.
> No. 10 Gp – 34 patrols.
> No. 11 Gp – 49 patrols; 26 Defiant, 10 Beaufighter, 7 Hurricane, 6 Blenheim;
>   5 E/A seen but no intercepts.
> No. 12 Gp – 24 patrols; Blenheim from Digby claim one damaged near
>   Swaffham.
> No. 13 Gp – 10 patrols.
> No. 14 Gp – 3 patrols.

1941 – Consolidation and new strategies

Whilst maintaining defensive cover for Britain, including coastal shipping, the Command also went looking for the enemy with offensive operations over France. It was to be a difficult year with a great deal of flying and little result, the Germans choosing not to take the bait of Fighter Command Wings and Circuses unless the conditions were just right.

Some time in late 1940 or very early 1941, No. 13 Group issued its pilots with a fascinating little advice booklet. *Forget-me-nots* for fighters contained 'pearls of wisdom' from the experiences of the Battle of Britain and used cartoons to illustrate the points made. The booklet was issued during AVM Saul's tenure as AOC, and in his introduction he states: 'This book is the outcome of discussion amongst the Training Staff on the best and simplest way to bring to the notice of new Fighter Pilots certain salient points in air fighting, which it is essential that they should master before taking their places as operational pilots in Fighter Squadrons. The various points illustrated are by no means comprehensive, and it must be clearly understood that only the main points which a new Fighter Pilot should know before going into action are included. These have been compiled on the advice and guidance of many well-known and proved Fighter Pilots, who have willingly co-operated in placing their knowledge and experience at the disposal of their younger brother-pilots.

'In selecting the motto of the Three Musketeers – "all for one and one for all" – to put at the head of this Foreword, I have done so because it expresses what should be the creed of every Fighter Pilot. Never forget that you are an essential cog in the wheel, and if you break or fail it will let down your brother pilots, and the grimness of war allows for no such weakness.

'Air fighting is a combination of skill and courage, which, allied with confidence and experience, makes the Fighter Pilot master of his trade.'

The Westland Whirlwind was an interesting experiment for the Command and after a year of teething troubles from its introduction in July 1940 it eventually started to show promise. The first confirmed victory occurred on 8 February 1941 – and was marked by the Squadron being given a case of champagne by Westland. 'Today gave us our first confirmed victory . . . two aircraft of Blue Section took-off from Exeter at 0840 on a local practice flight. At 0900 they were vectored onto Raid 139. While orbiting 12 miles South of Start Point an Arado 196 was seen by Sgt Rudland, who came down on its tail, but seeing British roundels on the fuselage did not fire, and in fact formatted on it. The enemy went into cloud and reappeared flying East 1,000 yards to Port of Fg Off Hughes, who carried out an attack from the front quarter, ending in a beam attack, opening at

THE LATE MAN LETS THE TEAM DOWN

THERE OFTEN IS

THE ADVANTAGE OF HEIGHT.

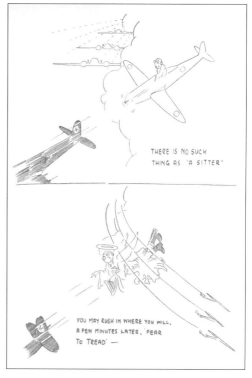

THERE IS NO SUCH THING AS 'A SITTER'

YOU MAY RUSH IN WHERE YOU WILL, A FEW MINUTES LATER, 'FEAR TO TREAD' —

450 and closing at 200 yards. A 5 second burst was fired, but no results were observed. Meanwhile Flt Lt Crooks and Plt Off Graham had taken off from St Eval. At Dodman Point Plt Off Graham was ordered to patrol below the cloud while Flt Lt Crooks patrolled above. Flt Lt Crooks came back down through the clouds. And just as he emerged, passed Plt Off Graham who was going West. He did a gentle left hand turn, intending to call Plt Off Graham and tell him to formate on him, but to his surprise

Whirlwind of 263 Squadron; The Westland Whirlwind was an interesting experiment for the Command and after a year of teething troubles from its introduction in July 1940 it eventually started to show promise. The first confirmed victory occurred on 8 February 1941 – and was marked by the Squadron being given a case of champagne by Westland.

found that Plt Off Graham had disappeared. Suddenly he saw an E/A come through the cloud on his left going lower and lower until it hit the water. Flt Lt Crooks had difficulty in identifying the E/A, but he saw floats uppermost on the water and black crosses on a piece of wing wreckage. Plt Off Graham did not return from the patrol. A Coastguard reported that two aircraft had crashed into the sea at 0950 three miles off the shore in flames' (263 Squadron ORB).

There was also occasional action at the other end of Fighter Command's domain.

On 2 March 1941 Hurricane of 3 Squadron was operating out of Sumburgh . . .'Two Hurricanes of Red Section, "A Flight", took-off from Sumburgh at 1427 on 2nd March to intercept Raid 252. When flying at 10 feet over sea at 1435, approximately 30 miles East of Sumburgh Red Section sighted a single Focke-Wulf 200 Condor about 5 miles ahead. E/A was flying 10 feet over the sea at about 220 miles per hour on a course of 130 degrees.

'Red One, P/O Crabb attacked first, closing to 400 yards and firing two 4-second bursts, breaking away at 150 yards. It is believe rear gunner of E/A was killed during this attack as after first few seconds of return fire from M/G ceased abruptly and Red 2 experienced no return fire when carrying out his astern attack. E/A increased speed to 270 mph and Red 1 climbing away to right delivered a diving attack from 800 feet directly to starboard firing a 3-second burst from 800 yards to 30 yards. Passing over and slightly behind E/A Red 1 delivered a similar attack from Port. No return fire from E/A experienced during either attack. Having run out of ammunition Red 1 made a dummy attack from front starboard to force E/A down on to sea. Heavy return fire experienced from front guns. Tracer seen to enter E/A on all three attacks. Red 1 then broke away and returned to base.

'Red Two, P/O Robertson followed Red 1 into attack flying astern and slightly above him. When Red 1 broke from his first attack Red 2 fired a 3-second burst from dead astern observing his tracer entering fuselage of E/A. Red 2 broke away as Red 1 delivered his starboard attack and climbing to the right delivered a diving beam from 200 feet above, firing a one-second burst. Red 2 had to break off his attack as Red 1 was firing from the opposite beam. He then delivered another astern attack firing a 6-second burst from approximately 200 yards and again saw tracer enter E/A. No return fire was experienced by Red 2 during these attacks. Red 2 then broke away and returned to base with Red 1.'

An interesting combat and testimony to the robust nature of the Condor, especially one that was flying only ten feet above the sea! This was one of the few 'highlights' for the Squadron; despite the fact that the Condor flew on, and a more usual routine was one of patrols and scrambles from Sumburgh and Castletown. There had been four other scrambles on 2 March, with five the next day and a Dusk patrol, with two scrambles and a Dusk Patrol the following day; the Patrol was flown by six aircraft from Castletown and found nothing of interest. At the end of the month the Squadron reunited at Castletown prior to a move south to Martlesham Heath and what all the pilots hoped would be more action. Initially, however, they were to be disappointed as the Hurricane IIs were still stuck with convoy patrols, although there was the odd combat with lone Do 17s or Ju 88s.

On 20 June 1941 White Section of 66 Squadron was ordered up to intercept a raid coming from the South. The two Spitfires, (piloted by Flt Allen and Sgt Large) climbed to 20,000 ft but were almost immediately ordered down to 6,000 ft by the controller. About 30 miles South of Bolt Head they spotted three He 111s at approximately 6,000 ft, with five Bf 109s as escort weaving above them at 7,000 ft. The Squadron ORB takes up

'Eagle' (121 Squadron) pilots; the Squadron formed in May 1941 and initially flew Hurricanes prior to re-equipping with Spitfires in October and becoming the 335th Fighter Squadron of the 4th Fighter Group in September 1942.

the story: 'White 1 then warned by White 2, who is not experienced, to gain height and look after his tail and dived to gain speed for attack. White 1 saw a 109 coming up at him, firing, but, although the shots were close, the aircraft was not hit, and in fact neither of our aircraft was marked as a result of this combat. After the first 109 had fallen away, White 1 fastened onto a pair of 109s rather below him and delivered a sharp quarter attack (2-secs at 150 yards) from the port side of the rear one, the engine of the E/A emitted white smoke and it slowed up and passed across the path of White 2 who gave

Spitfire Vb of 129 Squadron at Debden in November 1941. (Andy Thomas Collection).

it a quarter attack with three 2-sec bursts at 150 yards. More white smoke came out of the E/A and it crashed into the sea. Meantime White 1 saw another 109 coming towards him from behind and by dint of graceful manoeuvring himself came down on the E/A's tail and gave it a 3-sec burst in a quarter attack from 75 yards, as a result of which black smoke belched from its engine and the machine glided down. White 1 saw the pilot bale out and the parachute open and White 2 saw it go down, but they themselves were rather occupied with other matters. White 1 and White 2 then took evasive action, were unable to find the bandits again and returned to base.' The AOC of No. 10 Group sent a congratulatory message the following day: '... there is no doubt that this fine effort successfully frustrated an intended attack on our shipping and gave the Hun a lesson he will not forget in a hurry. I look forward with confidence to further successes by your Squadron.'

Night Defence

Amongst the new squadrons operational in 1941 was 255 Squadron, who entered the fray on 5 January and had three crews on standby each night. It was a frustrating first month with patrols and the occasional glimpse of the enemy but no success. However, 10 February was a very busy night and also brought the first successes. A number of patrols were flown in the Humber-Spurn Point area and two of these found targets:

> N1770 (F/L Trousdale/Sgt Chunn), patrolled Humber, sighted E/A at 2250 hours 200 yards to port, closed in and identified it as a He 111. Got in three bursts of fire, E/A disappeared diving steeply at 100 ft.
> N3335 (P/O Hall/Sgt Fitzsimmons), patrolled Humber, sighted E/A at approx 2315 flying at right angles to me and below, flying West, which proved to be a He 111. Got in three bursts, E/A descending all the time. Last attack delivered at 3,500 ft. E/A last seen diving towards the sea.

Amongst the new squadrons operational in 1941 was 255 Squadron, who entered the fray on 5 January and had three crews on standby each night. It was a frustrating first month with patrols and the occasional glimpse of the enemy but no success.

Air Ministry subsequently confirmed them as 'Probably Destroyed.' These first successful combats had a heartening effect on the whole Squadron.

The major attack on Liverpool on 12/13 March involved over 300 bombers and Fighter Command flew 178 sorties during that night, with claims being made for four destroyed. The Fighter Command log record of claims is shown in the table below:

Claims for 12/13 March 1941				
Group	*Squadron*	*Aircraft*	*Claim*	*Remark*
No. 9 Gp	96 Sqn	Hurricane	He 111 destroyed	Crashed at Wychbold
	307 Sqn	Defiant	He 111 damaged	South coast
No. 10 Gp	604 Sqn	Beaufighter	Ju 88 destroyed	Crashed at Warminster
			? Probable	Over sea
			Ju 88 damaged	South coast
			He 111 damaged	South coast
No. 11 Gp	264 Sqn	Defiant	He 111 destroyed	Crashed in sea
			He 111 destroyed	Crashed Beachy Head
	219 Sqn	Beaufighter	Ju 88 probable	Over sea
No. 12 Gp	255 Sqn	Defiant	He 111 probable	Retford
	151 Sqn	Hurricane	Ju 88 probable	Over sea

The 96 Squadron victory had been scored by Sgt McNair in Hurricane V7752 and the Squadron also claimed a probable, although this does not appear in the Fighter Command log. The 96 Squadron ORB for the night also stated: '18 trips hunting for the enemy and the result – no large numbers of enemy aircraft blazing on the ground, but just a drawing of the enemy blood in "probables", and a squadron with tails well up and a few gunsights and gun muzzles that had spat forth fire at the enemy machines. There was great enemy activity over Liverpool and several of our aircraft were in action for the first time. F/O Vesely was the first in action, having taken off in Defiant N1803 at 2155

New Zealand air gunners of 255 Squadron at Kirton-in-Lindsey.

with Sgt Heycock to patrol Cotton East at 15,000 ft. He saw an He 111 above on the port side and told the air gunner, but the guns failed to fire. He kept the Defiant in formation with the German aircraft and flew alongside and slightly below, expecting that the air gunner would get the guns to fire. Then the pilot of the Heinkel dived, followed by F/O Vesely, who manoeuvred to get on to the starboard side. He flew in formation again but

Defiant of 151 Squadron, Wittering; the Squadron operated Defiants for 18-months from December 1940.

the side gunner of the Heinkel got in two bursts. Pilot felt that he had been hit in the chest, shoulders and left arm. He lost consciousness and when he came round found the Defiant falling in a spin; however, he managed to recover and return to land despite his injuries.'

German aircraft were ranging far and wide at night and in the early hours of 8 April Sqn Ldr Simpson, OC of 245 Squadron, scrambled from Aldergrove, Northern Ireland:

> *I was in the Mess when news came that the Germans were dropping bombs on a town nearby. It seemed rather strange. The war had not come so close to Ulster before. Incendiaries had been dropped and high explosive bombs were on the way. I was next to patrol. It was about 1.15 in the morning, dark with a sickly moon shining through a mist. I took off and climbed to about 9,000 ft, passing above the clouds into another world, where the moon, in its second quarter, shone out of a blue-black sky.*
>
> *I was told that there were aircraft near me. My eyes searched the blackness. There was no horizon: no object upon which to fix one's eyes. And one had the illusion, travelling at 200 miles per hour, that every one of those brilliant stars was the tail light of an aircraft. I searched among that moving pattern of lights and my eyes rested upon two black objects. I could see them because, as they moved, they obliterated the stars. They were quite near when I recognised them as aircraft . . . whether enemy or not, I was unable to tell. So I flew nearer and learned soon enough. The rear gunners of both aircraft fired a shower of bullets at me, some with whitish-green light of tracer bullets, some glowing red. They missed me and for a minute I lost them. Then I saw them again, farther apart, moving against the white floor of the clouds below me. They were black and quite clear. The advantage was now mine for they were perfectly placed as targets. I crept down to attack the rear-most of them. They were flying slowly. It was difficult for me to withhold my speed so that I would not overtake him. At a distance of about 200 yards I opened fire from slightly below. Then came my next surprise . . . the blinding flash of my guns, in the darkness. In day time one does not see it. At night it is terrific and I was so blinded that I lost sight of my enemy. I broke away and lost him for a few seconds. I next saw him going into a gentle dive towards the clouds. The increase in speed made it easier for me to attack and I closed in to 80 yards. I opened fire once more. This time I was prepared for the flash and kept my eyes on the enemy. His rear gunner returned my fire, but only for a second. I had apparently got him for he was silent after that. I continued my fire, closing in to about 50 yards. Then I saw a comforting red glow in his belly. I was still firing when the Heinkel blew up, with a terrific explosion which blew me upwards and sideways. When I righted myself, I was delighted to see showers of flaming pieces . . . like confetti on fire . . . falling towards the sea. I was able to enjoy the satisfaction of knowing that I had brought him down before he had released his bombs.*

The second bomber escaped but a month later (6 May) Simpson claimed a Ju 88.

British cities were still vulnerable to night attacks and April witnessed a concentrated attack on Coventry. Night-fighters were still in short supply and Fighter Nights were a standard role for many of the day-fighter squadrons. With Coventry providing the

VIP visit to 245 Squadron at Aldergrove; the Squadron scored a number of night successes.

background illumination, 266 Squadron had four Spitfires over the City in the early hours of 9 April. The ORB records the four sorties:

P8187, P/O Thomas: Ordered to vector 265 deg and reached Coventry in about 15 mins at 16,000 ft. Climbed up to patrol height at 22,260 ft. Orbited at this height and after a short while saw one E/A silhouetted against fires a long way beneath. Dived after it but lost it when it went out of glow of the fires. Returned to patrol height. After about an hour ordered to return to base and land.

P8010, Sgt Cook: Vectored on 265 deg and after 15 mins arrived over Coventry at 15,000 ft. Climbed to 21,240 ft and orbited for an hour. No E/A seen. Ordered to return on vector 085 deg and to land.

P7992, S/Ldr Jameson: At 0144 hrs at 18,000 ft saw one E/A with one of our fighters formatting on it and trail of smoke from each engine. Turned to chase it and join in when saw an He 111 at about 17,000 ft. Made stern attack at 150 yds. There appeared to be four streams of return fire, one of them green, probably from the top turret. Fired two short bursts, but dazzled by bullets when the hit the E/A and broke away after first attack. Then carried out another stern attack and windscreen was obscured by oil from E/A. Great burning pieces came off the E/A which dived down through the clouds. No evasive action by the E/A.

P8185, F/Lt Armitage: Patrolled Coventry above fires at 27,000–28,000 ft. Visibility bad from 26,000 ft upwards due to haze. No E/A plotted at this height and no E/A seen.

The following night the Squadron was over Birmingham; Flt Lt Armitage was again one of the four pilots, but this time he found and engaged a target:

... after turning South saw a twin-engined aircraft about 200 ft beneath, travelling SW directly over the fires. Was able to identify it immediately as an He 111, but attacked too swiftly, partly through fear of losing it and partly in endeavour to get it before it dropped its bombs. As a result did not get sight on until 100 yds away with rather high overtaking speed. On opening fire was immediately dazzled,

probably by effect of De Wilde striking on E/A fuselage, which was certainly hit. After a burst of 2½ sec had to break-away violently. Made a thorough search in direction in which E/A had been going but could not find it again.

On 3 May the Squadron moved to Debden for night-fighter operations and a week later (10 May) the ORB recorded one of the most active nights: 'The Squadron took part on a Fighter Night operation during a heavy raid on London. The Squadron's allotted heights were from 22,000 ft upwards, and only four enemy aircraft were seen. Sqn Ldr Aitken gave a Ju 88 two short bursts of cannon fire, the second at extreme range, and saw explosive shells burst in its belly with a violent bluish-red flash. The Ju 88 took violent evasive action, making off East, and is claimed as damaged. Sgt Shaw, whilst making a starboard turn was confronted with an He 111 at 50 yards range beam on. He raked it with 60 rounds from his 12 machine-guns and saw incendiaries striking it amidships. The enemy aircraft fell away rapidly sideways and is claimed as probably damaged' (3 Squadron ORB).

May was to prove the busiest month of the year for Fighter Command's night defences, with almost 2,000 sorties flown and 96 enemy aircraft claimed as destroyed. Two-thirds of this effort (1,345 sorties) was by the single-engine squadrons. One of the latter, 255 Squadron, still at Kirton, had it busiest and most successful month: 'This moonlight period (till 17/5/41) was one of intense enemy "blitzing" of target areas in NE and Central England and in consequence a considerable strain was thrown on the Squadron. Each night one Flight was at "readiness" with the other "available", and on some occasions during the peak moonlight period as many as 16 planes have been at "readiness". From the assumption of this dusk state on 2/5/41 till the end of night state on 17/5/41 (15 nights) a total of 132 operational patrols were flown. In fact a total of 88 were flown in the 6 nights from midnight 4/5/41 till midnight 10/5/41, an average of more than 14½ patrols per night. The Squadron had it most successful night since formation. The most satisfactory aspect of these combats is that the losses inflicted on the enemy were all achieved at the loss of only one Defiant, both the occupants of which landed safely by baling-out of their burning machine.' The victories recorded for this period were:

> 5 May: S/Ldr Smith/P/O Farnes, Ju 88, Donna Nook.
> 7 May: Sgt Craig/Sgt Muir, He 111 damaged, near Goole.
> 8 May: Sgt Johnson/Sgt Aitchison, He 111, near Kirton. 'This actually occurred within sight of the 'drome, the pilots and A/Gs assembled at dispersal point having a grand-stand view of the E/A catching fire at 10,000 ft and coming down in flames.'
> P/O Dale (Hurricane), Do 17 damaged, Hull.
> 9 May: S/Ldr Smith (Hurricane), He 111, Hull.
> S/Ldr Smith (Hurricane), He 111 damaged, Hull.
> P/O Wyrill/Sgt Maul, He 111, Hull.
> P/O Wynne-Willson/Sgt Plant, He 111, Hull.
> P/O Wright/Sgt McChesney, Ju 88, Hull.
> F/Lt Trousdale/Sgt Chunn, He 111, Leconfield area.
> F/Lt Trousdale/Sgt Chunn, He 111, Leconfield area, crashed in sea.

The ORB quite rightly commented on the events of 9 May: 'This remarkable achievement – 6 enemy bombers destroyed, and one damaged inside half an hour with no loss to the Squadron's personnel or planes, evoked a deluge of congratulations.'

Summary of Fighter Command Night-Fighter Defensive Operations, 1941

Month	German sorties	Type	Sorties	Contacts	Combats	Claims	AAA or other
Jan	2,295	TE Aircraft	84	44	2	0	14
		SE Aircraft	402	34	9	3	
Feb	1,820	TE Aircraft	147	25	4	2	13
		SE Aircraft	421	33	9	2	
Mar	4,125	TE Aircraft	270	115	31	15	21
		SE Aircraft	735	34	25	7	
Apr	5,125	TE Aircraft	342	118	55	28	41
		SE Aircraft	842	45	39	20	
May	4,625	TE Aircraft	643	217	102	37	41
		SE Aircraft	1,345	154	116	59	
Jun	1,980	TE Aircraft	536	94	37	20	15
		SE Aircraft	942	24	15	7	
Jul	1,352	TE Aircraft	557	80	23	20	7
		SE Aircraft	338	25	18	6	
Aug	935	TE Aircraft	549	83	4	3	7
		SE Aircraft	592	5	1	0	
Sep	838	TE Aircraft	361	77	10	7	3
		SE Aircraft	344	7	3	1	
Oct	849	TE Aircraft	621	116	36	9	3
		SE Aircraft	496	10	3	2	
Nov	695	TE Aircraft	417	84	15	7	4
		SE Aircraft	345	8	0	0	
Dec	695	TE Aircraft	440	47	6	3	6
		SE Aircraft	211	2	0	0	
Totals	25,334		11,980	1,490	367	258	175

Note: SE – Single-engined, TE – Twin-engined.

Offensive Operations 1941

This was the year in which Fighter Command started to take its war to the enemy, by day and by night.

The Command's first recorded – official – offensive mission took place on 20 December 1940. Taking-off from Biggin Hill a pair of Spitfires from 66 Squadron (Flt Lt G P Christie and Plt Off C A W Bodie) flew across the Channel just below a bank of cloud that had a base of only a few hundred feet. They coasted in at Dieppe, turned inland near Criel and flew North at tree-top height until they came to an airfield, which they took to be Berck or Le Touquet. They flew low over the airfield, firing at anything that appeared to be a reasonable target, and were fired on by the airfield defences. Both aircraft returned safely. Only a few such *Rhubarbs* were flown each month and the first confirmed victory came on 9 April when Flt Lt O'Meara of 64 Squadron downed an He 59 off Dunkirk, and a Bf 109 falling to a 54 Squadron pilot later the same day.

10 January saw the first bomber *Circus*, with fighters escorting Blenheims to the Foret de Guisnes. The summary for *Circus No. 1* stated: 'at 1215 hours six Blenheims of 114 Squadron, No. 2 Group, Bomber Command, made rendezvous over Southend with six fighter squadrons – 56, 242, 249, 41, 64 and 611. From Southend the Blenheims flew in a tight formation at 12,000 ft to a point on the French coast just East of Calais. The Hurricanes of 56 Squadron flew in various situations around and amidst the formation of Blenheims; those of 242 and 249 squadrons about 1,000 ft below and to starboard,

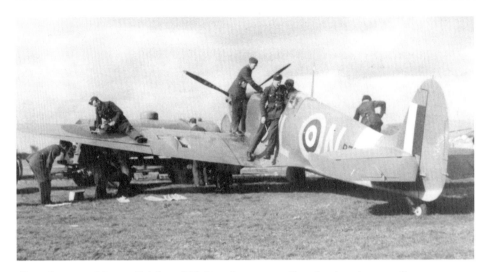

Groundcrew working on Spitfire of 91 Squadron; most pilots developed an excellent relationship with their regular groundcrew, who took pride in keeping 'their' pilot's aircraft in tip-top condition.

with the second of these squadrons a little above and to starboard of the first. The Officer Commanding RAF Station North Weald (Wg Cdr F V Beamish) flew with 249 Squadron. The Spitfires of 41, 64 and 611 squadrons flew in a stepped-up formation above and to port of the Blenheims, with 64 Squadron leading and 41 Squadron in the rear at 16,000 ft.

Spitfires of 611 Squadron; the Squadron flew as part of Circus No.1 *acting as fighter cover for the attacking squadrons.*

'On crossing the French coast the Blenheims changed to a more open formation, which they retained while over France. Taking gentle evasive action and coming down to 6,800 ft, they made a sweep round the target so as to approach it from the South-East. All six Blenheims dropped their bombs from 6,800 ft at 1249 hours; most of the bombs fell among the trees, where they seemed to start two fires.

'While the bombers were executing these manoeuvres, various things were happening to the fighters. The plan of the operation provided that 56 Squadron should stay with the Blenheims; the other two Hurricane squadrons were to engage the enemy's fighters, or, failing this, come down low and attack an aerodrome and landing ground at St Inglevert. The three Spitfire squadrons were to act as fighter-cover for the attacking squadrons throughout. Accordingly, 242 and 249 squadrons (with Wg Cdr Beamish) described two circles over the area between St Inglevert and Calais at 7,000 ft to 8,000 ft, but met no enemy fighters at this stage. Nevertheless, they refrained from making any concerted attack on the aerodrome and landing ground, both of which looked inactive. One pilot of 249 Squadron (Sgt Maciejowski) became separated from he rest of the formation and opened fire on five HS 126 aircraft standing on the edge of one of landing grounds beside the Foret de Guines. He then saw two Me 109s in the air, one of which he attacked and claims to have shot down. During this manoeuvre his throttle jammed in the fully-open position and he was compelled to return in this condition to Hornchurch, where he landed successfully by switching off his ignition.

'At various points the bomber and fighter squadrons were subjected to anti-aircraft fire, most of it inaccurate. Exceptionally accurate fire came from four boats standing three or four miles off Calais. On the homeward journey Wg Cdr Beamish raked their decks with machine-gun fire, and they stopped firing. Over the Channel a pilot of 249 Squadron (P/O McConnell) was attacked by an Me 109, wounded, and forced to bale out. Wg Cdr Beamish came to his assistance and opened fire on the Me 109, which was seen to fall into the sea.'

The Spitfire squadrons had a pretty uneventful mission, although '41 Squadron was approached from the rear by five Me 109s just as it was crossing the coast. A pilot of the rearguard Section (Sgt Baker) attacked one of these aircraft and may have destroyed it.'

The conclusions drawn from this first *Circus* stated that: 'This operation was generally considered a success. In most respects the plan conceived beforehand worked well; and the results, as far as they went, were satisfactory. A military objective had been bombed in daylight without the loss of a single bomber. At least two enemy aircraft were believed to have been destroyed; and our losses in combat amounted to a single Hurricane, whose pilot was in hospital with a broken leg. Incidentally, it had been discovered that German flak ships could apparently be silenced by raking their decks with machine-gun fire. On the other hand, as a test of superiority the operation had been inconclusive, since no major engagement had materialised. Moreover, there was a suspicion in some quarters that we had been lucky not to meet more energetic opposition, which the tendency of our squadrons to break up and come down low might have rendered dangerous. It was concluded that for some time we would be wise to go slowly, and content ourselves with attempts to surprise and confuse the enemy, without risking heavy losses.'

The latter comments were certainly valid and when *Circus 2* was planned, the option of going down low after ground targets was banned. Sqn Ldr A G 'Sailor' Malan led 74 Squadron on *Circus* No. 2; twelve aircraft of the Squadron were airborne at 1315 to be part of a large fighter escort for five Blenheims bombing Boulogne docks. The Blenheims

Douglas Bader (2nd from right) and pilots of 616 Squadron; Bader was an aggressive and effective air combat leader.

had an uneventful time and the Germans did make an appearance, with Malan and Sgt Payne each claiming a Bf 109 but with Sqn Ldr Michelmore failing to make it back.

Douglas Bader was soon in on the offensive operations act; on the morning of 12 January he took Stan Turner of 242 Squadron on a *Rhubarb,* and they found two ships near Calais:

> *... opened fire together at a height of 50 ft and speed of 200 mph, saw bullets strike water ahead of E-boat and then hitting E-boat. Got one burst from front guns of E-boat – no damage. E-boat ceased fire. Flt Lt Turner, having converged slightly on me, turned away to avoid slipstream as we passed over E-boat. Did not stop to observe damage to boats but E-boat must have had a lot as could see bullets from 16 guns hitting the boat.*

Hitting the target and running away was definitely the best tactic and failure to adopt this type of tactic was a common cause for losses – having been over the target once you will have woken-up the defences! Indeed, the Squadron flew two more similar missions that day, each with four aircraft and with one aircraft failing to return from each mission. The losses versus results statistics for the offensive missions of this sort often gave cause for concern – was the effort worth it – but it must be remembered that in part these missions were designed to give the fighters an aggressive, offensive spirit and to boost the morale of pilots who did not like sitting around in England waiting for something to happen. It was a definite case of taking the war to the enemy as part of the overall strategy of seizing and maintaining the initiative.

Wing Sweeps were mounted on a regular basis; a typical example being that of late afternoon (1600 take-off) 15 April by Spitfires of 65 and 266 squadrons and Hurricanes of 402 Squadron, a total of 34 aircraft. This was a Channel Sweep between Dungeness and Boulogne. 'W/Cdr Coope became separated due to minor engine trouble

Hurricane of 312 Squadron at Kenley, June 1941 where they had recently arrived to join the offensive operations over Europe.

but followed to rendezvous at Dungeness. When at 20,000 ft, 33 mins after leaving base (Wittering) he was turning to the left when attacked from port quarter by Me 109, turned and went into steep dive to evade, but was hit by two cannon shells, one of which went through parachute. Port aileron and petrol tank also hit. Came out of second dive at 5,000 ft and crash-landed at Manston. Pilot unhurt. Other nine aircraft (of 266 Squadron) had swept to Boulogne at 23,000 ft – Hurricanes being at 20,000 ft and 65 Squadron just above. 266 Squadron were spread out widely in pairs and were at 10,000 ft on return to coast and Hornchurch. When commencing to close in, four Me 109s dived on them from South out of sun. P7544 badly damaged by cannon fire, pilot (Sgt Barraclough) landed at Hornchurch unhurt. P8014 also badly damaged and crash-landed at Hawkinge, pilot (Sgt Whewll) receiving slight superficial injuries. P8185 (P/O Holland) fired 2 sec burst at Me109 which suddenly dived beneath on tail of Spitfire, but was full deflection shot, and thinking another Me 109 was on his own tail broke off with a steep climbing turn and did not again see E/A. Whilst this Me 109 is not claimed as damaged, three pilots saw an Me 109 dive past them at 300 mph at this time with wheels partially down. Seven Spitfires landed at Hornchurch to refuel and return to base.' (266 Squadron ORB).

This is a classic example of how quickly a peaceful piece of sky becomes a death trap for unwary fighter pilots – the 109s had set up a classic out-of-the-sun attack and in a quick pass had damaged at least two of the Spitfires. You could never relax when you were in the air as the famed 'Hun in the Sun' was always a threat.

The main role for 263 Squadron was convoy patrols, with a typical month (June 1941) involving 134 sorties of this type. However, the month also brought the first of what would become routine *Ranger* operations: 'This was a special operation known as "Warhead No. 1 Operation." Information had been received that there was a large concentration of Me 109s on the Cherbourg Peninsular; I and II JG2 and part of III JG26 (about 70 machines in all) at Quarqerville. It was decided to attack these machines on the ground at first light on 14th June.' Six Whirlwinds moved to Ibsley the day before, to operate in two pairs and with two spares, the targets being Quarqerville and Maupertus. 'There had been a slight hitch on the Intelligence side, and photographs of the target area had to be fetched by Spitfire from Middle Wallop, while a supply of French money was sent by dispatch rider from Fighter Command. All this kept us up rather late and we

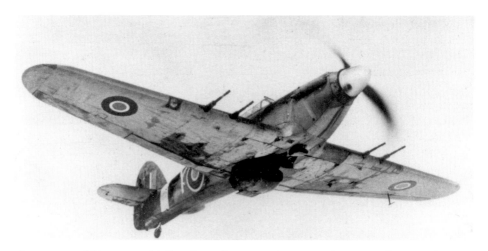

Cannon-armed Hurricane of 1 Squadron; these aircraft were used to great effect attacking ground targets during offensive sweeps.

weren't in bed until about midnight. We got up about 0315 to find conditions very nearly perfect. There was a certain amount of cloud in the South and a fairly clear moon. At 0445 Sqn Ldr Donaldson and Plt Off Rudland took off, followed a minute later by Flt Lt Pugh and Plt Off Mason.

'The former found their target without much difficulty and delivered an attack on the dispersal pans in a shallow dive from 1300 to 100 feet, They saw their shells hitting and exploding in the pans, but unfortunately these were covered with tarpaulins, and they could not see whether there were any machines in them or not. Sqn Ldr Donaldson then put a burst into a barrack block and had a shot at an oil tank; the latter he missed. ... Flt Lt Pugh and Plt Off Mason were clean out of luck as their target was covered by a thick morning mist.' The initial attack had stirred up a hornets nest and as the Whirlwinds landed an air raid warning sounded as six 109s attempted to return the favour ... 'but a short brush with 234 Squadron rather damped their ardour and they returned home. After an early breakfast we returned to Filton and made up for lost sleep.'

On 17 July the four Hurricanes of 3 Squadron took-off from Stapleford to attack E-boats – a popular target but a dangerous one. 'Blue and Green (one four-cannon and three 12 machine-gun aircraft) took-off to attack E-boats NE of Cap Griz Nez. They attacked a 1,500-ton armed ship in tow with two others, one a flak ship. The attack was made at zero feet out of the sun. Intense flak was experienced, but strikes were seen on the ships and some casualties on the flak ship. Blue Section then patrolled the coast and attacked an E-boat through intense flak, again seeing casualties on the boat.' All four aircraft returned safe and the ORB does not note any damage. However, the Command was starting to suffer increasing casualties from this type of attack.

The same day saw a number of Fighter Command squadrons on sweeps, including 308 (Polish) Squadron, led by Sqn Ldr Pisarak. His combat report stated: 'North of St Omer we were attacked from astern slightly on starboard side by about 15 Me 109s. I gave the order to circle to starboard – this stopped their attack. I then ordered the Squadron to resume formation with weavers and follow a zig-zag course towards the coast. Several times we had to re-form defensive circles owing to attempts by the numerous E/A to split up my squadron. I was able to keep my men together and after many times altering our direction and countering the enemy moves we approached Gravelines. I then heard P/O Blach call for assistance. I turned and saw several E/A behind him, one of which was about to dive on him. I delivered an attack on the E/A from below on the starboard side at 150/200 yds range, giving long bursts. The German began to dive and my No. 2, Sgt Schiele saw him going down with smoke pouring from the engine and gave him two short bursts – after which flames were seen and the E/A dived to the ground.' The *Luftwaffe* pilot had made the mistake of becoming fixated on his own target and thus fell victim to the sudden attack by Sqn Ldr Pisarak. A second 109 had been downed by Plt Off Retinger. At the height of the battle the Poles estimated that there were 50 enemy aircraft in the vicinity.

In July the Whirlwinds of 263 Squadron undertook weapon trials against tanks, and it was increasingly in the strafing role that they were employed. At last, in August 1941, the diarist was able to comment that: 'August has been a mensis memorabilis. The Whirlwind has at long last been completely vindicated and justified, having shown that it is an admirable machine for ground strafing, and also that it is a match for Me 109s. Many offensive sorties have been made during the month, mainly directed against enemy aerodromes. As a result of these, three Me 109s have been destroyed in combat, and one damaged. Five Ju88s, at least 7 JU 87s and some Me 109s have been destroyed on the ground, and others damaged. One E-boat has been sunk and another damaged. In addition, two tankers at sea, gun posts, lorries, wireless stations and enemy troops have been attacked and severe damage inflicted' (263 Squadron ORB).

Following a *Circus* mission on 20 August, the 66 Squadron ORB noted that the 'enemy aircraft were unusually aggressive.' The Squadron had sent eight aircraft to join similar numbers from 130 and 152 squadrons in escorting six Blenheims; the Wing was led by Sqn Ldr Forbes who reported: 'I was leading the Squadron, which was acting as high cover to six Blenheims. Some 20–30 miles from the coast I saw a Spitfire with a 109F on its tail at about 100 ft. I dived with my No. 2 from 600 ft and followed the 109, which had broken off its attack and had turned South, I had great difficulty in catching up with the 109 and staying in position. Three 2-sec bursts were fired and strikes observed. I then ran out of ammunition and broke away so that my No. 2 (Sgt Green) could attack. Whilst he was attacking I covered his tail. After 3 or 4 bursts from Sgt Green the 109 started to pour out black smoke, which turned white after a time. The 109 flew straight on for about half a mile and went into the sea nose first.'

Plt Off Oliver was No. 2 in another Section on the sortie:

Due to a dive after a 109 I had plenty of speed and was able to climb and shoot while practically vertical at a 109 which commenced a head-on dive. It turned away and my bullets entered its fuselage towards the tail … claim damaged. Another 109 attacked No. 1 of the Section (Flt Lt Allen) and myself head on. I was about 150 yards behind Allen and we both fired head on and as the 109 turned to starboard with a deflection shot. 109 continued to dive and shortly a lot of bluish smoke and oil started streaming out behind. Was unable to watch this E/A longer due to pressure of other E/A … claim probable.

The *Luftwaffe* was still active and the hunted could easily become the hunted. On 4 September 1941 Hurricanes of 302 Squadron were operating from Warmwell as high-cover for a Blenheim attack on Cherbourg docks. The fighters were at 14,000 ft when Sqn Ldr Witorzenc saw a pair of 109s attack the bombers; he closed on one, opening fire at 250 yards and closing at 80 yards, destroying the Messerschmitt. Meanwhile, Plt Off

Sporny went after another pair that he had seen moving in on the Whirlwind escort. He made a three-quarter attack, firing short bursts from 220 yards to 70 yards. The E/A turned on its back pouring smoke. He followed it down to 1,000 ft but was then bounced by two more enemy fighters. He dived to 300 ft and had to fly 10 miles inland, jinking and dodging, before he was able to turn back – still pursued – until he finally managed to get away.

For four successive months in late summer 1942, No. 452 (RAAF) Squadron was the top-scoring unit in Fighter Command, in large part due to the exploits of one of its Flight Commanders, Flt Lt Brendan Finucane. The Squadron claimed 40 aircraft destroyed between July and October, with Finucane scoring 15 of these, bringing his personal total to 20 and earning him two Bars to his DFC and a DSO. The citations read:

> Bar to DFC: Gazetted 9 September
> *This officer has led his flight with great dash, determination and courage in the face of the enemy. Since July, 1941, he has destroyed three enemy aircraft and assisted in the destruction of a further two. Flight Lieutenant Finucane has been largely responsible for the fine fighting spirit of the unit.*
>
> Second Bar to DFC: Gazetted 23 September
> *This officer has fought with marked success during recent operations over Northern France and has destroyed a further six enemy aircraft. Of these, three were destroyed in one day and two in a single sortie on another occasion. His ability and courage have been reflected in the high standard of morale and fighting spirit of his unit. Flight Lieutenant Finucane has personally destroyed fifteen hostile aircraft.*
>
> DSO: Gazetted 17 October
> *Recently, during two sorties on consecutive days, Flight Lieutenant Finucane destroyed 5 Messerschmitt 109s bringing his total victories to at least 20. He has flown with this squadron since June, 1941, during which time the squadron has destroyed 42 enemy aircraft of which Flight Lieutenant Finucane has personally destroyed 15. The successes achieved are undoubtedly due to this officer's brilliant leadership and example.*

Sadly Brendan Finucane was killed in action on 15 July 1942.

One pilot of 92 Squadron made comments in his log book that reflected the hazards of these offensive missions during this period of mid to late 1941; for example:

> *Bags of flak, horrible and twitchy.*
> *Heavily engaged by more 109s than was healthy; then caught the flak which was deadly.*
> *Hellish light flak, hit 36 times in tail.*
> *We got hammered. Blue Section were the lowest and were a little lower than intended. We watched as a bunch of 109s dived past us and despite the shouted warnings Blue Section took no evasive action and were well and truly bounced. Flt Lt Lund, Sgt Edge and Sgt Port went straight down.*
> *Another bad day – it was a shambles and involved another squadron being, as far as I was concerned, in the wrong place. Anyway we got bounced and lost Sgts Cox and Wood-Scawen.*

He summarised what had been a bad period for 92 Squadron. 'The Squadron had been taking such a beating for a long time and our aircraft were very tired despite the best

Pair of Spitfires of 306 Squadron getting airborne; many of the offensive sorties were flown as pairs under the Ramrod *or* Rhubarb *code-names.*

efforts of the groundcrew. The tiredness of the remaining aircrew, the overworked groundcrews and the aircraft themselves made a move necessary and on 20 October the Squadron moved to Digby and No. 12 Group.'

Night Intruders

On the night of 21 December 1940 six Blenheims of 23 Squadron flew offensive patrols having been 'on standby for nuisance raiding of aerodromes in French Occupied territory since the 16th'. Eight aircraft had actually been stripped of AI equipment on 10 December and placed on standby for 'special missions over French territory but this was postponed by Group mowing to unsuitable weather over France.'

The six Blenheims took-off between 2020 and 0155 and patrolled the areas around Abbeville, Amiens and Poix, three of the German night-fighter Sectors: according to the ORB: 'the airfields were beaten-up at heights down to 1,000 ft.' Seven aircraft were airborne the following night to the same areas, but this time one of the Blenheims ran out of fuel and the crew had to bale-out over the Channel. In this first intruder loss two of the crew drowned. The intruder role had been carried-out prior to this by aircraft of Bomber Command's No. 2 Group but from this date onwards it became the responsibility of Fighter Command, although this was by no means exclusive and Bomber Command continued to attack German airfields.

Of the two aircraft claimed as destroyed in September, one fell to Sqn Ldr Hoare of 23 Squadron, the ORB recording: 'S/L Hoare took-off for Melun, but seeing lights near Beauvais, turned aside to investigate and found the airfield lit up. He first chased an aircraft with navigation lights that was landing but gave it up in favour of an aircraft seen orbiting, and the air gunner put in a long burst at 75 yards range from underneath and to beam, but without visible result and the aircraft was then lost. Then another was seen and formatted on and the air gunner put in a long burst until blinded by a flash from his own gun. The E/A put out its lights and was lost. It was claimed as damaged. Yet a third aircraft was seen and followed as it turned in to land. The pilot opened fire at 100 yards causing both engines to smoke strongly as the E/A fell away to starboard in a vertical dive at 600 ft. It is claimed as destroyed.'

Intruder sorties and claims, 1941

	Nts	Blen.	Hav.	Bost.	Hurr.	Def.	Total	E/A seen	Claim	Afld attack	Loss
Jan	6	23	–	–	–	–	23	11	–	13	1
Feb	6	8	–	–	–	–	8	19	–	3	–
Mar	11	49	–	–	2	–	51	51	3	28	2
Apr	16	33	16	–	2	6	57	33	2	17	1
May	13	1	56	–	11	9	77	128	11	38	–
Jun	14	–	48	–	6	–	54	4	1	19	–
Jul	18	–	87	–	8	–	95	14	–	56	–
Aug	17	–	61	–	4	–	65	27	–	37	2
Sep	10	–	35	–	4	–	39	13	2	17	1
Oct	12	–	28	–	7	–	35	13	1	23	–
Nov	8	–	21	2	4	–	27	9	–	11	–
Dec	10	–	22	1	5	–	28	32	1	15	1
Totals	141	114	374	3	53	15	559	354	21	277	8

Note: Nts – Nights on which sorties flown; Blen – Blenheim; Hav – Havoc; Bost – Boston; Hurr – Hurricane; Def – Defiant; Afld attack – number of airfields claimed as attacked.

1942 – Losing the advantage

One of the major threats faced by the RAF's pilots in 1942 was the increased use by their opponents, especially JG26, of the Fw 190 – an aircraft that had the edge over the Spitfire V (the best of the RAF fighters at the time) in a number of crucial performance areas. Operating out of Bolt Head with 312 Squadron, Miroslav Liskutin recalled his first brush with the 190:

> We were directed to intercept four Focke Wulfs in the Torbay area. ... I spotted three aircraft low over the sea, but already heading back towards France after a hit and run attack against Torquay. We were some 5 miles from the enemy formation. After "cutting the corner" on them the distance was quickly reduced to under one mile. My engine was at full power with the boost over-ride beyond the gate and the propeller set at maximum revolutions. My Spitfire was gradually closing to about 700 yards when they spotted us. Until then we had no idea how the Spitfire VB would compare in a real-life race with an Fw 190. Our pilots knew that there was no great difference in the performance between these two aircraft, although the Fw 190 would have to be regarded as a marginal favourite. This occasion gave us proof that at sea level we were absolutely equal. ... Despite my earlier optimism, my distance behind the No. 3 Fw 190 became stabilised at about 650 yards. Joe (Pipa) tried some shots from this distance. It looked like the only effect of Joe's firing was a temporary slight slowing down of his aircraft, due to the recoil of his cannons. I was still hoping to close to at least 100 yards, to get a better chance with shooting.

Both formations were going all out, as evidenced by the black smoke from the German fighters. 'In these conditions my airspeed indicator was showing a steady 330 mph. There is no doubt that this was the true maximum speed of the Spitfire VB and the Fw 190 at sea level, in the summer of 1942.' The official RAF trials against a captured 190 were detailed in the previous Chapter and confirmed that the RAF pilots had to adapt their tactics when operating in areas prowled by 190s.

Combat film sequence of Spitfire V downing an Fw 190.

An August 1942 Air Tactics memo summarised the RAF's attitude: 'At the present stage of the war, the enemy in France is equipped with the Fw190, a fighter with an excellent rate of climb and good acceleration. To defeat this aircraft and to avoid casualties on our side, our aircraft must fly as fast as possible whenever they are in the combat zone.'

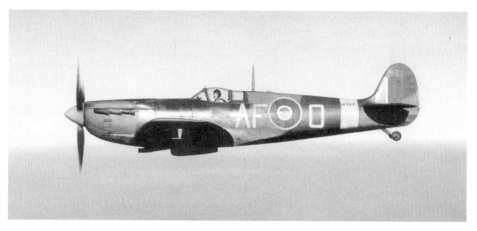

Spitfire V AA937 of 607 Squadron, November 1942; an August 1942 Air Tactics memo summarised the RAF's attitude: 'At the present stage of the war, the enemy in France is equipped with the Fw190, a fighter with an excellent rate of climb and good acceleration. To defeat this aircraft and to avoid casualties on our side, our aircraft must fly as fast as possible whenever they are in the combat zone.'

The same document included 'Prune's Guide for Living':

1. Don't loiter. When you can't keep up don't blame your leader; pull your finger out and cut the corners.
2. Low revs and high boost will bring you safely back to roost.
3. Don't wait until you see the Hun before you decide to get a move on. It will take a couple of minutes for your Spitfire to respond after you open up, and by that time whatever you do will be irrelevant. When you are liable to meet the enemy fly always at maximum cruising speed.
4. If you want to live on the other side, you must move fast, but equally, if you want to come back again you must save petrol. You will find your engine happier at, say, +4 lb and 1700 r.p.m. than at +1 lb and 2650 r.p.m. Both these adjustments give the same ASI but if you fly at +4 lb and 1700 r.p.m. you will save seven gallons of petrol an hour. It is possible to get full throttle and +4 lb above 10,000 ft by reducing the revs until the boost falls to +4 lb. Use full throttle and minimum revs above full throttle height for any desired ASI. This gives the best combination of fast cruising and minimum consumption.
5. When you are travelling at full throttle, and full power is suddenly wanted, it is only necessary to push the constant speed lever fully forward to get full revs and boost. To return to high speed cruising at best economical conditions, reduce your *revs* and not your boost.
6. When being briefed, always ask what revs and boost you should fly. This will naturally depend upon the length of the sweep, but don't forget that:
    a. When hard pressed you can fly +16 boost and 3,000 revs without any danger of blowing up, but
    b. Your consumption will be 150 gallons per hour.
7. Finally, when unlikely to be engaged always fly minimum revs and under 4 lb boost, but when in the vicinity of Huns, fly maximum everything and in *good time*.

In addition to the sorties shown in the table, the Command flew 37,478 shipping sorties by day and 2,709 by night.

In April 1942 'Spud' Spurdle became 'A Flight' Commander on 91 Squadron during what was a particularly busy period for the Squadron; in addition to the 'Jim Crow' shipping recce missions in which it specialised it also undertook the full range of Fighter Command tasks. Between 9 April and 26 May he flew 74 sorties; a few days later the first Spitfire VBs arrived. That was all very well but all too often the main opponent was the Fw 190 and 'I wanted to savour in full measure this victory as our Spit Vs were vastly inferior to the 190s and we'd been outnumbered 2 to 1'. The combat he was referring to took place on 26 July during a patrol intended to stop German weather-recce flights. Flying as Black Section with 'Knobby' Clarkson they spotted and engaged four 190s ...

Fighter Command Interception patrols, 1942			
Month	Day	Night	Total
Jan	1,313	681	1,954
Feb	1,816	580	2,396
Mar	1,548	586	2,134
Apr	2,863	1,569	4.432
May	3,482	1,123	4,605
Jun	3,929	1,725	5,654
Jul	3,558	1,899	5,457
Aug	4,350	2,035	7,385
Sep	3,136	1,534	4,670
Oct	4,419	1,028	5,447
Nov	2,742	746	3,488
Dec	2,484	647	3,131
Total	35,640	14,153	49,793

Note: Table is based on Form Y reports.

My Hun section was not turning fast and to avoid over-shooting I chopped the throttle and went into full fine pitch. I could just get a shot at the second Hun. I followed him round, the dot fair on his cockpit, then I tightened the turn. For an instant his black spinner hung steady against 'K's' nose. I pressed the gun-button and the machine-guns spluttered way out on the wings while the cannons thumped and coughed.

Not enough deflection. 'K' heaved around tighter and tighter. My vision browned with partial blackout and my hands grew heavy on the stick. The 190 was somewhere below me but I held the button down for a half-second then eased up. The second Hun whipped from under my nose and, chasing his leader, was off and away. They were going much too fast and slid up above, stall-turning for another attack. I couldn't overtake them – so far I had been trying to gain height and face them head-on. Here they come again. I pressed the button and the cannon's

One of the classic (and well-known) shots of a Spitfire; frontal view of a 92 Squadron aircraft.

thudding drowned the machine-gun's splutter. The leading Hun dipped, lifted. Suddenly a white cloud burst down its fuselage; his tail tore off and, dragging, whipped at the end of a tangle of cables. God! Hit his oxygen bottles! Blown his bloody tail off!

(*The Blue Arena*, Bob Spurdle, William Kimber). The pilot parachuted and was picked up by an RAF launch, with Bob Spurdle later meeting him in hospital.

Night Defence

The *Luftwaffe* had certainly not abandoned its night war over England, although the increasing effectiveness of the defences meant that it was less effective – and more hazardous. The attack on Liverpool on the night of 12/13 March was typical of many flown by the *Luftwaffe* during this period, with 169 bombers tasked against the city, of which 146 are recorded as having made attacks. The total enemy activity that night was just over 300 aircraft and the overall attacks lasted for about six hours from 2040 hours. Fighter Command flew 157 patrols (178 aircraft) as follows:

No. 9   Gp – 24 patrols, 32 aircraft.
No. 10 Gp – 19 patrols, 19 aircraft.
No. 11 Gp – 46 patrols, 59 aircraft.
No. 12 Gp – 48 patrols, 48 aircraft.
No. 13 Gp – 15 patrols, 15 aircraft.
No. 14 Gp – 5 patrols, 5 aircraft.

The majority of sorties were by Cats Eye single-engine fighters, who flew 140 sorties and claimed three destroyed, two probables and one damaged. Two of the destroyed were claimed by Defiants of 264 Squadron. The AI fighters claimed one destroyed, two probables and two damaged; the only confirmed success was by a 604 Squadron Beaufighter – the Squadron also claimed a probable and two damaged.

The raid had been quite successful: 'the Birkenhead and Wallasey areas suffered most in this raid, and many firms were affected by the loss of electricity supply. In Liverpool itself damage to house property was considerable and widespread and the problem of dealing with the numbers who had been rendered homeless was acute' (AHB Narrative).

A major German campaign was launched in April – the so-called Baedeker raids against British cultural centres, the first attack being on Exeter on 23/24 April. The Turbinlite-parasite teams were now part of the defence and on 29/30 April scored their only success of the campaign, a Hurricane of 253 Squadron operating with a Turbinlite Havoc of No. 1459 Flight. The ORB gave a brief account: 'Given vectors of 110 and told to climb to Angels 14, at Angels 8 were ordered to vector 060. On reaching Angels 14 further vector of 030, handed over to Reclo. After various vectors of a northerly direction made contact on 340 at a distance of 10,000 ft. Pilot Officer Scott brought them within 500 ft of the bandit's port side and identified as He 111. As Hurricane had clear visual, Turbinlite not used. Bandit took evasive action in a vertical dive, followed by Flt Lt Yapp, firing from approx 100 yards. Strikes observed as bandit dived and spiraled into cloud at approx 400 mph. Hurricane pulled out. Large fire seen below, lighting up the cloud. He 111 claimed as destroyed.'

By April 255 Squadron was operating from High Ercall and had completed its re-equipment with AI-equipped Beaufighter VIs; on the night of the 25th the first success with the new aircraft was made. 'F/O Wyrill (R/O Sgt Williams) on a non-operational

Beaufighter of 255 Squadron at Honiley; the Squadron operated Beaufighter VIs from this airfield for six months from June 1942 ,prior to departing to North Africa.

patrol, at 2300 hours was taken over by Honiley and passed to Comberton. After a series of vectors, a blip was obtained in the vicinity of Hereford at 12,000 ft, E/A being slightly below. After a burst of 2 seconds from dead astern, the E/A took violent evasive action, and visual was lost in the mist. Visual was regained and after a second burst of 4 seconds, E/A was seen to burst into flames and to dive vertically. There had been no return fire, A few seconds later, an open parachute was seen descending, and E/A was seen to hit the ground and explode. This success brought much encouragement to all members of the Squadron, as well as to the Station, and congratulatory messages cam from Group, Sector and various sections of the Station' (255 Squadron ORB). The victim was a Ju 88.

On 1 May a Beaufighter of 141 Squadron departed Acklington at 0244 for a patrol and was soon being vectored towards a target. '... obtained AI contact, which disappeared out of range. Further vector given at 12,500 ft, visual and AI contacts obtained simultaneously a head of port side 300–400 yds away at same level; E/A a Dornier 217 took evasive action by turning to starboard and diving. The Beaufighter, piloted by W/Cdr Heycock with R.Obs P/O Brandon, turned through 180 degrees, holding visual against background of cloud, and dived after E/A. E/A took double turn but AI contact and visual maintained and fighter opened fire at 3,000 ft. GCI could not help. After various vectors with fighter gaining height and travelling South, AI contact obtained on E/A below and to starboard, followed almost immediately by visual. E/A clearly seen to be a Dornier 217, was now dead ahead at 5,000 ft range. Fighter turned in for deflection shot and opened fire after closing in. Firing steady burst ending in line astern, strikes were seen all along starboard in towards engine, fuselage and tail. Blue sparks came out of E/A, which immediately went into a right-hand turn which increased to nearly vertical, and dive was so steep it could not be followed and E/A looked as if to crash. Fighter lost height as soon as possible, still keeping E/A in view, which was difficult as E/A was immediately below. E/A pulled out of dive and another attack was made and strikes were seen on the fuselage and tail, return fire from E/A's rear gun which burst to right and then hit nose of fighter. E/A was at that moment in a right-hand turn which was difficult to follow without overshooting. Able however, to see E/A going into cloud apparently out of control, approx 25 East of Blythe. Beaufighter landed Ouston 0405. Claim 1 Dornier 217 damaged.' This combat highlights a number of interesting points. The co-ordination between the GCI controller, the AI operator and the pilot was excellent, with the GCI controller manoeuvring the Beaufighter to a position where it could make an AI or visual acquisition. The AI operator was able to pick-up targets below the aircraft (not easy on the set fitted to the Beaufighter 1f) and give directions to the pilot, although in this case Wing Commander Heycock appears to be have been picking-up the Dornier – probably the same aircraft – fairly easily. The combat was recorded as indecisive, a claim being made for 'damaged' whereas in many other cases it would no doubt have gone down as a 'probable' because of the statements of 'steep dive' and 'apparently out of control'.

Defensive sorties in period of Baedeker Raids, April–August 1942					
Month	*Type*	*Sorties*	*Destroyed*	*Probable*	*Damaged*
April	AI	783	16	6	13
	Cats-eye	397	3	1	5
	Turbinlite	3	1	–	–
May	AI	547	14	3	5
	Cats-eye	187	–	1	1
	Turbinlite	37	–	–	–
June	AI	908	21	5	10
	Cats-eye	286	3	–	5
	Turbinlite	68	–	–	–
July	AI	1,231	36	8	20
	Cats-eye	655	?	?	?
	Turbinlite	117	?	?	?
August	AI	1,374	21	7	23
	Cats-eye	424	?	?	?
	Turbinlite	88	?	?	?

June 1942 at High Ercall – with 257 Squadron posing with one of their Hurricanes.

The Turbinlites remained active throughout this period and Leslie Holland was one of the 'unfortunate souls' to have been posted to this role, joining 534 Squadron at Tangmere.

> *I think it is true to say that nobody liked being on Turbinlites. Basically all the DB7 variants were very pleasant to fly, but they had never been intended to fly all the time with a load of a ton of batteries and a large arc-light installation in a very un-aerodynamic nose. I think part of the frustration of Turbinlite operations came from the fact that we carried no armament and would be dependent on the Hurricane to do the shooting – added to this was the knowledge that those German aircraft which did show their noses were always served up to the straight night fighters with their improved AI and much higher performance. The procedure of interception was exactly the same as for 'straight' night fighters including the drills for GCI and Searchlight Box. The difference came when approaching minimum range, when the light would be activated but the doors in the nose kept closed and the fighter directed by the code word 'boiling' to dive ahead, whereupon the light was exposed with the target hopefully slightly to one side in the flat beam. This would have the dual effect of putting it in front of the fighter and confusing a gunner in the E/A, who would be more than startled at the sudden dazzling illumination. Certainly 'friendlies' who were entertained with this treatment reported that looking towards the light was more blinding than a ground searchlight.*

Offensive Operations

Having formed at Warmwell at the beginning of March, 175 Squadron flew Hurricane IIBs on their first mission, a *Roadstead*, on 16 April when the CO, Sqn Ldr J R Pennington-Smith, led six aircraft to attack Maupertus airfield. One returned early with an engine problem and one (F/Sgt Foreman) had to ditch because of a glycol leak; sadly, the pilot was never found. More missions followed over the next few days and on the 30th the Squadron ORB recorded a day that concluded with the comment 'we are now starting to make the history which 175 Squadron wants to make.' The sortie that prompted this was against shipping at Isle de Batz, which involved eight aircraft led by the CO: 'Three destroyers and one merchant ship were attacked with 250 GP 3-second delay bombs and machine-gun fire, one destroyer was damaged but no confirmation concerning the others is to hand yet, at any rate the attack was severe and many casualties must have been inflicted on the crews. The lads consider it was a highly successful attack, they all come home very pleased with their first low level attack. W/O Emberg had his aircraft damaged by flak but managed to land at Portreath safely, otherwise, no casualties.' A few days later the ORB added: 'report from Group that one of the destroyers classed as casualty Category 3. As a first attempt at a shipping target we feel that we have made a good start at that kind of operation.'

On 23 July four Spitfires of 302 Squadron were airborne out of Heston on a *Rhubarb* in two pairs. 'Flying below 500 ft crossed over Dungeness and off Le Touquet. Fg Off Gorzula and Plt Off Czarnecki made landfall at Plage St Gabriel, north of Le Touquet while Fg Off Gladyth and Plt Off Nowakiewicz crossed south of the town. Gorzula and Czarnecki flew along east side of railway towards Etaples and near Lefaux saw a W/T Station consisting of one large building and five aerial masts all camouflaged with netting. They were unable to find target but attacked a large factory near Etaples. Bofors fire was seen from five points around the factory. Unable to find any other targets ...

Spitfires of 64 Squadron at Hornchurch, May 1942; Fighter Command flew 5,841 day offensive ops this month.

these two pilots returned via Rye and landed at base at 0645. Weather over France was 10/10 cloud at times down to ground and raining in places. Gladych and Nowakiewicz found themselves north of the Foret de Boulogne; they struck an army camp on a plateau. A number of Nissen huts camouflaged and a radio station of one hut and four aerial masts. Intense bofors fire from all round camp. Gladych attacked and silenced one gun post and after a wide turn attacked gun posts followed by Nowakiewiecz. Flashes and much dust and debris seen as results of hits. Flak continued all the time. After attack Nowakiewicz did not reply on R/T and Gladych flew south along railway line and found hutted camp at Etaples. His first attack showed many hits on huts but no AA was seen. After a left turn he came in again and saw many soldiers in camp, which he attacked and M/G fire opened up from west side of camp. His cockpit hood was hit near Foret de Boulogne. He made another wide turn followed by a third short attack with M/G. Landed Hawkinge 0725 and reported to Heston later. P/O Nowakiewicz missing' (302 Squadron ORB).

By mid 1942 trains had become a favourite target, the clearance for such attacks having been given in late 1941. For 32 Squadron's Hurricanes, late July was something of a train-busting month:

> 26 July: 'At 0115 Sgt R E Tickner took-off with instructions to search for trains in the Lens area. Pilot crossed Belgian coast near Ostend, and reached target area but no railway activity was observed. Pilot later proceeded North of target area and attacked two trains, resulting in damage to both locomotives. At 0115 P/O R S Davidson took-off for patrol in neighbourhood of Ypres, Bailleul and Lille; near Lille a train was observed, and after two attacks this appeared to be derailed and the engine damaged. Before returning to base an attack was

made on another locomotive, hits being observed, causing damage.'
Two other pilots were on similar Intruders that night but with no
success.

28 July: 'At 0055 P/O R S Davidson took-off for patrol over Lille aerodrome
where, however, no activity was observed; proceeding from the target
area in direction of Orchies pilot made three attacks on a train,
resulting in damage to the locomotive. P/O C Mehrof took-off at 0045
to patrol Leon area ... proceeded to Lens-Louvais area where an
attack on a train resulted in damage to the locomotive. Continuing
North of Lens pilot made an attack upon locomotive resulting in
damage.' Two more trains were attacked by other pilots that night,
with eight more being claimed as damaged the following night, Plt Off
Davidson reporting that one of his had 'blown up'. Sgt Dunn reported
'large clouds of steam and sparks' when he attacked a loco in the early
hours of 31 July.

It was always difficult to assess the amount of damage done during such attacks and
the reports of locomotives being damaged could not indicate the extent of the damage;
steam locos gave off a lot of steam at all times but should the boiler be hit by 20 mm
cannon fire then clouds of steam would often result – even then the damage may not have
been too significant. As we will see later, attacks on trains were to become one of the
main tasks in the D-Day period. They were never easy targets and as the Germans
became increasingly desperate to prevent the loss of locos, the defences increased and
flak traps were set for Allied pilots.

*Sqn Ldr Roberts in Typhoon of 257 Squadron; the Squadron converted to the Typhoon in
July 1942 and flew the type for the rest of the war.*

Fighter Command Offensive Operations, 1942			
Month	*Day*	*Night*	*Total*
Jan	273	36	309
Feb	906	60	966
Mar	2,083	72	2,155
Apr	7,651	207	7,858
May	5,841	198	6,039
Jun	5,895	366	6,261
Jul	3,341	376	3,717
Aug	6,802	227	7,029
Sep	2,137	102	2,239
Oct	2,888	78	2,966
Nov	2,648	115	2,763
Dec	2,800	107	2,907
Total	43,265	1,944	45,209

Note: Table is based on Form Y reports.

The source document for the offensive operations table and the one for defensive ops also include a figure for 'special patrols' but does make clear if these were defensive or offensive. However, they need to be added to the total of operations for the year, giving an extra 11,937 day and 580 night sorties. The Command's daytime total was therefore 128,420 sorties and 19,386 night sorties. However, the source document also states that from August 1942 sorties by USAAF units are included; the first USAAF Fighter Group to commence operations was the Spitfire-equipped 31st Fighter Group, which flew its initial missions with the RAF in late July.

Dieppe – Operation *Jubilee*

At 0445 on 19 August 1942 the first assault waves of Canadian troops went ashore at Dieppe under Operation *Jubilee*, a 'reconnaissance in force'. Air support was a vital element of *Jubilee* and 48 Spitfire squadrons (42 with Mark Vs and four with Mark IXs) were involved either with Close Air Support, 129 Squadron for example strafed ground targets in advance of the first landings, fighter cover to prevent German aircraft interfering with the operation, and escort for Allied bombers. It was the busiest day for many squadrons since the height of the Battle of Britain and some units flew four sorties during the day. The RAF flew some 3,000 sorties in the space of 16 hours on 19 August 1942. In response, the *Luftwaffe* flew just under 1,000 sorties.

Don Morrison was operating with 401 Squadron over Dieppe,

Just as we in Yellow Section arrived over the Dieppe area, I spotted a single 190 some 1,000–1,500 feet below and heading in the same direction. I did a wide, slipping barrel roll to lose height and levelled out about 150 yards behind him. As I closed up I opened fire with a two second burst of cannon fire. I saw strikes all along the starboard side of the fuselage and several pieces blew off from around the cowling. Just as we both went into a very thin layer of cloud he exploded with a terrific flash of flame and black smoke.

The first patrol by 124 Squadron was airborne at 0445; the ORB reporting that: 'The Hornchurch Wing were contacted soon after leaving Beachy Head; the patrolling squadrons were relieved at 0520 and the area of the anchorage was patrolled for thirty minutes at 3/500 ft, with Blue Section patrolling to the West, Red to the East and White in the centre. Assault and TLC were seen to be still arriving at Orange Beach. It was found impossible to contact Fighter Control by R/T. A Ju 88 was seen by Red 3 and shot into sea 5 miles NE of Dieppe by the fire from a destroyer, the E/A having dropped its bombs nearby. A ship of 6/800 tons was seen on fire 2 miles NE of Dieppe. Light flak was experienced from the Camp de Cesar and some heavy flak from the town. Approximately 3 E/A were seen in the vicinity, but no engagements eventuated.' The Squadron was back on the ground at 0622, but a second sortie, again of three Sections, was airborne at 1049 and was more productive: 'RV made with 616 Squadron in the Channel off Beachy Head. Squadron flew for 10 minutes at zero feet then climbed to

10,000 ft in the Dieppe area. Owing to great activity in that area the Squadron split into Sections to patrol the anchorage. Approx 20+ aircraft were seen, made up of Fw 190s, Do 217s and Ju 88s, some below and others at the same level. Combats took place as follows:

'F/L Gregson, Red 1 with Red 2 turned to assist Red 3 and 4 who were being dived on by 2 Fw 190s, coming from the South. The first Fw was attacked by Red 1 from the beam with a two second burst from 200 yards, which rapidly increased, while the second aircraft dived into France. Strikes were seen, and a small flash from underside of the enemy's port wing root. A panel appeared to rip backwards, the port leg dropped and hung at about 45 deg. The E/A continued to turn, dived away and was lost to sight. It is claimed as damaged. A little later Red 1 saw an Fw 190 pulling up out of a dive in front of him, and climbed up quickly behind the E/A who did not apparently see him, and thus took no avoiding action. Red 1 fired a quick burst with cannon and m.g. from astern at 300 yds for about 1 second. An explosion took place behind the E/A's cockpit, there was a large flash, and bits flew off followed by smoke and flame. The E/A went into a dive, slowly starting to spin, leaving a trail of smoke behind, and then crashed just off the beach, East of Dieppe, after having practically disintegrated in the air. It is claimed as destroyed.

'F/Sgt P E G Durnford DFM, White 3, attacked an Fw 190, from 200 yds with a one second burst on the port side. The E/A straightened out, and started diving, White 3 attacked again with a three second burst, from dead astern. The E/A started smoking and then caught fire. The E/A's pilot was not seen to bale out, or the E/A to crash. It is therefore claimed as probably destroyed but it is hoped that in view of the fact that the E/A caught fire it may be allowed as destroyed. Later, while flying at 5,000 ft over Dieppe, White 3 saw a Ju 88 flying at 2,000 ft, and closed to 300 yds. The E/A dived to tree-top level, and was attacked by White 3 from 250 yards, with a one second burst; strikes were seen around the port engine nacelle. After firing the remainder of his cannon ammunition White 3 saw the Ju 88 drop its bombs, and crash into a field with a dark smoke coming from its port engine, which had stopped before impact. This aircraft is claimed as destroyed; later reports from camera films identify the aircraft as a Do 217 and not a Ju 88.'

Plt Off Kilburn, Red 3, claimed a Fw 190 as probably destroyed and the Squadron's score for the action was three enemy aircraft but with Sgt Shanks failing to return.

The day was far from over for 124 Squadron and two more sorties were flown; the third sortie took-off at 1320, led by Sqn Ldr Balmforth, to patrol one of the convoys. During this sortie the Spitfires claimed an Fw 190 destroyed (P/O Hull), a Ju 88 probably destroyed (P/O Hull) and three Fw 190s damaged. One Spitfire was damaged and had to crash-land at Lympne but the pilot (Sgt Mirsch) was OK. The final sortie of the day was again led by Sqn Ldr Balmforth and was airborne at 1719 to patrol the same convoy. A group of 109s approached the convoy but turned away when the Spitfire moved towards them. The Squadron was back on the ground at 1847 after a hectic but successful day. 'Needless to say, celebrations took place in various places during the evening.' Sqn Ldr Balmforth had been on all four sorties and had led three of them, the first sortie having been led by Wg Cdr Duke-Woolley.

'Sammy' Sampson saw action twice in the Dieppe area. On one sortie he engaged a Dornier of KG2:

As I started to overhaul it I was completely put-off by the rear-gunner opening up on me and what looked like red tomatoes passed by me on either side. The result of this was that I opened-up far too early. However, I saw hits on the port wing and petrol started to pour out of the port wing tank. Then Johnny warned me of two 190s above and behind so I quickly broke off and rejoined him.

He attacked a second Dornier but with similar results and the exhaustion of his cannon ammunition. A sortie later in the day resulted in the destruction of an Fw 190 courtesy of the ideal set-up of sneak-up and shoot without being seen.

I don't think the Hun pilot saw me for very conveniently he turned to starboard, which enabled me to give him a 3-second burst from 150 yards and he went down on fire into the sea.

Plt Off Bob Large was airborne in a Spitfire VI of 616 Squadron on 2 October 1942 when he claimed an Fw 190 over St Omer. His combat report stated:

... as we were leaving the target area I reported about a dozen Fw 190s about 6,000 ft below us, proceeding north-west, and as the Squadron Commander had apparently not seen the E/A, I announced that I was going down. When about 800 yards away from the E/A the formation broke up in all directions and I closed in on a straggler, who broke to starboard. I opened fire at about 500 yards range, but as he turned sharply I pulled the nose of my aircraft ahead of him, blotting out the E/A from view and firing one 5-second burst and then allowing the nose of my aircraft to fall, to see the results of my fire. The E/A was diving very steeply to the NE with his port undercarriage leg hanging down and brown smoke pouring from him. Bright flashes were coming from the starboard side of his engine, which afterwards developed into flames. I continued to turn as other E/A were threatening Cooper and myself. I fired the remainder of my ammunition in a head-on attack on an Fw 190. FS Cooper came into line abreast, up sun, to my port wing and we recrossed the French coast north of Cap Griz Nez, being attacked most of the way out.

I warned FS Cooper of an attack from below and ordered him to break. FS Cooper was hit in the radiator but did not realise it and I told him that glycol was pouring from the radiator. FS Cooper baled out off Sangatte about 5 miles out to sea, and after 2 Fw 190s had made a final attack on me, they turned back to France. I remained with FS Cooper, giving Maydays, until I had to leave him owing to shortage of fuel, and returned to Hawkinge.

Bob Large had used 120 rounds of 20 mm and 1,250 rounds of 0.303 in ammunition during his combats.

November 1942 for 302 Squadron was typical of the routine of most of the Command's squadrons during this period:

2 Nov   Escort Bostons to Caen
3 Nov   Pair on *Rhubarb*
6 Nov   Escort to Caen
8 Nov   Sweep Ypres-Cassel-Gravelines
9 Nov   Escort to Le Havre
10 Nov   Escort to Le Havre
16 Nov   Two pair on *Rhubarb*, rail targets Amiens
17 Nov   Sweep to Cherbourg
19 Nov   Pair on *Rhubarb*, rail targets
22 Nov   Sweep and escort for Defiants.

The *Rhubarb* flown by Pilot Officers Wardzinski and Sniec on 3 November was productive: '*Rhubarb* operation to attack ground targets along the railway line Abbeville to Dieppe. Two factories attacked but results not seen. Aircraft continued and attacked large factory with four big camouflage containers about 30 ft high. One immediately exploded with smokeless flame and cover was blown off. Second attack made out of the sun and another container exploded; the first was still burning. The other two were visibly hit but showed no results. One machine-gun post opened fire but was silenced by fire from our aircraft' (302 Squadron ORB).

Night intruders

The pace of the night offensive work for the Command continued to increase in early 1942 and involved both single-engine and twin-engine fighters, the former could be provided by any squadron but were usually the Hurricane units that specialised in this task, and the latter were either AI-equipped or were acting as bombers.

Typical of the Hurricane intruder ops were those flown by 3 Squadron on the night of 31 May 1942. 'P/O B H Hay took-off in Hurricane Long-Range machine from Manston at 0030 hours to patrol Venlo. Arriving at Venlo P/O Hay orbited twice to port, wide of the town, changed orbit to starboard, and during this period he felt the slip stream of an aircraft but was unable to observe same. Whilst orbiting at 1500 ft south of Venlo, P/O Hay observed slightly above him and to starboard a twin engined aircraft silhouetted against the moon, at approximately 0130 hours. This twin engined aircraft was subsequently identified as a Ju 88. When on south side of Venlo, enemy aircraft opened fire with twin guns from the rear and above. P/O Hay closed to 80 yards and enemy turned from port to starboard still firing short bursts, which passed above Hurricane. P/O Hay was now astern 70 yards distance and he opened fire, strikes being observed along top side of fuselage. P/O Hay then lifted the nose of his machine and concentrated on the rear gunner, who ceased fire after one second. P/O Hay kept firing until long black smoke streams were observed from both engines, and a red glow in the cockpit. Large

Hurricane of 3 Squadron; 'P/O B H Hay took-off in Hurricane Long-Range machine from Manston at 0030 hours to patrol Venlo. Arriving at Venlo P/O Hay orbited twice to port, wide of the town, changed orbit to starboard, and during this period he felt the slip stream of an aircraft but was unable to observe same.'

pieces were also observed breaking off the enemy aircraft. At this point the Ju 88 had gone into a shallow dive, and P/O Hay was forced to take violent evasive action as he was caught in a cone of six blue searchlights and light concentrated flak. He then set a Westerly course where he attacked and extinguished six searchlights which endeavoured to locate him. P/O Hay then set course for the coast, and on arriving North of Antwerp he observed three barges all of which he attacked twice before emptying his guns. He returned to base at 0340 hours. He claims one Ju 88 as damaged and would like this machine confirmed as destroyed. Although the enemy aircraft was not observed to crash, P/O Hay considers that it is must unlikely to have sustained the attack.

'P/O D J Scott took-off from Manston in a Long-Range Hurricane at 2349 hours to patrol Deelen area. On arriving at Deelen aerodrome P/O Scott orbited at 1500 ft for 40 minutes. He then flew West and saw flarepath and searchlights some miles distant, which he believed to be Soesterburg. Several enemy aircraft appeared in area with navigation lights on, one of which (a Ju 88) was attacked by P/O Scott from 1,000 yards. Several strikes were seen and a large piece, probably the port wing, broke away. Immediately, enemy aircraft pulled up vertically and disappeared over head as P/O Scott continued straight on course to intercept another enemy aircraft in front. Whilst chasing second enemy aircraft a further aircraft approached from starboard slightly below at 1,000 ft, which P/O Scott engaged giving it a 4-second burst. The enemy aircraft evaded steeply to port followed by P/O Scott almost to ground level where visual contact was lost. P/O Scott then climbed to 2,000 ft, where he observed after 3 minutes the flarepath was again lit and numerous enemy aircraft were quickly seen flashing navigation lights. P/O Scott again attempted to make interception but failed to make contact. He then returned to base at 0305.' The Squadron sent four other Hurricanes out the same night to harass a number of other night-fighter airfields but with little to report.

These accounts illustrate the problems and potential for this type of 'airfield lurking' intruder. Acquisition of targets relied on visibility conditions, especially moonlight, and

The specialist night intruders of 23 Squadron were very active throughout 1943, operating a mix of Havoc Is and Boston IIIs, although between June and August 1942 these were replaced by Mosquito IIs.

The most successful night was 8/9 July when Sqn Ldr K Salisbury-Hughes was operating in a Mosquito and claimed an He 111 and Do 217; Mosquito DZ238 of 23 Squadron.

the use of lights by the airfield and the aircraft. Even when the sky seemed to be full of enemy aircraft it was difficult to get into a position to make a satisfactory attack, although if the port wing had been the large piece of debris it was a fine shot from 1,000 yards! Return fire from enemy gunners, and the searchlight and flak hazards certainly made this type of mission dicey but even when the fighters came back without confirmed results the disruption of the German night-fighter system was significant. What is never credited in this type of mission is the enemy aircraft that ran-out of fuel and crashed or was damaged and crashed or written-off on landing.

The specialist night intruders of 23 Squadron were very active throughout 1943, operating a mix of Havoc Is and Boston IIIs, although between June and August 1942 these were replaced by Mosquito IIs. July was a typical month, with the following operations being flown:

Intruder targets, 23 Squadron, July 1942		
Date	Aircraft	Targets
1/2 Jul	4	Evreux, St Andre
5/6 Jul	5	Amiens, Caen, Evreux, St Andre
6/7 Jul	1	Avard. one Do 217 destroyed
8/9 Jul	4	Chartres, Beauvais, Evreux, Orleans. One He 111 and one Do 217 destroyed
11/12 Jul	2	Evreux, Chartres
12/13 Jul	6	Caen, Rennes, Dinard, Evreux, Chartres
14/15 Jul	2	Rennes, shipping
19/20 Jul	1	Abbeville, Amiens
21/22 Jul	5	Chartres, Orleans, Rouen, Juvincourt, Criel
23/24 Jul	6	Chartres, Orleans, Juvincourt, Tours, Caen, Bretigny
25/26 Jul	2	Chartres, Orleans, Tours, Rouen
26/27 Jul	1	Juvincourt
27/28 Jul	6	Evreux, St Andre, Dreux, Chartres, Criel, Beauvais, Orleans
28/29 Jul	8	Chartres, Orleans, Amsterdam/Schiphol, Gilze-Rijen. Eindhoven, Soesterburg. One aircraft lost
30/31 Jul	9	Orleans, Bretigny, Orleans, Avord, Serquex. One E/A destroyed
31 Jul/1 Aug	6	Juvincourt, St Trond

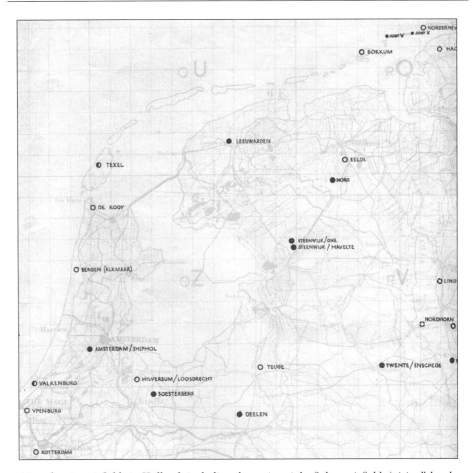

Map showing airfields in Holland, including the major night-fighter airfields 'visited' by the intruders.

The most successful night was 8/9 July when Sqn Ldr K Salisbury-Hughes was operating in a Mosquito and claimed an He 111 and Do 217. The busiest period was the end of the month, which corresponded with three large raids by Bomber Command. On the final night of July Bomber Command sent 630 aircraft to attack Dusseldorf but as with the previous raids in this period losses were high. There was increasing concern over bomber losses and the scale of offensive operation against night fighter airfields was increased, with the Squadron concentrating on four of the main bases in Holland – Deelen, Leeuwarden, Twenthe and Venlo – during October.

1943 – Putting on the Pressure

By 1943 the Allied emphasis was very much an offensive one with the invasion of Europe a possibility that year, although it was soon agreed by the Allied command that it would actually be in 1944. For Fighter Command the dual role of defending the homeland and supporting offensive operations remained throughout the year. In terms of defensive ops this was increasingly a night task, although the *Luftwaffe* attacks on England were few and ineffective.

Spitfire II in use with 276 Squadron for Air-Sea Rescue; Fighter Command had partial responsibility for the Air-Sea Rescue organisation.

Defensive Operations

On 17 April 1943 six patrols and two scrambles were flown by 266 Squadron in what proved to be a mixed day. 'On the first patrol, just after dawn, Sgt Eastwood was shot-down by a 65 Squadron Spitfire off Bolt Head; they had been escorting an MTB, and why on earth the Spitfire should break away from its formation and carry-out a long drawn-out attack on a Typhoon at short range is difficult to understand. Sgt Eastwood managed to fly his aircraft over land and baled-out successfully. He would obviously have crashed if he had tried to force-land as his aileron was shot-away. In the evening Sqn Ldr Green and Fg Off Deall were scrambled after two E/A at 18,000 ft over Plymouth.' The ORB sortie detail takes up the story, 'on arrival AA pointing South. Losing height flew due South for 12 mins, then vectored 220 deg and after 3 mins, saw 2 E/A going South on the "deck". Turned starboard, and then port, to get on their tails, and started chasing. Overtaking speed very small so fired at 1000/800 yards to make them weave. S/L Green seeing strikes claims one damaged, F/O Deall realised only one cannon was firing. S/L Green decided to attack the leading (fastest) E/A first so as to stand best chance of getting both, but in catching this one he overtook the other, which promptly attacked him. A general "dog-fight" ensued during which F/O Deall got strikes on his E/A, but S/L green did not see more strikes on his E/A. After about 5 mins of dog-fighting the E/A disappeared into the haze and Section returned to base.' Sqn Ldr C L Green DFC in EJ924 and Fg Off J H Deall in R8926.

There are two interesting points with this account; firstly, the continued problems of 'friendly fire' – and the RAF lost a fair number of aircraft to this throughout the war – with the Typhoon often being mistaken for an Fw 190; secondly, the fact that the Typhoons actually managed to catch the 190s. The overall performance of the 190 was such that Spitfires seldom had a chance of making up such ground in a tail-chase; the Typhoon may not have been the best dog-fighting aircraft but it did have some performance advantages.

Spitfire Vs of 130 Squadron at Ballyhalbert

On 11 June 1943 the Sergeants' Mess at Biggin Hill hosted a special dinner to 'celebrate the destruction of the one thousandth enemy aircraft from the Sector'. In addition to giving details of the menu (the main course being roast chicken), the menu card also gave a bit of background to the event: 'During this period, the number of enemy aircraft destroyed from this Sector has mounted with such rapidity that on 15th May, the splendid total of One Thousand was reached. It has been a hard and bitter struggle for air and ground personnel to achieve this figure, and we feel that tonight we are entitled to relax and celebrate an event which has never happened before in the history of the Royal Air Force, and may never be equalled.

'Out of our pride in this Thousandth Hun, let there be born the resolution that the lead which this Sector has established over all others shall not only be maintained, but increased day by day until a victorious peace is gained.'

Beaufighter of 604 Squadron; by 1943 the Command's night defences were highly efficient and the scale of German attacks had reduced.

The *Luftwaffe* was still active over Britain by night, albeit on a small-scale and in the face of what was now an effective defence equipped with Mosquitoes and with a proven and experienced Control and Reporting system. Bud Green of 410 Squadron had a successful engagement on 5 November:

> I was flying a patrol line in the middle of the Channel, with other Mosquitoes flying on my right and on my left. Ground control could only handle a limited number of aircraft; it was sited at Warding near Dungeness. I was instructed: 'Bandits on a southerly heading, height unknown, considerable numbers.' We were taken over by a controller who steered us towards them, then round them (at 18,000 ft), until we picked them up on our own radar. A classic interception.
>
> Once the navigator had picked up an aircraft on his AI, the ideal was for the pilot to come in below at a closing speed as slow as possible, but fast enough for evasive action if fired on. You had to match the speed before you got a visual contact, then open up the throttles to close in by eye. I came in too low, overtaking speed was not high enough. I had to pull up at full throttle, but was still too slow. Pointing upwards at 200 yards, I fired all four cannon and the four machine-guns: We were so close, I didn't need tracer or to allow for any deflection. He never knew what hit him. It was totally devastating as he just blew up. I thought it was an Me 410 but it turned out to be a Do 217.

Offensive Operations

Circus ops remained a standard task for the Command into 1943. On 15 February the Polish Wing (303, 306, 308, 315 squadrons) was airborne on Circus 266: 'Crossed English coast at North Foreland at 500 ft, climbed rapidly and crossed French coast West of Dunkirk at 15,000 ft, 303 leading. The bombers were already over Dunkirk, and dropped their bombs. Considerable ack ack was experienced. Squadrons recrossed French coast at 9,000 ft and flew along French coast to Calais and set course for Deal. They were attacked in mid-Channel by two groups of four Fws. Two pilots of 308 attacked these Fws and one was probably damaged, and one Spitfire was seen diving towards sea trailing smoke. No casualties experienced and W/O Piatowski claimed one Fw probably

Typhoon of 609 Squadron at Manston, March 1943; the Typhoon had found its true niche and in late 1943 became one of the main types with the new Tactical Air Force.

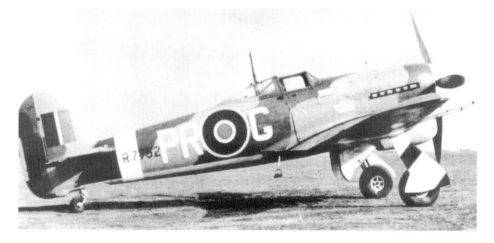

destroyed' (308 Squadron ORB). A number of similar missions were flown in February, with some days, such as 26th, having two such missions. The majority had little to report – meet up with the other fighters, watch the bombers drop their loads, usually with heavy anti-aircraft fire, and then escort them back again.

The table below shows the detail of the mission types, claims against the enemy and Fighter Command losses for the year to 14 November, the date at which Fighter Command became Air Defence of Great Britain.

Fighter Command/ADGB summary of day offensive operations, 1 Jan 1943–14 Nov 1943

| Mission | Days | Ops | Sorties | Claims | | | Losses | | |
				Dest.	*Prob.*	*Dam.*	*Lost*	*%*	*Dam.*
Escort	180	596	53,914	486	124	372	346	0.64	103
Roadstead	110	173	3,315	14	2	8	23	0.69	17
Bombing	11	11	90	0	0	0	5	5.56	8
Rhubarb	187	773	1,825	26	4	10	93	5.10	57
Ranger	98	184	291	15	1	1	9	3.09	6
Rodeo	101	188	7,211	61	21	60	31	0.43	11
Instep	158	294	1,295	29	5	18	8	0.62	5
Distil	22	22	120	0	0	0	2	1.67	0
Haunch	1	1	23	0	0	0	0	0	0
F.Roadstead	234	512	4,318	7	6	12	34	0.79	20
TacR	12	117	233	0	0	2	3	1.29	1
Photo Recce	130	1,091	1,179	0	0	0	14	1.19	4
Other	15	21	296	7	0	0	5	1.69	4
Total	1,259	3,983	74,110	635	163	483	573	0.77	236

Note: F.Roadstead – Fighter Roadstead and shipping recce; TacR – Tactical Reconnaissance; Bombing – unescorted bombing raid; % – percentage of the total effort (aircraft) lost on ops.

An additional 6,693 were flown to the end of the year, with claims for a further 47 enemy aircraft destroyed and a loss of 27 aircraft. Escort remained the most frequent mission and *Rhubarb* remained the most dangerous in terms of loss rate.

Airfields were amongst the most heavily-defended targets in Occupied Europe, bristling with quadruple 20 mm anti-aircraft guns. The gun positions were usually arranged to give murderous crossfire kill zones, and 'flak traps' were set up on the most likely lines of attack. In the face of such opposition it was very difficult for pilots to target aircraft on the ground, a fleeting pass with a burst or two being all that could be achieved. To stay in the area and make a second or third pass was to court disaster. 'Johnnie' Johnson recalled one such hairy occasion:

I led a section of Spitfires down to the deck to sweep the numerous airfields scattered around the circumference of the French capital. After 20 minutes at low level I was lost, although I knew we were a few miles south of Paris. I put the map away and concentrated on flying the various courses I had worked out before leaving base. About another five minutes on this leg and then turn to the west to avoid getting too close to Paris.

We crossed the complicated mass of railway lines which indicated that we were close to Paris. We sped across a wide river and ahead of us was a heavily wooded slope, perhaps rising 200 ft above the river. We raced up this slope, only a

Spitfire of 340 Squadron at Biggin Hill; Fighter Command flew over 74,000 offensive sorties between January 1943 and the change to Air Defence Great Britain in November, with the majority of those being flown by Spitfires.

Waiting for the next mission to Europe - 257 Squadron at Gravesend, August 1943.

'Circus' ops – 98 Squadron bombing the airfield at Caen/Carpiquet on 15 May 1943 to 'encourage' the Luftwaffe to come up and fight.

few feet above the topmost branches, and found ourselves looking straight across a large grass airfield with several large hangars on the far side.

The gunners were ready and waiting. The shot and shell came from all angles, for some of the gun positions were on the hangar roofs and they fired down on us. I had never seen the like of this barrage. Enemy aircraft were parked here and there, but our only thought was to get out of this inferno. There was no time for radio orders. It was every man for himself. It seemed that all our exits were blocked with a concentrated criss-cross pattern of fire from a hundred guns.

My only hope of a getaway lay in a small gap between two hangars. I pointed the Spitfire at this gap, hurtled through it and caught sight of the multiple barrels of a light flak gun swinging on to me from one of the parapets. Beyond lay a long, straight road with tall poplars on either side and I belted the Spitfire down the road with the trees forming some sort of screen. Tracer was still bursting over the cockpit. Half a dozen cyclists were making their way up the road towards the airfield. They flung themselves and their bicycles in all directions. I pulled up above the light flak and called the other pilots. Miraculously, they had all come through the barrage.

By late summer 1943 activity had increased; 302 Squadron had a very busy September:

302 Squadron operations, September 1942		
Date	*Aircraft*	*Mission*
2 Sep	12	Escort Marauders to Lille airfield
3 Sep	12	Escort Marauders to Beauvais airfield
	13	Escort Venturas to Foret D'Eperlecques
	14	Escort Marauders to Hazebroucke, cancelled after 20 minutes
4 Sep	14	Escort Mitchells to Rouen
	13	Escort Mitchells to Boulogne
	12	Escort Marauders to Hazebrucke airfield
5 Sep	12	Escort Marauders to Ghent
6 Sep	13	Escort Marauders to Amiens marshalling yards
7 Sep	14	Escort Marauders to Arras
8 Sep	12	Escort Marauders to Lille
		Escort Mitchells to Boulogne
11 Sep	13	Escort Mitchells to Rouen
13 Sep	12	Sweep Doullery–Abbeville
14 Sep	11	Escort Marauders to Woensdrecht airfield
15 Sep	13	Escort Marauders to Merville airfield
16 Sep	12	Escort Mitchells to Serquex airfield
18 Sep	14	Escort Marauders to Beauvais airfield
	13	Escort Marauders to Beaumont-le-Roger
19 Sep	12	Escort Mitchells to Lievin ammonia works
22 Sep	12	Sweep Amiens
23 Sep	12	Sweep Amiens
	12	Sweep Amiens
24 Sep	12	Sweep
	13	Escort Mitchells to St Omer
25 Sep	12	Escort Mitchells to St Omer
26 Sep	12	Escort Mitchells to Rouen
	12	Escort B-17s to near Beauvais
27 Sep	13	Escort Marauders to St Valery
	12	Escort Marauders to Conches airfield

Groundcrew of 56 Squadron at Matlask, 1943.

Pilots of 616 Squadron at Ibsley in June 1943; the Squadron continued to specialize in high-level ops with their Spitfire VIs, although in the absence of suitable targets were frequently employed as a normal fighter squadron.

Night Intruders

After a somewhat quiet but not uneventful tour on Turbinlites, Jack Cheney converted to Mosquitoes with 25 Squadron at Church Fenton in early 1943, although shortage of aircraft and other problems meant it was March before his crew was operational. April saw the start of the Intruder season for 25 Squadron and Jack Cheney flew his first such op on the 20th.

> *Manor 24 (our callsign) became airborne from Coltishall in the bright moonlight, with no cloud and visibility of four miles. We crossed the North Sea at 200 ft and after pinpointing Vlieland to starboard we climbed to 4, 500 ft …. We followed some railway lines to Papenburg and Leer, encountering moderate flak and searchlight activity on the way. A train was spotted entering Leer from the south and I turned to attack. Just as I did so, the aeroplane was illuminated by the glare of three searchlights for about half a minute. Considerable light flak, again pretty accurate was thrown at us and I had to break off the attack with some violent evasive action. … West of Bremen a fast-moving train was spotted. I gently pushed the stick forward and made a head-on pass at it, starting at 1,300 ft and, with Mike shouting out the height, down to about 400 ft. Cannon strikes were observed on the locomotive and we broke away and headed for Cloppenburg. I followed the railway tracks south to Quackenbruck and Furstenau and soon we came upon another train near Bippen. This time I attacked from astern and to starboard, opening up with a long five-second burst. The slow-moving train was hit in a concentrated strike and the flash from the explosions was blinding. The engine became enveloped in clouds of steam and smoke, grinding to a halt and lit up with a vivid red glow.*

(From 'Night Fighter Pilot's Diary, Alastair Goodrum, FlyPast magazine). Jack Cheney and 'Mike' Mycock flew a number of operational sorties before they were listed as missing from an *Instep* mission over the Bay of Biscay on 13 June.

With Bomber Command having suffered heavily during its Battle of the Ruhr (March to July 1943) there were calls on Fighter Command to increase its night intruder work. Having spent May and the early part of June training at Drem with its new AI Beaufighter VIs, 141 Squadron was at Wittering on 11 June when it was visited by the AOC of No. 12 Group, Air-Vice Marshal Andrew, who wished them luck with their forthcoming operational period. The Squadron was led by one of the RAF's great night-fighter aces and leaders, Wg Cdr R D Braham and it was he who was to fly the first op – and score the first victory. The ORB recorded for 14 June: 'First night of Squadron's Intruder operations. W/Cdr Braham with F/L Gregory as Navigator Radio took-off at 2355 hours to patrol Deelen, which they did uneventfully, and at 0210 whilst returning to the Dutch coast saw an Me 110 coming up behind. A dog-fight in bright moon-light ensued in which W/Cdr Braham with the assistance of F/L Gregory completely outmanoeuvred the enemy aircraft, which received a 5-second burst of cannon and machine-gun fire. Strikes were observed on fuselage and port engine, which caught fire. The Me 110 dived vertically and crashed on the ground in flames North of Stavoren.' Four more of the Squadron's aircraft were on similar missions but none found any 'trade'. The Bomber Command target that night was Oberhausen and 17 of the 197 Lancasters failed to return, a loss rate of 8.4%, an indication that the Command was continuing to suffer unsustainable loss rates. The night intruder effort continued to increase and Braham and 141 Squadron were always in the thick of it. On 1 October 1943

'W/Cdr Braham with F/L Gregory as Navigator Radio took-off at 2355 hours to patrol Deelen, which they did uneventfully, and at 0210 whilst returning to the Dutch coast saw an Me 110 coming up behind. A dog-fight in bright moonlight ensued in which W/Cdr Braham with the assistance of F/L Gregory completely outmanoeuvred the enemy aircraft.' One of the most successful night-fighter crews: Wg Cdr Bob Braham and Flt Lt Gregory.

he was posted and the ORB noted the impact he had made: 'He joined the unit at a time when it was at its very lowest ebb. By his magnificent example and good organisation, and despite the fact that all the experienced crews were posted away, the morale and work of the Squadron started to improve immediately. He succeeded in communicating a fine offensive spirit, which showed itself to such an effect while the Squadron was at Predannack, that they were eventually chosen from all the Night Fighter squadrons of Fighter Command to undertake the present extremely important tasks. During the nine months he has led the Squadron, he has succeeded in destroying eight enemy aircraft and damaging two others. While at Predannack he shot-up a Motor Torpedo Boat in a convoy, and on another occasion seriously damaged a submarine, both in the Bay of Biscay. Over France in Ranger Operations he seriously damaged a train, and a lorry. He has succeeded with his last victory in beating the score of W/C Cunningham and leaves the Squadron as the Ace Night Fighter Pilot.'

Fighter Command summary of night offensive operations, 1 Jan 1943–14/15 Nov 1943

				Claims			Losses		
Mission	*Nights*	*Ops*	*Sorties*	*Dest.*	*Prob.*	*Dam.*	*Lost*	*%*	*Dam.*
Intruder	189	1,951	1,951	50	5	32	28	1.44	12
Serrate	53	334	334	13	1	8	4	1.20	0
Mahmoud	31	100	100	2	1	0	2	2.00	1
Night Ranger	63	583	594	2	0	0	16	2.69	7
Night Rhubarb	24	37	153	1	0	0	3	1.96	0
Ship Recce	67	100	328	1	0	0	6	1.83	2
Other	5	6	18	0	0	0	1	5.56	0
Total	432	3,111	3,478	69	7	40	60	1.75	22

Notes
1. % – percentage of the total effort (aircraft) lost on ops.
2. Under its ADGB title the Command flew a further 234 sorties to the end of year, claiming five aircraft and losing five.

1944 – Year of the Invasion

Once again it was offensive missions that occupied the bulk of Fighter Command (Air Defence of Great Britain) flying, although by this time it had lost a large part of its strength to the 2nd Tactical Air Force. The one exception to this was the sudden need from June onwards to provide an effective defence against the new German assault on London by the V-1 'pilotless aircraft' (flying bombs).

Defensive Operations – Second Blitz
The first V-1 Flying Bombs hit England on 13 June and the Fighter Command defence plan against these *Divers* swung into action – and immediately revealed the problems of catching and shooting-down these small, fast targets.

Although 501 Squadron was the last of the Tempest units to enter the campaign, it became one of the most successful. By 29 July the Squadron had received its full complement of Tempest Vs, and was taken off operations to carry out intensive training in *Diver* techniques, but was tasked to specialise in the night role. The squadron, under the command of V-1 ace Squadron Leader Joe Berry, moved to Manston on 2 August and two days later the ORB recorded that Sqn Ldr Rougetelle, a controller from Biggin Hill Sector, 'told us what was to be our function with the new aircraft with which we had been equipped; it was to chase flying-bombs between the coast and the North Downs, to keep a Section Patrol from Folkestone to Manston and to operate under Sandwich Control.'

The first kill went to Flying Officer Bill Polley in Tempest EJ598 on 5 August, F/Sgt Ryman (EJ585) also downed a V-1 as part of the same engagement, Bill Polley later recalled some of the problems of attacking these weapons:

> *Very often we were too close to our targets before we got the opportunity to fire, and the big danger was getting an airburst. On one occasion I was chasing a V-1 too quickly and I knew that I was overhauling the bomb too quickly and that I was very close to the armoured balloons. I fired a long burst and pulled up steeply to starboard, almost above the V-1, just as it exploded. The blast caught my left wing and tumbled the aircraft in a series of snap rolls. After what seemed an eternity, the aircraft regained its stability. . . . As my gyros had tumbled it was many ageing moments before I realised that I was upside down.*

There was a significant risk of self-damage when the bomb exploded. Joe Berry made his stance very clear. 'The squadron must consider itself expendable, and thus will take off and try to effect interception in every weather condition . . . even though all other squadrons are grounded.' The Tempest pilots flew along set patrol lines, the ends of which were marked by searchlights, and each patrol lasted some two hours. The sector controller provided positions of target and fighter, with the aim of putting the latter in an advantageous position to achieve a kill. The first intense night for 501 Squadron was 11/12 August, with the first patrol airborne at 2215; by 0140 they had claimed eight Divers, three falling to Flt Lt Thornton and three to Flt Officer Miller (an American). By

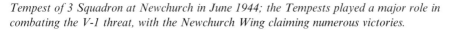

Tempest of 3 Squadron at Newchurch in June 1944; the Tempests played a major role in combating the V-1 threat, with the Newchurch Wing claiming numerous victories.

the end of the month the Squadron score was 38, four of these fell on the night of 26/27 August to Flt Lt G L Bonham – 'three of them, having expended his ammunition on the first, by tipping them over with his wing' (501 Squadron ORB). Sadly he was killed in a flying accident a month later.

Mosquito units were also active during the night hours, using radar to locate their targets.

Whilst the Allied ground offensive gradually rolled over the V-1 launching sites, putting many targets in England out of range, the Germans had already started using air-launch from an He 111. The air-launched V-1s were proving a problem and the ideal solution was to hunt down and destroy the launch aircraft. On 14 October the Mosquitoes of 25 Squadron, the unit primarily employed on this task, claimed the destruction of four He 111s, with two more probables and two damaged.

The V-1 campaign also involved the RAF's first jet fighters, the Gloster Meteors of 616 Squadron scoring a number of successes. Flt Lt Graves landed off his 3rd August sortie cursing a Mustang pilot who had got in his way just as he was setting up to finish off a 'bomb'. Success eventually came the next day with 616 destroying two of these weapons. Mid afternoon 'Dixie' Dean was airborne patrolling under the control of Kingsley 11 (Biggin Hill) ... at 1616 he spotted a bomb at 1,000 feet near Tonbridge and was cleared to give chase. Diving down from 4,500 feet and reaching 450 mph he soon

Fighter Command statistics – night operations by AI aircraft over UK and NW Europe

Date	Sorties	Contacts	Visuals	Combats	Destroyed	Probable	Damaged
Jan 1943	562	79	27	20	10	0	8
Feb 1943	554	25	11	11	7	2	2
Mar 1943	767	158	60	34	21	5	2
Apr 1943	552	50	17	8	6	0	2
May 1943	687	79	24	13	11	1	1
Jun 1943	690	74	27	16	9	1	4
Jul 1943	612	63	23	16	11	0	3
Aug 1943	860	82	27	24	16	4	3
Sep 1943	865	56	17	12	10	1	1
Oct 1943	799	145	46	24	14	1	4
Nov 1943	866	62	27	13	11	1	0
Dec 1943	495	41	11	8	4	0	3
Jan 1944	755	78	31	25	16	3	4
Feb 1944	1,102	256	81	47	26	3	10
Mar 1944	1,402	259	91	58	44	3	5
Apr 1944	1,519	208	75	47	32	4	4
May 1944	1,922	150	60	37	24	6	6
Jun 1944	2,545	262	155	112	90	7	14
Jul 1944	2,314	155	89	59	44	3	6
Aug 1944	757	162	97	75	58	3	9
Sep 1944	577	44	16	14	12	2	0
Oct 1944	813	82	31	22	20	1	1
Nov 1944	1,360	99	38	25	18	2	3
Dec 1944	263	38	6	4	2	0	1
Jan 1945	101	8	1	1	1	0	0
Feb 1945	153	1	0	0	0	0	0

Note: Table based on March 1949 Air Ministry record.

caught up with his quarry and positioned to attack it from astern ... at which point his cannon failed. Determined that it shouldn't get away he flew alongside and positioned his wingtip under the wing of the 'bomb' and then pulled up sharply; this sent the weapon out of control and it crashed about 4 miles south of Tonbridge. Another historic event had been notched up – the first jet air-to-air victory. The second 'bomb' fell at 1640 in a more conventional mode as the 20 mm cannon of Fg Off Rodgers delivered two 2 second bursts causing the weapon to explode. Dean added to his '*Diver*' score by downing another on the 7th; three days later he shot down his third. Success against '*Divers*' continued to mount and by the end of the month the squadron total stood at twelve and a half.

Offensive Operations

Mustangs joined the fray in early 1944. The 19 Squadron Operational Record Book recorded the unit's first mission with the new type: 'We now have sufficient aircraft operational to put a squadron in the air, and everyone was very keen to test out our new machines against the wily Hun. Unfortunately, the weather intervened and the show did not come off'. However, the following day, 15 February, it was different ... 'Offensive fighter sweep of Holland/Northern France by three flights of four (White, Dick, Green) led by S/L N J Durrant. Take-off 0950 and climb to 26,500 ft and cross the coast near Flushing. To avoid smoke trails angels were reduced to 25 and the Squadron swept the area Antwerp-Brussels-Cambrai without any enemy reaction and crossed out just south of Boulogne. Although uneventful, everybody felt very happy with their new kites and our cruising speed at altitude was very high (approx 250 IAS).' The Squadron flew another uneventful sweep in the afternoon.

Whilst the anti-*Diver* operations referred to above were a vital element in countering this threat, there was also an offensive element with the *Noball* and *Crossbow* operations. There were two parts to this: the routine of fighter escort to bombers attacking these targets, which was the main effort, and the employment of fighters and fighter-bombers. Once again this is where the operations of the squadrons belonging to Fighter Command

Mustang of 2 Squadron at Sawbridgeworth; this Army-Cooperation squadron was attached to the Air Spotting Pool during the D-Day landings.

Tactical air power was used to attack a wide range of targets in and around the invasion area, with radar sites being a frequent target.

(or ADGB as it now was) and the AEAF become difficult to separate. The same type of escort and offensive ops were flown by both organisations, using the same types of aircraft, although by now most Typhoons were with the AEAF.

Having spent some time with No. 85 Group of AEAF, 124 Squadron was transferred to No. 11 Group, ADGB in mid August 1944, but as the introductory comments to the ORB for that month show, this made no difference to the work being undertaken by the Spitfires. 'This month saw a great increase in the amount of operational work of the Squadron, and a corresponding increase in the enthusiasm of the pilots. At the beginning of the month with the Detling Wing we carried out a number of sweeps and close escorts to Lancasters and Halifaxes bombing Noball sites and in particular the large dumps in the caves at Creil, North of Paris. The Squadron's work was definitely now long-range; 90 Gallon tanks being invariably fitted, and needed. Chiefly escort work, such as Lancasters to Tours, and Blous (our deepest penetration), sweeps to Evreux, Nogent and the Lisieux Falaise pocket, and the Squadron strafing on return any suitable ground target – mainly MT vehicles and barges. On 15.8.44 we went to Coltishall to escort the heavies bombing all the airfields in Holland – the Squadron being allocated the Gilze-Rijen box. Some more escorts – heavies to Noball targets and mediums to strategic targets such as bridges on the Seine and one or two Rodeos, but with no luck ... these were to Mezieres, Rheims, Beauvais and Criel areas. Squadron then concentrated on practice ground attacks for a special target which had been allocated to us, but the actual attack never came off.

'On 27th August we went to Manston and then escorted the Lancasters which bombed the synthetic oil plant at Homberg-Mierbeck in the Ruhr. It was on this sortie that we first saw the jet aircraft Me 163, which attacked one of the bombers, and also

'We couldn't see much. The sky was full of American fighters, in pairs. They were wandering about rather haphazard, and showed a tendency to come and sniff at us from very close to; when they seemed too aggressive we showed our teeth and faced them.' The American fighters were not always welcome!

our Wing Leader W/Cdr Checketts. On the last day of the month we did target cover for 1½ hours over Noball areas near Amiens, and came out near Le Touquet at zero feet; F/L Melia being badly shot-up, but he managed to make landfall, and crash land at Lydd, himself unhurt but his aircraft a write-off. During the same evening an Armed Recce with some good results on MT Barges.' The Squadron flew 675 operational hours in the month. The Command's contribution to the maritime war, or rather the protection of Allied shipping against German naval, primarily submarine and E-boat, activity was also stepped-up in early 1944.

During the first week in January the Mosquitoes of 157 Squadron were operating out of Predannack on Box protection and patrols, one of which included escorting a Tsetse Mosquito (75 mm cannon) of 248 Squadron in an unsuccessful search for a damaged submarine. On 7 January the Squadron came across a pair of Ju 88s, the rear of which was engaged by Fg Off Huckin and F/Sgt Graham

> *... strikes were seen and a few minutes later the Ju 88 crashed into the seas in flames. F/O Huckin called on R/T that he was hit and was making for base, and a few minutes later called again saying both engines had failed and he was ditching. Mosquito was later seen in sea about 1½ miles from where Ju 88 had crashed, with what appeared to be a dinghy alongside it, with two occupants who waved. Dinghy was late seen in position 4708N 0730W at 1634.*

It was standard practice for squadrons to mount search patrols for aircraft that had ditched like this and at 0720 the following day, 'B Flight' was airborne. Having found nothing they returned to base. 'A Flight' was already airborne and heading for the same area and after a square search of the area found the dinghy at 1205.

> *Warwick was given a vector and successfully dropped lifeboat within 50 yards of dinghy. F/O Huckin appeared quite cheerful, both he and Graham waving frantically to the Mosquitoes. News came through later from the Warwick crew that Huckin and Graham were in lifeboat and had set course. At 1434 S/Ldr Chisholm, F/L Smyth and F/O Whitlock were airborne to give cover to F/O Huckin in case the Huns sent any aircraft to interfere with rescue operations. At 1614, 7 Ju 88s were sighted and engaged. F/O Whitlock's guns would not fire and he sustained several strikes on the windscreen. F/Lt Smyth's guns also did not fire due to a short in the electrical system. S/Ldr Chisholm closed in and engaged, and received hits in port engine and wing, he made a second attack during which his port engine seized, he made another attack and strikes were see on 88's fuselage and behind cockpit. He set course for base, coming back on one engine and made a good landing.*

On the following day the ORB continued the story: 'Nothing further heard from Huckin, but no undue concern is felt as the lifeboat they are in has ample supplies of clothing and emergency rations.' No flying was possible because of bad weather.

And on the 10th: 'S/Ldr Tappin and F/L Stevens located at 1515 F/O Huckin. They had set sail but did not appear to be moving; they both appeared to be well and waved to the Mosquitoes. Coastal Command had the Warwick out again but bad weather set in and it was recalled. Launches were known to be within 7 miles of last known position.'

Attacks on locomotives were intensified as part of the plan to shut-down German railway movement.

The following day the ORB noted that the crew had been picked-up by a naval launch 36 miles South-East of the Scillies. It was very reassuring to the aircrew to know that such efforts would be made to find and rescue them; sadly, the happy outcome relayed here was by no means always the case, although by 1944 the Air-Sea Rescue service was very efficient. For 157 Squadron their time with Fighter Command was almost over as in March they went to Valley to re-equip with Mosquitoes and AI Mk. X prior to joining No. 100 Group.

Much of the period from April onwards was spent in preparatory operations for the D-Day landings, with fighters and fighter-bombers of ADGB and 2nd TAF. A typical record of an RAF unit involved during the day was that of 602 Squadron. One of its pilots later recorded his impressions of the evening patrol:

> We flew along the Cotentin peninsula. There were fires all along the coast, and a destroyer surrounded by small boats was sinking near a little island. Our patrol zone was the area between Montebourg and Carentan. We were covering the 101st and 82nd American Airborne Divisions while the 4th Division, which had just landed, marched on Ste Mere Eglise.
>
> We couldn't see much. The sky was full of American fighters, in pairs. They were wandering about rather haphazard, and showed a tendency to come and sniff at us from very close to; when they seemed too aggressive we showed our teeth and faced them. One Mustang coming out of a cloud actually fired a burst at Graham, whose shooting was as good as his temper was bad, who opened fire in return, but luckily for the Mustang, he missed.

Jerry Jarrold was flying with 80 Squadron:

> The Squadron flew two missions on D-Day; the first involved two flights of four aircraft acting as cover for a convoy over North Foreland, with the first

Pilots of 80 Squadron at West Malling, July 1944; the Squadron was one of a number that returned from overseas to boost the UK-based fighter strength in the invasion period. (Jerry Jarrold)

four airborne at 1100 and down at 1340, and the second four, with me as No. 2, airborne at 1205 and down at 1355. It was exceptionally bad weather, and we didn't see much of the ships we were supposed to be patrolling and our patrol saw no action, but the earlier one had spotted a Ju 88 attempting to attack the ships and Fg Off Anderson had given chase, but with no result. The Squadron sent 12 Spitfires up at 1950 as escort to Albemarles towing gliders to St Aubin, with the fighters flying at 3–4,000 ft; I was not on this op.

A similar shipping cover operation was carried out by the section I was in on 7th June, but this time it was over the beachhead. We were able to observe the truly enormous number of ships of all sorts, assembling off the Normandy coast. Many big ships – I recall the massive US Battleship 'Mighty Mo' (the Missouri) with its huge guns belching out flame and smoke as it fired rounds off in the direction of Normandy. It was possible to see where the shells landed with large explosions well into France, which was a truly memorable sight. We didn't see any enemy aircraft, but the massive number of Allied fighters over the beachhead, at their allocated levels, was very impressive. Our height was 18,000 feet. As usual, the Yanks wouldn't keep to their allotted altitude and were diving about all over the place and, at times, moving into our air space. I remember 'Spud' Spurdle firing warning shots in their direction whenever they came into our allotted air space.

During the next few weeks every available aircraft was thrown into the bridgehead area to help secure the area and assist the breakout; the primary role of virtually very fighter type was to attack anything enemy that moved by land, sea or air – or anything that looked remotely suspicious. Within days, Allied fighter types were operating from rough airstrips in the beach-head area, which provided a significant boost in capability as they could rearm and refuel in the front line rather than flog back across the Channel. And so it continued for the next few months as the Allies gradually moved further inland and the role of Fighter Command in support reduced. Escort of medium and heavy

Spitfire IX MK264 of 308 Squadron; black-and-white identification stripes were painted on all tactical aircraft in the 48-hours preceding 6 June.

Mosquito of 85 Squadron at Castle Camps, April 1945; this Cambridgeshire airfield spent its entire war as home to night-fighter units.

bombers remained important, and the advent of the Mustang into the Command meant it at last had an aircraft with a good combat range.

On 7 October 1944 the North Weald Mustang Wing (129, 306, 315 squadrons) were tasked to escort the Lancasters of 617 Squadron during an attack on the Kembs Dam, on the Rhine just North of Basle. 'The first wave of bombers was to attack at 8,000 ft and the second at zero feet. No. 129 Squadron provided top cover, 315 Squadron covered the low-flying force and 306 Squadron was detailed to silence flak positions defending the dam. The approach to the target was uneventful and enemy opposition was not aroused until the first two Lancasters of the low-flying force went in to attack. The second bomber was hit by flak after crossing the dam. Meanwhile, 306 Squadron had temporarily subdued the anti-aircraft gunfire enabling the remainder of the force to place their delayed action bombs accurately. The fighters covering the target area did not turn for home until the last bomb was dropped and landed at dusk after being airborne for four and a half hours' (AHB Summary). The Lancaster of the low force dropped 12,000 lb *Tallboy* bombs and these succeeded in breaching the gates of the dam. According to Bomber Command records two of the Lancasters were shot down.

On 12 December the German fighters made a concerted attempt to disrupt the bombing attack on Witten. The escort comprised eight Mustang squadrons from Andrews Field and North Weald and in the target area, at 1400 hours, the formations were attacked by 40+ enemy fighters, a mix of 109s and 190s. The enemy was more aggressive than they had been for a while and managed to shoot down four Lancasters. Five of the attackers were shot down by the Mustangs and a further five by the bombers.

The final months
V-1s continued to land on the UK in the early months of 1945 and Dick Leggett, flying Mossies with 125 Squadron, recalled the problems of engaging the air-launched weapons.

Once the ram-jet of the flying bomb had ignited, the pilot [of the Heinkel] would quickly descend to his original height and head for home, using low stratus or sea fog to cover his retreat. During the few minutes taken to launch the missile the enemy aircraft was vulnerable to attack from the numerous night fighters which would always be in the area due to the prior warning given to us from intelligence sources. However, as winter set in, the German pilots became more adept at cutting their exposure time to a minimum, thereby avoiding interception during the launching period.

It was under these circumstances that Operation Vapour *was evolved, in early 1945, so that the Heinkels could be intercepted and destroyed whilst at low altitude. Prior to this tactic, life had been more difficult as the Heinkel could happily cruise at a speed well below the stalling speed of a Mosquito XVII. On one particular intercept, each time visual contact was attempted the severe turbulence from the slipstream of the Heinkel destabilised my aircraft and created an incipient stall. Throughout the interception my Nav/Rad, Egbert Midlane, miraculously held radar contact with the target and repeatedly guided me into his minimum AI range of 100 yards, but cloud and darkness prevented a visual sighting. We decided to wait for the greyness of dawn and were eventually rewarded by the destruction of the Heinkel as it approached Den Helder. Some 55 minutes had elapsed from the first radar contact to firing the four 20 mm cannon.'*

In the early hours of 26 March Flt Lt Jimmie Grottick of 501 Squadron made the last V-1 kill by a fighter:

It was a clear night, but without a moon. It wasn't long before I could see the 'jet light' of a V-1 at about 1,000 ft and traveling very, very fast. It was some distance ahead and about 2 miles off to the port side. I turned towards it and eventually came in through a 180 degree approach. I recollect that at the bottom of my dive and on the final approach I was clocking 580 mph! Allowing the distance to decrease, throttling back as I came into range, and then at about 300 yards down to about 200 yards I opened fire with a 3–4 second burst. There were immediate strikes and then the flame feathered ... it veered off course and dived into the ground near North Weald.

This brought to a close what had been a good record by 501 Squadron against the V-1s, with almost 100 destroyed in the period August to December 1944. The Tempests generally had proved themselves in this campaign, the three squadrons of the Newchurch Wing (3, 56 and 486) in particular having played a major role, although of the Tempest units 501 served the longest in this role.

German fighters could still be found in the latter weeks of the war even for squadrons operating from Scotland, and 19 Squadron, by this time operating Mustangs from Peterhead, recorded their 40th victory since D-Day (to bring the Squadron total to 143½) on 12 March. 'Another show was laid on escorting 44 Mosquitoes to the Kattegat. The Mosquitoes rendezvoused with us over base at 1320 and set course out to sea. Unfortunately there was a layer of 10/10 over the Kattegat and the Mosquitoes chose to patrol above it, so there was no strike, no ships being seen. They turned and set course for base and as everyone was settling down to go home, F/L Butler leading White Section, saw some aircraft passing him head on. The visibility was bad down on the sea, making it hard to identify the aircraft but they turned out to be about 10 Me 109s. A dog-fight started at once, Green and Tonic Sections also being attacked by three others.

Unfortunately, White 2, S/L M R Hill, was shot down in the melee. Also Green 2 (P/O Avery) was shot up in the first bounce and got some shell splinters in the back, however, he got back safely and is now rapidly recovering. F/L Shirreff, Green 1, was unlucky enough to have his reflector-sight bulb fuse at the critical moment. The Squadron destroyed one (the CO) and one Probable (F/L Butler)' (19 Squadron ORB).

1946–1968 – The Cold War

Until the introduction of a long-range bomber capability by the new enemy, the Russian-dominated Warsaw Pact, it could be argued that Fighter Command did not take part in any operations. Indeed, even with that threat established it did not actually take part in operations as such but was required to maintain a 24 hours a day 365 days a year capability to protect the UK from air attack, the main concern from the late 1950s being air-launched nuclear weapons.

This role became encapsulated in the maintenance of a QRA (Quick Reaction Alert) force.

As already mentioned, one of the major problems for Fighter Command in the early 1950s was the short range of its jet fighters and the lack of any real all-weather capability, although in terms of the likely threat – which until the mid 1950s was seen as minimal in terms of the UK itself – this presented few problems. The fighters 'rehearsed' with the bombers and invariably managed to 'shoot down' enough to prove that the fighter defence was effective. What was effective was the ability of the defenders to find their targets, as the control and reporting system was excellent. The situation looked a little less secure when the RAF introduced a bomber, the Canberra that out-performed the fighters!

In addition to its defensive role the Command was called on to deploy aircraft in support of other operations, such as Suez, to provide base defence or area defence. Most of these deployments were fairly low key and whilst operational in one sense did not

Meteor F8s of 56 Squadron at Waterbeach; the RAF undertook no combat ops with the Meteor but a number of Fighter Command pilots served with Australian Meteor squadrons in the Korean War.

Javelins of 23 Squadron out of Coltishall with tanker to El Adem. November 1962; the ability to rapidly deploy fighter aircraft to other theatres brought a new capability – and commitment – to Fighter Command.

involve actual combat, with the exception of the pilots loaned for ops with the Australian and American squadrons in Korea.

The creation of Strike Command in 1968 did not bring the fighter mission to an end and for the next 20+ years the main role remained that of defending British airspace against aggressors. On a routine basis this involved QRA (Quick Reaction Alert) fighters scrambling to intercept and shadow long-range Russian bombers and reconnaissance aircraft. The primary threat was from such bombers launching stand-off nuclear weapons (shades of the He 111s launching V-1s in late 1945) and the air defence network was optimized for this.

The Lightning prototype was a revolution in terms of aircraft performance and the supersonic interceptor entered service with a new Fighter doctrine of intercepting Soviet bombers some distance from the coast.

CHAPTER THREE

Operational Groups

The RAF's command structure is organised into Commands, Groups, Wings and Squadrons (with some operational units also being designated as Flights). All parts of this command structure applied to Fighter Command. Wings were employed by Fighter Command throughout the war, initially as named Wings that did not always carry a unified command responsibility but were often only a geographic grouping, and later with numbered Wings. Between 1940 and 1942 reference is made to named Wings such as the Duxford Wing and the Kenley Wing, whilst from 1943 onwards reference is made to the likes of No. 127 (Fighter) Wing. The latter Wings were often a renaming of the grouping that had been designated as an Airfield for mobile operations, so No. 127 Airfield became No. 127 Wing, and most were associated with the new Groups that became part of the Tactical Air Force.

This chapter focuses on the Groups as they were the main operational command elements. With the formation of Fighter Command in May 1936 a new series of Groups was created from the old regional groupings and was based on the perceived threat at the time and the number of airfields and squadrons in each region, the intention being to create a logical and workable command structure. When the Command formed it had a single Group – No. 11 Group – but this was joined in April 1937 by No. 12 Group. Unlike Bomber Command where the Groups specialised in particular aircraft types, the Fighter Groups maintained a mix of day and night fighters types in accordance with the strategic need, a policy that continued throughout the war as other operational Groups came and went. No. 13 Group was formed in September 1939 and the Command entered the war with the UK divided between the three Groups; however, three more were formed in 1940 as the number of airfields and squadrons continued to increase. By August 1940 the Command had six operational Groups, although those in the South-East remained the largest in terms of numbers of squadrons. Each Group was commanded by an air-ranking officer, usually of Air Commodore or Air-Vice Marshal rank, although it tends to be only those of Battle of Britain 'vintage' in No. 11 and No. 12 Group whose names are well-known; indeed only Park (No. 11 Group) and Leigh-Mallory (No. 12 Group) are well-known names, in part because of the disagreements over tactics employed in the Battle of Britain.

The Group structure remained virtually unchanged, although actual strength of squadrons varied, until mid 1943, by which time the threat to the UK had diminished and the Command was increasingly offensive oriented. First to disband was No. 14 Group, which was absorbed into No. 13 Group in July 1943. No. 9 Group vanished the following year but the other four survived to the end of the war, although No. 10 Group disbanded in May 1945 and No. 13 Group in May 1946. The latter re-formed in the mid 1950s but for most of the post-war period Fighter Command had two operational Groups – No. 11 and No. 12. The latter disbanded in March 1963 as part of a restructuring that gave it the new title of East Anglian Sector; a similar renaming took place throughout the Command – a poor decision as the 'names' did not carry the ethos of the wartime history of the Groups. When this decision was reversed the only Group number to be resurrected was No. 11 Group and it duly became part of RAF Strike Command when Fighter Command disbanded in 1968.

No. 9 (Fighter) Group

Badge: No badge was awarded.

No. 9 (Fighter) Group began to form on 9 August 1940, when it became apparent that the geographic area assigned to No. 12 Group was too unwieldy. The new Group was given the operational area of the Irish Sea, including the Isle of Man, and NW England/N Wales. This area was divided into sectors based on Jurby, Millom, Speke, Ternhill, Baginton, Harlech and Rhosneigr (later known as Valley), each of which would be allocated two fighter squadrons. This initial plan was put into effect, with the exception of the Millom and Harlech sectors. AVM W A McCloughy was appointed as the first Air-Officer-Commanding and established his HQ at Barton Hall, near Preston. This site had been requisitioned in July as home to the North-West Filter Room and so its adoption for the new Group was a logical move. The Group's first operational station was Speke (Liverpool), which opened on 24 September, with Baginton coming on line

Crews of No.1456 Flight, Honiley; the Flight was part of No.9 Group in 1942.

the following day. The Hurricane-equipped 308 (Polish) Squadron had been at Speke since 12 September but moved to Baginton on the 25th as the first of No. 9 Group's operational units.

    One of the major tasks was the defence of Liverpool and its vital docks, as well as the convoys that came and went from this port. The city had become one of the major trans-shipment ports and the flow of war material into the UK via Liverpool was absolutely essential. The Group's first success came on 8 October when Hurricanes of 312 (Czech) Squadron shot down a Ju 88 of KGr.806, which crash-landed near Bromborough Dock, three of its crew being taken prisoner. Although No. 9 Group only became operational towards the end of the Battle of Britain, its squadrons scored a number of successes against German bombers.

    Liverpool was not the only important city to be covered by the Group: Manchester and Birmingham were also afforded protection. Day and night patrols were flown by the Hurricanes and by the limited number of Beaufighters that were available, and in late 1940 the Group had an average daily availability of 80 aircraft. This pattern of activity, with an increased emphasis on night-fighter patrols, continued throughout 1941. A few successes were recorded by 68 Squadron operating out of High Ercall and 219 Sqn out of Valley, both equipped with AI Beaufighters and, from June 1941, operating under GCI control. On 3 August 1941, the Sector names were changed with Jurby becoming Andreas, Speke changing to Woodvale, Ternhill to Atcham, Baginton to Honiley, and Valley remaining unchanged. Following the formation of the USAAF's 31st Pursuit Group at Atcham in June 1942, the Group was able to call on its aircraft from time, although this unit was not under RAF operational control. No. 9 Group was also the command authority for the strike-based Merchant Ship Fighter Unit.

Penrhos was one of the airfields under the operational control of the Group during 1941.

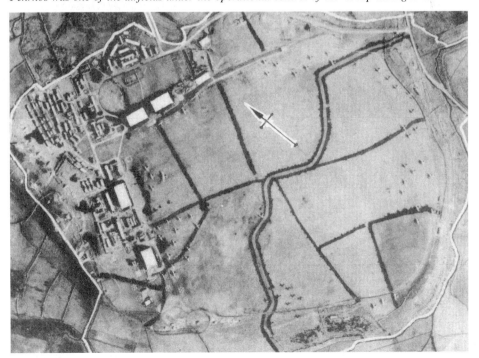

An important functional change came in April 1943 when the OTUs which had been part of No. 81 Gp were transferred on the disbandment of that Group. With 12 OTUs, numbered 51 to 62, this was an extensive training organisation, although a number of these units subsequently became Tactical Exercise Units (TEU) during 1944. First to form was No. 2 TEU, from No. 58 OTU, followed by No. 3 TEU, initially from No. 55 OTU.

As there was little or no air threat to this part of the UK, there was little need for an operational network and with the departure of 198 Squadron's Typhoons from Woodvale to Ludham on 13 May no operational day fighter squadrons were left within No. 9 Group. Thus the primary role became fighter training (OTU and TEU), as well as a continued commitment for Air-Sea Rescue. In November the number of Sectors was reduced to two, Honiley and Woodvale, the former also being home to No. 3 TEU. When the last night-fighter unit, 68 Squadron, was withdrawn in November 1944 the Group had no operational aircraft left and in the event of operational need it either used aircraft from the training units or borrowed aircraft from neighbouring Groups.

All operational commitments were transferred to No. 12 Group on 4 August 1944, but it retained control of its OTUs and TEUs. However, this was short-lived and on 17 September the Group was disbanded, the remaining units also being transferred to No. 12 Group. During its period of operation, its squadrons had claimed 36 enemy aircraft destroyed, ten probable and 27 damaged.

Air-Officer-Commanding No. 9 Group

Command from:

16 Sep 1940	AVM W A McClaughry DSO MC DFC
26 Jun 1942	Air Cdre W F Dickson CB DSO OBE AFC
18 Oct 1942	AVM W F Dickson CB DSO OBE AFC
2 Nov 1942	Air Cdre C R Steele DFC
10 Nov 1942	AVM J Whitworth Jones CB
6 Jul 1943	AVM L N Hollinghurst CB OBE DFC
11 Oct 1943	Air Cdre C A Stevens MC
7 Dec 1943	AVM D F Stevenson CBE DSO MC
15 Aug 1944	Air Cdre S D Macdonald

No. 9 Group Order of Battle, August 1940–September 1944

	Feb 1941	*Apr 1942*	*Apr 1943*
Andreas	–	452	–
Baginton	308	79	–
Cranage	96	–	–
High Ercall	–	255	41, 247
Honiley	–	246, 1456 Flt	96, 255, 285
Jurby	258	–	–
Penrhos	312	–	–
Speke	229, 312	MSFU	MSFU
Squires Gate	307	256	–
Ternhill	306	–	–
Valley	–	131, 275, 456	256, 275, 456
Woodvale	–	–	195
Wrexham	–	96, 285	–

No. 10 (Fighter) Group

Badge: A Sword Sable and a Sword Argent in saltire enfiled with an Astral Crown Or.
Motto: *Challenge*

The swords represent day and night activity and are in the shape of the Roman numeral X (10). They also indicate the fighting spirit of the Group. The Astral Crown appears to represent the RAF and was also used by No. 11 Group and No. 12 Group; it also probably signifies the realm as part of the protectors of the country symbology.

No. 10 Group had originally formed in April 1918 as a Marine Operational Group based at Calshot; it survived into the post-war period, disbanding in February 1932. In its role with Fighter Command No. 10 Group was formed – though with limited facilities – on 31 May 1940, at Rudloe Manor, Box (it did not become operational until 8 July). Accommodation was initially in tents – and just as the camp neared completion, orders were issued for it to be moved into the cover of nearby undergrowth, a task that took another week. The Group's official history details its establishment thus: 'Unusual activity began to be seen in a disused barn in the grounds of an old manor house a few miles outside Bath. Covered and guarded lorries delivered strange equipment, and RAF officers and men busied themselves around the old building. In the old barn the advance party improvised a Fighter Operations Room, with its intricate and secret apparatus for the control of aircraft, reception of warnings of approaching hostile raiders, and liaison with all the other services concerned with the defence of this country against any form of enemy attack. When No. 10 Group's skeleton organisation was established – this was done within a few hours of the arrival of the advance party – a handful of fighter squadrons from Britain's small resources were transferred, together with their airfields, to the operational and administrative control of the new Group.'

The Air-Officer-Commanding, AVM Sir Quintin Brand, was instructed to look for suitable airfields, and although Sector stations were under construction at Colerne and Middle Wallop he had to make temporary use of Exeter, Pembrey, St Eval and Warmwell. The Sector Operations Room was located at Filton. On formation, the Group had acquired four squadrons – 92 at Pembrey, 87 and 213 at Exeter, and 234 at St Eval – all from No. 11 Group. The first success came on the Group's first operational day, 8 July, when Blue Section of 234 Squadron shot down a Junkers Ju 88 off Land's End.

By mid-July there were seven squadrons in the Group – up from one the previous month. New radar stations were also entering service and by late July four Chain Home stations, west of the Isle of Wight, had been linked to the filter room at Group headquarters. To complete the warning and reporting chain, an expansion of the Observer Corps saw the establishment of an Observer Group in Devon and a sub-Group in Cornwall.

No. 10 Group was tasked with defending the entire Western and South-Western sectors of England, and its area included a number of significant military and industrial targets, such as Plymouth. August was a hectic month and according to the Group history: 'on one day in mid-August the Group flew more than 70 defensive patrols, 508 enemy aircraft were encountered and 48 were destroyed. Fifty-six more *Luftwaffe*

Hurricanes of 79 Squadron; the Squadron was part of No.10 Group whilst based at Pembrey in early 1941.

machines were destroyed in three weeks by one squadron alone; the cost was six of our pilots – four killed and two taken prisoner.'

The Group's ORB for August shows the intensity of ops in the last week of August:

August 21: 41 patrols totalling 104 aircraft were flown during the period. 60 EA operated over the Group area. Enemy losses: 234 Sqn – one Ju 88 destroyed, 152 Sqn – one Ju 88 destroyed, 238 Sqn – two Ju 88s destroyed. Our losses: 152 Sqn – one Spitfire badly damaged, 238 Sqn – one Hurricane damaged.

August 22: 31 patrols totalling 72 aircraft were flown during the previous 24 hours [note – the entry is timed at 2100 each day so it refers to the activity of the 24 hours preceding that time]. 40 EA operated over the Group's area. Enemy losses: 213 Sqn – one Ju 88 destroyed, 152 Sqn – one Ju 88 and one Do 17 destroyed. Our losses: 152 Sqn – one Spitfire damaged, pilot safe. There were no bombs dropped in the Group area during this period.

August 23: 43 patrols totalling 93 aircraft were flown. Some 152 EA operated over the Group area. Enemy losses: 152 Sqn – one Ju 88 destroyed. Our losses: one Spitfire of 152 Sqn temporarily u/s. Bombs were dropped in the following areas: Filton, Bath, Bristol, Blandford, Gloucester, Cirencester and Barry. St Eval aerodrome received nearly 1,000 incendiary bombs at 2100 hours August 22 but little damage was done.

August 24: 48 patrols involving 145 aircraft were flown. 160 EA operated in the Group area. Enemy losses: 234 Sqn – two Me 109s destroyed, one Me 109 probable, one Me 109 and one Me 110 damaged, 249 Sqn – one Me 109 destroyed. Our losses: 234 Sqn – one Spitfire Cat 3, pilot safe, 609 Sqn – one Spitfire Cat 1 and one Spitfire Cat 3, pilots safe. Bombs were reported from a number of places in S Wales and Cornwall. St Eval aerodrome was again attacked at 2119 on August 23 but little or no damage.

August 25: 44 patrols involving 129 aircraft were flown. Some 360 EA operated over the Group area. Enemy losses: 609 Sqn: four Me 109s and two Me 110s destroyed, five Me 110s probable; 92 Sqn – one Dornier type destroyed; 87 Sqn – two Ju 88s, four Me 109s and four Me 110s destroyed, one Do 17 and two Me 109s probable and three Me 109s damaged; 213 Sqn – three Me 109s, one Me 110 and one Ju 88 destroyed, two Me 110s damaged; 152 Sqn – two Me 109s and one Me 110 destroyed, one Ju 88 probable. Our losses: 609 Sqn – one Spitfire Cat 3, one Spitfire Cat 2; 92 Sqn – one Spitfire Cat 3 (Flt Lt Tuck wounded); 152 Sqn – two Spitfires missing (Plt Off Hogg, Plt Off Wildblood); 87 Sqn – one Hurricane missing (Sgt Wakeling); 213 Sqn – two Hurricanes missing (Plt Off Atkinson, Plt Off Phillipart), three Hurricanes damaged.

August 26: 46 patrols flown totalling 165 aircraft. Some 300 EA operated over the Group area. Bombs were dropped indiscriminately over a wide area. Enemy losses: 234 Sqn – six Me 109s destroyed. Our losses: one Spitfire force-landed (pilot safe).

As with the other Fighter Command Groups the post Battle of Britain period brought two major tasks – night defence and offensive operations. It is with the latter that the Group played a specific part, as its operational area was closely linked with naval activities and especially the campaign against the U-boats. The Group history records that: 'the offensive area was only limited by the range of its aircraft; far out into the Bay

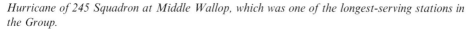

Hurricane of 245 Squadron at Middle Wallop, which was one of the longest-serving stations in the Group.

of Biscay and over NW Europe. One of the Group's most valuable contributions to the war effort was to sweep the skies over the SW Approaches clear of German long-range raiders intent on severing our shipping lanes.' Close co-operation was maintained with Coastal Command and many joint operations were flown.

Whilst offensive sweeps and bomber escort had been part of the standard tasks since mid 1941 it was with the pre D-Day 'softening up' campaign that the Group's Spitfires and Typhoons joined other tactical aircraft in attacking targets along the French coast. Radar sites, lines of communication, bridges and vehicles were hammered on an almost daily basis. In July 1944 the Group had a strength of 12 squadrons, one of which specialised in Air Sea Rescue.

With the Allies ashore and moving towards Germany the offensive role reduced and the main tasks of the Group were protection of shipping – and attacks on enemy shipping – plus the continued, but little tested, defence of its area. No. 10 Group was disbanded on 2 May 1945. Its wartime tally, according to its official history was 839 destroyed, 243 probable and 423 damaged.

Air-Officer-Commanding No. 10 Group
Command from:

Jun 1940	Air Cdre C J Q Brand KBE DSO MC DFC
22 Jul 1941	AVM A H Orlebar AFC
4 Nov 1942	AVM W F Dickson CB DSO OBE AFC
5 May 1943	AVM C R Steele DFC
10 Jul 1944	AVM B Cole-Hamilton CB CBE
1 Nov 1944	Air Cdre A V Harvey CBE

Plan of Warmwell, 1944.

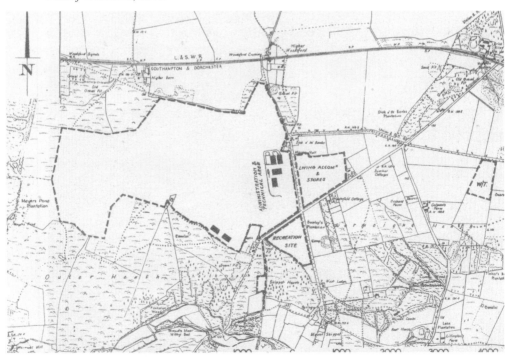

No. 10 Group Order of Battle, September 1939–July 1944

	Aug 1940	Feb 1941	1942	Apr 1943	Jul 1944
Angle	–	–	312	–	–
Bolt Head	–	–	–	307, 310	263
Boscombe Down	–	–	–	–	–
Castle Camps	–	–	–	–	68
Charmy Down	–	87	87, 1454 Flt	–	–
Chilbolton	–	238	–	–	–
Church Stanton	–	–	306	312, 313	–
Colerne	–	256	125, 286	264	–
Culmhead	–	–	–	–	126, 131, 616
Defford	–	–	–	–	–
Exeter	87, 213	263, 504	307, 308	266	–
Filton	–	501	–	–	–
Fairwood Comm.	–	–	263, 402, 615	125, 412	–
Friston	–	–	–	–	41, 610
Harrowbeer	–	–	267, 302	193, 276	–
Ibsley	–	32	118, 234, 501	129, 504, 616	–
Lympne	–	–	–	–	1, 165
Middle Wallop	238, 604, 609	93, 604	245, 604, 1458 Flt	164, 406	–
Odiham	–	–	–	174, 175	–
Pembrey	92	79, 316	–	–	–
Perranporth	–	–	130, 310	19, 130, 602	–
Portreath	–	–	66	1449 Flt	276
Predannack	–	–	247, 600, 1547 Flt	141	151, 1449 Flt
St Eval	234	234, 247, 263	–	–	–
St Mary's	–	–	1449 Flt	–	–
Warmwell	152	152, 609	175	257, 263	–
Weston-S-Mare	–	–	–	184, 286	–
Winkleigh	–	–	–	–	406

Notes
1. Chain Home – Hawks Tor, Haycastle, Warren, Worth.
2. Chain Home Low – Carnaton, Drytree, Rame Head, Strumble Head, St Twynells, West Prawle.

No. 11 (Fighter) Group

Badge: The clock tower of the Houses of Parliament proper enfiled with an Astral Crown.
Motto: *Tutela Cordis*

The tower represents London, the heart of the Empire with whose safety the Group was charged. The hands are at 11 o'clock to symbolise the time of the armistice of the Great War and the Group's number.

No. 11 (Fighter) Group was formed on 1 May 1936, under the command of AVM Sir Phillip Joubert de la Ferte. This was achieved by effectively renaming the old Fighting Area headquartered at Uxbridge. Eight main fighter stations came under its command: Biggin Hill, Duxford, Hornchurch, Kenley, Northolt, North Weald, Tangmere and Hawkinge, each with two established squadrons. Little was changed between this time and the outbreak of war other than the loss of a number of airfields and squadrons to No. 12 Group when that organisation was

Hurricanes of 111 Squadron at Northolt, with the pre-war 'code' system of having the squadron number on the aircraft.

formed in May 1937. As tension increased following the Munich Crisis in September 1938, the Group was called on to increase its state of readiness: the Operations Room was manned up on 20 March 1939, and the War Preparedness plan instituted. This lasted a week before the Group 'commenced to return quietly to normal routine', though it did give the Group what turned out to be a final chance to refine its command and control procedures. When General Mobilisation was ordered at 1630 hours on 1 September the Group had 19 operational squadrons, most of them equipped with Spitfires or Hurricanes, at eight main airfields, although satellite airfields were an important part of the Group's deployment strategy and a number of these were available.

Four squadrons were scrambled on 4 September 1939 following reports that a large number of German aircraft were massing over Holland, but no enemy aircraft were found, an indication that the control and reporting chain – and radar – were still in early days. Two days later there was further evidence that the reporting system was still not reliable. Twenty raids were plotted, based on information from RDF and the Observer Corps, indicating a major *Luftwaffe* attack up the Thames Estuary, aimed at London. Fighters were sent to intercept these aircraft, but again no Germans were found. However, at least four of the fighter formations were fired at by anti-aircraft guns and one aircraft was hit. Even worse, two Hurricanes from North Weald were shot down by Spitfires from Hornchurch, and Plt Off Houlton-Harra was killed – the so-called Battle of Barking Creek.

A number of the Group's Hurricane squadrons were deployed to France in support of the British Expeditionary Force, where they gained very useful combat experience. Although units remained officially within No. 11 Group, they were passed to the operational control of the Air Officer Commanding the Air Component of the British Expeditionary Force. However, the *Luftwaffe* seldom appeared over England and by the end of 1939, only three combats had been recorded. This situation continued for the first

Sqn Ldr Leigh, 66 Squadron, Gravesend 1940; Gravesend was a fighter base from, January 1940 but despite its key location was not attacked by the Luftwaffe during the Battle of Britain.

four months of 1940 and gave No. 11 Group valuable time to improve the reporting system, train more pilots and expand its operational capability. During the Phoney War the Group's main tasking comprised standing patrols and convoy patrols, the latter including protection for lightships and the fishing fleets, aircraft on the latter task being referred to as 'Kipper Kites'.

With a continued requirement for standing patrols, convoy and other shipping tasks, the strain on the limited resources of No. 11 Group began to tell. At the same time the organisation of the Group and of Fighter Command continued to evolve and by August 1940, No. 11 Group was operating seven Sectors: Biggin Hill, Debden (added in early August), Hornchurch, Kenley, Northolt, North Weald and Tangmere. The geographic area of responsibility had been reduced in July with the creation of No. 10 Group to cover the South-West of England, although it was a few weeks before this Group was fully operational. By that time the RAF – and No. 11 Group – was facing their real test as the *Luftwaffe* at last appeared in strength to contend for air superiority. The Battle of Britain had commenced.

Throughout the Battle of Britain, the bulk of the enemy air effort was made against targets within the area covered by No. 11 Group. At the start of the Battle, the Group fielded 21 operational squadrons, plus the Fighter Interception Unit, at 13 main stations, though only six of these squadrons were equipped with Spitfires, and 12 had Hurricanes. The course of the Battle, the rotation of squadrons to maintain the operational effectiveness of No. 11 Group, and the general management of Fighter Command were all covered in the introduction and operations chapters. For those few months in late summer and autumn 1940 the fate of the War, and in the opinion of many historians, of Western Europe, lay in the hands of a few hundred fighter pilots. Airfields such as Biggin

Hill, Hornchurch, Kenley and North Weald became household names and thousands of civilians looked up over South-England to watch the air battles and await the news bulletins that would give the daily 'scores'. According to the Group's statistical records it claimed the destruction of 2,033 enemy aircraft during the period of the Battle, including 115 of the 178 that were claimed on 'Battle of Britain Day', 15 September. The Group lost a number of aircraft that day but only eight pilots.

The removal of Keith Park in December 1940 and his replacement by Trafford Leigh-Mallory is often seen as an expression of displeasure with the former and agreement with the policies of the latter, and perhaps arose out of the Big Wing controversy. Keith Park went on to another seemingly hopeless case, the defence of Malta, and once again proved his credentials. Leigh-Mallory led Fighter Command onto the offensive and as the RAF's rising star he later became commander of the Allied Expeditionary Air Force, but that is moving ahead of this story.

The Wing concept was very much in evidence once Leigh-Mallory was in command and by February 1941 a policy had been devised whereby Wings of two or three squadrons, which also sometimes operated as two or more Wings (this larger grouping being referred to as a *Circus*), became the standard tactic to be employed whenever possible. A 17 February 1941 memorandum stated that: 'To make these operations successful, it is essential that circuses and wings be able to form up in the shortest possible time at the height required. It is intended that each Sector should produce its own wing, but the following will normally supply the wings comprising circuses:

North Weald/Debden	Hurricane Wing
Hornchurch	Spitfire Wing
Kenley	Hurricane Wing
Tangmere	Spitfire Wing

For the purposes of training and operations, the Debden wing and North Weald wing and the Hornchurch wing will be affiliated, and the Kenley and Tangmere wing will be affiliated.' This was very much the old Duxford 'Big Wing' writ large.

As the Germans did not reappear in force by day these arrangements saw no defensive employment, though when the Group turned its attention to offensive operations the Wing concept became the standard tactic. Defensive operations were still important in order to counter the not inconsiderable German night bombing, which at times involved hundreds of aircraft in a single night. By late 1940 the Group had increased its night strength to seven squadrons, some of which were 'cats eye' (no radar) and some of which were equipped with Airborne Interception (AI). Day fighter squadrons were also tasked to provide aircraft, especially when 'Fighter-nights' were called for, but in general terms these proved ineffectual, although there were a number of successes. With the night offensive continuing well into 1941, the effectiveness of the defenders gradually increased and during a large-scale raid on the night of 3/4 May the fighters claimed 12 enemy aircraft. Introduction of improved AI, better training and the Beaufighter turned the tide of the night war and by late 1941 the *Luftwaffe* raids were on a much smaller scale and incurred heavy losses in percentage terms.

Offensive operations, day and night, continued throughout the war and a number of new aircraft types (or variants) entered service, most notably the Spitfire IX as a counter to the Fw 190, and the Hawker Typhoon. No. 11 Group was heavily involved in the August 1942 Dieppe Raid, flying more than 2,000 sorties during which claims were made for 90 enemy aircraft destroyed. Throughout 1942 and 1943 the Group continued to grow and by late 1943 it comprised 57 squadrons, the bulk of which were employed

Meteor of 500 Squadron at West Malling.

on offensive operations, including the escort of light and medium bombers. Indeed of the 739 enemy aircraft claimed for 1943, offensive sorties accounted for 581, of which 54 were at night.

In mid-1944 the Group was once more called on to repel a major German offensive, this time in the form of unmanned flying bombs – the V-1s. This new campaign involved placing squadrons at airfields on the line of the approach of the V-1s, with pilots developing tactics to destroy these small, fast – and very explosive – targets. Griffon-engined Spitfires, along with Mustangs and Tempests, were all employed in the role, as was the RAF's first Meteor jet squadron, 616 Squadron. The invasion by the Allies in June 1944 brought to an end the main V-1 threat when the launching sites were over-run. It is worth noting that during the immediate period of D-Day, No. 11 Group had operational control of no fewer than 150 squadrons, including USAAF units, although this number rapidly declined as tactical aircraft moved to Europe with the 2nd TAF and IXth Air Force. In respect of the V-1s, tactics were continually being refined to cope with the threat from air-launched weapons, and on 14 November the Group issued Operational Instruction 42/1944 on the 'employment of night fighter squadrons' in regard to anti-Diver standing patrols

Air-Vice Marshal Keith Park was AOC of No. 11 Group from April to December 1940 – the most critical period for this Group and for Fighter Command.

AVM T G Pike took command of No. 11 Group in January 1950.

and readiness. In part this stated: 'The exact positioning of the out to sea patrols is left to the discretion of the North Weald controller ... it should be borne in mind by all controllers and aircrews that the primary function of the out to sea patrols is the destruction of the enemy launch aircraft; the shooting down of flying bombs being left to the overland patrols and the anti-aircraft guns.' Although the He 111 launch aircraft were small in number, they were a nuisance that Fighter Command was determined to counter.

The latter months of the war saw very little activity over England and no claims were made against German aircraft; indeed, only 72 were claimed during offensive patrols. In the period from September 1939 to February 1945, No. 11 Group aircraft claimed an impressive number of enemy aircraft – 6,540 destroyed, 1,685 probable and 2,617 damaged.

No. 11 Group remained at Uxbridge until August 1949 when it moved to Hillingdon, by which time it was organised in two Sectors – Southern and Metropolitan. Its primary task remained the home defence of Britain and jet fighters rapidly replaced the stalwart piston types which had fought the war. In July 1958 the Group HQ moved to Martlesham Heath where it remained until disbandment on 31 December 1960; this was a 'paper' disbandment, as the Group number-plate was transferred to No. 13 Group at Ouston. Despite various moves and renaming/renumbering, this historic Group has continued to be at the forefront of Britain's air defence.

The No. 11 Group title was eventually resurrected in April 1968 – but after the formation of Strike Command. It continued to be the main fighter command for the RAF.

Air-Officer-Commanding No. 11 Group
Command from:

6 Jun 1936	AVM P B Joubert de la Ferte CMG DSO
7 Sep 1936	AVM E L Gossage DSO MC
1 Feb 1940	AVM W L Welsh CB DSC AFC
20 Apr 1940	AVM K R Park MC DFC
18 Dec 1940	AVM T Leigh-Mallory CB DSO
28 Nov 1942	AVM H W L Saunders CBE NC DFC MM
1 Nov 1944	AVM J B Cole Hamilton CB CBE
20 Jul 1945	AVM D A Boyle CB AFC
24 Apr 1946	AVM S D Macdonald CBE DFC
1 Jun 1948	AVM S F Vincent CB DFC AFC
9 Jan 1950	AVM T G Pike CB CBE DFC

5 Jul 1951   AVM The Earl of Bandon CB DSO
1 Nov 1953   AVM H L Patch CB CBE
16 Jan 1956   AVM V S Bowling CBE
12 Jan 1959   AVM A Foord-Kelcey CBE AFC
1 Jan 1961   AVM H J Maguire CB DSO OBE
12 Jan 1962   AVM G T B Clayton CB DFC
As No. 11 (Northern) Sector
1 Apr 1963   Air Cdre C J Mount CBE DSO DFC
11 Jan 1964   Air Cdre W T Brooks DSO OBE AFC
1 Apr 1965   Air Cdre R J P Prichard CB CBE DFC AFC
As No. 11 Group
30 Apr 1968   AVM R I Jones CB AFC (As part of Strike Command)

No. 11 Group Order of Battle, Aug 1940–Jul 1944

	Aug 1940	Feb 1941	Apr 1942	Apr 1943	Jul 1944
Biggin Hill	32, 610	66, 74, 264	72, 124	1, 340, 611	–
Bradwell Bay	–	–	418	23, 157	219, 278
Castle Camps	–	–	157	605	–
Coltishall	–	–	–	–	229
Croydon	111	605	287	287	–
Debden	17	85	65, 111, 350	–	–
Fairlop	–	–	–	350	–
Ford	–	23	FIU	418, 604, FIU	96, 456
Friston	–	–	–	–	350, 501
Gravesend	501	141	401	277	–
Harrowbeer	–	–	–	–	64, 611
Hawkinge	–	91	91	91	–
Hendon	–	–	24, 116	–	–
Heston	–	–	1422 Flt	303, 515, 1422 Flt	–
Hornchurch	41, 65, 74	–	122, 313	64, 122	–
Hunsdon	–	–	3, 85, 1451 Flt	3, 85	–
Hurn	–	–	–	–	125
Kenley	64, 615	1, 615	485, 602	402, 403, 421	–
Lee on Solent	–	–	–	–	26, 63
Lympne	–	–	–	–	33, 74, 127
Manston	600	92	23, 32, 174, 607	137, 609	137, 605
Martlesham Heath	25, 85	17, 242, 605	71	132, 182	–
Merston	–	–	340	485	130, 303, 402
Northolt	–	303, 601	303, 316, 317	308, 315, 316	–
North Weald	56, 151	56, 259	121, 222, 403	124, 331, 332	–
Predannack	–	–	–	–	234
Redhill	–	–	457	–	–
Shoreham	–	–	–	–	277, 345
Southend	–	64	64	453	–
Stapleford Tawney	–	–	277	–	–
Tangmere	1, 266, 601, FIU	65, 145, 219	1, 23, 219	129, 486	–
Warmwell	–	–	–	–	275
West Malling	–	–	29, 264, 1452 Flt	29	80, 274
Westhampnett	145	302, 610	41, 129	165, 610	–

Radar Stations, 1940
Chain Home – Bawdsey, Bromley, Canewdon, Dunkirk, High Street, Pevensey, Rye, Ventnor
Chain Home Low – Beachy Head, Dover, Dunwich, Fairlight, Foreness, Poling, Truleigh, Walton

No. 11 Group Order of Battle, Jul 1945–Jan 1961

	Jul 1945	Apr 1953	Jan 1961
Andrews Field	306, 309, 315	–	–
Bentwaters	64, 65, 118, 126	–	–
Biggin Hill	–	41/253, 600, 615	–
Breighton	–	–	112
Carnaby	–	–	247
Castle Camps	25	–	–
Chilbolton	183	–	–
Chivenor	–	–	229 OCU
Colerne	74	–	–
Dunholme Lodge	–	–	141
Duxford	–	64, 65	–
Filton	–	501	–
Harrowbeer	275, 329	–	–
Leconfield	–	–	19, 72
Leeming	–	–	228 OCU
Leuchars	–	–	29, 43, 151
Llandow	–	614	–
Manston	29, 310, 312, 313	–	–
Middleton St George	–	–	33, 92
Misson	–	–	94
North Coates	–	–	264
North Weald	–	72, 601, 604	–
Odiham	–	54, 247	–
Predannack	151, 406	–	–
Tangmere	–	1, 22/29	–
Waterbeach	–	56, 63	–
Wattisham	–	257, 263	–
West Malling	–	25, 85, 500	–
Woodhall Spa	–	–	222

Air photo of North Weald with runways highlighted to show layout in late 1944.

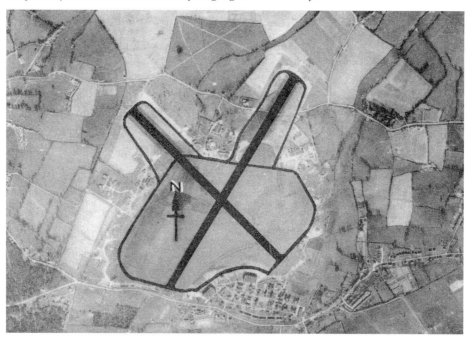

No. 12 (Fighter) Group

Badge: A Sword in pale point downwards Argent hilted Or
enfiled with an Astral Crown Or.
Motto: We Fight to Defend

The Crown represents the RAF, whilst the sword indicates
the operational function of the Group.

No. 12 (Fighter) Group was formed on 1 April 1937, at
Uxbridge under the command of Air Commodore J H
Tyssen, and in May the HQ staff moved to Hucknall. Initial
establishment was five squadrons and the main Stations were
Catterick, Church Fenton and Duxford. In December,
Trafford Leigh-Mallory arrived as Air-Officer-Commanding
and was to lead the Group through the Battle of Britain – with no small amount of
controversy.

Throughout 1938 the Group practised for its task of defending Central England and
the East coast, with Sector Operations Rooms having been established at Catterick,
Church Fenton, Digby and Duxford. The main training effort took place with the weekly
Tactical Exercise during which Bomber Command provided a 'live' enemy. The scale of
these exercises was increased at the end of the year with the introduction of the Fighter
Command Minor Air Exercise. It was a similar pattern into 1939 although on the
outbreak of war the Group began to focus on its wartime tasks of patrols and scrambles,
the former primarily involving convoy work.

The Group HQ had moved to Watnall on 8 May 1940, and this remained its home
throughout the war. With the retreat of the British Expeditionary Force, the Group was
amongst the Fighter Command organisations tasked to provide air cover in the Dunkirk
area and on 2 June 1940, five squadrons were ordered to be over the beaches at 0700. The
Group ORB recorded the day's events: 'several Group squadrons were again in action
over the Dunkirk area, with very satisfactory results. Squadrons 266, 32, 92, 611 and 66
were ordered to patrol the Dunkirk area at 0700 hours. Squadron 92 were in the main
ordered to attack the bombers and the other four squadrons were to act as an escort and
deal with the enemy fighters. On arriving over their patrol area several formations of
Ju 87s and He 111s escorted by Me 109s were sighted and in the battles that followed
some of the squadrons became split and individual combats took place. It is estimated
that at least 16 E/A were destroyed and a further 26 either probably destroyed or
damaged severely. Eight of our aircraft are missing.'

Over the next few days the Group forward-deployed squadrons, with four stationed
at Martlesham in case further such patrols were required. Although the *Luftwaffe*
was not yet attacking Britain by day it had opened its night offensive and the Group
ORB for 19 June recorded that: 'there was considerable hostile activity over the East
Coast especially in East Anglia during the night 18/19 June. Bombs were dropped near
Scunthorpe, King's Lynn, Waddington and Louth. However, the enemy suffered several
casualties during these night operations, as there was very successful co-operation
between the searchlights and our fighters. In all, five He 111s were shot down and two
more probably did not reach their home base.'

The ORB recorded victories for Flt Lt Duke-Woolley (23 Sqn), Fg Off Barnwell and
Plt Off Humphries (both 29 Sqn) and Fg Off Ball and Fg Off Petre (both 19 Sqn).

Hurricane of 151 Squadron at Digby; the Squadron arrived here in September 1940.

During a conference at Fighter Command on 3 July 1940, Dowding proposed changes that would affect No. 12 Group; the minutes of the conference state his view that: 'what was proposed [in terms of area of responsibility] was too big a job for No. 12 Group, especially if there were heavy operations in the East and West simultaneously. He proposed that No. 13 Group should take control of Church Fenton and Squires Gate and that No. 12 Group be split down the middle so that it would control a long narrow strip facing east [and a new Group – No. 9 Group – would take the area to the West].'

No. 9 Group formed in July 1940 but its was some weeks before it took operational control of all the airfields within its area, with responsibility remaining with No. 12 Group until the AOC of the new organisation was happy to assume control. This was particularly important in respect of key locations such as Liverpool and Manchester. In a 27 September memo, Fighter Command stated that: '. . . attention is drawn to the great importance of improving the fighter defences of Liverpool without delay. AOC No. 12 Group is instructed to maintain a full fighter squadron at Ringway or Ternhill. He should support this with the equivalent of at least a Flight of Blenheims or Defiants for night interception.' It was not until 1 December that No. 9 Group finally took control of the Speke and Ternhill Sectors.

The Battle of Britain opened for No. 12 Group with a continuation of the well-established, and invariably unproductive, convoy patrols. During July the Group's squadrons flew 1,100 such patrols, involving 2,668 operational flights. Activity increased during August as the Germans began a period of intense operations designed to cripple Fighter Command. The number of large-scale raids within the Group's area was limited, although on 15 August the ORB recorded: 'there was tremendous enemy activity all around the coast of England today and for the first time they paid a mass daylight visit to the Group – a day they will probably remember. Raid 10 was first plotted as 20 plus, then as 30 plus aircraft. The object of this attack was Driffield aerodrome. Squadron 616 and 73 ("A" Flight) dealt with it. The enemy consisted of about 40 Ju 88s escorted by Me 110s who apparently completely failed in their mission as only a few were seen by our pilots. Some of the enemy bombers reached their objective and in all about 80 bombs fell on and around the aerodrome. Three hangars were fired and the Officers' Mess and

Defiant of 151 Squadron wrapped up against the snow at Wittering.

AA HQ were severely damaged. However, the losses inflicted on the enemy by these two squadrons were tremendous – 15 Ju 88s were destroyed, 7 probably destroyed and 4 more badly damaged. In addition at least six more Ju 88s were shot down by the ground defences.'

Whilst, as usual, the actual number of losses was not as great as claimed, it was certainly a decisive victory for the defenders, and the *Luftwaffe*'s hope that the battles in the South had drawn away Fighter Command's squadrons was convincingly negated. Whilst Driffield might have suffered on this occasion, the threat to the airfields within No. 11 Group was far more serious and led to acrimony between the commanders of the two Groups, the essence of which has been previously outlined.

Typical of the ORB entries for No. 12 Group is that for 30 August: 'there was again intense activity in No. 11 Group and squadrons 242, 611, 310 and 19 were despatched to assist. Of these only 242 Squadron contacted the enemy and this they did in no uncertain manner claiming 8 Me 110s and 4 He 111s destroyed plus 3 probable He 111s.'

There are very few references in No. 12 Group's documents to the relationship with its neighbour, and certainly none (that the author found) that are as outspoken as those issued by Keith Park. The first entry in the ORB for the 'Big Wing' type of operation occurred on 7 September: 'a new and highly successful policy was begun when a No. 12 Group Wing was formed to assist No. 11 Group. This Wing consisted of three squadrons based at Duxford.' And again a few weeks later, 9 September: 'during the day only one raid crossed the coast in the Group area but the Wing were again despatched to 11 Group where they fought a most successful action.'

The three squadrons, led by Douglas Bader, were 19, 242 and 310 and they claimed 21 destroyed, five probable and two damaged for the loss of four aircraft. 'The method of attack was that 19 Squadron should attack the fighters, and squadrons 310 and 242 should deal with the bombers.'

Park argued that all too often the Wing was too late in getting airborne, didn't go where he asked and most times did not even make contact with the enemy. There is some truth in this and the records of No. 12 Group show that on many occasions no contact was made, they also show high levels of claims when contact was made.

Although No. 12 Group was the second busiest of Fighter Command's operational Groups its overall level of activity relative to its southerly neighbour is demonstrated by the operational flying hours for August 1940 when No. 11 Group flew 12,853 hours and No. 12 Group only a third of that at 4,076 hours. With the exception of the Wing operations, there was very little daylight activity over the Group area for 1940 or 1941, but it was a different story at night. The scale of the night attacks varied from a few isolated raiders to concentrated attacks against a single target by 50 or more bombers. Countering the night attacks on Britain's industrial heartland became one of the Group's major tasks and one for which it was at first ill-equipped. Although the Battle of Britain officially ended on 31 October the night war continued well into 1941. The night of 15 November was recorded as: 'the enemy launched by far his biggest attack on the Group area during the night and Coventry was the main objective. Wave after wave of bombers attacked this city from about 1915 hours till 0530 hours from heights varying from 10–20,000 ft. Our fighters were sent up but had no success, but the AA with a limited number of guns put up as heavy a barrage as they could. The weather was perfect with a full moon and good visibility.' Considering the weather conditions and the number of enemy aircraft the poor performance of the defenders illustrates the limited capability. Indeed so desperate did the defence become that Bomber Command Hampdens were called on to fly defensive patrols over some cities in the Midlands. From mid to late December Liverpool was the focus of the attack but again the defenders achieved few successes. One of the problems in this area was lack of RDF and a number of new stations became operational in early 1941 to try to fill in the blind spots. Heavy night attacks continued into 1941 and it was only the gradual improvement in GCI, along with better aircraft (Beaufighters and Mosquitoes), that the tables eventually turned and the night skies over England were made secure.

Javelin of 85 Squadron at Stradishall; No.12 Group was disbanded on 31 March 1963, when it was re-designated as East Anglian Sector.

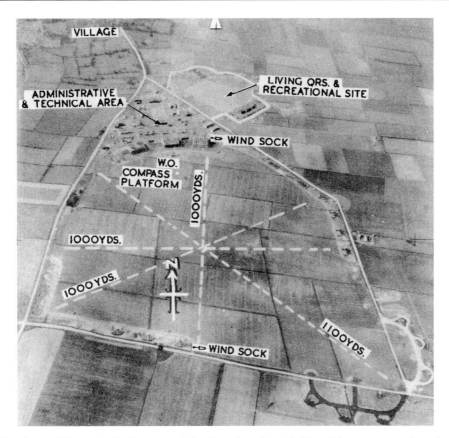

Air photo of Kirton-in-Lindsey, one of the Group's main airfields and home to a number of day and night squadrons.

Offensive operations by day and night, the former primarily being Wing sweeps 'looking for trouble' became the routine, and whilst activity was never on the scale of that by No. 11 Group, the general principles were the same. In this way No. 12 Group saw out the rest of World War Two, providing aircraft for the major operations such as D-Day.

During the 1950s, the Group's Sectors were reorganised to become Eastern Sector and Western Sector and its squadrons re-equipped with the first generation of jet fighters. No. 12 Group was disbanded on 31 March 1963, when it was redesignated as No. 12 East Anglian Sector.

It was based at Horsham St Faith (Norwich) until 29 May 1963 when it moved to Neatishead, which also became one of the main Fighter Control stations in the RAF. The No. 12 designation was lost on 1 April 1968 when, on the formation of Strike Command, the Sector became part of No. 11 Group as Sector North; a sad and almost unremarkable end to a famous fighter Group.

Air-Officer-Commanding No. 12 Group
Command from:

    1 Apr 1937   Air Cdre J H S Tysson MC
    4 Dec 1937   AVM T L Mallory DSO

17 Dec 1940   AVM R B Saul CB DFC
29 Nov 1942   AVM J O Andrews CB DSO MC
26 Jul 1943   AVM R M Hill CB MC AFC
22 Nov 1943   AVM M Henderson CBE CIE DSO
1 Jan 1945   AVM J W Baker CB MC DFC
5 May 1946   AVM T C Traill OBE DFC
17 Nov 1948   AVM G Harcourt-Smith CB CBE MVO
1 Jan 1951   AVM R L R Atcherley CB CBE AFC
13 Nov 1953   AVM W J Crisham CB CBE
25 Jun 1956   AVM H P Fraser CB CBE AFC
20 Jul 1959   AVM Sir Christopher H Hartley CBE DFC AFC BA KCB
1 Jan 1961   AVM R N Bateson DSO CB DFC
As No. 12 (East Anglian) Sector
1 Apr 1963   AVM F D S Scott-Malden DSO DFC*
25 Mar 1964   Air Cdre A C Deere DSO OBE DFC*

Air-Vice Marshal Trafford Leigh Mallory was AOC of No.12 Group from December 1937 to December 1940 and was an exponent of the 'Big Wing' tactic. He is seen here later in the war.

No. 12 Group Order of Battle, Aug 1940–July 1944

	Aug 1940	Feb 1941	Apr 1942	Apr 1943	Jul 1944
Church Fenton	–	–	885 FAA	25, 183	307
Collyweston	23		–	–	–
Coltishall	66, 242		68, 154, 278	56, 68, 118, 278	25
Digby	29, 46, 611	2 RCAF, 29, 46	288, 409, 411, 412, 609	288, 410, 411	504
Driffield	–	1 RCAF	–	–	–
Duxford	–	19, 310	266, 609	–	–
Fowlmere	19		154	–	–
Hibaldstow	–	–	253, 1459 Flt	–	–
Hutton Cranswick	–	–	19	306	–
Kingscliffe	–	–	616	–	–
Kirton-in-Lindsey	222, 264	71, 255, 616	133, 486	302, 317	–
Ludham	–	–	610	167	–
Matlask	–	–	137	–	–
Snailwell	–	–	56	181	–
Wittering	229	25, 151, 266	151, 1453 Flt	151	–

Radar Stations, 1940

Chain Home – Easington, Stenigot, Staxton Wold, Stoke Holy Cross, West Beckham
Chain Home Low – Flamborough Head, Happisburgh, Ingoldmells

No. 12 Group Order of Battle, July 1945–Jan 1961

	Jul 1945	Apr 1953	Jan 1961
Abbotsinch	–	602	–
Acklington	19		–
Aldergrove	–	502	–
Chilbolton	26		–
Church Fenton	125	19/152, 609	–
Coltishall	303, 307, 316	23, 141	23, 74, AFDS
Digby	441, 442		–
Dyce	–	612	–
Duxford	–	–	64, 65
Finningley	–	616	–
Honiley	–	605	–
Hooton Park	–	610, 611	–
Horsham St Faith	–	74/34, 245	–
Hutton Cranswick	–	124	–
Leuchars	–	43/17, 151, 222	–
Linton-on-Ouse	–	66, 92, 264, 275	–
Ludham	–	1, 91	–
Marham	–	–	242
Ouston	–	607	–
Rattlesden	–	–	266
Ringway	–	613	–
Stradishall	–	–	1, 54
Thornaby	–	608	–
Turnhouse	–	603	–
Warboys	–	–	257
Waterbeach	–	–	25, 46
Wattisham	–	–	41, 56, 111
Watton	–	–	263
West Raynham	–	–	85, CFE
Woolfox Lodge	–	–	62
Wymeswold	–	504	

No. 13 (Fighter) Group

Badge: A Pomme pierced by an Arrow Or
Motto: *Non cramben sed carnem* – Not cabbage but meat.

The badge symbolises the high standard of accuracy and marksmanship within the Group, comparable to that of William Tell (or Robin Hood?). With the words prefaced by 'We want' the motto is intended to convey the same idea as the Russian Marshal Budenny's war cry of 'We are not vegetarians!' A strange choice and with no obvious reason.

No. 13 (Fighter) Group was officially formed at Kenton Bar, Newcastle-upon-Tyne, on 24 July 1939, under the command of Air Vice Marshal R E Saul DFC, as part of the reorganisation of Fighter Command. The Group had existed in the latter part of World War One, having been formed in Birmingham in April 1918 and subsequently designated No. 13 (Training) Group before merging with No. 3 (Training) Group in October 1919.

When it re-formed in 1939 in the fighter role, the Group had responsibility for the air defence of the UK from North Yorkshire northwards. Initially it comprised four Sectors (M, O, P and S) with four main Stations – Catterick, Church Fenton, Turnhouse and Usworth – housing seven fighter squadrons, three of which were equipped with Spitfires, the others flying Gladiators (two squadrons), Blenheims or Hinds. Two AA Divisions were affiliated to the Group: 2nd AA Division covering the Tyne and Tees area and 3rd AA Division covering the Firth of Forth and Clyde area. With the outbreak of war the squadrons came to high readiness and a number of scrambles took place, most without a sight of the enemy. However, on 16 October 1939, aircraft of 602 and 603 Squadrons intercepted a German raid over the Firth of Forth and shot down two He 111s – the first German aircraft destroyed over the UK since 1918. The first German bomber fell to a combined attack by Flt Lt Gifford, Fg Off McDonald and Plt Off Robertson of 603 Sqn; 15 minutes later the second one was shot down by the Hurricanes of 602 Sqn. The auxiliaries had scored the first aerial victories over Britain. Fears were expressed about the need for more co-ordination of friendly aircraft: 'movement of heavy bombers of No. 4 Group caused many false raid reports this day, resulting in many patrols being despatched' (No. 13 Group ORB 24 November 1939). The Group sent up ten patrols, totalling 31 aircraft, with Turnhouse the most active station, despatching six patrols of three aircraft each.

Patrol activity and convoy escort continued into 1940 and by August the Group had 12 operational squadrons dispersed at eight main locations, covering a very large geographic area which included Northern Ireland (245 Squadron's Hurricanes were based at Aldergrove.) In addition to the huge area to be covered, the Group also encountered problems over the condition of many of its airfields and there is frequent reference in the records to an airfield being unserviceable for either day or night operations or being limited to certain aircraft types. Although patrol activity, including shipping standing patrols, was maintained throughout the winter, it was generally a quiet period. In February a new patrol was instigated to protect the Grimsby fishing fleet, a day sweep by Blenheims being alternated between No. 13 Group and No. 12 Group.

In the summer of 1940 the pace of activity increased, initially with more shipping patrols. The *Luftwaffe* attempted a number of raids into the Group area: a large raid

Hurricanes at Wick, an airfield initially allocated to No.13 Group but later transferred to No.14 Group. (Andy Thomas Collection).

of more than 100 bombers with an escort of over 50 fighters was intercepted west of the Firth of Forth on 15 August by Spitfires of 72 Squadron, four other squadrons subsequently joining in the combat. On this one day of intense activity, the Group's squadrons claimed to have destroyed 91 enemy aircraft, with a further 44 claimed as probably destroyed and 28 damaged.

In the period 3 September 1939 to 10 October 1940, the Group's squadrons claimed 95 enemy aircraft destroyed and 46 damaged (there was no 'probable' category for most of this period.)

With the ending of the Battle of Britain and the termination of large-scale daylight attacks, the main enemy activity comprised minelaying, both by day and night, and night bombing attacks on industrial centres. At times the latter could be on a significant scale, with over 100 aircraft operating in a single night: one of the major changes in the Group's Order of Battle was an increase in night fighter units. In mid-1940 the night-fighter force comprised one squadron of Defiants (141 Sqn) and one squadron of Blenheims (219 Sqn) but by late 1941 this had been increased by a further three units, with the AI-equipped Beaufighter as the main type.

The geographic area covered by No. 13 Gp was very large and in order to provide fighter cover it made use of a number of airfields that were not under its command,

Typhoon of 1 Squadron at Acklington, 1942; the Squadron spent the last six months of 1942 at Acklington. (Peter Green Collection)

or which were only under command for a short period of time. Usworth, for example, was used by the Hurricanes of 607 Squadron between August 1939 and January 1941, 43 Squadron taking its place from September to December 1940. Other airfields, like Montrose, were used for a brief period by one or more fighter detachments.

With a general lowering of the threat during 1942, the number of squadrons was reduced. By January 1943, the Group had nine squadrons, of which seven were

Map showing airfields used by No's.13 and 14 Groups, plus destruction of enemy aircraft.

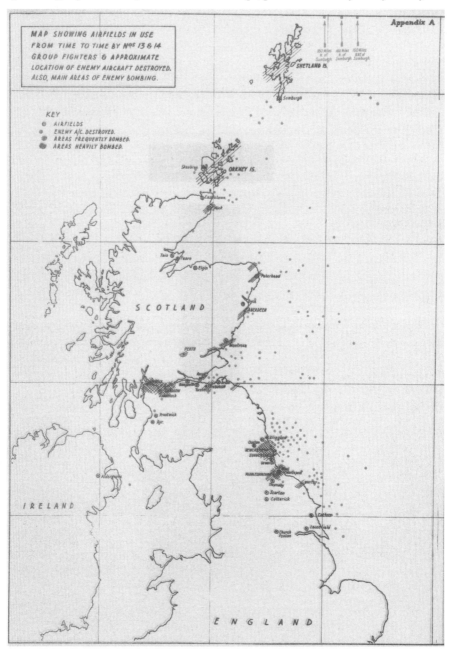

front-line operational units: four of these were in the night fighter role. However, in June the Group was boosted by the acquisition of No. 32 Wing with its Army Co-operation units, this Command having been absorbed by Fighter Command. This development included the acquisition of three new Stations – Macmerry, Kirknewton and Findo Gask. Two months later No. 13 Group moved its HQ from Newcastle to Inverness.

The number of combat opportunities had decreased from late 1940 onwards and whilst the Group claimed the destruction of almost 100 enemy aircraft in the year to 14 October 1940, it only claimed 73 over the next three years. Statistics for the period 1 October 1940 to 15 July 1943, were 73 destroyed, seven probable and 34 damaged.

The general reduction in operational units continued as air assets were moved south in 1944 for D-Day; by June only two squadrons were still on strength. A new role was acquired when these squadrons, soon joined by a third, began operating in conjunction with Coastal Command on offensive operations, primarily as escort to strike aircraft such as Beaufighters and Mosquitoes, against enemy shipping and U-boats in the North Sea and off Norway. Ground targets in Norway were also attacked by the Mustang III squadrons. These tasks continued to the end of the war – Wick, in NE Scotland, having become the main operational base. For the period from 15 July 1943 to VE Day (8 May 1945), the Group claimed 33 enemy aircraft destroyed, six probable and seven damaged.

A move from Inverness to Dalcross was brought about by the return to peace-time considerations. The ORB states: 'Like many HQ units No. 13 Group was entirely accommodated, both for office and domestic accommodation, in requisitioned property. On the cessation of hostilities and the reversion of the Country to normal peacetime conditions this HQ has of necessity to move to a fresh location and RAF Dalcross has been selected.' There appeared to have been no hurry, however, and although the move was promulgated in August it was not due to take effect until 7 December. The move

Air photo of Skeabrae.

actually took place in November, by which time the Group had five squadrons at two Stations: Wick (91, 122 and 316 Sqns) and Turnhouse (164 and 303 Sqns). The Group disbanded on 20 May 1946, but was subsequently re-formed on 4 April 1955, at Watnall, again in the fighter role. On 1 January 1961, it was merged with No. 11 Group.

Air-Officer-Commanding No. 13 Group
Command from:

24 Jul 1939	AVM R E Saul DFC
4 Feb 1941	AVM J O Andrews DSO MC
27 Nov 1942	AVM M Henderson CB CIE DSO
15 Nov 1943	Air Cdre S F Vincent DFC AFC
26 Jan 1944	Air Cdre J A Boret CBE MC AFC
3 May 1945	Air Cdre T B Prickman CBE CB
Apr 1955–Jan 1961	No details available.

No. 13 Group Order of Battle

	Aug 1940	Feb 1941	Apr 1942	Apr 1943	Jul 1944
Acklington	72, 79	72, 315	43, 141, 1460 Flt	198, 409	–
Aldergrove	245	245	–	–	–
Ayr	–	–	134, 406	222, 488	–
Castletown	504, 808 FAA	–	–	–	–
Catterick	54	54, 68, 600	332	219, 401	–
Church Fenton	73, 249	–		–	–
Drem	602, 605	43, 603	410, 611	65, 197	309
Grangemouth	263	–		–	–
Leconfield	616	–		–	–
Leeming	219	–		–	–
Ouston	–	–	281, 410, 1423 Flt	281	–
Prestwick	141	602		–	–
Skeabrae	–	–	–	–	118
Sumburgh	232	–		–	–
Turnhouse	253, 603	–	81, 289	289, 341	–
Usworth	607	–		–	–
Wick	3, 804 FAA	–		–	–

Radar Stations, 1940
Chain Home – Anstruther, Bamburgh, Danby Beacon, Doonues Hill, Drone Hill, Hillhead, Nether Burton, Ottercops Moss, Shotton, St Cyrus, Thriumster
Chain Home Low– Cockburnspath, Cresswell, Douglas Wood, Fair Isle, Rosehearty, School Hill

---

No. 14 (Fighter) Group

Badge: No badge was awarded.

The Group originally formed in April 1918 as a Marine Operational Group at Pembroke, although this was short-lived as it disbanded in May 1919. It re-formed on 20 June 1940 by renumbering No. 60 Wing. However, with the collapse of the RAF's operations in France the Group disbanded in May. It re-formed again on 1 August at the Drumossie Hotel, Inverness.

On 1 September the Group took operational control of Castletown and Skeabrea as well as the Sector Station at Wick and Sector HQ at Dyce; however, it was not until October that a squadron in this Group made an operational flight.

The first three operational patrols in response to plotted raids were made on 14 October: '3 operational patrols were carried out by 7 aircraft. Communications with Wick was difficult, owing to the changing over of Service lines. No. 3 Squadron moved from Wick to Castletown and 232 Squadron from Castletown to Skitten.' On 16 October the Group ORB noted the first bombs dropped in its area, with a number of patrols flown but no contact with the enemy. The Sector Operational Control moved from Wick to Kirkwall the same day.

Raids were plotted each day for the rest of October but despite patrols and scrambles no contact was made, although the attack on Montrose airfield on 25 October and that on Lossiemouth the following day caused casualties and damage. It was a similar story of day and night raids, all small-scale, plus attacks on shipping, in early November but it was not until 13 November that the Group ORB claimed a success: 'A He 111 was intercepted and shot-down in the sea 40 miles SE of Aberdeen. The personnel engaged were P/O P J Simpson, Sgt Kucera and Sgt Mansfeld.' The next intercept took place on 25 November when Blue Section of 3 Squadron engaged a Whitley. There were suspicions that it was a captured aircraft and after warning had been ignored the fighters attacked and damaged the port engine: 'No. 1 (fighter) opened his hood and pointed towards Wick. The Whitley then turned and went in that direction. At this point the Whitley fired the correct signals and flashed correct colour of the day. The Whitley made a crash-landing on Wick aerodrome; none of the crew were injured.'

Interceptions of friendly but unidentified aircraft became routine for fighters in the Group's area, as did frequent fruitless patrolling. On many days there was no enemy activity recorded, on others it was a 'routine' reconnaissance flight observed passing through the area, and from December 1940 it was the increasing number attacks on shipping. On 22 December a convoy was attacked off Oban and 24,000 tons of shipping sunk – with no apparent response from the defenders. However, it has to be remembered that this was a large operational area and had few fighter squadrons.

The usual 'customers' were Ju 88s and He 111s, with both attacking a variety of targets, most often as a single aircraft hit-and-run attack.

This low level of activity continued throughout 1941 with shipping as the most frequent targets, although aircraft occasionally bombed airfields or towns. It must have been very frustrating for No. 14 Group's controllers and pilots as patrols were made but there were very few records of combat – and even fewer notes of any success. By early 1942 there was very little aerial activity directed at this area – perhaps 5 or 6 days a month when 'raids plotted' and it was more usual for the ORB to note 'the Atlantic and North Sea recce were plotted as usual'. On 2 March 1942 one of the latter was 'intercepted by a Coastal Beaufighter under Fighter Control from Sumburgh. The Beaufighter opened fire but no results were observed and the E/A escaped into cloud.'

The ORB for October 1942 recorded: 'Enemy activity in the Group area was mainly confined to the 2 weather recces which were plotted on most days. From 6th instant, Beaufighters of 125 Squadron attached from No. 10 Group operated from Sumburgh with a main objective of intercepting these recces. They were armed with 4 cannon and 6 MGs. Of a total of 8 interceptions affected during the month 5 were made by this squadron. The results were 4 interceptions without combat, 4 combats in one of which the E/A was probably destroyed, in 2 the E/A was damaged and in the other case no claim was made.' The Squadron continued its success in November: 'During the month,

Spitfires of 123 Squadron at Castletown, December 1941. (Andy Thomas Collection).

4 interceptions took place, 2 of which resulted in combats. The enemy North Sea Zenit was destroyed on these occasions by Beaufighters of 125 Squadron.' However, the month also saw a decrease in size of the Group when 'Sector Stations at Tain, Tiree and Stornoway were put on a care and maintenance basis at the end of the month', although Fordoun had become operational on 2 November (but was used by a training unit).

The ORB for February 1943 noted:' during the month there was slight increase in the number of hostile recces in the Group area and for the first time since 7.8.42 bombs were dropped. For the first time Typhoon aircraft (245 Squadron) made their appearance in the Group area.' The bombs were dropped on Fraserhead and Peterborough on

Air photo of Castletown.

20 February. On the last day of the month the Group moved its HQ to Raigmore. The next few months remained quiet and on 7 June a meeting was held with officers from No. 13 Group concerning the proposed amalgamation of the two Groups. A week later (15 March) the ORB noted:' Turnhouse Sector commenced operating under No. 14 Group from 0830 hours. The Group area now covers the whole of Scotland.' The final entry was for 15 July:' There was no evidence of enemy activity up till 0800 hours at which time the amalgamation of 13 and 14 Groups took effect and 14 Group ceased to exist.'

With the reduction in the air threat to the UK, Fighter Command reorganised its structure in July 1943, part of which saw No. 14 Group disband to be amalgamated with No. 13 Group, with effect from 15 July.

Air-Officer-Commanding No. 14 Group
Command from:

31 Jul 1940	AVM M Henderson CB CIE DSO
28 Jan 1942	Air Cdre W H Dunn DSC
21 Mar 1942	AVM Collishaw CB DSC DSO DFC OBE

No. 14 Group Order of Battle, 1940–1943

	Feb 1941	Apr 1942	Apr 1943
Castletown	3, 213		131, 282
Dyce	111		–
Elgin	232		–
Montrose	111		–
Peterhead			245
Skarbrae	253, 260		66, 234
Sumburgh	3		–

CHAPTER FOUR

Aircrew Training

W hat makes a fighter pilot? This question was addressed by the major conference that took place in early 1942 to discuss aircrew training; the report opened with a series of statements as to what was required of a fighter pilot.

'Except for greater speed, higher ceiling, fire-power and armour, there is essentially little difference between aerial combat to-day and that in the latter part of the last war. Speed has been gained at the expense of manoeuvrability, but the fleeting instants in which targets present themselves are compensated for by greatly-increased fire-power. Thus, the first requirement of a pilot who has learned to handle his aircraft is an ability to seize his limited opportunities, and, having done so, to shoot accurately when an opportunity is presented. Such work calls for an instant response from hand and eye, together with the capacity to endure a considerable strain concentrated into a short but decisive period of time'.

The report went on to address a number of key elements, extracts of which are included below.

Aircraft performance: 'A good fighter pilot must feel himself part of his aircraft. He must be well aware of its powers of manoeuvrability at all altitudes and in every condition of weather, its offensive power, and its vulnerability to attack.'

Gunnery: 'He should have a capacity for taking infinite pains to perfect the tactical side of flying and most important of all, gunnery. In the last war the most successful fighter pilots spent much time on the ground in perfecting their gunnery and in devising new methods of attack; and no system of training can fully succeed if it does stimulate the same interest and enthusiasm.'

Fuel awareness: 'While the speed of a fighter is great, its endurance is small and the constant concern of a pilot is his petrol consumption. ... a pilot cannot achieve an economical standard unless he is trained to understand the capabilities and limitations of his engine and can extract the best performance from it.'

Aircraft recognition and lookout: 'It is vital that a fighter pilot should be trained to recognise friend from foe at the first glance and at maximum distance. This entails constant practice, and intensive study of models and photographs throughout the training period. The importance of "rubbernecking" must be instilled into every pupil from the very beginning of his training, so that the whole time he is flying he is studying the sky and making a mental note of the type, position, course and height of every aircraft he sees. He must be made to realise that for every aircraft he doe see there is probably another he does not; and that he must be watchful and alert from the moment that he enters his aircraft.'

Oxygen and Blacking-out: 'The rate of climb, ceiling and speed of fighter aircraft are responsible for several problems, principal among them are oxygen and blacking-out. One object of training should be to kill the fallacy that oxygen is necessary for height only. It is, of course, essential at high altitudes, but it is also necessary long before the need for it becomes physically apparent to the pilot if his mental alertness is to be kept at concert pitch. Pilots must realise that oxygen has as its principal function the improvement of fighting efficiency at all altitudes, and that the correct drill is vital to safety and success. In blacking-out it is not generally realised that many successive tight turns or immoderate weaving have accumulative effect on the circulation, tending to early fatigue and possible blackout. Training should teach the pilot to realise instinctively what he can and cannot do without incurring the risk of blackout.' (Extracts from SD349: Aircrew Training: Report on the Conference held in the United Kingdom January/February 1942.)

Many of these points were made with the benefit of two years of wartime hindsight and by the time they were written most were already being addressed in the training of fighter pilots. It was a very different situation at the start of the war.

Pre-war Training

The RAF's pre-war flying training system was based on principles that had been developed in the latter stages of World War One and in terms of producing a competent pilot the system was good. Selection process was rigorous and pupil pilots went through a structured course of elementary and advanced flying, the latter usually being known as Service Flying, before being sent to squadrons were they learnt to fly and operate the squadron aircraft type. In peacetime this process was fine as the squadrons had time to provide the training, much of it centred on formation flying and, for fighters, what virtually amounted to choreographed attacks, the Fighter Attacks mentioned in a previous chapter. However, this lack of an operational element to the training was to prove a major problem when war finally came.

This chapter on aircrew training will only focus on the operational flying elements, the Operational Training Units and specialist training units. However, before moving on to the operational side of training it is appropriate to give a brief mention to the

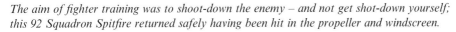

The aim of fighter training was to shoot-down the enemy – and not get shot-down yourself; this 92 Squadron Spitfire returned safely having been hit in the propeller and windscreen.

Elementary Flying Training School (EFTS) and Service Flying Training (SFTS) elements as these formed the foundation skills to which the operational elements were added.

There was no shortage of young men wanting to be pilots, and the RAF selection process was rigorous, weeding out some that would later reapply, succeed and go on to become aces. Having been selected and survived the Initial Training Wings with 'square bashing' and academics, the first real flying training took place at the EFTS. The EFTS was where prospective pilots first took to the air and where a great many of them ended their flying careers, either being 'washed out' (failing the course for one reason of another) or ending up as a statistic – KIFA (Killed in Flying Accident). The EFTS underwent numerous changes during the war, especially in the first two years, with much of this flying moving overseas as part of the British Commonwealth Air Training Plan. The length of the course and the syllabus changed a number of times, but these aspects are omitted from this chapter. Most pupil pilots wanted to be fighter pilots, although some were keen on bombers as a way of hitting back at the enemy. Personal choice was not the main basis for selection to role, although it was noted, and pilots were selected according to ability and the needs of the RAF for pilots in particular roles. As night fighters became more important those assessed as having excellent night vision often found themselves pointed in that direction.

The course was hard and many of the instructors, the majority being on rest tours, were even harder. It was a case of work hard, keep your nose clean and hope you were lucky with your instructor and Flight Commander. Jerry Jarrold underwent this stage of training in summer 1941, by which time the syllabus was well established and the RAF flying training system was turning out thousands of pilots.

On 9th July 1941, a small number of us were posted to RAF Peterborough and No. 17 EFTS (Elementary Flying Training School) and so started our first insight into flying – in the world-famous DH82A, better known as the De Havilland Tiger Moth. The School had only moved to Peterborough that month from its original base at North Luffenham and as a Class A + 1 School it catered for 150 pupil pilots and had 90 Tiger Moth IIs on strength.

My first-ever experience of flying was as a passenger in Tiger Moth T5698 on 19th July 1941; Sergeant Reed was my instructor and the first flight was called Air Experience and Familiarity with cockpit layout, and lasted just 20 minutes. I had another 30-minute flight in the same aircraft, the same day, with the same instructor – 'Effect of Controls and Taxying'. All very exciting stuff I seem to remember. Next day was in a different aircraft (T7026) but the same instructor and another 30-minute flight, this time 'Effect of Controls and Straight and Low Level Flight'. On 21st July I flew with Sgt. McDonald on 'Climbing, Side Slipping and Stall', which lasted 40 minutes. I was with Sgt. McDonald again the next day for another 40 minutes on 'Medium Turns and Taking-off into Wind'. This type of instruction continued for another eleven or twelve flights, mostly with Sgt. McDonald, although I flew with a Sgt. Spiers on 2nd August. The latter was for me a big, big day, for after 9 hours of instruction I was given a 25-minute test by Pilot Officer Roxburgh, who passed me for my first solo flight. It lasted just 10 minutes in Tiger Moth T5840 – oh, what joy that I could at last fly on my own. I landed without incident and was passed OK. It was a great feeling to go solo but a bit like treading water as you came in to land, half a hiccup and you bounce all over the place! I made two more flights that day, with one solo of 15 minutes, and

'If you lot think you are good enough ....' 'Pep talk' for new pupil pilots!

one with Sgt Spiers with 35 minutes of low flying. Wonderful day, the 2nd of August 1941 – I flew 5 times; two of which were solo. This carried on until 20th August, flying solo or instruction, mostly now with Sgt Spiers.

Jerry passed out as 'Average' with 50 hour and 5 minutes flying time, of which 25 hours was dual.

The SFTS stage of training also varied in terms of hours and syllabus at various periods during the war but essentially was designed to provide a bridge between the simple aircraft and basic flying of the EFTS and the operational types and flying of the OTU. Those who reached this stage were by no means safe and the 'wash-outs' and fatalities continued. Jerry Jarrold went to No. 8 STFS at Montrose.

For me, flying started on 15th September in a Miles Master Mark I with Sgt Griffiths as my instructor. After nine flights in just six days I was tested and went solo (21st September). There followed a further 80 or so flying hours, including approximately 43 solo flights, in Miles Master I and II aircraft under various instructors before completing the Course on 26th February 1942. Night flying was the worse time and was the cause of many accidents – and deaths. I recall on one night solo trip I overshot to make another circuit, entered cloud and became disoriented. This was a very dangerous situation and was often put down as the cause of fatal crashes. I don't remember how much I panicked or how I got out of it, but somehow I cheated fate and ended back on the runway in one piece! The Master II was an excellent training aircraft and after the Tiger Moth it seemed to us to be like a fighter, and had the same exhilaration when you flew it solo – which of course was the whole point. It seemed a massive aircraft and far more solid after the Tiger and very fast. We always made 3-point landings and you had to

Another Spitfire night landing (and the same in the background); night flying on type was just one of many skills that new pilots had to learn when they arrived on their squadrons, as previous training had been minimal.

> *settle it in, which was good training for a Spitfire as the technique was the same; by the end of my Spitfire period I could drop the aircraft down on a spot. There were a few Hurricanes at the School and in the latter stages of the Course some chaps got to fly these, which, as we all thought we were heading for fighters, would have been a nice end to the Course.*

Having completed the SFTS course the new RAF pilot – now proudly wearing his wings – was sent to an Operational Training Unit. Before looking at the role and development of the Fighter Command OTUs, which is the main part of this chapter, it is important to mention the training role of the squadrons themselves.

Training on the Squadron
The role of the squadrons in providing training was crucial, especially in the first few years of the war before the formal training system had become well established. New pilots arrived on a squadron with little, if any, flying time on the operational type of the squadron and certainly with no tactical or 'operational' training. It was the job of the squadron to teach these elements and to bring each pilot, and the squadron in general to the appropriate level of competence. In the mid 1930s this was a reasonably sound (or at least acceptable) way of doing things, there was plenty of time on the squadron for this and the training schools were not staffed with the right number or type of instructors for this work. Where it started to fall down was with the rapid expansion of the Command and the consequent diluting of experience on each squadron and the increasing complexity of aircraft – plus the likelihood that these pilots would indeed have

to fire their guns in combat. Of all the comments made by pilots in the early part of the war the most frequent and heartfelt is the lack of gunnery training; many commented that they never fired their guns until they were on a squadron, and for many that was days or hours before going into actual combat.

On 27 April the Hurricane-equipped 253 Squadron was declared operational day and night – and just over two weeks later was sending aircraft to France. The Squadron had formed in October 1939 but far from having six months to 'get up to speed' its early period was not what one could consider truly appropriate for a front-line fighter squadron. Extracts from the ORB illustrate the point and the problems faced by Fighter Command in equipping and training squadrons:

30 Oct 1939: Formed and given establishment of 16 Blenheims, actually had one Magister.

18 Nov 1939: Told by Air Ministry that the Squadron would equip with Battles and not Blenheims – as a temporary measure; by 23 November had 15 Battles on strength but 'during first fortnight had great difficulty in maintaining aircraft batteries owing to fact that no starter trolleys available.'

Jan 1940: Fighter tactics co-operation with 79 Squadron; dummy sights painted on windscreens; plenty of formation practice. Told on 15 January that to re-equip with Hurricanes and 'all pilots spent a short time in a Hurricane cockpit to learn the lay-out.' Fighter Command attacks rehearsed.

14 Feb: Now have 10 Hurricanes on strength.

21 Mar: All guns harmonised to 250 yards; new type of microphone received at end of month, two cine-camera guns borrowed from 604 Squadron.

3 Apr: Commence operational flying.

14 Apr: Air-to-ground firing at Dengie Flats.

27 Apr: Declared operational; 'repeated demands for equipment are slowly having desired effect; modifications on aircraft are being gradually effected, most important being the arrival of variable pitch airscrews and reflector sights.'

Over two days in May the Squadron lost six pilots in France.

One of the classic scenes in the 'Battle of Britain' film is when a Spitfire pilot makes a hash of his landing – given a Very to wave him off because the undercarriage wasn't down, followed by a bouncing landing. When met by the CO with the question 'how many hours do you have on Spitfires?' his answer was '10½ sir'. 'Let's make it 11 before Jerry has you for breakfast.' As they walk to their aircraft the other pilots make the comment 'spring chicken to shite hawk in one easy lesson'. The point is, however, a very valid one for 1940 and not only were pilots arriving with very little tactical training they were arriving with very few flying hours on type.

In July 1940 the CO of 249 Squadron received a signal from AOC No. 13 Group congratulating the Squadron on flying over 1,000 hours of training in June: 'I do not remember a case where a Squadron has ever passed the 1,000 hour mark in a month, and this intensive effort to become operational at the earliest possible moment reflects great credit on all concerned.' The ORBs of fighter squadrons show that a great deal of effort was expended on increasing or maintaining the skills of pilots, especially with formation flying and squadron attacks, although 'cloud flying' was a regular activity for solo pilots.

During the last few days a considerable amount of practice flying has been carried out and much attention paid to beam attacks and dog-fighting practice (249 Squadron ORB August 1940)

A general comment made by many fighter pilots is that they were given very little tactical training, either in training or on the squadron. In 1940 Spitfires and Hurricanes were in short supply and were needed in the squadrons; there were very few to spare for the training units and pilots had to make do with whatever types were available. However, the policy of leaving such additional type experience and tactical training to the squadrons was massively flawed. It was workable in 1939 and even into early 1940 with the Phoney War, although it very much depended on the attitude of the CO and his senior pilots, some of whom saw 'sprog' pilots as more trouble then they were worth.

In August 1940 Johnnie Johnson was posted to 19 Squadron at Duxford with a total of 205 hours in his logbook, of which 23 were on Spitfires. The promised extra training was not forthcoming as the Squadron was having problems with its new cannon armament: 'I don't know how we shall find time to train you chaps. We've simply got to get these things working first.' The concept of on-squadron training was totally flawed, especially at a time when the squadrons were hard-pressed to maintain operational status. Most Flight and Squadron Commanders did the best they could and tried to shield new boys from ops until they had built-up a few more hours and had flown a few mock combats. Sadly, for many a bright young fighter pilot his first combat experience was often his last.

The situation varied from unit to unit and depended to a large degree on the attitude of the Squadron Commander, and to a lesser extent the Flight Commanders or even

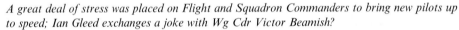

A great deal of stress was placed on Flight and Squadron Commanders to bring new pilots up to speed; Ian Gleed exchanges a joke with Wg Cdr Victor Beamish?

senior (experienced) pilots. 'We had a great deal of respect for "Crash" Curry (Sqn Ldr John Harvey Curry DFC). He set about really putting us through our paces with "tail-chasing". A small formation of say four aircraft went off and he would do all sorts of attacks on us, "out of the sun", "up and under" and really gave us a hard time. He was a magnificent pilot, nobody could touch him – he had his own "Flying Circus" in Texas before the war. He did not approve of the RAF gun-sight and had his own built into his aircraft. He was out "polishing" his Spitfire almost every day until it gleamed, and no airman was allowed to go near it.' (Jerry Jarrold, 80 Squadron)

Without skilled groundcrew the aircraft would not be fit to fly or operationally ready and the groundcrew went through an equally rigorous selection and training process.

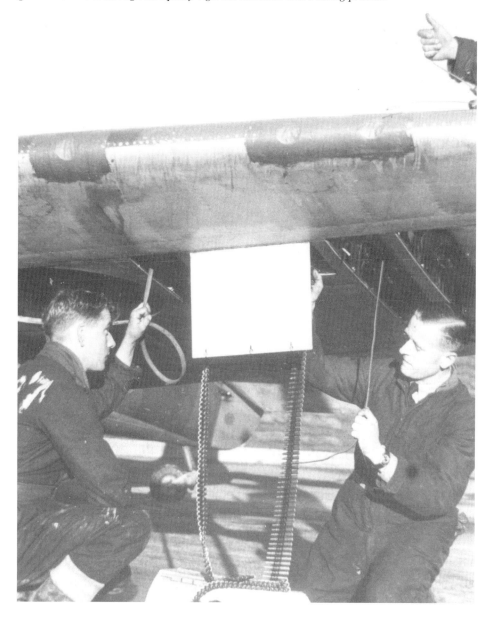

Whilst the role of experienced pilots, Flight Commanders and COs remained vital throughout the war, from 1942 onwards the basic 'product' they received from the training system was far better trained, although the reduction in real combat opportunities meant that for many their experience was still too theoretical – there is nothing like a real dog-fight to ram home lessons. Nevertheless, the system of Operational Training Units adopted by all the RAF Commands was an excellent one and produced good results. With the specialist training units providing leadership and tactical training the overall system was perhaps the best of any of the fighting air forces.

Operational Training Units

Bomber Command addressed the problem of operational training and the provision of a trained pool of aircrew through the formation of a number of Group Pool squadrons, each operational Group being provided with one such squadron, the squadrons themselves being 'operational' units that had been redesignated to the training role. Fighter Command appeared reluctant to follow this process and at the outbreak of war had only one such unit, the No. 11 Fighter Group Pool. This was formed on 14 January 1939 at Andover and was equipped with 11 Hurricanes and 22 Battles, the latter were not ideal but provided experience with the Merlin engine as well as providing valuable flying time. Pilots would join the Pool prior to being posted to a squadron, although this only applied to those pilots who were not found immediate places on squadrons and so the principle was one of maintaining flying currency rather than giving operational training. Nevertheless, the Pool was seen as being able to supply pilots at short notice to make good casualties in front-line units; it was little short of a recipe for disaster but it was better than nothing. As an Air Historical Branch summary makes clear, one of the problems was Dowding's priority on the build-up of his operational squadrons. 'The Commander-in-Chief, Fighter Command, correctly appreciating the vital struggle which was about to take place, was concentrating on increasing at all costs his first line strength and in "working up" to full operational pitch. He was therefore most reluctant owing to the time factor and shortage of aircraft, to devote any resources to operational training. For this reason he resisted proposals to create a second Fighter Group Pool, and proposed instead that the aircraft were needed to make two half-squadrons of Blenheim fighters. It was pointed out, however, by the Air Ministry that lack of Fighter Group Pool would mean lack of casualty replacements when fighting became intense and that, in emergency, operational training aircraft could be used. Fighter Command therefore reluctantly agreed to the formation of a second Group Pool (No. 12 Group) on 25 September 1939. Both Pools were handicapped by lack of camera guns, reflector sights, armoury and radio telephonic facilities. There was also a shortage of fully-equipped aircraft. This made them only capable of producing half the planned output of 1,100 pilots a year. In fact they hardly met, in quality or quantity, the requirements of the fighter squadrons in France. At the end of April 1940, the Air Ministry overruled Fighter Command's objections to the diversion of resources into the operational training organisation, and two more fighter OTUs were formed and the entire establishment of the four OTUs was increased.'

The latter reference to Operational Training Units moves beyond where we are in this overview. The No. 12 Group Pool formed at Aston Down with 11 Gladiators, seven Harvards and three Blenheims – so with the exception of the latter, the C-in-C was certainly not allocating front-line aircraft.

Spitfire pilots await the next mission; a great deal of experience could be passed from pilot to pilot, although in some units this was actively discouraged.

Those squadrons re-equipping with Blenheims were provided with an Oxford to help with conversion to twin-engined flying and Bomber Command was requested to 'make available Blenheim pilots to visit the units in order that instruction in flying Blenheims may be given to the pilots of these squadrons. A dual control set for a Blenheim will be allotted to each squadron' (Memo 2 December 1938 on re-equipment of Fighter Command). The Blenheim squadrons in question were 600, 601 and 604 at Hendon with a plan to re-equip them by mid February. With the assistance of Blenheim Conversion Flight at Hendon (short-lived), the two Group Pool were expected to supply the needs of whole of Fighter Command, including the squadrons deployed to the Continent. Their estimated output in early 1940 was 44 pilots a month.

An organisational memo of February 1940 gave details of the expansion of fighter Operational Training Units: 'Fighter Group Pools will become Operational Training Units and no longer be affiliated to a particular Group. This will avoid the necessity of establishing all types of aircraft at each OTU.

'The No. 11 Group Pool will move to Sutton Bridge as No. 6 Operational Training Unit, with effect from 6 March 1940. Establishment will be 48 Hurricanes, 4 Defiants, 2 Gladiators and 13 Harvards or Battles. The No. 12 Group Pool at Aston Down will become No. 5 Operational Training Unit. Establishment will be 34 Spitfires, 20 Blenheims and 10 Harvards or Battles.' (SOM 141/40)

The entire aircrew training system was being reviewed at this time, not so much out of any concern for Fighter Command but very much focused on the problems and needs of Bomber Command; however, it focused attention on all parts of the training system and led to specialisation at the Service Flying Training Schools, the output of which went to the OTUs. The problem had been exasperated by poor weather over the winter of 1939/40 and the generally poor condition of many of the training airfields. A suggestion of reducing night flying for pilots destined for day-fighter squadrons was vetoed by Fighter Command but it was agreed that the SFTS course for fighter pilots should be different. It was decided that No. 12 SFTS at Montrose would be the first to specialise in fighter pilot training, with a 12-week course, after which the pilot would go to an OTU. In June 1940 the decision was taken to form four of these Group Service Flying Training Schools: By September 1940 the Montrose School had an establishment of 108 Masters and was using a number of satellite airfields, including Edzell and Stracathro. It remained one of the major fighter Schools for the next two years.

Let's go back and look at the continued development of the OTUs, as these were the real key to providing squadrons with 'operational' pilots. The February 1940 decision gave the Command two OTUs, formed out of the old Group Pools, with a third subsequently added ... but the war was placing increasing demands on the Command, especially with the commitment – and losses – in France. The AHB account neatly summarises this difficult period on 1940: 'The problem of converting a hastily trained output so that it would be fit to take its place in the fighting line became urgent. By June 1940 the vigorous efforts which had been made to complete Fighter Command's preparations now made it all the more imperative that the squadrons should be supported by a proper backing for operational training, and it was agreed that every pilot should go through an OTU on the same basis as that to which Bomber Command had already been working. ... Their backing in operational training resources was extremely slender. By that time they only had three OTUs behind them. These OTUs were all under the direct control of one of the operational Groups (No. 10). The Battle of Britain was to show most clearly how essential was organised operational training. It was only by a most drastic shortening of courses that the flow of pilots to squadrons was maintained, and had the Service Flying Training School organisation been properly geared to the programme for first line expansion the Fighter OTUs would have formed a most severe bottleneck. As it was it was necessary to resort to many expedients in order to give the pilots their conversion.'

In October the numbering system of the OTUs was changed, with Aston Down becoming No. 55 OTU, Sutton Bridge No. 56 OTU and Hawarden No. 57 OTU. By late 1940 the Fighter Command plan was to have one OTU for every ten fighter squadrons, with each OTU turning-out 34 pilots a month from a six-week course. The AHB summary stated: 'The average casualty rate per ten squadrons was 26 a month over a year. On this basis the OTU output would be eight pilots per month more than was likely to be required. The task of forming an adequate OTU organisation was considerable, and the AMSO had been compelled to suggest that the operational training should to some extent be carried out in the squadrons themselves. It was impossible, therefore, at this stage to increase the ratio of fighter OTUs to squadrons to more than one to ten.'

One of the important elements of this equation was the loss rate in the squadrons, which included both casualties and routine 'losses' through such things as postings. An intrinsic part of this was tour lengths (the Operational Tour Policy); this was covered in the Overview chapter – but in essence Fighter Command averaged its tour lengths at 200 hours 'operational time' rather than a number of sorties. However, there was great variation on this and decisions were often taken at squadron level. Overall the anticipated loss rates for Fighter Command and therefore the replacement numbers required seemed about right and the Command did not suffer the same massive variations in losses that faced Bomber Command. In an effort to keep squadrons up to established manning levels, the pilot establishment per squadron was reduced from 26 to 23 – a neat way of making the numbers work! However, the training system was still hard-pressed to meet the demands and into the early part of 1941 the average pilot strength per squadron was 21.

It was hoped that the combined output of the four OTUs would be 60 pilots a week, which was almost five times that of just 10 months previously – but it was still not enough as it was not just supplying Fighter Command but was also supplying fighter squadrons in the Middle East. According to the AHB summary, 'wastage from all causes, including postings to other Commands, averaged 58 a week in October 1940. During the first few weeks of November Fighter Command found itself called upon to supply more than 100 pilots to the Middle East alone, although its own strength was already below establishment. It was obvious that even the expanded organisation would not be able to make good such a drain as this. Shortly before leaving the Command, therefore, Air Chief Marshal Dowding asked the Air Ministry to sanction the formation of two more OTUs. He also suggested that all Fighter OTUs should be incorporated into an operational Training Group within his Command.' At the end of December the OTUs joined the newly-formed No. 81 (Training) Group, which had formed on 16 December to control all Fighter Command's OTUs and was commanded by Air Commodore F J Vincent. The other change at the end of the year was the formation of a night-fighter OTU, which was in response to a reorganisation of the night defences instituted by the new C-in-C, Air Marshal Sholto Douglas. The new Unit formed, No. 54 OTU, at Church Fenton in late November with a large and diverse aircraft establishment comprising Blenheims (17 + 6), dual-control Blenheims (6 + 2), Defiants (18 + 6), Havocs (4 + 2), Masters (7 + 3), Oxfords (4 + 2) and four target-tow aircraft.

When No. 81 Group formed it had command of the six OTUs that were already functioning or in the process of formation, as shown in the table below:

Fighter Command OTUs, No. 81 Group, December 1940		
Unit	*Parent airfield*	*Main type(s)*
54 OTU	Church Fenton	Blenheim, Defiant
55 OTU	Aston Down	Hurricane, Master
56 OTU	Sutton Bridge	Hurricane, Master
57 OTU	Hawarden	Spitfire, Master
58 OTU	Grangemouth	Spitfire, Master
59 OTU	Turnhouse	Hurricane, Master

All pilots did some night flying but for those at Church Fenton's night fighter OTU this was a significant part of the course. Harold Stone (later 418 Sqn) was one of those who had a frightening experience during his training:

I was at Church Fenton doing my OTU course. I should point out that at this time I had only 120 hours flying under my belt and the Blenheims we now flew were so teased out that if you had to wait for the runway to clear for take-off the ground crew had to put chocks under the wheels to allow us to rev the engines to prevent them from oiling up. I had 6 hours dual before going solo and that was all any instructor was prepared to fly in these bombers. Even the 2 hours dual night flying check done was in an Oxford and single engined practice was also a solo effort!

Blenheim of No.54 Operational Training Unit, the first of the specialist night-fighter training units.

> *So when it came to practicing use of oxygen I was told to fly as high as I could. I got to 21,000 ft before the aircraft started to wallow and lose height every time I tried to gain extra altitude. To return to base I had to descend through a solid layer of cloud during which I lost the starboard engine and some instruments iced up. I broke cloud at approx. 2,000 ft but was able to maintain height until I was in sight of base. Unfortunately before I was able to rejoin the circuit the port engine also decided enough was enough and gave up the struggle. I called to clear the 'drome for an emergency landing and was just able to reach the main runway but just as I was about to touch down another aircraft took off across my bows and I had to leap frog over it and land with a rather sickening thud. Believe it or not, when I reported in I was given a rocket for landing on the wrong runway. This then is an example of a prolonged state of anxiety. Despite the above – the CO – W/C (Batchy) Atcherley was kind enough to assess me as 'A good type of N.C.O pilot with enthusiasm and ability.*

The Miles Master was the main trainer within the Fighter Command OTUs and first entered service in May 1939 as a two-seat advanced trainer. Three variants of the Master were used (I to III) and nearly 3,500 were produced – very few RAF single-seat pilots avoided the Master. It was a rugged and reliable trainer with a retractable undercarriage and reasonable performance, making it far better than other trainer types of the period. Miles aircraft played a major role in RAF training not only with the Master but also with the Magister, primarily used at the EFTS stage but also as squadron 'hacks' and comms aircraft, and the Martinet target-tower. Pilots sent to fire at aerial drogues were often aiming at a sleeve target being dragged around by a Martinet.

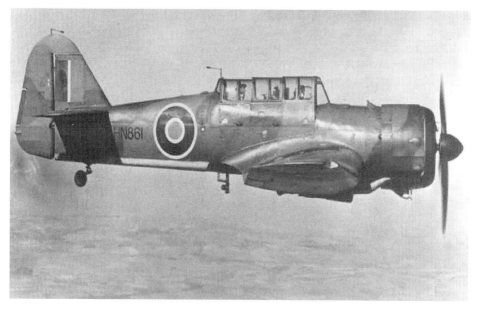

Miles Master HN861; the Master was one of a series of Miles aircraft that played a vital role in fighter-pilot training.

1941 – More problems

The expansion of the training system continued in 1941, with a plan approved in May to have eight day and three night Operational Training Units. By this time three more had already been added: No. 52 at Debden and No. 53 at Heston starting to form in mid February, and a second night unit, No. 60 starting to form in April at Leconfield. The aircraft establishment of the training units also continued to be subject to modification throughout this period; for example, the establishment of No. 53 OTU changed in May to 51 + 17 Spitfires, 17 + 5 Masters and 4 + 2 target-tow types. There were frequent changes in the aircraft establishment, in terms of types and numbers, throughout the war and it is not the intention of this chapter to track all such changes; mention will only be made where it is considered significant. One such change in June saw the Defiants leave No. 54 OTU to join No. 60 OTU, leaving the Church Fenton unit to concentrate on twin-engine night-fighter training, although it was another year before the promised replacement of the Blenheims by Beaufighters commenced.

This expansion of the training system did not solve the Command's problems as pilot output was still being drained away to various places, and, more tellingly, the supply of pilots from Flying Training Schools to No. 81 Group was drying up. Indeed, in the week to 14 April the Command received only 35 pilots from the FTS system whereas its requirement was 245 pilots. The C-in-C complained that his Command was not being given the priority it deserved – and was told that Fighter Command was 'quite all right'. It must be remembered that this was a period of massive expansion and heavy losses in Bomber Command and that the bomber battle was seen as the No. 1 priority.

The average OTU course by mid 1941 was 40 hours on type – four times more than it had been in 1940, although tactics and gunnery were still not significant parts of the syllabus. A great deal of time was spent honing the skills of pilots to enable them to manoeuvre in attack and defence, and it is strange that so little was done to ensure that they had a good standard of marksmanship. Less than three of the 40 hours were spent on actual firing, and cine-gun, whilst very useful, was of limited use in comparison.

Miroslav Liskutin, a Czech pilot, was on No. 10 Course at No. 58 OTU, Grangemouth in summer 1941. He was one of 30 pilots on the 6-week course – and six of them were killed in flying accidents, a higher than usual rate but a fact of life at training units such as this. In his biography 'Challenge in the Air' (William Kimber, 1988) he recalled:

> the ground school instructors gave us the principles for using our aircraft's guns for combat. This was followed by lectures on local firing practice and the air firing followed in great haste. It is difficult to describe my pleasant surprise when, on my first attempt at firing onto a flying target I achieved 16% of hits. My result had turned out to be one of the best at Grangemouth at that time.

He was right to be pleased with that percentage as for most pilots an average score was nearer to 5%.

By June 1941 the Command was operating nine OTUs, all being controlled by No. 81 (Training) Group, as shown in the table below.

Fighter Command OTUs, No. 81 Group, June 1941		
Unit	*Parent airfield*	*Main type(s)*
52 OTU	Debden	Hurricane
53 OTU	Heston	Spitfire
54 OTU	Church Fenton	Blenheim, Defiant
55 OTU	Usworth	Hurricane, Defiant
56 OTU	Sutton Bridge	Hurricane
57 OTU	Hawarden	Spitfire
58 OTU	Grangemouth	Spitfire
59 OTU	Crosby-on-Eden	Hurricane
60 OTU	Leconfield	Blenheim

Jack Cheney arrived at Church Fenton in August 1941 to join No. 11 course at No. 54 OTU, having been selected during SFTS for training as a night fighter pilot. He was teamed up with his Observer, Sgt James Mycock, the following month and the routine of day flying in Blenheims and night flying in Oxfords continued: 'blokes were killing themselves right, left and centre in those ropey Blenheims, which we had now also begun to fly by night. Together with our Observers we put in a tremendous amount of both day and night flying in an effort to become an efficient team and yet again the end of the course was rushed.' Just as the course was coming to an end in mid October his friend Tosh Bramely was killed in a flying accident – the fourteenth casualty in the space of three months.

By the end of the year the Command had its full complement of eleven OTUs, the new additions being: No. 51 OTU, which started to form at Debden in late July as a night unit and moved to its planned home at Cranfield on 17 August; and No. 61 OTU, which formed out of No. 53 OTU at Heston in June as a day unit. Thus by the end of the year the Command's capacity to train pilots had been transformed: in 1941 the organisation flew 263,604 hours and trained 4,242 pilots – an average output of 350 a month. There were, perhaps, still questions to be asked as to the content of the training, although this too had been greatly improved since the dark days of 1940.

Navigators of No.2 Course of No.60 OTU; this night-fighter training unit re-formed in May 1943 at High Ercall.

P9386 started life with 19 Squadron and served with a number of squadrons before being sent to training duties, where it served with three OTUs before crashing in May 1941 whilst with No.57 OTU.

1942 – Maximum Effort

By 1942 the Command's had 12 units, three of which specialised in night fighters. It must be appreciated that in many cases these OTUs did not just supply Fighter Command but also served overseas commands and other commitments.

Fighter Command OTUs, No. 81 Group, 1942		
Unit	Parent airfield	Main type(s)
12 OTU	Cranfield	Beaufighter, Havoc
52 OTU	Aston Down	Spitfire
53 OTU	Llandow	Spitfire
54 OTU	Charter Hall	Beaufighter, Blenheim
55 OTU	Annan	Hurricane
56 OTU	Tealing	Hurricane
57 OTU	Eshott	Spitfire
58 OTU	Grangemouth	Spitfire
59 OTU	Milfield	Hurricane
60 OTU	East Fortune	Beaufighter, Blenheim
61 OTU	Rednal	Spitfire
62 OTU	Usworth	Anson

Jerry Jarrold went to No. 55 OTU at Usworth; by the time he arrived at Usworth his log book showed a total of 126 hours and 35 minutes day flying, of which nearly 68 hours were solo, plus a mere 4 hours and 55 minutes of night flying, only 2 hours and 35 minutes of which were solo.

Flying started on the 24 March, with a sector reconnaissance in a DH82A (Tiger Moth) piloted by a Flt Lt Askew. The next day was dual instruction in a Miles Master Mark I by Flt Lt Rippon with so called 'dual landings' for just 25 minutes. Then it was off to the Hurricane and in total awe of the aircraft when first seen close up; the first thing being to sit in the cockpit and get used to the controls and layout. There was no dual-control Hurricane, so you were on your own from the first flight. This was followed immediately by my first flight in Hawker Hurricane Mark I (6622) for circuits and landings lasting one hour 10 minutes; later the same day I was up again in the same Hurricane Mk I for 'experience on type and sector recce', a trip that lasted one hour 35 minutes. Quite a day! Once you opened the throttle it pushed you into the seat as you roared off down the runway. As always, landing was the trickiest part and we tended to land rolling on main wheels, so it was important to keep the nose up and the brakes off, or an embarrassing tip-up on the nose would result (and maybe worse). It was also important to remember to put the undercarriage down, so you always kept a look-out for a red Very from the ground that would wave you off, usually because the gear was not down! Formation flying was tricky until you were experienced, and on early flights you tended to pump the throttle and see-saw until you settled down.

Looking back after all these years, it's now pretty hard to remember much of the nature of the very short periods devoted to air-to-air and air-to-ground firing. The old Hurricane Is' armament consisted of eight 0.303-in machine guns – four mounted in each wing and it was only on a couple of occasions that live ammo was used against ground targets; I can only assume that we shot at drogues for air-to-air. Ground firing (I think) was low level approach (not diving) onto the target on firing ranges, and, of course air-to-air required allowing for deflection. Most of the other firing – air-to-air – was cine camera. Again, if I remember correctly, most of us were concerned that not enough time was devoted to the subject of firing and gunnery on the Course, which for potential fighter pilots was extremely bad.

In July 1942 new establishments were promulgated for three of the OTUs:

> No. 51 OTU 20 + 6 Havoc, 10 + 3 Blenheim (AI), 10 + 4 Blenheim (Solo), 9 + 3 Blenheim (Dual), 3 + 1 Havoc I, 3 + 1 Oxford, 3 + 1 Target Tower.
>
> No. 54 OTU 20 + 6 Beaufighter (AI), 10 + 3 Blenheim (AI), 9 + 3 Blenheim (Dual), 10 + 4 Blenheim (Solo), 3 + 1 Beaufighter, 3 + 1 Oxford, 3 + 1 Target Tower.
>
> No. 60 OTU was given the same establishment as No. 54 OTU.

Ralph 'Sammy' Sampson went through No. 53 OTU in early 1942 and initially had a poor reception as his SFTS flying had been on Oxfords and under normal circumstances he would have been destined for night fighters and not Spitfires. Having had a check ride in the Master he was let loose a few days later on a Spitfire II:

Log-book extract for Jerry Jarrold during his time with No.55 OTU, March 1942.
(Jerry Jarrold)

YEAR 1942		AIRCRAFT		PILOT, OR 1ST PILOT	2ND PILOT, PUPIL OR PASSENGER	DUTY (INCLUDING RESULTS AND REMARKS)	SINGLE-ENGINE AIRCRAFT					DAY 1ST PILOT
MONTH	DATE	Type	No.				DAY DUAL	DAY PILOT	NIGHT DUAL	NIGHT PILOT	DUAL	
				55 OTU VSWIOER		TOTALS BROUGHT FORWARD	58·50	69·45	2·20	2·35		
MARCH.	24	D.H. 89A	7374	F/LT. ASKEW	SELF.	SECTOR RECCO						
MARCH	25	MASTER. 1.	8767	F/O RIPPON	SELF	DUAL LANDINGS.						
MARCH	25	HURRICANE.1.	6622	SELF.	–	3. FIRST SOLO, CIRCUITS.	0·25					
MARCH	25	HURRICANE.1.	6622	SELF	–	4. EXP. ON TYPE AND SECTOR RECCO		1·10				
MARCH	27	HURRICANE.1.	6798	SELF.	–	CIRCUITS AND LANDINGS.		1·35				
MARCH	27	HURRICANE.1.	7285	SELF.	–	5 D.F. HOMINGS 10A CROSS COUNTRY		1·05				
MARCH.	27	HURRICANE. 1.	6883	SELF	–	4. 10A		1·40				
MARCH.	28	HURRICANE.1.	1563	SELF.	–	7. FORMATION.		1·15				
MARCH.	30	HURRICANE.1.	1563	SELF.	–	7. FORMATION		1·30				
APRIL	1	HURRICANE.1.	1563	SELF.	–	10A. 18 CLOUD FLYING.		0·45				
APRIL	1	HURRICANE.1.	7068	SELF.	–	STEEP TURNS. FORCED LDGS 26.		1·40				
APRIL	1	HURRICANE1.	6798	SELF.	–	18a CLOUD FLYING 26 FORCED LDGS.		1·15				
APRIL	2	HURRICANE.1.	6798	SELF.	–	6. CLIMB 18000'		1·05				
APRIL	2	HURRICANE.1.	6798	SELF.	–	CIRCUITS AND LANDINGS.		1·30				
APRIL	2	HURRICANE. 1.	6798	SELF.	–	20. CROSS COUNTRY (NAV. II)		0·10				
APRIL	10	HURRICANE.1.	968	SELF	–	18a CLOUD FLYING.		1·50				
APRIL	12	MASTER. 1.	9015	SGT. LEVINSON	SELF	AIR-AIR AIR-GROUND DUAL		1·35				
APRIL.	12	HURRICANE. 1.	4196	SELF.	–	12 AIR TO GROUND FIRING	0·45					
APRIL.	12	HURRICANE.1.	6803	SELF.	–	CAMERA ASTERN.		1·15				
APRIL	14	HURRICANE.1.	1563	SELF	–	16 AEROBATICS.		1·00				
APRIL	14	HURRICANE.1.	1563	SELF	–	25a LOW FLYING SOLO		1·35				
APRIL	15	HURRICANE.1.	3227	SELF.	–	7 FORMATION FLYING		1·30				
						21a SECTION ATTACKS 4000'						
						21b. SECTION ATTACKS 10000 - 15000'		1·45				
				GRAND TOTAL [Cols. (1) to (10)] 157 Hrs. 50 Mins.		TOTALS CARRIED FORWARD	1·10	25·10				
							60·00	92·55	2·20	2·35		

Unlike the previous three types I had flown, the Spitfire was like a race horse once it was airborne, gathering terrific speed where the others were clambering into the air. As I left the ground, I selected wheels-up and with my eyes glued to the horizon ahead but with an occasional glance at the instruments, gained height. When I reached 1,000 ft I turned my head to look at the aerodrome and it was not in sight. This then was the difference between a fighter aeroplane and the training planes I had flown. Speed and power. I flew for 15 minutes, thankfully relocated the airfield and landed. It was a tremendous feeling of achievement. I had finally made it. (Spitfire Offensive, R W F Sampson, Grub Street).

The East Fortune unit (No. 60 OTU) was disbanded in November 1942, its aircraft and personnel being transferred to No. 132 OTU of Coastal Command, although some of the Beaufighters went to No. 51 OTU to form a fourth squadron at that Unit, which had only started to receive Beaus in August. The Unit was also taking an increasing role in the training on intruder crews.

During 1942 the following statistics were recorded for the Command OTUs:

Total hours flown	390,236
No of accidents	1,242
Fatal accidents	189
Pilot intake	4,993
Pilot output	4,353
Wastage rate	13%

Accidents were always a matter of great concern, especially if they were caused by flying indiscipline – and there are frequent entries in the records of flying training units of pilots being suspended, the commonest offence being illicit low flying. This was more of a problem in the earlier stages of training and by the OTU stage, where low flying was a routine part of the course, the more frequent problems were those of airmanship. As a typical month of accidents for a Spitfire OTU, the following incidents were recorded by No. 61 OTU at Rednal for December 1942, a month when the weather was only fit for flying for half the month.

1 Dec: Spitfire P7973 (Sgt Menuge), heavy landing, undercarriage collapsed.
Spitfire P7746 (P/O Rivett), swung on take-off.

14 Dec: Spitfire ? (P/O Degail), flew into hill, pilot killed.

16 Dec: Spitfire X4776 (Sgt Crawley), taxiing too fast, undercarriage collapsed.
Spitfire R7125 (Sgt Veys), heavy landing, undercarriage collapsed.
Lysander T1655 (F/L Walker), on search for lost Spitfire, flew into hill, pilot killed.

19 Dec: Spitfire R7151 (Sgt Robson), took-off in coarse pitch, hit railway bank.
Spitfire P8389 (Sgt Veys), pilot on air firing over range failed to appreciate how much fuel he was using, with only 25-gallons left pilot should not have attempted a further 200 minutes flying, but should have landed at one of available dromes. Accident attributed to an error of judgement through inexperience.

27 Dec: Spitfire P8693 (Sgt Girardon), attempted half-roll at 3,000 ft, failed to pull-up before hitting tree. Sent to Aircrew Refresher School at Brighton.

1943 – Reorganisation

By 1943 the training machine for fighter pilots was running well and as there was not such a panic for pilots they were being allowed enough training time and flying hours, although there was still some concern over the amount of gunnery.

On 15 April 1943 the training organisation passed to No. 9 Group as part of a restructuring of Fighter Command. By June the training organisation comprised 14 OTUs, as shown in the table below.

Fighter Command OTUs, No. 9 Group, June 1943		
Unit	Parent airfield	Main type(s)
41 OTU	Hawarden	Mustang
43 OTU	Old Sarum	Auster
51 OTU	Cranfield	Beaufighter
52 OTU	Aston Down	Spitfire
53 OTU	Kirton-in-Lindsey	Spitfire
54 OTU	Charterhall	Beaufighter
55 OTU	Annan	Hurricane/Typhoon
56 OTU	Tealing	Hurricane
57 OTU	Eshott	Spitfire
58 OTU	Grangemouth	Spitfire
59 OTU	Millfield	Hurricane
60 OTU	High Ercall	Mosquito
61 OTU	Rednal	Spitfire
62 OTU	Usworth	Anson

No. 60 Operational Training Unit re-formed at High Ercall on 5 May 1943 as directed by No. 9 Group, the nucleus of the unit coming from No. 2 (Intruder) Training Squadron of No. 51 OTU. Under the command of Wg Cdr Hoare DSO DFC* it was equipped with 24 Mosquito IIs and IIIs and two Ansons and was tasked with training Mosquito crews for intruder operations. The first intake of pupils arrived in mid May to go through two phases of training. The first was with No. 1 (Conversion) Squadron, which gave a 4-week conversion to the Mosquito, plus formation flying and instrument flying. This was followed by 8-weeks with No. 2 (Advanced) Squadron when pupils crewed-up and flew 15 day and 25 night hours. To quote the ORB 'this was mainly cross-country but considerable time would be devoted to camera-gun exercises, air-to-air firing and air-to-ground firing, as well as practice attacks and practice intruders.' Course size varied, No. 1 Course had 12 crews whilst others had as few as three crews. Failure rates were very low and on most courses all crews graduated, although there are a few notes of 'suspended' or 'taken off course'. Likewise, casualty rates were low.

This was part of a general reorganisation of night-fighter training promulgated in early September 1943 'in order to overcome the present deficiency of night fighter AI crews and to meet future requirements of night fighter AI and Intruder crews, it has been decided to reorganise the night fighter OTUs in No. 9 Group, Fighter Command, as follows:

1. Increase the intake of the two night fighter (AI) OTUs – Nos 51 and 54 – from 32 to 40 crews every four weeks.
2. Reduce No. 60 (Intruder) OTU to approximately half size.

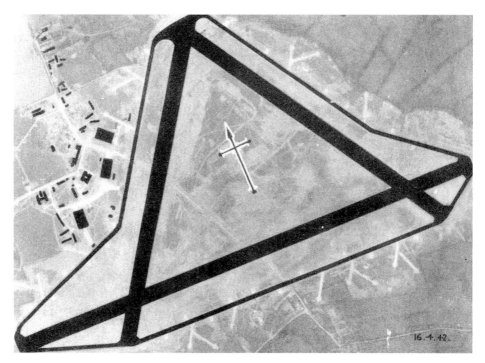

Rednal was home to No.61 Operational Training Unit, which formed at Heston in June 1941 to train day fighter pilots and moved to Rednal in April 1942. It remained here to the end of the war, primarily equipped with Spitfires until Mustangs took over in late 1944.

    3. Form No. 63 (AI) OTU with intakes of 20 crews every four weeks.
    4. Expand No. 62 (AI) OTU to train 100 Navigators/Radio per four weeks.

'The crew intakes at No. 51 OTU (Cranfield, with satellite at Twinwood Farm) and No. 54 OTU (Charter Hall, with satellite at Winfield) will be increased from 32 to 40 every 4 weeks. The training organisation of each of these OTUs will be:

    a. Length of course – 12 weeks.
    b. Population – 120 crews.
    c. Outputs – 34 crews every four weeks.

'The aircraft establishment of these OTUs will be amended as follows:

No. 51 OTU: Beaufighter IF increased from 40 + 14 to 50 + 18 and Beaufort dual 9 + 3 to 11 + 4.

No. 54 OTU: Beaufighter II increased from 40 + 14 to 50 + 18 and Beaufort dual from 9 + 3 to 11 + 4.

'No. 60 OTU will now train Intruder crews only. It will be reduced to half size and will remain at High Ercall, but Honiley will become home for No. 63 OTU. The training organisation of No. 60 OTU will be:

    a. Length of course – 12 weeks.
    b. Intakes – 18 crews every four weeks.
    c. Population – 54 crews.
    d. Outputs – 16 crews per four weeks.

'No. 63 OTU will start to form forthwith as a night fighter (AI) OTU at Honiley. Its training organisation will be:

a. Length of course – 12 weeks.
b. Intakes – 20 crews every four weeks.
c. Population – 60 crews.
d. Outputs – 17 crews per four weeks.

'Its aircraft establishment will be 25 + 9 Beaufighter II, 2 + 0 Blenheim V duals, 8 + 2 Beaufort duals, 2 + 1 Martinets, 2 + 0 Magister.

'No. 62 OTU at Ouston will be expanded forthwith to train 100 Navigators/Radio per four weeks. Its training organisation will be:

a. Length of course – 6 weeks.
b. Intakes – 53 every two weeks.
c. Population – 159.
d. Outputs – 100 per four weeks.'

A second major reorganisation took place in October, this time affecting the Fighter Gunnery Flights; these numbered Flights were disbanded and a series of Armament Practice Camps were established, although this was essentially a re-designation of the old Flights. The effective date for this change was 18 October, with ten Flights becoming eight APCs, as shown in the table below.

Formation of APCs, October 1943

Fighter Gunnery Flight	APC	Airfield	Group
1487 Flt	11 APC	Fairwood Common	10 Gp
1498 Flt			
1486 Flt	12 APC	Llanbedr	9 Gp
1492 Flt	13 APC		
1490 Flt	14 APC	Ayr	13 Gp
1491 Flt	15 APC	Peterhead	13 Gp
1489 Flt	16 APC	Hutton Cranswick	12 Gp
1488 Flt	17 APC	Southend	11 Gp
1493 Flt	18 APC	Gravesend	11 Gp

The establishment for each of the APCs was 6 + 1 target-tow aircraft, usually Lysander or Martinet, and 3 + 1 Master. It was intended that fighter squadrons would spend 14 days with the APC for intensive training. This is one reasons why airfields such as Llanbedr and Fairwood Common keep appearing in squadron records as 'bases'; the Squadron was detached to the APC for this short training period.

1944

In January 1944 the Millfield unit (No. 59 OTU) flew 1,435 hours and its aircraft strength was 77 Hurricanes, 18 Masters, 15 Martinets, six Typhoons and one each of the Tiger Moth and Dominie. Flying ceased on 26th of the month as the Unit was disbanding and in early February 1944, the AOC of No. 9 Group sent the following message: 'The closing down of No. 59 OTU has brought to an end the existence of an Operational

Training Unit with a very fine record of achievement. In the 34 months of its life, no less than 101,335 hours have been flown and 1,485 pupils trained. This represents a contribution to the war effort of a considerable magnitude and it has only been made possible by the hard work and devotion to duty, not only of the instructors and staff of the OTU but of the entire strength of the Station.

'At no time has life been easy, for the training commitment has always been a little greater than the resources of the OTU could normally meet, and it has meant a sustained effort on the part of everybody to provide the training which has been required.'

In was not actually the end as far as Millfield, the aircraft or the staff were concerned, as the resources were used to form the Fighter Leaders School, which also absorbed the Specialised Low Attack School.

With the use of fighters as fighter-bombers the art of bombing was introduced to some of the OTUs, including No. 53 OTU at Kirton-in-Lindsey, which now had three phases to its course:

1. 20-hours familiarisation on Spitfire Vb.
2. 20-hours gunnery and bombing.
3. 20-hours formation, tactics and night flying.

Peter Rivington recalled his time with the OTU:

we now turned to armament training – air-to-air and air-to-ground firing, and dive-bombing with practice bombs. The ranges for air-to-ground firing were just off Spurn Head, while the air-to-air firing took place out to sea off the Point. We fired at drogues towed by a Martinet ... quite a number of our exercises were carried out with camera gun only, and one's films were then analysed and criticised by an instructor. We also practiced dive-bombing using an off-shore target. The Spitfire was not an ideal aircraft for this exercise, as with its clean lines and absence of dive-brakes it picked up speed very quickly when going down hill! I see from my Log Book that my best effort produced an average error of 97 yards for eight bombs, so I imagine that a few fell quite a bit closer than that.

With the armament phase of the course completed the final two or three weeks were spent once more at Kirton [the armament phase was flown from Hibaldstow] in tactical training, formation flying, in Flights and as a squadron, dog-fighting and ground-attack. Following the pattern of the air war being waged at that time, great stress was placed on the latter. (Adventures on the Infinite Highway, Peter Rivington, ed Rod Priddle, Woodfield.)

By June 1944 the Command had 13 training units under No. 9 Group, as shown in the table on the right:

With fighter-bombing now a standard role for most fighter units there was a requirement to increase the training for this role. ... No. 59 Operational Training Unit re-formed at Acklington, in No. 12 Group, for this task on 26 February 1945 as a half-strength OTU to train Typhoon pilots in the fighter-bomber role, primarily for 2nd Tactical Air Force. No. 1 Course, of 22 pilots, assembled on 20 March and were briefed that they were to 'consider themselves as qualified pilots on a conversion course to fly and fight in Typhoons.' It was explained that 'absolute obedience was expected in the air and that breaches of flying discipline would not be tolerated.' Flying started on 23 March and was in phases but was somewhat disrupted by VE Day celebrations. By the end of

Fighter Command Training Units, No. 9 Group, June 1944

Unit	Parent airfield	Main type(s)
13 OTU	Bicester	Mitchell
41 OTU	Hawarden	Mustang
51 OTU	Cranfield	Beaufighter, Mosquito
53 OTU	Kirton-in-Lindsey	Spitfire
54 OTU	Charter Hall	Beaufighter, Mosquito
55 OTU/3 TEU	Annan, Honiley	Hurricane, Typhoon
56 OTU/1 TEU	Tealing	Hurricane
57 OTU	Eshott	Spitfire
58 OTU/2 TEU	Grangemouth	Spitfire
60 OTU	High Ercall	Mosquito
61 OTU	Rednal	Spitfire
62 OTU	Ouston	Anson
FLS	Milfield	Spitfire, Typhoon

Note: TEU – Tactical Exercise Unit; FLS – Fighter Leaders School.

the course the average flying hours per pilot were 56 day and four night; for the OTU it was a one-off course as it disbanded in June.

As the war drew to a close there were 15 training units, but as had been the case for some time they were not all directly related to the needs of Fighter Command and a great deal of the output was destined for the Tactical Air Force. Reorganisation had seen No. 9 Group disband in September 1944 and the training had been placed back under command of the operational Groups, with No. 12 Group in particular as most of the units were within its operational area. The training units are detailed in the table below.

Fighter Command Training Units, May 1945

Unit	Parent airfield	Main type(s)
No. 11 Group		
13 OTU	Harwell	Mitchell, Mosquito, Boston
1335 CU	Colerne	Meteor
No. 12 Group		
41 OTU	Chilbolton	Spitfire, Hurricane
51 OTU	Cranfield	Mosquito
53 OTU	Kirton Lindsey	Spitfire
54 OTU	Charter Hall	Mosquito
55 OTU	Aston Down	Typhoon, Hurricane
56 OTU	Milfield	Tempest, Typhoon
57 OTU	Eshott	Spitfire
58 OTU	Hawarden	Spitfire
59 OTU	Acklington	Typhoon
61 OTU	Rednal	Spitfire, Mustang
62 OTU	Ouston	Wellington, Hurricane
80 (French) OTU	Morpeth	Spitfire
CFE	Tangmere	various

By November the total was down to six OTUs plus No. 1335 Conversion Unit and the Central Fighter Establishment, with most coming under No. 12 Group.

Specialist Schools

Whilst the OTUs were without doubt the most important part of the operational training for the Command's pilots, the role played by a number of specialist training schools was highly significant, especially in the development of leadership and tactical training. These specialist schools were staffed by experienced fighter pilots on rest tours from operational flying and 'new boys' rubbed shoulders with many of the great names of air combat, not all of whom wanted to be there and not all of whom were suited to the training role. Nevertheless, as forums of excellence they proved invaluable and lessons were distilled and passed on. This brief overview will not mention all the schools of this type.

Tactical development and instruction in tactics became increasingly well-established from 1943. In theory, those who attended a specialist course not only improved their own skills, especially in leadership, but also imparted the latest tactical wisdom to the rest of the squadron. The theory was sound but it was by no means always applied.

The Central Gunnery School (CGS) was formed at Warmwell in November 1939 as the centre of excellence for all air gunnery matters in order to improve standards and provide specialist training. The School operated a range of aircraft types from trainers to front-line fighters, and selected pilots went through the short course, the intention being that they would pass on the wisdom gained to other members of their squadron.

By 1944 Spitfires were the main fighter type with CGS; by the following year the establishment included 20 Spitfire XVIs, although the actual strength in terms of numbers and Marks varied.

In January 1943 the Fighter Leaders School was formed at Chedworth (out of No. 52 OTU); with an establishment of 36 Spitfires its role was to teach Flight and

Bf 109 in RAF 'service'; the use of captured aircraft for trials was essential but they also undertook tours of squadrons to give pilots a close-up view of the enemy.

Spitfire of the Central Gunnery School at Catfoss, 1944.

Squadron Commanders tactical employment of fighter aircraft, for both air fighting and ground-attack. The FLS was staffed by very experienced pilots and although it was a short course it was intensive with theory, a great deal of discussion, and as much flying as could be packed in.

The School continued to grow and by October 1943 its official designation was No. 52 OTU (Fighter Command School of Tactics). It reverted to the FLS title in January 1944, by which time it was at Millfield and has grown both in size and diversity of aircraft, with 69 Spitfires, 18 Typhoons, 11 Hurricanes and 8 Masters. In December 1944 the FLS became part of the Central Fighter Establishment's (CFE) Day Fighter Wing at Wittering. The CFE gradually acquired most of the Fighter Command specialist units that performed this type of role, such as the Day Fighter Development Wing, which had originally formed at Milfield in September with a Fighter Training Squadron, a Fighter-Bomber Training Squadron and an Air Support Development Squadron.

It was a similar situation with night fighter training and by 1944 the CFE had absorbed most other specialist units in this sphere as well. The Night Fighter Development Wing (NFDW) formed at Ford on 16 October 1944, incorporating the well-established Fighter Interception Unit. It operated three main sub-units: Fighter Interception Development Squadron (FIDS), Night Fighter Training Squadron (NFTS) and the Naval Fighter Interception Development Unit (NFIDU). The main type operated by the NFDW was the Mosquito, in a number of NF variants. Moving to Tangmere in July 1945 the Wing then moved to West Raynham that October to join the rest of the CFE at its new home. With that move came a change of designation for the NFTS, becoming the Night Fighter Leaders School.

Cold War

There had been a major reorganisation of OTUs during 1946 and by the end of the year Fighter Command had four such units, although three of these were only cadres, plus the first Operational Conversion Unit, No. 226, although that too was only a cadre. The details are shown in the following table.

Fighter Command Training Units, December 1946		
Unit	*Parent airfield*	*Main type(s)*
No. 11 Group		
226 OCU	Bentwaters	Various
No. 12 Group		
13 OTU	Middleton St George	Mosquito
43 OTU	Andover	Auster
54 OTU	Leeming	Mosquito
61 OTU	Keevil	Spitfire

The nomenclature applied to the main training units changed in the late 1940s, with Operational Training Units becoming Operational Conversion Units and the primary role becoming conversion to type rather than simply a tactical or operational orientation to role. This carried with it a more focused training role on taking crews from advanced flying training, converting them to the specific aircraft type and providing weapon and tactical training. The first of the newly-designated units was No. 226 OCU at Molesworth, which formed within No. 11 Group on 15 August 1946 to provide operational training for fighter pilots. Its establishment was not wonderfully impressive and comprised three Tempest IIs, two Hornets, two Meteor IIs and single examples of Vampire, Oxford and Harvard. It moved to Bentwaters in October, still with a mixed but limited aircraft collection, although it now had six Meteor IIIs. By August 1949 it was at Driffield but that same month it became No. 203 Advanced Flying School. To confuse the issue, No. 203 AFS at Stradishall became No. 226 OCU! The Vampire element departed the following year to form No. 229 OCU at Leuchars. The Stradishall Unit disbanded in June 1955 but the OCU was resurrected on 1 June 1963 at Middleton St George from the Lightning Conversion Squadron. Having moved to Coltishall in April 1964 this designation survived into the period of Strike Command.

June 1949, Operation Foil; in the post-war period some of the most effective training took place during major Exercises and annual 'Operations' such as Foil, as realistic combined training was possible using multiple units and 'real' targets.

The post war creation, movement and renumbering of training units was somewhat convoluted, as demonstrated above and I do not propose to go through each one in details; however, in summary:

No. 228 OCU formed 1 May 1947 at Leeming to train night fighter crews, for which task it initially used Mosquitoes. The role changed to training all-weather crews and the equipment also changed. The OCU disbanded in September 1961 but re-formed at Leuchars in May 1965 to train Javelin crews, although this lasted only just over a year with disbandment in December 1966.

No. 229 OCU formed on 15 December 1950 at Leuchars to provide operational training for fighter pilots, for which it used Vampires as its main type, plus a few Meteors. Having moved to Chivenor in March 1951 its basic role survived into the Strike Command period.

No. 233 OCU formed on 1 September 1952 at Pembrey to provide operational training for fighter pilots, with Vampires as the main type. The role continued to disbandment in September 1957.

No. 238 OCU formed on 15 June 1952 at Colerne to train night fighter radar operators; it used Brigands and Meteors for this work, along with Valetta 'flying classrooms'. The OCU moved to North Luffenham in January 1957 and disbanded in March 1958.

Central Fighter Establishment
The principle of having specialist schools also survived into the post war period, with the Central Fighter Establishment retaining its pre-eminence, and with the sub-units carrying appropriate titles, which changed from time to time to better match the actual work being carried out. The CFE moved to West Raynham in October 1945 and remained at the Norfolk base until a final moved to Binbrook in October 1962. This incredible unit disbanded on 1 February 1966.

Whilst units as the CFE had a training role, it is important to realise that their main function was evaluation of aircraft and weapons and the determination of tactics, which were then transmitted to operational units either as documents, briefings or short courses. The following brief notes include an insight into, but not a history of, the post war CFE.

On 15 March 1958 the DFLS became the Day Fighter Combat Squadron within the CFE and in the same year shadow squadron numbers were adopted, the original plan for this having been agreed in 1954. This was part of the concept of strengthening the front-line and the two squadrons would become operational, using instructors, as required. Elements of the CFE were therefore designated as 63 Squadron and 122 Squadron, although the policy was that these numbers could only be used when activated and that for routine duties the training designations were to be used. Fighter Command extended the overall plan in 1956 and designated eight such potential squadrons to form from its training units, although this was reduced to five the following year. There was debate as to the numbers to be used, the original sequence being 122, 124, 127, 129, 131, 137, 165 and 176, but those who favoured the allocation of squadron numbers with an 'appropriate history' won the case and 63, 145, 219, 234 and 253 were allocated. Over the next few years there were some changes to this but the generally policy of shadow squadron numbering has survived to the present day.

Fighter Command use of Shadow Squadron numbers

Squadron	Main unit	Sub unit	Airfield	Aircraft	Dates
11	228 OCU	–	Leuchars	Javelin	11 Jan 1966–23 Dec 1966
63	CFE	DFCS	West Raynham	Hunter	30 Nov 1958–1 Jun 1963
	229 OCU	–	Chivenor	Hunter	1 Jun 1963–(2 Sep 1974)
79	229 OCU	–	Chivenor	Hunter	2 Jan 1967–(2 Sep 1974)
122	CFE	DFLS	West Raynham	Hunter	11 Jan 1956–30 Nov 1958
124	APS	–	Acklington	Meteor	11 Jan 1956–27 May 1956
127	229 OCU	–	Chivenor	Hunter	11 Jan 1956–22 Oct 1958
129	233 OCU	–	Pembrey	Hunter	11 Jan 1956–1 Sep 1957
131	FWS	–	Leconfield, Driffield	Meteor	11 Jan 1956–15 Mar 1958
	229 OCU	–	Chivenor	Hunter	15 Mar 1958–22 Oct 1958
137	228 OCU	–	Leeming	Javelin	11 Jan 1956–15 Sep 1961
145	229 OCU	–	Chivenor	Hunter	22 Oct 1958–1 Jun 1963
	226 OCU	–	Middleton St George	Lightning	1 Jun 1963–13 Apr 1964
		–	Coltishall	Lightning	13 Apr 1964–1 Sep 1970
165	238 OCU	–	North Luffenham	Meteor	11 Jan 1956–13 Mar 1958
176	CFE	NFLS, AWFLS	West Raynham	Meteor, Venom, Javelin	11 Jan 1956–22 Oct 1958
219	CFE	AWFCS	West Raynham	Javelin	22 Oct 1958-1 Jul 1962
		JOCU	West Raynham	Javelin	1 Jul 1962-31 Oct 1962
234	229 OCU	–	Chivenor	Hunter	22 Oct 1958-(2 Sep 1974)

Note: DFCS – Day Fighter Combat Squadron; DFLS – Day Fighter Leaders School; NFLS – Night Fighter Leaders Squadron; AWFLS – All-Weather Fighter Leaders Squadron, AWFC – All-Weather Fighter Combat Squadron; JOCU – Javelin Operational Conversion Unit.

No.228 Operational Conversion Course – course June-September 1960.

The Ingpen Trophy was awarded annually to the' night all-weather squadron in Fighter Command which is declared to be the most proficient in weapon training.' Competitions such as this were many and varied and played an important role in the training cycle of fighter squadrons.

244 FIGHTER COMMAND 1936-1968

The All-weather (AW) designations started to be used in the 1950s as new concepts and aircraft types, such as the Javelin, were given this role title to reflect their day/night/ poor weather capability. First user within the CFE was the A-W Fighter Leaders School (AWFLS), which formed in July 1950 within the NFLS, initially equipped with Meteor NF.11s but with Javelins arriving in 1957. This became the March 1958 when the A-W Fighter Combat School in March 1958 as part of a general change in nomenclature. This sub-unit became the Javelin Operational Conversion Squadron in July 1962.

The A-W Development Squadron (AWDS) formed in February 1956 to evaluate the Javelin and determine tactical and operational procedures.

In the post-war period, which has essentially been a period of peace, the wartime pressures of an operational squadron were no longer a factor and far more routine training could be conducted at squadron level. Essentially, every day and every sortie increased the experience of individual pilots and crews and the Squadron as a whole. This was a structured process of building new skills and maintaining and improving, through experience, existing skills.

CHAPTER FIVE

Operational Aircraft

The primary purpose of Fighter Command for its 30 years of existence was to protect the UK airspace from enemy aircraft (and missiles) and when it formed in 1936 the only experience of having to do this was back in World War One – when the bombers seemed to have the upper hand. The bombers in question were airships and long-range bombing aircraft, both of which carried only light bomb loads and very little in the way of defensive armament, and appeared over Britain unescorted, with operations taking place at night, mainly the airships, and by day. Although the defences eventually made the attacks unprofitable it had not been a comfortable period and air doctrine between the wars was based on the effectiveness of the bomber but with little regard to providing an effective defence against the bomber, and with no expectation of having to face enemy fighters *with* the bombers.

By the time the Command formed in 1936 this doctrine had started to change but it would be some years before that change became effective; Fighter Command entered the war with new and effective aircraft – but only just made it – and even then the aircraft had been primarily designed as bomber destroyers, with the tactics based almost solely on this concept. During the six years of war the Command continued to defend Britain, playing a large part in staving off the threatened German invasion in 1940 and then turning to the offensive. The Spitfire ended the war as the darling of the RAF's fighters and in terms of its employment by and significance for Fighter Command this is a very fair assessment; the capabilities of the aircraft increased as the war progressed but it remained limited in range, its major restriction, and fire-power, especially when adapted to the fighter-bomber role, although new types such as the Typhoon and new organisations, such as the 2nd Tactical Air Force, took on that role.

Jet fighters appeared in mid 1944 but the number of Meteors and their operational participation remained limited; however, in the immediate post-war period the Meteor – in both day- and night-fighter variants became the mainstay of the Command through much of the 1950s. Performance continued to increase with the introduction of the Hunter, the next 'mainstay' of the Command, ably supported in the night/all-weather role by the Javelin. The latter also saw the introduction of effective air-to-air missiles, the weapon that would become the main element in a fighter's arsenal. In the mid 1940s the average top speed of a fighter was 400–450 mph, only 15 years later the RAF introduced the supersonic Lightning with a notional speed of Mach 2 (twice the speed of sound) – or well over 1,000 mile an hour, although the aircraft's thirsty engines and lack of fuel gave it speed but not range or endurance. The introduction of the Lightning in 1960 had been preceded by the introduction of the RAF's first Surface-to-Air Missile (SAM), the Bloodhound, which to many heralded the future of air defence – missiles not manned aircraft. However, when Fighter Command became part of Strike Command in 1968 the manned aircraft was very much still part of the Order of Battle, as indeed it still is with the recent introduction of the Eurofighter Typhoon.

This chapter is divided into the same three periods we have used throughout the book: Pre 1939, the Second World War, and the Cold War (1945–1968). All the operational types, and the one SAM, are included but there is no mention of training types unless this was a secondary role of one of the operational types. This is not to decry the role of the trainers but is simply a question of space; trainer types are referred to in the Aircrew Training chapter. Aircraft tables and the write-ups concentrate on the use with Fighter Command, although wider reference is occasionally made, and the entries are not, therefore, mini-histories of each type. The tables do not show individual Marks of aircraft; for example, a Spitfire is a Spitfire.

Summary of Operational Types			
Aircraft	*Period*	*Sqns*	*Crew*
Pre 1939			
Bulldog	(1929)–Jul 1937	10	1
Fury	(May 1931)–Jan 1939	6	1
Gauntlet	(May 1935)–Dec 1939	19	1
Demon	(Jul 1932)–Auf 1939	12	2
Gladiator	Feb 1937–Feb 1941	19	1
Second World War			
Hurricane	Dec 1937–Mar 1944	65	1
Blenheim	Dec 1938–May 1941	16	2
Spitfire	Aug 1938–Nov 1951	91	1
Defiant	Dec 1938–Jun 1942	13	2
Beaufighter	Sep 1940–Aug 1944	19	2
Whirlwind	Jul 1940–Dec 1943	2	1
Havoc	Feb 1941–Jan 1943	15	2
Airacobra	Aug 1941–Mar 1942	1	1
Typhoon	Sep 1941–Sep 1945	9	1
Mosquito	Jan 1942–May 1949	23	2
Tempest	Jan 1944–Oct 1946	11	1
Mustang	Dec 1943–May 1946	16?	1
1945–1968			
Meteor	Jul 1944–Jun 1959	44	1 or 2
Hornet	Feb 1946–Mar 1951	4	1
Vampire	Apr 1946–Mar 1957	19	1 or 2
Venom	Nov 1953–Nov 1957	8	2
Sabre	Jan 1954–Apr 1956	2	1
Swift	Feb 1954–Mar 1955	1	1
Hunter	Jul 1954–Apr 1963	16	1
Javelin	Feb 1956–Apr 1965	11	2
Lightning	Jun 1960–(Apr 1988)	7	1
Bloodhound	Dec 1958–(1994)	14	SAM

Notes
1. Only those units that were part of Fighter Command are included in the lists.
2. Period of service refers to the numbered squadrons (the only exception being the Fighter Interception Unit – FIU); in some cases aircraft entered RAF service before this date or left after this date. The squadrons and dates are those which served with Fighter Command and the brackets show dates outside of the Fighter Command date range of 1936–1968.
3. The airfield details are in chronological order but each location is only listed once, so if a unit was, for example, at Biggin Hill, on more than one occasion the subsequent occasions are not listed – this is not intended as a detailed history of the movements of each unit but as an indication of location and the frequency of movement, as well as being a pointer to further research sources.
4. In late 1943 and early 1944 the situation with the fighter and fighter-bomber types was confusing in respect to allocation of squadrons to Commands and there is in the lists shown here, especially for the Spitfire and Typhoon, inevitable cross-over between Fighter Command/ADGB and the AEAF and its tactical units.

Pre 1939

When Fighter Command formed in 1936 it was still a biplane force – in terms of equipment, doctrine and training; three years later it was comprised of high-speed monoplane fighters with double the fire-power, an amazing transformation, although doctrine and tactics had not kept pace with the technical developments. The 1920s and 1930s was the era of agile biplanes that were, usually, a delight to fly, looked good when painted in squadron colours and appeared impressive at the various public displays; none of which had much value in operational terms. The era was dominated by Bristol, Hawker and Gloster and for the pilots of the period it seemed an almost idyllic life, as the lumbering bombers were easy to 'shoot down' on exercises and the threat of *real* combat was simply not there.

Bristol BULLDOG

The Bristol Bulldog entered service in June 1929 with 3 Squadron at Upavon and its twin Vickers machine-guns provided the same firepower as carried by the types it was to replace, the Gamecock and the Siskin. The Bulldog was one of a number of designs for Specification F9/26 and the prototype flew on 17 May 1927, with the Mark II (the one that entered production) flying the following January. The RAF eventually acquired 301 Bulldogs, the majority of which served with fighter units in Britain, six of which were still equipped with the type in early 1936. The table of units shows all the Bulldog squadrons, although as can be seen some had re-equipped pre 1936 and all but one had given up the type by the end of 1936 – so the Bulldog only just makes it into the Fighter Command list.

In addition to its machine-guns the aircraft could carry four small (20 lb) bombs and its Bristol Jupiter engine gave it a performance of 174 mph (at 10,000 ft) and a ceiling of just over 29,000 ft. Agility was its main attribute and it was certainly well-liked by its pilots. The Bulldog was declared obsolete in September 1937 but some, including a number of the dual-control trainers, remained in second-line roles for a few more years. The trainers were primarily used by the Service Flying Training Schools.

For most of the operational squadrons the replacement type was the Gloster Gauntlet.

Bristol BULLDOG
Prototype, first flight: Mk.II J9480, 21 January 1928
Entry to service: 3 Sqn, June 1929

Squadron	Dates	Airfields
3 Sqn	(June 1929)–Jul 1937	Upavon, Sudan, Kenley
17 Sqn	(Oct 1929)–Aug 1936	Upavon, Kenley
19 Sqn	(Sep 1935)–(Jan 1935)	Duxford
23 Sqn	(Jul 1931)–(Apr 1933)	Kenley
29 Sqn	(Jun 1932)–(Apr 1935)	North Weald
32 Sqn	(Jan 1931)–Jul 1936	Kenley
41 Sqn	(Oct 1931)–(Aug 1934)	Northolt
54 Sqn	(Apr 1930)–Sep 1936	Hornchurch
56 Sqn	(Oct 1932)–May 1936	North Weald
111 Sqn	(Jan 1931)–Jun 1936	Hornchurch, Northolt

The Bulldog entered service in June 1929 and served with ten squadrons, surviving just into the Fighter Command period.

Hawker FURY

The Fury was one of a delightful family of aircraft to appear from Hawkers in the 1920s, with the Hart and Hind light-bombers being the best-known but with the Fury definitely playing its part – it was, for example, the first RAF fighter with a speed of over 200 mph. The aircraft originated with a prototype to Specification F20/27, which duly became the Hornet and then the Fury when the name was changed, with the true prototype Fury (K1926) flying on 25 March 1931. By this time the type had been chosen as one of the RAF's standard fighters and it entered service with 43 Squadron in May 1931 at Tangmere. Other than its increase in speed, which of course was important, and came courtesy of good aerodynamics and the superb Kestrel engine, the Fury was still carrying

One of the delightful series of Hawker biplanes, the Fury, with two variants, the I and II in service between 1931 and 1939.

only a pair of guns. The RAF acquired 117 Fury Is and these served with three front-line squadrons (1, 25 and 43) and a number of other units.

Having been impressed with the early showing of the Fury the Air Ministry issued Specification 14/32 for the improved Fury II; the new variant had a more powerful kestrel engine and a few aerodynamic tweaks, such as wheel spats, which gave an increase in speed to 223 mph and an improved rate of climb ... but still only two guns. The first production Mk. II Fury (K7263) flew on 3 December 1936 in response to a production order from Specification 6/35. Deliveries began immediately to 25 Squadron and by the time production ceased some 112 Fury IIs had been built, 89 of these by General Aircraft. Five squadrons of Fighter Command used the Fury II but for all of them it was a fairly short association as the aircraft was *definitely* obsolete by this date; nevertheless, it was early 1939 before the last ones had left front-line service. For most of the squadrons the replacement type was the Gloster Gladiator. The Fury survived in support roles, mainly training, for a number of years.

Hawker FURY
Prototype, first flight: Production, K1926, 25 March 1931
Entry to service: 43 Sqn, May 1931

Squadron	Dates	Airfields
1 Sqn	(Feb 1932)–Nov 1938	Tangmere
25 Sqn	(Feb 1932)–Oct 1937	Hawkinge
41 Sqn	Oct 1937–Jan 1939	Catterick
43 Sqn	(May 1931)–Jan 1939	Tangmere
73 Sqn	Mar 1937–Jul 1937	Mildenhall, Debden
87 Sqn	Mar 1937–Jun 1937	Tangmere, Debden

Gloster GAUNTLET

Glosters produced rugged aircraft but they did not produce attractive aircraft and their biplanes of this period did not have the same lines as those from Hawkers. However, it was Gloster products – the Gauntlet and the Gladiator – that provided Fighter Command with its last biplane fighters and which, with the Gladiator, saw operational service.

The first production Gauntlet (K4801) flew on 17 December 1934 but it was the end product of a development line that had started some time before and had been ordered into production by the Air Ministry under Specification 24/33. In essence the Bristol Mercury-powered aircraft had a similar performance to the Fury, with a top speed of 230 mph but its ceiling was better as was its range and endurance. It also was still limited to two Vickers machine-guns. However, it appeared at a time when the RAF's expansion was underway and hence gained significant orders for equipping new squadrons. The Gauntlet I, of which only 25 were produced, was followed by the Gauntlet II, of which 204 were ordered. The type entered service with 19 Squadron in January 1935 and eventually equipped 19 squadrons in the UK within Fighter Command and the Auxiliary Air Force. Despite looking somewhat bulky the Gauntlet kept the agility that was inherent in biplane fighters and it was liked by its pilots, although by this time some were looking at the monoplane fighters and reading accounts of Bf109s in the Spanish Civil War and wondering how their aircraft would fare in combat. For Fighter Command that

Gauntlet … The type entered service with 19 Squadron in January 1935 and eventually equipped 19 squadrons in the UK within Fighter Command and the Auxiliary Air Force.

problem never arose and the majority of Gauntlets had gone by the outbreak of war; indeed only 616 Squadron had a few of the type still in use in late 1939. The Gauntlet did see some combat but that was in East Africa with No. 430 Flight.

Gloster GAUNTLET

Prototype, first flight: J9125; first production K4801, 17 December 1934
Entry to service: 19 Sqn, January 1935

Squadron	Dates	Airfields
17 Sqn	Aug 1936–Jun 1939	Kenley, North Weald
19 Sqn	(Jan 1935)–Mar 1939	Duxford
32 Sqn	Jul 1936–Oct 1938	Biggin Hill
46 Sqn	Sep 1936–Mar 1939	Kenley, Digby
54 Sqn	Aug 1936–May 1937	Hornchurch
56 Sqn	May 1936–Jul 1937	North Weald
65 Sqn	Jul 1936–Jun 1937	Hornchurch
66 Sqn	Jul 1936–Dec 1938	Duxford
74 Sqn	Mar 1937–Feb 1939	Hornchurch
79 Sqn	Mar 1937–Nov 1938	Biggin Hill
80 Sqn	Mar 1937–May 1937	Kenley, Henlow
111 Sqn	Jun 1936–Jan 1938	Northolt
151 Sqn	Aug 1936–Mar 1939	North Weald
213 Sqn	Mar 1937–Mar 1939	Northolt, Church Fenton
504 Sqn	Nov 1938–Aug 1939	Hucknall
601 Sqn	Dec 1938–Mar 1939	Hendon
602 Sqn	Jan 1939–May 1939	Abbotsinch
615 Sqn	Dec 1938–Sep 1939	Kenley
616 Sqn	Jan 1939–Dec 1939	Doncaster

Hawker DEMON

Whilst the Fury had a loose connection to the Hart, the Demon was a direct derivative of the highly-successful day-bomber; of particular significance was that fact that it remained a two-seater, the first inter-war two-seat fighter for the RAF, and included a variant with a gun turret. The Demon started life as the Hart Fighter and prototype J9933 flew in March 1931 to Specification 15/30. Renamed Demon in July 1932 the aircraft went to 23 Squadron for evaluation, which appears to have been satisfactory. By the time production ended the RAF had received 234 aircraft, 106 of these from Boulton Paul at Wolverhampton.

Standard armament was two forward-firing Vickers guns and a single Lewis for the gunner, with underwing bomb-racks for light bombs, so in essence it was not real improvement in terms of combat effectiveness – especially as top speed had reduced to 182 mph (at 16,400 ft) and all other performance figures had also come down. Nevertheless, the type served with a number of Fighter Command squadrons from mid 1932 to mid 1939, with some of those squadrons taking the type on operational deployments overseas.

The Turret-Demon was a development that appeared in October 1936 when a number of aircraft served with 29 Squadron; the modification involved a Frazer-Nash hydraulic turret in place of the standard rear cockpit, although this was not really a turret as such but rather an enhanced and powered shield for the gunner, who still only had a single gun. Nevertheless, it pointed the way for a series of aircraft that the RAF was keen to have – the turret fighter.

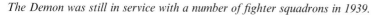

The Demon was still in service with a number of fighter squadrons in 1939.

Hawker DEMON
Prototype, first flight: J9993, March 1931; first production K2842, 10 February 1933
Entry to service: 23 Sqn, July 1932

Squadron	Dates	Airfields
23 Sqn	(Jul 1932)–Dec 1938	Kenley, Biggin Hill, Northolt, Wittering
25 Sqn	Oct 1937–Jun 1938	Hawkinge
29 Sqn	(Mar 1935)–Dec 1938*	North Weald, Debden
41 Sqn	(Jul 1934)–Oct 1937*	Northolt, Catterick
64 Sqn	(Mar 1936)–Dec 1938*	Martlesham Heath, Church Fenton
65 Sqn	(Aug 1934)–Jul 1936	Hornchurch
74 Sqn	(Sep 1935)–Apr 1937*	Hornchurch
600 Sqn	Feb 1937–Apr 1939	Hendon, Kenley
601 Sqn	Aug 1937–Dec 1938	Hendon
604 Sqn	(Jun 1935)–Jan 1939	Hendon
607 Sqn	Sep 1936–Aug 1939	Usworth
608 Sqn	Jan 1937–Mar 1939	Thornaby

Note: 29 Sqn – Turret Demon Oct 1936–Dec 1938; 41 Sqn – in Aden Oct 1935–Sep 1936; 64 Sqn – in Egypt to Sep 1936; 74 Sqn – in Malta to Sep 1936.

Gloster GLADIATOR

The only RAF biplane fighter to see combat in World War Two (with the exception of the limited use of the Gauntlet mentioned above) the Gloster Gladiator introduced a number of firsts to Fighter Command. The Gladiator was the first enclosed cockpit fighter and, more importantly, it had double the armament with four machine-guns, with the Browning having been chosen as the standard RAF rifle-calibre (0.303 in) weapon.

The Gladiator was a major type with Fighter Command in the late 1930s and survived in operational service into the early part of the war.

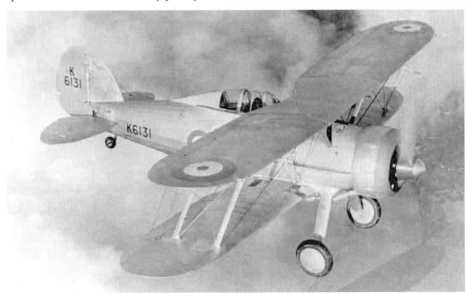

The prototype (K5200) flew on 12 September 1934 and was given a production order, under Specification 14/35, the following summer. By the time production ceased in early 1940 the RAF had received over 490 Gladiator Is and IIs, all powered by Mercury engines. The type entered service with 72 Squadron at Tangmere in February 1937 and eventually equipped a large number of Fighter Command squadrons, as well as serving with squadrons overseas. Despite its enclosed cockpit, four guns and top speed of 253 mph (at 14,500 ft) the Gladiator was still an obsolete type by the time it entered service and as with its predecessors the only thing it had going for it was agility. Most had left Fighter Command by the outbreak of war, giving way to Hurricanes and Spitfires but a number of the Command's squadrons did take them into active service. The operations in Norway by 263 Squadron were a brief interlude in which the aircraft had few combats but met with some success, whilst 247 Squadron used Gladiators in the Battle of Britain to defend Plymouth and the naval dockyards, eventually being the last Fighter Command squadron to re-equip from Gladiators (February 1941). The type more famously saw action in Malta, the Western Desert and Greece.

The Shuttleworth Collection, Bedfordshire operates the world's only airworthy Gladiator.

Gloster GLADIATOR
Prototype, first flight: K5200, 12 September 1934; first production K6129
Entry to service: 72 Sqn, February 1937

Squadron	Dates	Airfields
3 Sqn	Mar 1937–Mar 1938	Kenley
25 Sqn	Jun 1938–Feb 1939	Hawkinge, Northolt
54 Sqn	Apr 1937–Apr 1939	Hornchurch
56 Sqn	Jul 1937–May 1938	North Weald
65 Sqn	Jun 1937–Apr 1939	Hornchurch
72 Sqn	Mar 1937–May 1939	Tangmere, Church Fenton
73 Sqn	Jun 1937–Jul 1938	Debden, Digby
80 Sqn	May 1937–(Nov 1940)*	Henlow, Debden
85 Sqn	Jun 1938–Sep 1938	Debden
87 Sqn	Jun 1937–Aug 1938	Debden
152 Sqn	Oct 1939–Jan 1940*	Acklington
247 Sqn	Aug 1940–Feb 1941	Roborough, St Eval
263 Sqn	Oct 1939–Jun 1940	Filton, Norway
603 Sqn	Mar 1939–Oct 1939	Turnhouse
605 Sqn	Apr 1939–Nov 1939	Castle Bromwich
607 Sqn	Dec 1938–May 1940	Usworth
615 Sqn	Jun 1939–May 1940	Kenley, Croydon, France

Notes
* 80 Sqn – Egypt from Apr 1938.
* 152 Sqn – Plus detachments at Leconfield, Sumburgh.

WORLD WAR TWO

Like all major military conflicts, World War Two saw a tremendous increase in military technology, especially in the sphere of military aviation. The review of Fighter Command's pre-war aircraft showed that most were biplanes of around 230 mph and carrying two machine-guns; by the end of the war the performance and fire-power of fighters had been transformed and the jet age had arrived. Cannon, radar, g-suits and a whole host of advances that were almost undreamt of when Fighter Command formed in 1936 were in service and the capability of fighters, or more accurately the air defence network, had taken a quantum leap forward. That is not to say that the period was without its problems and for the first years of the war the Command suffered from lack of equipment, or at least lack of the appropriate equipment as it continued a rapid expansion programme. By 1942 day-fighter environment was dominated by the Spitfire, with the Hurricane serving in other roles or other theatres of war. The continued development of the Spitfire from the Mk I to the later Griffon-powered with four cannon was perhaps the best reason for the type to be called 'legendary', an epithet certainly not justified just by its Battle of Britain performance. The night war was incredibly difficult for Fighter Command until AI (Airborne Intercept – radar) came of age, a development initially with the Blenheim but taken-over by the Beaufighter and then that exponent of the art, the Mosquito. Amongst the Command's other types the Airacobra, Defiant, Havoc and Whirlwind had mixed fortunes and were never truly successful, although the Defiant in particular played a key role in the expansion of the night-fighter force. Jets arrived in 1944 but saw little operational service; nevertheless they pointed to the post-war future.

Hawker HURRICANE

The Hurricane has lived in the 'shadow' of the Spitfire throughout its career and all too often its importance has been overlooked. The Hurricane was the most numerous fighter in the Battle of Britain, and it destroyed more enemy aircraft than all other defences combined. True, in some respects it was not so well able to deal with the

Hurricane P3428 only served with 245 Squadron and was written-off after a flying accident in June 1941.

Hurricane BE485 carrying underwing bombs; although Fighter Command made little use of Hurri-bombers, this did become a major role of the aircraft in other theatres of war.

German escort fighters as well as its partner but it was liked by its pilots for its sturdy construction and reliability. In the bigger picture of the aircraft's career, albeit outside of the Fighter Command period, it developed new roles and become a major contributor to the war effort in the Middle East and Far East theatres.

The aircraft's origins can be traced to October 1933, with the prototype (K5083) of Camm's design taking to the air on 6 November 1935. It was an obvious success from the start, bearing in mind that the RAF was still introducing biplanes of just over 200 mph and with two guns, and an order for 600 aircraft was placed – orders that by September 1944 had totalled 12,950 in a variety of marks. The first squadron to re-equip was 111 Squadron, which gave up its Gauntlets in December 1937.

By late 1941 the main period of Hurricane use by Fighter Command was over.

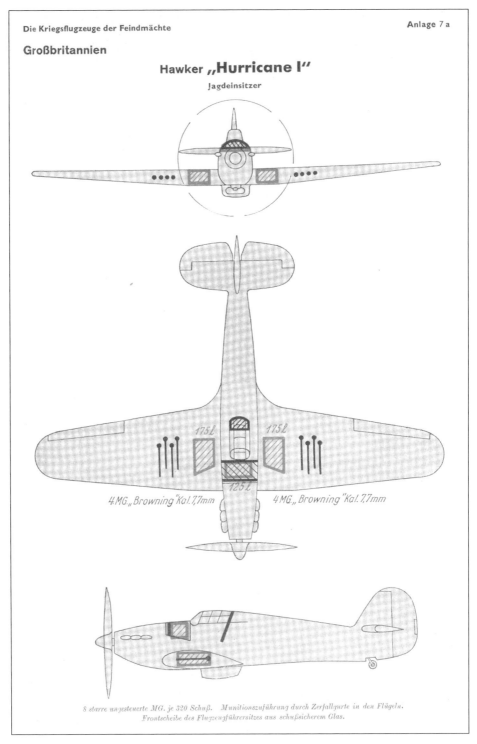

Die Kriegsflugzeuge der Feindmächte   Anlage 7 a

Großbritannien

Hawker „Hurricane I"

Jagdeinsitzer

175ℓ   175ℓ

4 MG.„Browning"Kal. 7,7mm   4 MG.„Browning"Kal. 7,7mm

125ℓ

8 starre ungesteuerte MG. je 320 Schuß.   Munitionszuführung durch Zerfallgurte in den Flügeln.
Frontscheibe des Flugzeugführersitzes aus schußsicherem Glas.

Hurricane 3-view; as with all the 3-views in this chapter, this is a German document that highlights the armament, armour plate and fuel tanks of the aircraft – information of great use for the attacker.

By July 1939 the Hurricane I was in service with twelve squadrons, and with six of the Auxiliary Air Force squadrons scheduled to re-equip. The aircraft was an enormous advance in all respects on the biplanes it was replacing – at over 100 mph faster (316 mph at 17,000 ft) and with eight Brownings, but nevertheless was inferior in most key respects to its main *Luftwaffe* opponent, the Bf 109. The latter could out-climb, out-run and out-dive the Hurricane but lost out in the turns, a significant factor in combat terms. This was OK if the aircraft joined combat at the same altitude or if the German aircraft stayed in to fight, especially at low lever, but the slashing, diving attack from a position of advantage left the Hurricane with few options. Lessons were learnt during the months in France; some were applied, for example, new propellers, armour plate, and a change in gun harmonisation. Another of the saving graces of the aircraft was its construction which enabled it to take a tremendous amount of punishment and yet keep on flying. The Hurricane has been called a 'Bulldog', as against the 'greyhound' of the Spitfire, and a range of similar sobriquets that suggest it was somewhat less appealing than its 'rival'; a Fighter Command study in 1941 simply called it 'the versatile Hurricane'. Captain Eric Brown flew the Hurricane and told the author:

> the Hurricane had a better rate of role, a distinct manoeuvring asset. However, it had a somewhat nasty abrupt stall, which could spell trouble if it occurred while pulling a lot of 'g' in combat. This might result in a spin, and spin recovery was not the Hurricane's strong point; indeed, deliberate spinning was prohibited.

As a gun platform the Hurricane was excellent and its roomier cockpit made it more comfortable for the pilot, although the 'ironwork' of the canopy gave a restricted view, although the forward view was better than that of the Spitfire.

As the data table shows, a large number of Fighter Command squadrons used Hurricanes, most of these in the day-fighter role, although some flew dual-role with day and night ops, with a few, such as 87 Squadron specialising in the latter and even painting their aircraft black. By late 1941 the main period of Fighter Command operations was over as more Spitfires became available and whilst some units continued to operate Hurricanes to as late as 1944 it was by then a minor element of the Command.

The Hurricane has not survived as well as other wartime fighters in terms of preservation in airworthy or museum condition and the world airworthy population is probably as low as six or seven, most of which are in the UK. The best place to see the type in the air is at one of the Duxford (Cambridgeshire) air shows.

Hawker HURRICANE
Prototype, first flight: K5083, 6 November 1935; first production L1547
Entry to service: 111 Sqn, December 1937

Squadron	Dates	Airfields
1 Sqn	Oct 1938–Sep 1942	Tangmere, France, Northolt, Hawkinge, Wittering, Kenley, Croydon, Redhill, Acklington
3 Sqn	Mar 1938–Feb 1943	Biggin Hill, Croydon, Manston, Kenley, Wick, Castletown, Turnhouse, Skeabrae, Martlesham Heath, Stapleford Tawney, Hunsdon
17 Sqn	Jun 1939–Nov 1941	North Weald, Croydon, Debden, Martlesham Heath, Hawkinge, Kenley, France, Castletown, Elgin, Tain, Catterick, (Far East)

32 Sqn	Oct 1938–Nov 1942	Biggin Hill, Manston, West Malling, Friston, Honiley, Baginton, (Middle East)
43 Sqn	Dec 1938–Oct 1942	Tangmere, Acklington, Wick, Usworth, Drem, Crail, Kirton-in-Lindsey, (Middle East)
46 Sqn	Mar 1939–May 1941	Digby, Acklington, Norway, Stapleford Tawney, North Weald, Church Fenton, Sherburn-in-Elmett, (Middle East)
56 Sqn	Apr 1938–Mar 1942	North Weald, Martlesham Heath, France, Digby, Boscombe Down, Middle Wallop, Duxford
71 Sqn	Nov 1940–Aug 1941	Church Fenton, Kirton-in-Lindsey, Martlesham Heath, North Weald
73 Sqn	Jul 1938–Nov 1940	Digby, France, Church Fenton, Castle Camps, (Middle East)
79 Sqn	Nov 1938–Mar 1942	Biggin Hill, Manston, France, Digby, Hawkinge, Sealand, Acklington, Pembrey, Fairwood Common, Baginton, (Far East)
81 Sqn*	Jul 1941–Dec 1941	Leconfield, Russia, Turnhouse
85 Sqn	Sep 1938–Apr 1941	Debden, Aldergrove, France, Croydon, Castle Camps, Church Fenton, Kirton-in-Lindsey, Gravesend
87 Sqn	Jul 1938–Nov 1942	Debden, France, Church Fenton, Exeter, Charmy Down, Colerne, (Middle East)
96 Sqn	Dec 1940–May 1941	Cranage, Wrexham
111 Sqn	Dec 1937–Apr 1941	Northolt, Acklington, Drem, Wick, Digby, North Weald, Croydon, Dyce
121 Sqn	May 1941–Nov 1941	Kirton-in-Lindsey, Digby
133 Sqn	Aug 1941–Dec 1941	Coltishall, Duxford, Collyweston, Fowlmere, Eglinton
134 Sqn*	Jul 1941–Dec 1941	Leconfield, Russia, Catterick
136 Sqn	Aug 1941–Nov 1941	Kirton-in-Lindsey, (Far East)
137 Sqn	Jun 1943–Jan 1944	Southend, Manston, Lympne, Colerne
145 Sqn	Mar 1940–Feb 1941	Croydon, Filton, Tangmere, Westhampnett, Drem, Dyce
151 Sqn	Dec 1938–Jan 1942	North Weald, Martlesham Heath, France, Manston, Stapleford Tawney, Digby, Bramcote, Wittering
164 Sqn	Feb 1943–Feb 1944	Fairwood Common, Middle Wallop, Warmwell, Manston, Fairlop, Twinwood Farm
174 Sqn	Mar 1942–Apr 1943	Manston, Fowlmere, Warmwell, Odiham, Chilbolton, Grove, Zeals, Gravesend
175 Sqn	Mar 1942–Apr 1943	Warmwell, Harrowbeer, Gatwick, Odiham, Stoney Cross, Lasham Colerne
182 Sqn	Sep 1942–Oct 1942	Martlesham Heath
184 Sqn	Dec 1942–(Mar 1944)	Colerne, Chilbolton, Grove, Zeals, Eastchurch, Merston, Manston, Kingsnorth, Newchurch
186 Sqn	Aug 1943–Jan 1944	Ayr
213 Sqn	Jan 1939–May 1941	Wittering, Biggin Hill, Exeter, Tangmere, Leconfield, Driffield, Castletown, (Middle East)
229 Sqn	Mar 1940–May 1941	Digby, Wittering, Northolt, Speke, (Middle East)
225 Sqn	Jan 1942–May 1942	Thruxton
232 Sqn	Jul 1941–Nov 1941	Sumburgh, Castletown, Skitten, Drem, Elgin, Montrose, Abbotsinch, Ouston, (Middle East)
238 Sqn	Jun 1940–May 1941	Middle Wallop, St Eval, Chilbolton, Pembrey, (Middle East)
239 Sqn	Jan 1942–May 1942	Gatwick
242 Sqn	Feb 1940–Nov 1941	Church Fenton, Biggin Hill, France, Coltishall, Duxford, Martlesham Heath, Stapleford Tawney, Manston, Valley, (Far East)
245 Sqn	Mar 1940–Jan 1943	Drem, Turnhouse, Aldergrove, Ballyhalbert, Chilbolton, Warmwell, Middle Wallop
247 Sqn	Jan 1941–Mar 1943	Roborough, St Eval, Portreath, Predannack, Exeter, High Ercall
249 Sqn	Jun 1940–May 1941	Church Fenton, Leconfield, Boscombe Down, North Weald, (Malta)
253 Sqn	Feb 1940–Nov 1942	Manston, Northolt, Kenley, France, Kirton-in-Lindsey, Turnhouse, Prestwick, Leconfield, Skeabrae, Hibaldstow, Shoreham, Friston, (North Africa)

255 Sqn	Mar 1941–Jul 1941	Kirton-in-Lindsey, Hibaldstow
257 Sqn	Jun 1940–Sep 1942	Hendon, Northolt, Debden, Martlesham Heath, Coltishall, Honiley, High Ercall
263 Sqn	Jun 1940–Nov 1940	Drem, Grangemouth
302 Sqn	Jul 1940–Jul 1941	Leconfield, Northolt, Westhampnett, Kenley, Jurby, Church Stanton, Warmwell, Ibsley
303 Sqn	Aug 1940–Oct 1941*	Northolt, Leconfield, Speke
306 Sqn	Aug 1940–Jul 1941	Church Fenton, Ternhill, Northolt
308 Sqn	Oct 1940–Apr 1941	Baginton
310 Sqn	Jul 1940–Dec 1941	Duxford, Martlesham Heath, Dyce
312 Sqn	Aug 1940–Dec 1941	Duxford, Speke, Valley, Jurby, Kenley, Martlesham Heath, Ayr
315 Sqn	Feb 1941–Jul 1941	Acklington, Speke, Northolt
316 Sqn	Feb 1941–Nov 1941	Pembrey, Colerne, Church Stanton
317 Sqn	Feb 1941–Nov 1941	Acklington, Ouston, Colerne, Fairwood Common, Exeter
331 Sqn	Jul 1941–Nov 1941	Catterick, Castletown, Skeabrae
401 Sqn	Mar 1941–Sep 1941	Digby
402 Sqn	Mar 1941–Mar 1942	Digby, Martlesham Heath, Ayr, Southend, Warmwell, Colerne
438 Sqn	Nov 1943–Jan 1944	Digby, Wittering, Ayr
439 Sqn	Jan 1944–Feb 1944	Wellingore, Ayr
440 Sqn	Feb 1944–Mar 1944	Ayr
486 Sqn	Mar 1942–Jul 1942	Kirton-in-Lindsey, Wittering
501 Sqn	Mar 1939–May 1941	Filton, Tangmere, France, Croydon, Middle Wallop, Gravesend, Kenley, Colerne
504 Sqn	May 1939–Nov 1941	Hucknall, Digby, Debden, Martlesham Heath, France, Manston, Wick, Castletown, Catterick, Hendon, Filton, Exeter, Fairwood Common, Chilbolton, Ballyhalbert
601 Sqn	Feb 1940–Jan 1942	Tangmere, Middle Wallop, Tangmere, Debden, Exeter, Northolt, Manston, Matlask
605 Sqn	Jun 1939–Nov 1941	Castle Bromwich, Tangmere, Leuchars, Wick, Hawkinge, Drem, Croydon, Martlesham Heath, Ternhill, Baginton, Honiley, (Far East)
607 Sqn	Mar 1940–Mar 1942	France, Croydon, Usworth, Tangmere, Turnhouse, Drem, Macmerry, Skitten, Martlesham Heath, Manston. (Far East)
615 Sqn	Apr 1940–Mar 1942	France, Kenley, Prestwick, Northolt, Kenley, Valley, Manston, Angle, Fairwood Common, (Far East)

Notes

1. Where a location is shown in brackets (e.g. Far East),the second date in the date column is that on which the squadron departed the UK for the overseas theatre and left Fighter Command; in most cases they continued to operate Hurricanes for some time.
2. 81 and 134 Sqns formed No. 151 Wing for service in Russia.
3. 303 Sqn, no Hurricanes on establishment Jan-Aug 1941, equipped with Spitfire.

Brewster BUFFALO

In September 1940 a dumpy new fighter appeared at Church Fenton for trials with 71 Squadron – and was promptly rejected as unsuitable for the European war. The Brewster Buffalo was one of the few types that the RAF Purchasing Commission had been able to get hold of in the panic phase of buying almost anything and was a version of the US Navy F2A-2 that had been ordered by the Belgians but had not been delivered before the Germans overran Belgium, which meant that aircraft for available for the RAF. The RAF eventually placed orders for 170 aircraft but other than the brief (six weeks) flirtation with 71 Squadron the type played no role with Fighter Command, although it did have a less than successful career in the Far East.

Bristol BLENHEIM

The Blenheim stunned the aviation world when it first appeared in 1936 as it was superior in performance to the current front-line fighters of the RAF – and it was intended as a bomber. The Blenheim was under development in the early 1930s at a period when the RAF was desperate for new aircraft and it looked so impressive on paper that 150 were ordered 'off the drawing board' in August 1935, the prototype (K7033) not making its first flight until 25 June 1936. Destined to join Bomber Command as a light bomber the first Blenheims went to 114 Squadron at Wyton in March 1937 and the type became standard equipment for No. 2 Group. However, its potential as a night-fighter had also been recognised and the Blenheim IF was developed into this role, the first of the type entering Fighter Command service with 25 Squadron at Hawkinge in December 1938.

To be effective as a fighter the aircraft needed two things – better forward armament, for which it was given an under-fuselage gun-pack with four 0.303 in Brownings, and an air intercept (AI) radar. The Blenheim played a significant role in the development of AI and night-fighter tactics and despite its poor showing in the early months of the war this vital link in the development of what would become effective equipment and tactics must not be overlooked; that is not to say that the Blenheims were unsuccessful, a number of night claims were made, the first AI 'kill' being recorded on the night of 22/23 July 1940.

As the unit list shows, a significant number of the Command's night-fighter units used Blenheims before 'graduating' to Beaufighters or Mosquitoes; the main period of Blenheim ops was over by early 1941. The list also includes the Fighter Interception Unit,

Blenheim of 25 Squadron; the Squadron introduced the Blenheim into Fighter Command service in December 1938.

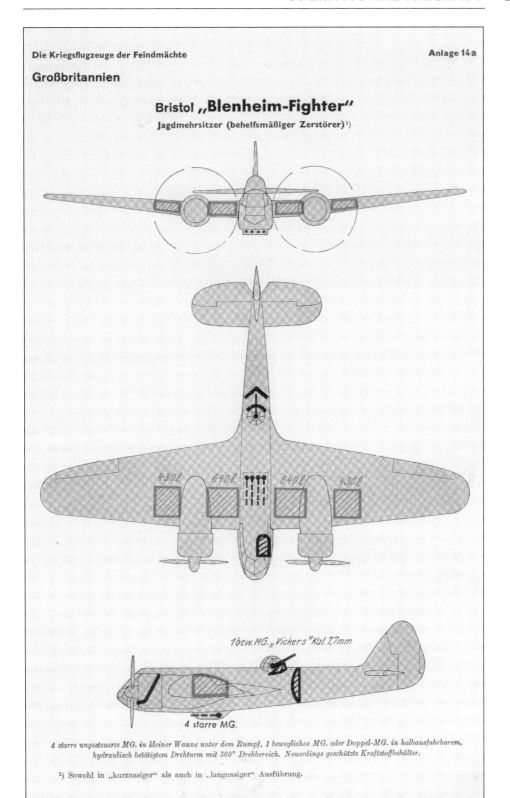

Großbritannien

Bristol „Blenheim-Fighter"
Jagdmehrsitzer (behelfsmäßiger Zerstörer)[1]

1 bew. MG. „Vickers" Kal. 7,7 mm

4 starre MG.

430 ℓ   640 ℓ   640 ℓ   430 ℓ

4 starre ungesteuerte MG. in kleiner Wanne unter dem Rumpf, 1 bewegliches MG. oder Doppel-MG. in halbausfahrbarem, hydraulisch betätigtem Drehturm mit 360° Drehbereich. Neuerdings geschützte Kraftstoffbehälter.

[1] Sowohl in „kurznasiger" als auch in „langnasiger" Ausführung.

a trials unit that also took part in operations. The majority of fighter Blenheims were Mark Is, although a number of Mark IVs for converted for the role.

There is only one airworthy Blenheim, which operates out of Duxford and regularly changes its colour scheme and markings to reflect different users. Sadly there are not too many Blenheims preserved in museums, although Canada has a reasonable collection of Bolingbroke versions.

Bristol BLENHEIM
Prototype, first flight: K7033, 25 June 1936; Blenheim IF L1424
Entry to service: 25 Sqn, December 1938

Squadron	Dates	Airfields
23 Sqn	Dec 1938–Apr 1941	Wittering, Collyweston, Wittering, Ford
25 Sqn	Dec 1938–Jan 1941	Hawkinge, Northolt, Filton, North Weald, Martlesham Heath
29 Sqn	Dec 1938–Feb 1941	Debden, Drem, Digby, Wellingore
64 Sqn	Dec 1938–Apr 1940	Church Fenton, Duxford
68 Sqn	Jan 1941–May 1941	Catterick, High Ercall
92 Sqn	Oct 1939–Mar 1940	Tangmere, Croydon
141 Sqn	Nov 1939–May 1940	Grangemouth, Prestwick
145 Sqn	Oct 1939–May 1940	Croydon
219 Sqn	Oct 1939–Feb 1941	Catterick
222 Sqn	Oct 1939–Mar 1940	Duxford
234 Sqn	Nov 1939–Mar 1940	Leconfield
242 Sqn	Dec 1939	Church Fenton
600 Sqn	Jan 1939–Oct 1941	Hendon, Northolt, Hornchurch, Rochford, Manston
601 Sqn	Jan 1939–Feb 1940	Hendon, Biggin Hill, Tangmere
604 Sqn	Jan 1939–May 1941	Hendon, North Weald
FIU	Apr 1940–?	Tangmere, Shoreham, Ford

Vickers-Supermarine SPITFIRE

In May 1940 A Spitfire I was evaluated against a captured Bf 109E-3, with Plt Off Adolf 'Sailor' Malan detached from 74 Squadron as the Spitfire pilot. The overall conclusion of the evaluation was that the Spitfire was generally superior in all areas; however, a similar evaluation by the Germans told a different story. The evaluation was conducted by one of the leading fighter exponents, Werner Molders who said that:

> it handles well, is light on the controls, faultless in turns, and has a performance approaching that of the Me 109. As a fighting aircraft, however, it is miserable. A sudden push forward on the stick will cause the motor to cut ... in a rapidly changing air combat situation the motor is either over-speeding or else is not being used to the full.

The is without doubt a fair slice of bias in the assessments plus the important element of lack of expertise in the flying of the enemy type – and combat effectiveness is a result of training and experience as well as the actual aircraft and weapon.

The Spitfire is nevertheless the best-known British fighter of all time and has a unique place in the annals of aviation, and has often been called 'legendary'. Designed by R J Mitchell, the prototype Spitfire (K5054) first flew in March 1936 but early production difficulties meant it was two years before deliveries began to the first squadron – 19 Squadron at Duxford in August 1938. By September 1939 only nine squadrons had been re-equipped, although this number had doubled by the start of the Battle of Britain.

Spitfire Vb October 1941; this Mark was produced in large numbers and a number of sub-variants and was the mainstay of the Command from mid 1941 to mid 1942.

To many people the Spitfire is the essence of the Battle of Britain, the sleek fighter with its throaty engine, against the masses of German bombers. Of course this is a very unrealistic picture but the appeal of the aircraft both at the time and since has ensured the survival of the myth. The 'invincibility' of the Spitfire was part of the morale boosting ethos current during the Battle – 'Spitfire' funds sprang up throughout the country with the news that for £5,000 you could 'buy' a Spitfire for one of the squadrons.

The classic lines of the Supermarine fighter as seen from underneath.

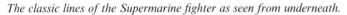

Die Kriegsflugzeuge der Feindmächte   Anlage 9 a

Großbritannien

Supermarine „Spitfire I"

Jagdeinsitzer

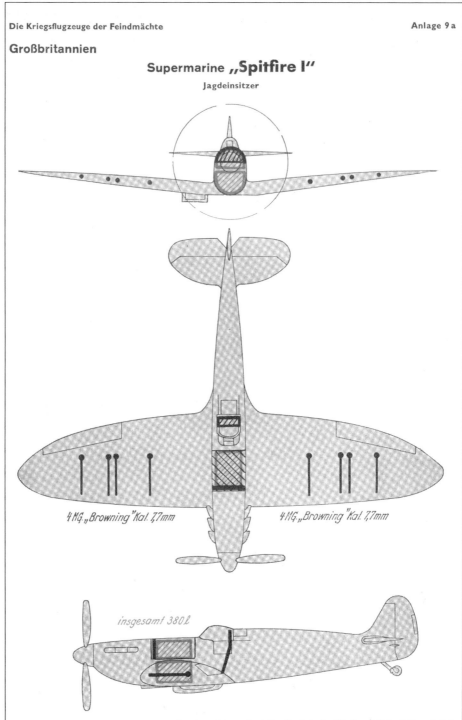

4 MG. „Browning" Kal. 7,7mm   4 MG. „Browning" Kal. 7,7mm

insgesamt 380 l

8 starre ungesteuerte MG. Je MG. 320 Schuß. Munitionszuführung durch Zerfallgurte in den Flügeln. Auffallend die große Entfernung der MG. von der Längsachse. Abstand des äußersten rechten MG. vom äußersten linken MG. 7,8 m. Frontscheibe des Flugzeugführersitzes aus schußsicherem Glas.

A speed of around 350 mph (at 19,000 ft) and a ceiling of 34,000 ft were by no means startling and as with the Hurricane, the Spitfire lost out to the Bf 109 in most performance criteria, with the exception of the turn. An overall improvement was made to the Spitfire Is by fitting of variable-pitch constant-speed propellers. Aircraft armament remained a vexed question with the argument over cannon or machine-guns. The standard eight 0.303 inch Browning machine guns fitted to the Spitfire were certainly reliable but against the latest large bombers they lacked hitting power and range. Cannon had greater range but less accuracy and a lower rate of fire, although they had greater hitting power – a single hit from a 20 mm shell being far more effective than numerous 0.303 strikes. Whilst the Spitfire IA kept the traditional armament, the IB was given 20 mm Hispano cannon. It turned out to be a very troublesome arrangement, mainly due to problems with fitting the system into the Spitfires very thin wing, and was not liked by the crews sent to try it out because of this unreliability. The only other mark to see service during the Battle of Britain was the IIA which, with its Merlin XII engine, brought an overall improvement in performance.

Whilst the Hurricane had largely vanished from Fighter Command by early 1941, the Spitfire went from strength to strength, as can be seen from the unit list below, with dozens of squadrons operating the type. The Spitfire was a fighter through and through although it undertook many other roles as well, from ground attack to its superlative role as a photo-recce aircraft.

Spitfires were used as 'Cats-Eye' night-fighters during the Night Blitz, with occasional success but with many problems – it was not really suited to night ops and landing accidents were frequent. With the Command turning to the offensive the Spitfire's limited radius of action became a problem – but there was little that could be done despite the use of external fuel tanks. With ground-attack – strafe and then bombing – an increasing part of the routine the aircraft also revealed another 'defect'; it was prone to self-damage from bullet ricochet or bomb fragments, as indeed was the P-51.

Although maintaining its basic form, the Spitfire went through numerous transformations to keep it in line with what was required – a good example being the development of the Mk. VIII/IX to counter the Fw 190. Fighter Command used various Merlin and Griffon versions of the Spitfire during the ten years the type operated with the Regular squadrons comprising (but not including sub-variants): Merlin variants – I, II, V, VI, VII, VIII, IX, XVI and Griffon variants – XII, XIV, XVIII, 21, 22, 24. Many of these came with LF (for low-altitude fighter) or HF (for high-altitude fighter) and this brief overview of the aircraft is not the place to go into details – that would require a complete, and very large, book. Total output of Merlin-engined alone *Spits* was over 18,300! The Spitfire II was powered by a single 1,150 hp Merlin XII giving a max speed of 357 mph. A further 2,042 Griffon-engined Spits were built, of which the Mk. XIX had a top speed of 460 mph.

Spitfires remained in service with Fighter Command in the post-war period with the F.20 series equipping a number of Auxiliary squadrons, although the Regular units were soon re-equipped with jets – often to the annoyance of the pilots.

A reasonable number of airworthy Spitfires have survived and more are being restored each year; the 'average' number of airworthy examples worldwide is 50 and there are numerous others in aviation museums. In the UK you are never too far from a Spitfire and most air displays include at least one *Spit*, often featuring the Battle of Britain Memorial, which has the finest collection of the type.

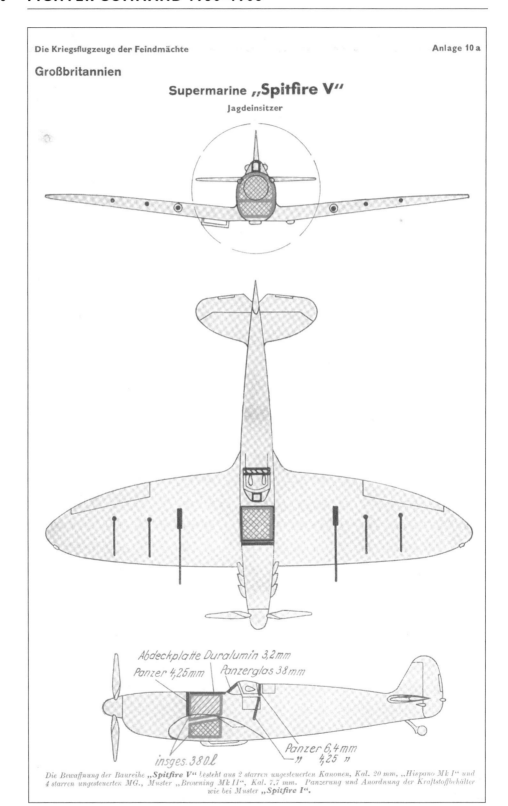

Die Kriegsflugzeuge der Feindmächte   Anlage 10 a

Großbritannien

Supermarine „**Spitfire V**"

Jagdeinsitzer

Abdeckplatte Duralumin 3,2mm

Panzer 4,25mm   Panzerglas 38mm

Panzer 6,4mm
„   4,25 „

insges. 380 l

Die Bewaffnung der Baureihe „**Spitfire V**" besteht aus 2 starren ungesteuerten Kanonen, Kal. 20 mm, „Hispano Mk I" und 4 starren ungesteuerten MG., Muster „Browning Mk II", Kal. 7,7 mm. Panzerung und Anordnung der Kraftstoffbehälter wie bei Muster „**Spitfire I**".

Vickers-Supermarine SPITFIRE
Prototype, first flight: K5054, 5 March 1936
Entry to service: 19 Sqn, August 1938

Squadron	Dates	Airfields
1 Sqn	Apr 1944–Oct 1946	North Weald, Ayr, Predannack, Harrowbeer, Detling, Lympne, Manston, Coltishall, Ludham, Hutton Cranswick, Tangmere, Acklington
19 Sqn	Aug 1938–Jan 1944	Duxford, Horsham St Faith, Hornchurch, Fowlmere, Matlask, Ludham, Hutton Cranswick, Perranporth, Middle Wallop, Fairlop, Digby, Gravesend, Kingsnorth, Weston Zoyland, Gatwick
19 Sqn	Mar 1946–Nov 1946	Molesworth, Wittering, Biggin Hill
26 Sqn	Aug 1944–Dec 1944	Lee-on-Solent. Hawkinge, Tangmere, Manston
41 Sqn	Jan 1939–Sep 1945*	Catterick, Wick, Hornchurch, Merston, Martlesham Heath, Merston, Hawkinge, Debden, Longtown, Llanbedr, High Ercall, Biggin Hill, Friston, Westhampnett, Southend, Lympne, *Europe*
	Apr 1946–Aug 1947	Wittering
54 Sqn	Mar 1939–Jun 1942	Hornchurch, Rochford, Catterick, Southend, Martlesham Heath, Castletown, Wellingore, (Australia)
63 Sqn	May 1944–Jan 1945	Woodvale, Lee-on-Solent, North Weald, Manston
	Sep 1946–May 1948	Middle Wallop, Thorney Island
64 Sqn	Apr 1940–Nov 1944	Church Fenton, Usworth, Kenley, Leconfield, Biggin Hill, Coltishall, Hornchurch, Southend, Drem, Turnhouse, Fairlop, Predannack, Ayr, Gravesend, West Malling, Deanland, Harrowbeer, Bradwell Bay
65 Sqn	Mar 1939–Jan 1944	Hornchurch, Northolt, Kirton-in-Lindsey, Turnhouse, Tangmere, Oulton, Debden, Great Sampford, Gravesend, Drem, Perranporth, Fairlop, Selsey, Kingsnorth, Ashford, Gatwick, Gravesend
	Feb 1946–Oct 1946	Spilsby, Horsham St Faith
66 Sqn	Oct 1938–Apr 1945*	Duxford, Horsham St Faith, Coltishall, Kenley, Gravesend, West Malling, Biggin Hill, Exeter, Perranporth, Portreath, Ibsley, Zeals, Skaebrae, Church Stanton, North Weald, Hornchurch, Southend, Bognor, Castletown, Funtingdon, Ford, *Europe*
	Sep 1946–Mar 1947	Duxford
71 Sqn	Aug 1941–Sep 1942*	North Weald, Martlesham Heath, Debden, Gravesend
72 Sqn	Apr 1939–Nov 1942	Church Fenton, Leconfield, Drem, Acklington, Gravesend, Biggin Hill, Croydon, Coltishall, Matlask, Leuchars, Lympne, Morpeth, Ayr, Ouston, (Middle East)
74 Sqn	Feb 1939–Apr 1942	Hornchurch, Rochford, Leconfield, Wittering, Kirton-in-Lindsey, Biggin Hill, Gravesend, Acklington, Llanbedr, Long Kesh, Atcham, (Middle East)
	Apr 1944–May 1945	North Weald, Lympne, Tangmere, Selsey, Southend, Tangmere, *Europe*
80 Sqn	Apr 1944–Aug 1944	Sawbridgeworth, Hornchurch, Detling, Merston, Gatwick, West Malling
91 Sqn	Jan 1941–Oct 1946	Hawkinge, Lympne, Honiley, Wittering, Westhampnett, Tangmere, Hutton Cranswick, Castle Camps, Drem, West Malling, Deanland, Biggin Hill, Manston, Ludham, Fairwood Common, Dyce, Duxford
92 Sqn	Mar 1940–Feb 1942	Croydon, Northolt, Hornchurch, Pembrey, Biggin Hill, Manston, Gravesend, Digby, (Middle East)
118 Sqn	Feb 1941–Jan 1945	Filton, Colerne, Warmwell, Ibsley, Tangmere, Zeals, Wittering, Coltishall, Merston, Peterhead, Castletown, Detling, Skaebrae, Westhampnett, Manston, Bentwaters
121 Sqn	Oct 1941–Sep 1942*	Kirton-in-Lindsey, North Weald, Southend, Debden

122 Sqn	May 1941–Feb 1945	Turnhouse, Ouston, Catterick, Scorton, Hornchurch, Fairlop, Martlesham Heath, Eastchurch, Bognor, Kingsnorth, Ashford, Brenzett, Weston Zoyland, Gravesend
	Aug 1945–Apr 1946	Dyce, Wick, Hawkinge, Wick, Dalcross
123 Sqn	May 1941–Apr 1942	Turnhouse, Drem, Castletown (Middle East)
124 Sqn	May 1941–Aug 1945	Castletown, Biggin Hill, Gravesend, Eastchurch, Martlesham Heath, Debden, Tangmere, Westhampnett, North Weald, Drem, Croughton, Duxford, West Malling, Southend, Church Fenton, Bradwell Bay, Manston, Coltishall, Hutton Cranswick, Molesworth
126 Sqn	Apr 1944–Mar 1946	Sawbridgeworth, Culmhead, Harrowbeer, Bradwell Bay, Hethel
127 Sqn	Apr 1944–Apr 1945	North Weald, Lympne, Tangmere, Southend, Funtingdon, Ford, *Europe*
129 Sqn	Jun 1941–Apr 1944	Leconfield, Westhampnett, Debden, Ipswich, Thorney Island, Grimsetter, Skaebrae, Ibsley, Tangmere, Hornchurch, Peterhead, Heston
	May 1945–Sep 1946	Bentwaters, Dyce, *Norway*, Molesworth, Hutton Cranswick, Spilsby, Church Fenton
130 Sqn	Jun 1941–Oct 1946	Portreath, Harrowbeer, Warmwell, Perranporth, West Freugh, Thorney Island, Drem, Ballyhalbert, Honiley, West Malling, Catterick, Scorton, Ayr, Acklington, Lympne, Horne, Westhampnett, Merston, *Europe*, North Weald, Dyce, *Norway*, Manston, Charterhall, Odiham
131 Sqn	Jun 1941–Nov 1944	Ouston, Catterick, Ternhill, Atcham, Llanbedr, Valley, Merston. Tangmere, Ipswich, Thorney Island, Westhampnett, Castletown, Exeter, Redhill, Church Stanton, Colerne, Harrowbeer, Culmhead, Friston, (Far East)
132 Sqn	Jul 1941–Dec 1944	Peterhead, Skaebrae, Grimsetter, Martlesham Heath, Hornchurch, Zeals, Eastchurch, Perranporth, Gravesend, Newchurch, Detling, Castletown, Ford, *Europe*, (Far East)
133 Sqn	Oct 1941–Sep 1942*	Eglinton, Kirton-in-Lindsey, Biggin Hill, Lympne, Gravesend, Martlesham Heath, Great Sampford
152 Sqn	Dec 1939–Nov 1942	Acklington, Warmwell, Portreath, Snailwell, Swanton Morley, Coltishall, Eglinton, Angle, Collyweston, Wittering, (North Africa)
154 Sqn	Nov 1941–Nov 1942	Fowlmere, Coltishall, Church Stanton, Hornchurch, Fairlop, Ipswich, Wellingore, (North Africa)
	Nov 1944–Feb 1945	Biggin Hill
164 Sqn	Apr 1942–Feb 1943	Peterhead, Skaebrae, Fairwood Common
	Jun 1945–Aug 1946	Turnhouse, Fairwood Common, Tangmere, Middle Wallop
165 Sqn	Apr 1942–Jan 1945	Ayr, Eastchurch, Gravesend, Tangmere, Martlesham Heath, Peterhead, Ibsley, Exeter, Kenley, Church Stanton, Colerne, Culmhead, Predannack, Harrowbeer, Detling, Lympne, Bentwaters
	May 1945–Sep 1946	Bentwaters, Dyce, *Norway*, Charterhall, Duxford, Middle Wallop
167 Sqn	Apr 1942–Jun 1943	Scorton, Castletown, Ludham, Kidlington, Fowlmere, Digby, Hornchurch, Westhampnett, Woodvale
186 Sqn	Feb 1944–Apr 1944	Tain, Lympne
222 Sqn	Mar 1940–Dec 1944	Duxford, Digby, Kirton-in-Lindsey, Hornchurch, Coltishall, Matlask, Manston, Southend, North Weald, Winfield, Drem, Biggin Hill, Ayr, Martlesham Heath, Woodvale, Catterick, Acklington, Selsey, Coolham, Funtingdon, *Europe*, Predannack
234 Sqn	Mar 1940–Oct 1944	Leconfield, Church Fenton, St Eval, Middle Wallop, Warmwell, Ibsley, Predannack, Portreath, Charmy Down, Perranporth, Grimsetter, Skaebrae, Church Stanton, Honiley, West Malling, Southend, Hutton Cranswick, Church Fenton, Coltishall, Bolt Head, Deanland, North Weald
	Aug 1945–Feb 1946	Bentwaters, Molesworth

238 Sqn	May 1940–Jun 1940	Tangmere, Middle Wallop
242 Sqn	Apr 1942–Oct 1942	Turnhouse, Ouston, Drem, North Weald, Manston, Digby, (North Africa)
243 Sqn	Jun 1942–Nov 1942	Ouston, Turnhouse, (North Africa)
249 Sqn	May 1940–Jun 1940	Leconfield
257 Sqn	May 1940–Jun 1940	Hendon
266 Sqn	Jan 1940–Jul 1945	Sutton Bridge, Martlesham Heath, Wittering, Eastchurch, Hornchurch, Collyweston, Kingcliffe, Duxford
274 Sqn	Apr 1944–Aug 1944	Hornchurch, Detling, Merston, Gatwick, West Malling
302 Sqn Polish	Oct 1941–Dec 1946*	Ibsley, Harrowbeer, Warmwell, Heston, Croydon, Ipswich, Kirton-in-Lindsey, Hutton Cranswick, Perranporth, Fairlop, Tangmere, Northolt, Llanbedr, Deanland, Southend, Chailey, Appledram, Ford, *Europe*, Fairwood Common, Hethel
303 Sqn Polish	Jan 1941–Apr 1945	Northolt, Speke, Kirton-in-Lindsey, Redhill, Heston, Debden, Martlesham Heath, Ballyhalbert, Horne, Westhampnett, Coltishall, Andrewsfield
306 Sqn Polish	Jun 1941–Apr 1944	Northolt, Speke, Church Stanton, Kirton-in-Lindsey, Hutton Cranswick, Catterick, Gravesend, Friston, Heston, Llanbedr, Coolham
308 Sqn Polish	Mar 1941–Dec 1946*	Baginton, Chilbolton, Woodvale, Exeter, Hutton Cranswick, Redhill, Heston, Ipswich, Northolt, Church Fenton, Hutton Cranswick, Llanbedr, Deanland, Chailey, Appledram, Ford, *Europe*, Hethel
310 Sqn Czech	Oct 1941–Aug 1945	Montrose, Perranporth, Predannack, Warmwell, Exeter, Redhill, Castletown, Ibsley, Llanbedr, Mendlesham, Southend, Appledram, Tangmere, Lympne, Digby, North Weald, Bradwell Bay, Manston, (*Europe*)
312 Sqn Czech	Oct 1941–Aug 1945	Ayr, Fairwood Common, Angle, Warmwell, Harrowbeer, Redhill, Church Stanton, Skaebrae, Llanbedr, Ibsley, Mendlesham, Southend, Appledram, Tangmere, Lympne, Coltishall, North Weald, Bradwell Bay, (*Europe*)
313 Sqn Czech	May 1941–Aug 1945	Catterick, Leconfield, Portreath, Warmwell, Hornchurch, Southend, Fairlop, Church Stanton, Peterhead, Hawkinge, Ibsley, Woodvale, Ayr, Mendlesham, Southend, Appledram, Tangmere, Lympne, Skaebrae, North Weald, Bradwell Bay, Manston, (*Europe*)
315 Sqn Polish	Jul 1941–Apr 1944	Northolt, Woodvale, Hutton Cranswick, Ballyhalbert, Heston, Llanbedr, Coolham, Holmsley South, Ford, Brenzett, Andrewsfield, Coltishall, Peterhead, Fairwood Common
316 Sqn Polish	Oct 1941–Apr 1944	Church Stanton, Northolt, Heston, Hutton Cranswick, Acklington, Woodvale, Coltishall, West Malling, Friston, Andrewsfield, Fairwood Common, Wick, Hethel
317 Sqn Polish	Oct 1941–Dec 1946*	Exeter, Northolt, Croydon, Woodvale, Kirton-in-Lindsey, Martlesham Heath, Heston, Perranporth, Fairlop, Southend, Deanland, Chailey, Appledram, Ford, *Europe*, Hethel
318 Sqn Polish	Aug 1946–Dec 1946	Coltishall
322 Sqn Dutch	Jun 1943–Oct 1945*	Woodvale, Llanbedr, Ayr, Hawkinge, Acklington, Hartford Bridge, West Malling, Deanland, Fairwood Common, Biggin Hill, *Europe*
329 Sqn French	Feb 1944–Nov 1945*	Perranporth, Ayr, Merston, Llanbedr, Funtingdon, Selsey, Tangmere, *Europe*, Turnhouse, Skaebrae, Harrowbeer, Fairwood Common, Exeter
331 Sqn Norway	Nov 1941–May 1945*	Skaebrae, North Weald, Manston, Ipswich, Llanbedr, Southend, Bognor, Tangmere, Funtingdon, Ford, *Europe*, Dyce, *Norway*
332 Sqn Norway	Jan 1942–May 1945*	Catterick, North Weald, Manston, Martlesham Heath, Llanbedr, Southend, Bognor, Tangmere, Ford, *Europe*, Dyce, *Norway*

340 Sqn French	Nov 1941–Nov 1945*	Turnhouse, Drem, Ayr, Redhill, Westhampnett, Ipswich, Hornchurch, Biggin Hill, Turnhouse, Drem, Merston, Llanbedr, Merston, Funtingdon, Selsey. Tangmere, *Europe*
341 Sqn French	Jan 1943–Nov 1945*	Turnhouse, Biggin Hill, Merston, Llanbedr, Funtingdon, Selsey, Tangmere, *Europe*
345 Sqn French	Mar 1944–Nov 1945	Ayr, Shoreham, Deanland, Fairwood Common, Biggin Hill, *Europe*
349 Sqn Belgian	Jun 1943–Oct 1946	Wittering, Collyweston, Kingscliffe, Wellingore, Digby, Acklington, Friston, Southend, Hornchurch, Llanbedr, Selsey, Coolham, Funtingdon, Tangmere, *Europe*
350 Sqn Belgian	Nov 1941–Oct 1946	Valley, Atcham, Warmwell, Debden, Gravesend, Martlesham Heath, Kenley, Redhill, Southend, Hornchurch, Heston, Fairlop, Acklington, Ouston, Digby, West Malling, Hawkinge, Llanbedr, Peterhead, Friston, Westhampnett, Lympne, *Europe*
401 Sqn RCAF	Sep 1941–Jun 1945	Digby, Biggin Hill, Gravesend, Eastchurch, Martlesham Heath, Lympne, Kenley, Catterick, Redhill, Staplehurst, Fairwood Common, Tangmere, *Europe*
402 Sqn RCAF	Mar 1942–Jul 1945	Colerne, Fairwood Common, Kenley, Redhill, Ipswich, Martlesham Heath, Digby, Ayr, Wellingore, Horne, Westhampnett, Merston, Hawkinge, *Europe*
403 Sqn RCAF	May 1941–Jul 1945	Baginton, Ternhill, Hornchurch, Debden, Martlesham Heath, Northolt, Southend, Catterick, Manston, Kenley, Lashenden, Headcorn, Kenley, Hutton Cranswick, *Europe*
411 Sqn RCAF	Jun 1941–Mar 1946	Digby, Hornchurch, Southend, Shawbury, Kidlington, Fowlmere, Kenley, Redhill, Stapleford, Biggin Hill, Peterhead, Fairwood Common, *Europe*
412 Sqn RCAF	Jun 1941–Mar 1946	Digby, Wellingore, Martlesham Heath, North Weald, Merston, Tangmere, Redhill, Kenley, Angle, Fairwood Common, Hurn, Odiham, Lasham, Perranporth, Friston, Staplehurst, Biggin Hill, Hutton Cranswick, *Europe*
416 Sqn RCAF	Nov 1941–Mar 1946	Peterhead, Dyce, Martlesham Heath, Hawkinge, Redhill, Kenley, Wellingore, Digby, Merston, Tangmere, *Europe*
417 Sqn RCAF	Nov 1941–Apr 1942	Charmy Down, Colerne, Tain, (*Middle East*)
421 Sqn RCAF	Apr 1942–Jul 1945	Digby, Fairwood Common, Warmwell, Exeter, Ibsley, Kenley, Angle, Zeals, Redhill, Lashenden, Headcorn, Hutton Cranswick, Tangmere, *Europe*
441 Sqn RCAF	Feb 1944–May 1945	Digby, Holmsley South, Westhampnett, Hutton Cranswick, Funtingdon, Ford, *Europe*, Hawkinge, Skeabrae, Hawkinge, Hunsdon
442 Sqn RCAF	Feb 1944–Mar 1945	Digby, Holmsley South, Westhampnett, Funtingdon, Hutton Cranswick, Ford, *Europe*, Hunsdon
443 Sqn RCAF	Feb 1944–Mar 1946	Digby, Holmsley South, Hutton Cranswick, Westhampnett, Funtingdon, Ford, *Europe*
451 Sqn RAAF	Dec 1944–Jan 1946	Hawkinge, Manston, Matlask, Swannington, Lympne, Skeabrae, Lasham, *Europe*
452 Sqn RAAF	Apr 1941–Jun 1942	Kirton-in-Lindsey, Kenley, Redhill, Andreas, (*Australia*)
453 Sqn RAAF	Jun 1942–Jan 1946	Drem, Hornchurch, Southend, Martlesham Heath, Westcott, Newmarket, Ibsley, Perranporth, Skeabrae, Detling, Hutton Cranswick, Peterhead, Ford, *Europe*, Coltishall, Matlask, Swannington, Lympne, Lasham, *Germany*
457 Sqn RAAF	Jun 1941–Jun 1942	Baginton, Jurby, Andreas, Redhill, Kirton-in-Lindsey, (*Australia*)
485 Sqn RNZAF	Mar 1941–Aug 1945	Driffield, Leconfield, Redhill, Kenley, Kingscliffe, West Malling, Kirkistown, Eglinton, Westhampnett, Merston, Biggin Hill, Hornchurch, Drem, Llanbedr, Selsey, Coolham, Funtingdon, Tangmere, *Europe*, Predannack, *Holland*

501 Sqn	Apr 1941–Apr 1944	Colerne, Chilbolton, Ibsley, Tangmere, Warmwell, Middle Wallop, Hawkinge, Ballyhalbert, Westhampnett, Woodvale, Southend, Friston
	Oct 1946–May 1949	Filton
504 Sqn	Oct 1941–Mar 1945	Ballyhalbert, Kirkistown, Middle Wallop, Ibsley, Church Stanton, Redhill, Castletown, Peterhead, Hornchurch, Llanbedr, Digby, Lympne, Detling, Manston, Hawkinge, Colerne
	May 1948–Mar 1950	Hucknall, Wymeswold
602 Sqn	May 1941–May 1945	Abbotsinch, Grangemouth, Drem, Dyce, Westhampnett, Prestwick, Ayr, Kenley, Redhill, Peterhead, Skeabrae, Perranporth, Lasham, Fairlop, Bognor, Kingsnorth, Newchurch, Detling, Llanbedr, Ford, *Europe*, Coltishall, Matlask, Swannington, Ludham
	Oct 1946–May 1951	Abbotsinch, Leuchars
603 Sqn	Sep 1939–Apr 1942	Turnhouse, Prestwick, Dyce, Drem, Hornchurch, Southend, Fairlop, Peterhead, (*Egypt*)
	Jan 1945–Aug 1945	Coltishall, Ludham, Turnhouse, Drem, Skeabrae
	Oct 1946–Jul 1951	Turnhouse
604 Sqn	Oct 1946–May 1950	Hendon, North Weald
607 Sqn	Nov 1946–Jun 1951	Ouston
609 Sqn	Aug 1939–May 1942	Yeadon, Catterick, Acklington, Drem, Kinloss, Northolt, Middle Wallop, Warmwell, Biggin Hill, Gravesend, Digby, Duxford
	Apr 1948–Feb 1951	Yeadon, Church Fenton
610 Sqn	Sep 1939–Mar 1945	Hooton Park, Wittering, Prestwick, Biggin Hill, Gravesend, Acklington, Westhampnett, Leconfield, Hutton Cranswick, Ludham, Castletown, Perranporth, Bolt Head, Fairwood Common, Exeter, Culmhead, Harrowbeer, West Malling, Friston, Lympne, *Europe*, Warmwell
	Nov 1946–Aug 1951	Hooton Park
611 Sqn	May 1939–Mar 1945	Speke, Duxford, Digby, Southend, Hornchurch, Drem, Kenley, Martlesham Heath, Redhill, Ipswich, Biggin Hill, Matlask, Ludham, Coltishall, Manston, Ford, Deanland, Harrowbeer, Predannack, Bolt Head, Bradwell Bay, Skeabrae, Hawkinge, Hunsdon
	Nov 1946–Nov 1951	Woodvale, Hooton Park
612 Sqn	Nov 1946–Jun 1951	Dyce
614 Sqn	Dec 1946–Mar 1951	Ringway
615 Sqn	Oct 1946–Oct 1950	Biggin Hill
616 Sqn	Oct 1939–Aug 1944	Leconfield, Rochford, Kenley, Coltishall, Kirton-in-Lindsey, Tangmere, Westhampnett, Kingscliffe, West Malling, Great Sampford, Ipswich, Ibsley, Harrowbeer, Exeter, Fairwood Common, Culmhead

Notes
41 Sqn, from Dec 1944 to Mar 1946 the Squadron was in Europe (Not FC).
66 Sqn, from Aug 1944 to Apr 1945 the Squadron was in Europe (Not FC).
71 Sqn, became 334th Fighter Squadron/4th Fighter Group USAAF.
74 Sqn, from Aug 1944 to May 1945 the Squadron was in Europe.
121 Sqn, became 335th Fighter Squadron/4th Fighter Group USAAF.
133 Sqn, became 336th Fighter Squadron/4th Fighter Group USAAF.
302 Sqn, from Aug 1944 to Oct 1946 the Squadron was in Europe.
308 Sqn, from Aug 1944 to Oct 1946 the Squadron was in Europe.
317 Sqn, from Aug 1944 to Oct 1946 the Squadron was in Europe.
322 Sqn, from Jan 1945 to Oct 1945 the Squadron was in Europe.
331 Sqn, from Aug 1944 to Apr 1945 the Squadron was in Europe.
332 Sqn, from Aug 1944 to Apr 1945 the Squadron was in Europe.
340 Sqn, from Aug 1944 to Nov 1944, Feb 1945 to Nov 1945 the Squadron was in Europe.
341 Sqn, from Aug 1944 to Nov 1945 the Squadron was in Europe.

The Spitfire XIV had a top speed of around 450 mph and entered service, with 610 Squadron, in January 1944.

The Spitfire XXI was only produced in small numbers (120) and entered service in January 1945 with 91 Squadron; it only served with eight squadrons.

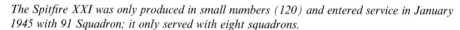

Boulton-Paul DEFIANT

In the mid 1930s the RAF expressed interest in a 'turret fighter' that could fly alongside enemy bombers and use its 'heavy' firepower of four machine-guns to destroy the enemy. Various evaluations suggested the concept was viable and required that as a bomber-destroyer the aircraft would prove invaluable; it was a concept that by the late 1930s was seriously flawed. The only turret-fighter to enter service was the Boulton Paul Defiant and its combat career was somewhat mixed.

The Defiant was developed against Specification F9/35 and the prototype (K8310) flew on 11 August 1937; by the time the first aircraft joined 264 Squadron in December 1939 the concept was already being called into question for a day fighter. However, they duly took the aircraft to war in May 1940 – and it was an immediate success; it appears that the enemy thought they were standard fighters with only forward-firing guns, and by the end of May the Squadron had made claims for over 60 aircraft. Losses had been reasonable and the aircraft appeared to be justifying itself. This optimism proved unfounded and in summer 1940 the Defiants were shot out of the sky by German fighters, which led to their relegation to the night-fighter role, in which they were to play a significant role. The 303 mph speed and 30,000 ft ceiling were adequate for night ops.

On 16 June the CO of 264 Squadron (Sqn Ldr Hunter) took a Defiant to Farnborough for evaluation against a Bf 109. His report was positive and concluded that: 'should an Me 109 attack a Defiant, if the pilot of the latter goes into a really steep turn, he will prevent the pilot of the 109 bringing his guns to bear, and will eventually, if the pilot of the 109 follows him into the turn, be able to get into a suitable position to deliver his own attack. If conditions are the same for both aircraft, that is to say, if the Me 109 does not have a height advantage, the general manoeuvrability of the Defiant compares very favourably with that of the 109, the Defiant being able to turn in a much smaller turning circle and still have full control. To conclude, it is thought that the Defiant fitted with a constant speed airscrew should be able to deal with the Me 109

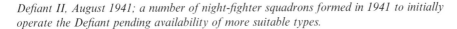

Defiant II, August 1941; a number of night-fighter squadrons formed in 1941 to initially operate the Defiant pending availability of more suitable types.

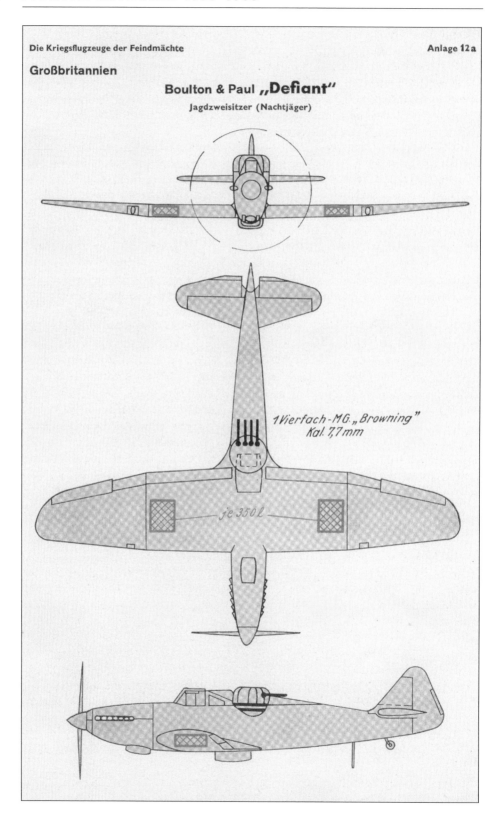

Die Kriegsflugzeuge der Feindmächte

Anlage 12a

Großbritannien

Boulton & Paul „**Defiant**"

Jagdzweisitzer (Nachtjäger)

1 Vierfach-MG. „Browning"
Kal. 7,7 mm

je 350 ℓ

very satisfactorily at all times.' Sadly this was to prove an over-estimation of the combat equation between the two types.

The unit list shows a number of squadrons forming in 1940 and 1941 as part of the growing night-fighter force. Guided by ground controllers or free-lancing, and equipped with AI radar the Defiants scored a number of successes at night but more important was the experience gained by the crews in night operations, which they were able to put to good use when re-equipped with better aircraft.

Although production totalled 1,064 aircraft (ceasing in February 1943), operationally the aircraft had a limited career; however, it served in a variety of other roles, many in support of Fighter Command, including target-towing and Air-Sea Rescue.

There are no airworthy Defiants and very few preserved in museums.

Boulton-Paul DEFIANT

Prototype, first flight: K8310, 11 August 1937

Entry to service: 264 Sqn, December 1939

Squadron	Dates	Airfields
85 Sqn	Jan 1941–Feb 1941	Debden
96 Sqn	Mar 1941–Jul 1942	Cranage, Wrexham
125 Sqn	Jun 1941–May 1942	Colerne, Charmy Down, Fairwood Common
141 Sqn	Apr 1940–Sep 1941	Turnhouse, Grangemouth, Prestwick, West Malling, Dyce, Drem, Gatwick, Gravesend, Ayr
151 Sqn	Dec 1940–Jul 1942	Bramcote, Wittering, Coltishall
153 Sqn	Oct 1941–Apr 1942	Ballyhalbert
255 Sqn	Nov 1940–Sep 1941	Kirton-in-Lindsey, Hibaldstow
256 Sqn	Nov 1940–Jun 1942	Catterick, Pembrey, Colerne, Squires Gate
264 Sqn	Dec 1939–Jul 1942	Martlesham Heath, Duxford, Fowlmere, Kirton-in-Lindsey, Hornchurch, Southend, Debden, Gravesend, Biggin Hill, West Malling, Colerne
307 Sqn Polish	Sep 1940–Aug 1941	Kirton-in-Lindsey, Jurby, Squires Gate, Colerne, Exeter
409 Sqn RCAF	Jul 1941–Sep 1941	Digby, Coleby Grange
410 Sqn RCAF	Jun 1941–May 1942	Ayr, Drem
456 Sqn RAAF	Jun 1941–Nov 1941	Valley

Bristol BEAUFIGHTER

The Bristol Beaufighter took on many roles during its wartime career and played a major role in each of them; however, in Fighter Command it was responsible for honing the capabilities of the night-fighter squadrons by providing them with the first truly effective radar-based aircraft with performance and firepower. The Bristol Beaufighter was a private venture not developed to a military specification but when the prototype (R2052) flew on 17 July 1939 it was obvious that this was going to be a successful aircraft, and it had already been given a production Specification (F17/39) by the Air Ministry as a long-range day-fighter. Production Beaufighter F.1s joined the Fighter Interception Unit (FIU) at Tangmere in mid August 1940, with the first operational unit, 25 Squadron, receiving aircraft the following month. Whilst the type did serve in the long-range fighter role this was with other Commands and for Fighter Command its significance was as a night-fighter equipped with, initially, AI Mk. IV. The first success came on 19 November when a 604 Squadron Beaufighter shot-down a Ju88.

Improvements in equipment were steadily introduced, the Beaufighter IIF joining 600 Squadron in April 1941, to be followed in 1942 by the Mark VIF, one of the major

In all the roles in which it was employed the Beaufighter was a success; in conjunction with the Control and Reporting system, the type was responsible for bringing Fighter Command's night defences to a peak of efficiency.

variants in terms of production numbers and roles. The Beaufighter VIF had two Bristol Hercules engines, a top speed of 333 mph (at 15,600 ft) and a ceiling of 26,500 ft; it also had good endurance – and ten guns (four 20 mm cannon and six 0.303 in machine-guns). The ability to hit a target hard was especially important at night when you might only get fleeting opportunities to find and engage the enemy. As different AI variants were introduced so the noses of the Beaufighter changed, from the simple 'feathered arrow' aerials of the early sets to the 'thimble' noses and radomes that hid the later sets.

As the night war progressed, the squadrons were employed in an intruder role to hunt the enemy, in the air and on the ground, in his own territory. This tactic met with considerable success both with material returns ('kills') and the disruption of the enemy air effort. With Fighter Command the Beau gradually gave way to the Mosquito and the type had vanished from the Command's front-line by mid 1944. Like other types it had

Beaufighter VI with Hercules engines, January 1942; the introduction of the more powerful aircraft and the adoption of centimetric radar gave the RAF the best night-fighter of the time.

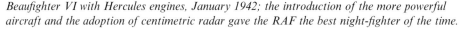

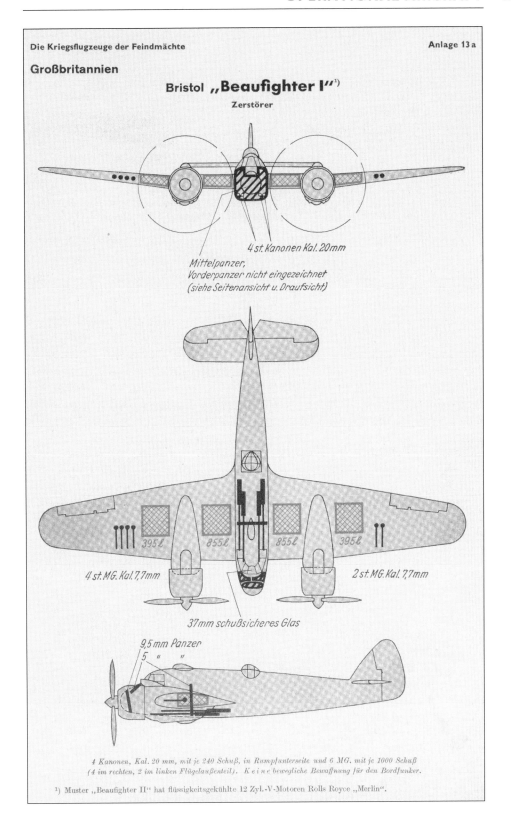

Die Kriegsflugzeuge der Feindmächte

Anlage 13 a

Großbritannien

Bristol „Beaufighter I"[1]
Zerstörer

4 st. Kanonen Kal. 20mm

Mittelpanzer,
Vorderpanzer nicht eingezeichnet
(siehe Seitenansicht u. Draufsicht)

395 ℓ   855 ℓ   855 ℓ   395 ℓ

4 st. MG. Kal. 7,7mm   2 st. MG. Kal. 7,7mm

37mm schußsicheres Glas

9,5mm Panzer
5 "   "

4 Kanonen, Kal. 20 mm, mit je 240 Schuß, in Rumpfunterseite und 6 MG. mit je 1000 Schuß
(4 im rechten, 2 im linken Flügelaußenteil). K e i n e bewegliche Bewaffnung für den Bordfunker.

[1] Muster „Beaufighter II" hat flüssigkeitsgekühlte 12 Zyl.-V-Motoren Rolls Royce „Merlin".

also served the Command in a 'support' role in the training system. It also saw extensive and distinguished service with other Commands, especially Coastal, and in other theatres.

There are no airworthy Beaufighters but one is under rebuild (to fly) at Duxford as part of the Fighter Collection. A number survive in museums, including the RAF Museum.

Bristol BEAUFIGHTER
Prototype, first flight: R2052, 17 July 1939
Entry to service: 25 Sqn, September 1940

Squadron	Dates	Airfields
25 Sqn	Sep 1940–Jan 1943	North Weald, Debden, Wittering, Ballyhalbert, Church Fenton
29 Sqn	Sep 1940–May 1943	Wellingore, West Malling, Bradwell Bay
68 Sqn	May 1941–Jul 1944	High Ercall, Coltishall, Coleby Grange, Fairwood Common, Castle Camps
96 Sqn	May 1942–Nov 1943	Wrexham, Honiley, Church Fenton, Drem
125 Sqn	Feb 1942–Mar 1944	Colerne, Fairwood Common, Exeter, Valley
141 Sqn	Jun 1941–Jan 1944	Ayr, Acklington, Tangmere, Ford, Predannack, Wittering, West Raynham
153 Sqn	Jan 1942–Dec 1942	Ballyhalbert, Portreath, (*North Africa*)
219 Sqn	Sep 1940–May 1943	Catterick, Redhill, Tangmere, Acklington, Scorton, (*North Africa*)
255 Sqn	Jul 1941–Nov 1942	Hibaldstow, Coltishall, High Ercall, Honiley, (*North Africa*)
256 Sqn	May 1942–May 1943	Squires Gate, Woodvale, Ford, (*Malta*)
307 Sqn Polish	Aug 1941–Jan 1943	Exeter, Pembrey
406 Sqn RCAF	Jun 1941–Aug 1944	Acklington, Ayr, Scorton, Predannack, Middle Wallop, Valley, Exeter, Winkleigh
409 Sqn RCAF	Aug 1941–Apr 1944	Coleby Grange, Acklington
410 Sqn RCAF	Apr 1942–Jan 1943	Drem, Ayr, Scorton, Acklington
456 Sqn RAAF	Sep 1941–Jun 1943	Valley, Middle Wallop
488 Sqn RNZAF	Jun 1942–Sep 1943	Church Fenton, Ayr, Drem
600 Sqn	Sep 1940–Nov 1942	Hornchurch, Redhill, Catterick, Drem, Fairwood Common, Colerne, Predannack, (*North Africa*)
604 Sqn	Sep 1940–Apr 1944	Middle Wallop, Warmwell, Predannack, Ford, Scorton
FIU	Aug 1940–	Tangmere, Shoreham, Ford, Wittering

Westland WHIRLWIND

Only two squadrons operated this most unusual of RAF fighters and by the time the aircraft's problems had been overcome it was deemed not worthy of further effort. The first aircraft arrived with 263 Squadron at Grangemouth on 6 July 1940 and there were three on strength by the end of the month – and 'a considerable amount of what the makers are pleased to call 'teething troubles' had been encountered' (263 Squadron ORB). It was a problematic period and by early September when the Squadron moved to Drem it still only had seven aircraft, all in 'A Flight': 'the engines have still not yet surmounted their teething troubles. The guns, however, are now firing satisfactorily' (263 Squadron ORB).

The first Whirlwinds arrived with 263 Squadron at Grangemouth on 6 July 1940 and there were three on strength by the end of the month - and 'a considerable amount of what the makers are pleased to call 'teething troubles' had been encountered'

The Westland Whirlwind prototype (L6844) flew on 11 October 1938 to Specification F37/35 and a production order for 400 aircraft was placed in January. At this stage it all looked very promising; the two Rolls-Royce Peregrine engines and the sleek airframe promised a speed of 360 mph and the nose-mounted 20 mm cannon promised a mighty punch, whilst the pilot had a good all-round view from the canopy that sat on top of the fuselage. Sadly, development problems meant that the first aircraft did not reach 263 Squadron until July 1940 and even then the teething troubles had only just started. The Whirlwind never recovered from these problems, although in subsequent ORB entries the Squadron was to sing the praises of the type as 'having come of age' in the roving fighter-bomber role. Only 112 aircraft were built and only one other squadron used the type.

Westland WHIRLWIND
Prototype, first flight: L8644, 11 October 1938
Entry to service: 263 Sqn, July 1940

Squadron	Dates	Airfields
137 Sqn	Feb 1941–Jun 1943	Charmy Down, Coltishall, Matlask, Drem, Snailwell, Manston, Southend
263 Sqn	Jul 1940–Dec 1943	Grangemouth, Drem, Exeter, St Eval, Portreath, Filton, Charmy Down, Warmwell, Harrowbeer, Zeals, Manston

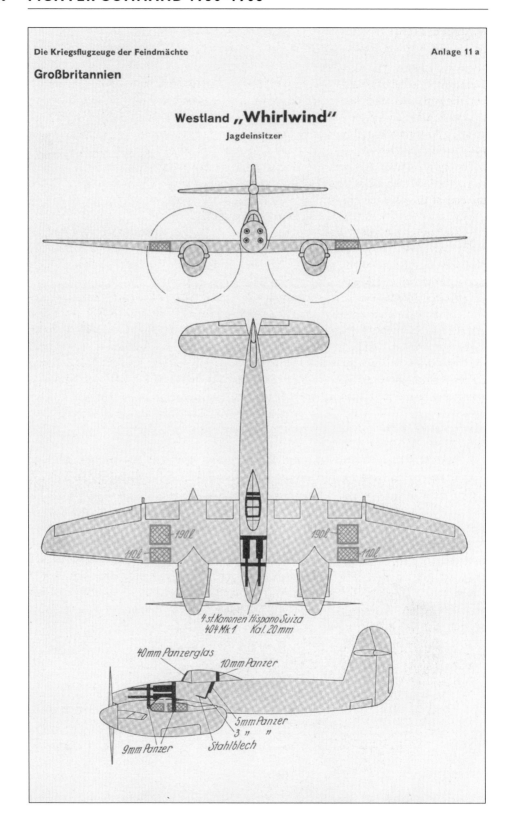

Die Kriegsflugzeuge der Feindmächte   Anlage 11 a

Großbritannien

Westland „**Whirlwind**"
Jagdeinsitzer

190ℓ

190ℓ

110ℓ

110ℓ

4.st.Kanonen Hispano Suiza
404 Mk 1   Kal. 20 mm

40mm Panzerglas

10mm Panzer

5mm Panzer
3 "   "

9mm Panzer   Stahlblech

Douglas HAVOC

In summer 1940 the first Douglas Bostons (DB-7s) arrive for the RAF, the intention being to employ the American type as a light-bomber to supplement/replace the Blenheim; this did not take place until the following year with the arrival of Boston IIs but the type did enter service in late 1940 as the Havoc for use as a night-fighter. Conversion to the fighter role, including an AI radar and eight-gun nose fitting took place at Burtonwood and the first Havoc Is went to 85 Squadron at Debden in February 1941 to replace Defiants. The following month a number of Havoc II entered service, including a number that went to 23 Squadron as fighter-bombers for night intruder work, the first such use taking place in April. From their entry to service in April 1941 to the end of the year the Havocs were the busiest of the night intruder types, flying 374 sorties, the majority of these being attacks on airfields.

This latter variant was sometimes referred to as the Moonfighter as it had no radar and carried only four forward guns and a small bomb-load. Again this was only produced in small numbers, as was the variant supplied to 93 Squadron for use with the Long Aerial Mine (LAM).

The Turbinlite version was delivered in larger numbers (70) and was an interesting concept in which the Havoc carried a Helmore searchlight in the nose, with which it was intended to illuminate the enemy so that an accompanying fighter, usually a Hurricane, could 'step forward' and destroy the enemy. A number of specialist Flights were formed for this work from June 1941 but as discussed in the operations chapter it was never a success, although the Flights were raised to squadron status before the idea was eventually abandoned in January 1943.

The Havoc served in two roles with the Command – night intruder (with 23 Squadron) and airborne searchlight (Turbinlite).

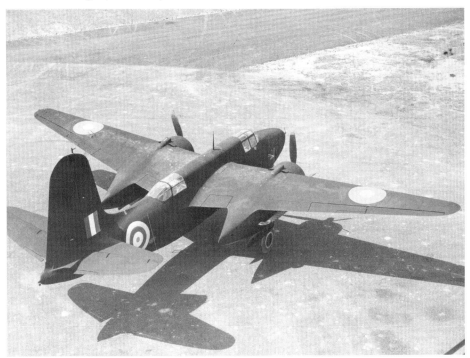

Douglas HAVOC
Prototype, first flight: BJ464
Entry to service: 85 Sqn, Feb 1941

Squadron	Dates	Airfields
23 Sqn	Mar 1941–Aug 1942	Ford
25 Sqn	Jul 1941–Aug 1941	Wittering
85 Sqn	Feb 1941–Sep 1942	Debden, Hunsdon
93 Sqn	Dec 1940–Nov 1941	Middle Wallop
1451 Flt/530 Sqn	May 1941–Jan 1943	Hunsdon
1452 Flt/531 Sqn	Jul 1941–Jan 1943	West Malling, Debden
1453 Flt/532 Sqn	Jul 1941–Jan 1943	Wittering, Hibaldstow
1454 Flt/533 Sqn	Jun 1941–Jan 1943	Colerne, Charmy Down
1455 Flt/534 Sqn	Jul 1941–Jan 1943	Tangmere
1456 Flt/535 Sqn	Nov 1941–Jan 1943	Honiley, High Ercall
1457 Flt/536 Sqn	Sep 1941–Jan 1943	Colerne, Predannack, Fairwood Common
1458 Flt/537 Sqn	Dec 1941–Jan 1943	Middle Wallop
1459 Flt/538 Sqn	Sep 1941–Jan 1943	Hunsdon, Hibaldstow
1460 Flt/539 Sqn	Dec 1941–Jan 1943	Acklington
605 Sqn	Jul 1942–Aug 1942	Ford

Note: This includes the Boston as in essence both were the same for Fighter Command as they operated in the Intruder role.

Bell AIRACOBRA

Like the Buffalo, the Airacobra (Bell P-39) was an American aircraft seized on by the British Purchasing Commission in 1940, and like the Buffalo it was not a success, although it did at least enter (briefly) operational service with Fighter Command. The P-39 was, on paper, a promising type with a speed of 358 mph (at 15,000 ft), a range of over 1,000 miles (over twice that of the Hurricane and Spitfire) and good armament, comprising a spinner-mounted 20 mm cannon and six machine-guns. The RAF eventually ordered 675 aircraft, initially benefiting from an undeliverable French order, and aircraft arrived with the Air Fighting Development Unit (AFDU) in July 1941 and 601 Squadron, at Matlask, the following month.

The Squadron was initially enthusiastic but soon expressed concern over the unreliability of their aircraft, in part caused by the unusual rear engine arrangement and

The Airacobra was used for a short period by a single Fighter Command squadron and flew very few operational sorties.

Die Kriegsflugzeuge der Feindmächte

Großbritannien und USA.

Bell „Airacobra" (P 39)[1]

Jagdeinsitzer

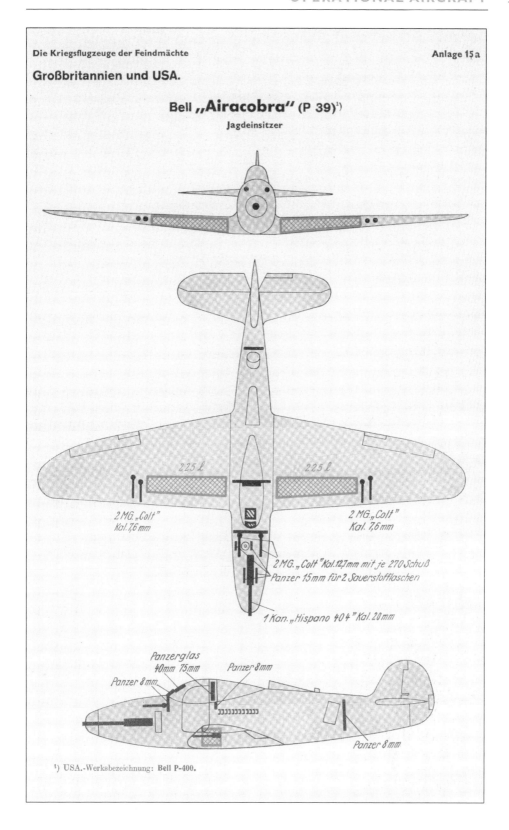

225 ℓ

225 ℓ

2 MG. „Colt"
Kal. 7,6 mm

2 MG. „Colt"
Kal. 7,6 mm

2 MG. „Colt" Kal. 12,7mm mit je 270 Schuß
Panzer 15mm für 2 Sauerstofflaschen

1 Kan. „Hispano 404" Kal. 20 mm

Panzerglas
40mm 75mm   Panzer 8mm

Panzer 8mm

Panzer 8mm

[1]) USA.-Werksbezeichnung: Bell P-400.

the tricycle undercarriage. Work-up took longer than expected and without pressure from the Squadron Commander it is likely that the type would never have seen action. Having moved to Manston as a forward base in early October, the Squadron flew its first *Rhubarb* three days later. This routine was followed for a few days and there appear to have been few problems and some action, with attacks on ground targets. However, it had already been decided that the teething troubles were more trouble than they were worth, a view enhanced by a series of accidents, some of them fatal, and the aircraft were taken out of service in March 1942.

In fairness to the P-39 it did have a reasonable combat career with other users, including the USAAF and the Russians.

Bell AIRACOBRA
Prototype, first flight
Entry to service: 601 Sqn, August 1941

Squadron	Dates	Airfields
601 Sqn	Aug 1941–Mar 1942	Matlask, Duxford, Acaster Malbis

Hawker TYPHOON

Designed as a heavily-armed and fast day-fighter the Hawker Typhoon was scheduled to enter service in summer 1940 and had it done so and had it met its specification it would have given a new perspective to the Battle of Britain. In the event, development was slower and performance less than predicted. The type had its origins in Specification F18/37 for fighters equipped with the developmental engines predicted to yield 2,000hp, which in the case of the Typhoon was the Napier Sabre. Perhaps not surprisingly there were delays and problems with the engines; the prototype Typhoon (P5212) flew on 24 February 1940 but it was over a year before the first production aircraft took the air, with deliveries to the first unit, 56 Squadron at Duxford, not taking place until September 1941.

It still looked promising with its 412 mph speed – the first RAF fighter to exceed 400 – and four 20 mm cannon; by this time the RAF had settled on the 20 mm cannon as its standard fighter armament. However, other fighter performance elements were poor, including rate of climb and some elements of manoeuvrability, as well as a distinct drop-off in performance with height. Nevertheless, it was the reliability of the Sabre engine that caused 56 Squadron its major headaches and called the aircraft into question.

Combat ops commenced with the Typhoon flying defensive missions against the hit-and-run fighter-bombers, where its speed was a major advantage, and offensive missions with sweeps over Europe. All of this proved that the aircraft was viable, especially at low-level and especially with the addition of external weapons as the RAF turned its attention to fighter-bombing. Indeed, it was in the latter role with a steady increase in bomb-load to an impressive 2,000 lb and the fitting or rails for Rocket Projectiles (RPs) that gave the Typhoon its true place in the RAF as a ground-attack machine. It was here that the boundaries with Fighter Command become somewhat blurred as new squadrons formed primarily in this role; some initially operated with the Command whilst others were part of the tactical Groups or 2nd Tactical Air Force formed as part of the build-up to D-Day.

The Typhoon entered Fighter Command service with 56 Squadron in September 1941.

The list of Typhoon operators shown below is limited to those with a known connection with Fighter Command, although the precise allocation of a unit in the period summer 1943 to summer 1944 can be confusing. The total list of Typhoon units would be much longer as at least 23 squadrons operated with 2nd TAF – causing mayhem amongst German ground forces in Europe.

Hawker TYPHOON
Prototype, first flight: P5212, 24 February 1940
Entry to service: 56 Sqn, September 1941

Squadron	Dates	Airfields
1 Sqn	Jul 1942–Apr 1944	Acklington, Biggin Hill, Lympne, Martlesham Heath, North Weald
3 Sqn	Feb 1943–Apr 1944	Hunsdon, West Malling, Manston, Swanton Morley
56 Sqn	Sep 1941–May 1944	Duxford, Snailwell, Manston, Matlask, Manston, Martlesham Heath, Bradwell Bay, Scorton, Acklington, Ayr, Scorton, Newchurch
175 Sqn	Apr 1943–Sep 1945	Colerne, Lasham, Appledram, Lydd, Westhampnett, Holmsley South, *Europe*
181 Sqn	Sep 1942–Sep 1945	Duxford, Snailwell, Gravesend, Lasham, Appledram, New Romney, Odiham, Merston, Eastchurch, Hurn, *Europe*
182 Sqn	Sep 1942–Sep 1945	Martlesham Heath, Sawbridgeworth, Middle Wallop, Fairlop, Lasham, Appledram, New Romney, Merston, Odiham, Eastchurch, Hurn, *Europe*
266 Sqn	Mar 1942–Aug 1945	Duxford, Matlask, Warmwell, Exeter, Harrowbeer, Bolt Head, Tangmere, Needs Oar Point, Eastchurch, Hurn, *Europe*
486 Sqn RNZAF	Jul 1942–Apr 1944	Wittering, North Weald, West Malling, Tangmere, Beaulieu, Drem, Castle Camps, Ayr
609 Sqn	Apr 1942–Sep 1945	Duxford, Bourn, Biggin Hill, Manston, Matlask, Lympne, Fairwood Common, Tangmere, Acklington, Thorney Island, Llanbedr, Funtingdon, *Europe*

De Havilland MOSQUITO

The Mosquito was without doubt one of the great British aircraft of the war and it performed astoundingly well in a variety of roles with the three main operational Commands – Bomber, Coastal and Fighter. The Mosquito was produced in an impressive number of Marks and served into the post war period; with Fighter Command it primarily served as a night-fighter and from 1942 was the main operational type in this role, although its intruder and fighter-bomber work were also important.

The de Havilland Mosquito started life in late 1938 as a private venture for a high-speed, unarmed all-wooden bomber and there was little initial interest from an Air Staff that was looking towards a heavy bomber force. The prototype (W4050) flew on 25 November 1940 and its startling performance convinced any doubters that this aircraft had a future, and fighter and photo-reconnaissance variants prototypes were soon underway. Indeed, the original contract for 50 bombers was almost immediately changed to 30 fighters and 20 bombers. The fighter version was given the impressive armament of four 20 mm cannon and four 0.303 in machine guns, a mighty punch and one that meant that the nose of the aircraft had to be strengthened, as were the wing spars to make it suitable for fighter manoeuvres. The prototype night-fighter (W4052)

The Mosquito F.II entered service with Fighter Command in early 1942, 157 Squadron at Castle Camps being the first unit; eventually some 466 of this variant were built, the majority serving with Fighter Command.

flew on 15 May 1941 as the Mosquito II and it was also fitted with the AI Mk IV, one of the early series of air-to-air radars. Early trials proved promising and the F.II entered service with Fighter Command in early 1942, 157 Squadron at Castle Camps being the first unit; eventually some 466 of this variant were built, the majority serving with Fighter Command.

Improvements in the radar increased the effectiveness of the aircraft, with the Mark XII being the first to have centimetric radar (AI Mk VIII); all were conversions from Mark IIs and this also involved the removal of the machine guns to make way for the radar nose that would be the distinguishing feature of all subsequent NF variants. The Mosquito NF.XII entered service with 85 Squadron at Hunsdon in February 1943 and over the next few years it was followed by a succession of night-fighter variants. The main differences between variants lay in the engines or radar.

However, the success of the F.II in its offensive role as an intruder, pioneered by 23 Squadron from April 1942, led to the development of a true fighter-bomber, the Mosquito VI. This was used by Fighter Command for day and night offensive operations and carried an internal bomb-load as well as wing hard-points for bombs or fuel tanks. It was an undoubted success and was adopted by other operational Commands. Although not equipped as a night-fighter it also performed this role with some success.

Night-fighters maintained offensive and defensive patrols and in the former role the aircraft were adopted by the specialist squadrons of No. 100 Group, with aircraft of this Bomber Command Group and Fighter Command tasked with disrupting German night-fighter operations to support the bomber offensive. In terms of pure night-fighters the last variant to enter service during the war was the Mark XXX and by the latter months of the war this was the main version with Fighter Command. The wartime record of the *Mossie* as a fighter included over 600 enemy aircraft and 600 flying-bombs, virtually all of these kills being at night.

Two further night-fighter versions entered service with the Command in the post-war period, the NF.36 and the NF.38, which were essentially the same except for the radar. The NF.36 flew in May 1945 and the NF.38 in November 1947; it was an example of the latter that was the last production Mosquito, VX916 being built at Chester in

In Fighter Command service the NF.36 was the final version and the final few squadrons gave up their Mosquitoes in the early 1950s, the last one being 23 Squadron at Coltishall, the Vampire NF.10 taking its place.

November 1950. However, in Fighter Command service the NF.36 was the final version and the last few squadrons gave up their Mosquitoes in the early 1950s, the final one being 23 Squadron at Coltishall, the Vampire NF.10 taking its place.

The Mosquito continued in RAF service into the mid 1950s and with overseas air forces even longer than that. A reasonable number of airframes have survived, with the collection at the Mosquito Aircraft Museum being particularly impressive. Sadly there is no airworthy aircraft at present, or at least not one that actually flies, although a number of restorations are underway.

De Havilland MOSQUITO
Prototype, first flight: W4050, 25 November 1940
Entry to service: F.II; 157 Sqn, January 1942

Squadron	Dates	Airfields
23 Sqn	Jun 1942–Dec 1942	Ford, Manston, Bradwell Bay, *Malta*
	Sep 1946–Jun 1952	Wittering, Coltishall, Church Fenton, Horsham St Faith
25 Sqn	Oct 1942–Oct 1951	Church Fenton, Acklington, Coltishall, Castle Camps, Boxted, West Malling
29 Sqn	May 1943–Aug 1951	Bradwell Bay, Ford, Drem, West Malling, Hunsdon, Colerne, Manston, Spilsby, Acklington, Tangmere
68 Sqn	Jul 1944–Apr 1945	Castle Camps, Coltishall, Wittering, Church Fenton
85 Sqn	Aug 1942–Oct 1951	Hunsdon, West Malling, Swannington, Castle Camps, Tangmere, Acklington, Church Fenton
96 Sqn	Oct 1943–Dec 1944	Drem, West Malling, Ford, Odiham
125 Sqn	Feb 1944–Nov 1945	Valley, Hurn, Middle Wallop, Coltishall, Church Fenton
141 Sqn	Jun 1946–Dec 1951	Wittering, Acklington, Coltishall, Church Fenton
151 Sqn	Apr 1942–Oct 1946	Wittering, Colerne, Middle Wallop, Predannack, Castle Camps, Hunsdon, Bradwell Bay, Exeter, Weston Zoyland
157 Sqn	Jan 1942–(Aug 1945)	Castle Camps, Bradwell Bay, Hunsdon, Predannack, Valley, Swannington, West Malling
219 Sqn	Feb 1944–Sep 1946	Woodvale, Honiley, Colerne, Bradwell Bay, Hunsdon, *Europe*, Acklington, Spilsby, Wittering
264 Sqn	May 1942–Aug 1945	Colerne, Predannack, Fairwood Common, Coleby Grange, Church Fenton, Hartford Bridge, Hunsdon, *Europe*, Colerne, Odiham
	Nov 1945–Jan 1952	Church Fenton, Spilsby, Linton-on-Ouse, Acklington, Wittering, Coltishall
307 Sqn Polish	Dec 1942–Nov 1946	Exeter, Fairwood Common, Predannack, Drem, Coleby Grange, Church Fenton, Castle Camps, Horsham St Faith
409 Sqn RCAF	Mar 1944–Jun 1945	Acklington, Hunsdon, West Malling, *Europe*
410 Sqn RCAF	Oct 1942–Jun 1945	Acklington, Coleby Grange, West Malling, Hunsdon, Castle Camps, Hunsdon, Zeals, Colerne, *Europe*
418 Sqn RCAF	Mar 1943–Sep 1945	Ford, Holmsley South, Hurn, Middle Wallop, Hunsdon, Blackbushe, *Europe*
456 Sqn RAAF	Dec 1942–Jun 1945	Valley, Middle Wallop, Colerne, Fairwood Common, Ford, Church Fenton, Bradwell Bay
488 Sqn RNZAF	Aug 1943–Apr 1945	Drem, Bradwell Bay, Colerne, Zeals, Hunsdon, *Europe*
604 Sqn	Feb 1944–Apr 1945	Scorton, Church Fenton, Hurn, Colerne, Zeals, *Europe*, Predannack, Odiham
605 Sqn	Feb 1943–Aug 1945	Ford, Castle Camps, Bradwell Bay, Manston, Blackbushe, *Europe*
	May 1947–Sep 1948	Honiley
608 Sqn	Jul 1947–Jun 1948	Thornaby
609 Sqn	Apr 1947–Sep 1948	Yeadon
616 Sqn	Sep 1947–May 1949	Finningley

Die Kriegsflugzeuge der Feindmächte   Anlage 28

Großbritannien

De Havilland D. H. 98 „Mosquito"
Mehrzweckeflugzeug (Aufklärer, leichtes Kampfflugzeug und Zerstörer)

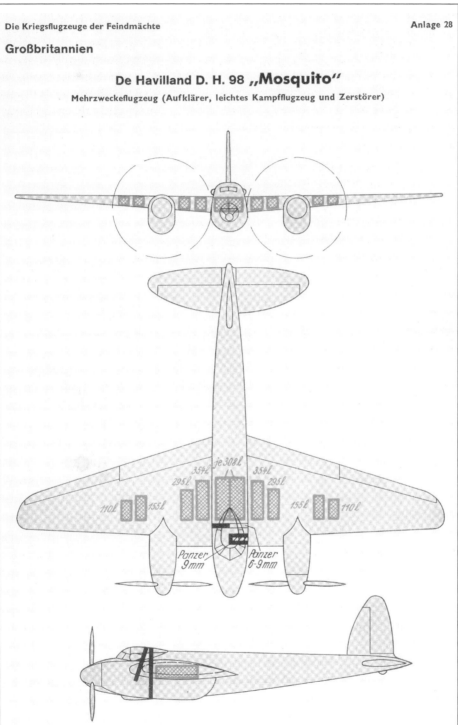

*Als Aufklärer und leichtes Kampfflugzeug **ohne** Bewaffnung, als Zerstörer 4 Kanonen, Kal. 20 mm, und 4 starre MG., Kal. 7,7 mm, im Rumpf. Keine bewegliche Bewaffnung. (Bilder des Flugzeugs noch nicht vorhanden.)*

Hawker TEMPEST

Derived from the Typhoon but with aerodynamic improvements, including a new wing, the Hawker Tempest was designed to have longer range and to operate as a pure fighter. The initial problems with the Sabre engine had been largely ironed-out by the time prototype HM595 (a converted Typhoon V) flew on 2 September 1942 but it was still June 1943 before the first production example of the Tempest V flew – and this was the only Mark to see operational service in World War Two. With a top speed of 435 mph the Tempest was the fastest RAF fighter and its all-round performance was good, including a normal range of over 700 miles and an extended range of over 1,500 miles. Tempests entered service with 486 Squadron in January 1944 and within months there was a Tempest Wing of three squadrons.

The aircraft's initial operations were the same as those of all the other fighters and fighter-bombers – attacking anything enemy that moved air and ground in Europe. However, with the launch of the V-1 attacks on Britain the Tempests became part of the anti *Diver* defences, the speed and firepower of the aircraft proving effective. The aircraft also operated offensively over Europe to the end of the war and even scored a number of jet 'kills' on Me262s.

The post-war period saw Tempest IIs and VIs in service with the RAF, the former in RAF Germany and with Fighter Command and the latter primarily in the Middle East and Africa. As with other fighter types the Tempest also served with a number of training and support units, some in support of Fighter Command, and the last ones left No. 233 OCU (Pembrey) in July 1955.

With a top speed of 435 mph the Tempest was the fastest RAF fighter and its all-round performance was good, including a normal range of over 700 miles and an extended range of over 1,500 miles.

Hawker TEMPEST
Prototype, first flight: LA602, 28 June 1943
Entry to service: 486 Sqn, January 1944

Squadron	Dates	Airfields
3 Sqn	Feb 1944–(Apr 1948)	Manston, Bradwell Bay, Newchurch, Matlask, *Europe*
54 Sqn	Nov 1945–Oct 1946	Chilbolton, Odiham
56 Sqn	Jun 1944–(Apr 1946)	Newchurch, Matlask, *Europe*
80 Sqn	Aug 1944–(Feb 1948)	Manston, Coltishall, *Europe*
183 Sqn	Oct 1945–Nov 1945	Fairwood Common, Chilbolton
222 Sqn	Jan 1945–Oct 1945	Predannack, *Europe*, Weston Zoyland, Molesworth
247 Sqn	Sep 1945–May 1946	Chilbolton
274 Sqn	Aug 1944–Sep 1945	Manston, Coltishall, *Europe*
349 Sqn	Feb 1945–Apr 1945	Predannack, *Europe*
486 Sqn	Jan 1944–Sep 1945	Tangmere, Beaulieu, Drem, Castle Camps, Newchurch, Matlask, *Europe*
501 Sqn	Jul 1944–Apr 1945	Westhampnett, Manston, Bradwell Bay, Hunsdon

North American MUSTANG

The P-51 Mustang was another of the fighter types that truly deserved its wartime epithets; the combination of a superb aerodynamic airframe and the Merlin engine created a superlative fighter that was produced in large numbers for the USAAF but also saw service with the Allies. Fighter Command was late in acquiring the Mustang and by autumn 1944 had only four squadrons of Mustang IIIs for the long-range escort role; however, the numbers continued to increase, partly through an exchange of units with 2nd TAF, and by April 1945 the Order of Battle included 16 Mustang units.

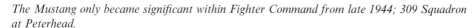

The Mustang only became significant within Fighter Command from late 1944; 309 Squadron at Peterhead.

The RAF had ordered the Alison-powered Mustang in 1940, the first aircraft flying the following April, the original intention being that it would go to Fighter Command. However, performance deficiencies above 15,000 ft, the introduction of better Spitfires and a lowering of the immediate German threat led to a rethink; the Mustang I entered service with Army Co-operation Command in the Tactical Reconnaissance role in early 1942, the first unit being 26 Squadron. It performed well with this Command and the RAF eventually had 16 squadrons in this basic role. The USAAF also took an interest in the aircraft, which led to improvements in the aircraft and to a reluctance to let anyone else have any! The main part of the Mustang story was very much an American one and the large numbers of P-51s that served with the VIIIth and IXth Fighter Commands, but that is outside of the scope of this book. However, the success of the P-51 in long-range escort and the failings of the Spitfire in this regard led to a reappraisal by Fighter Command and a decision to acquire Mustangs. At the end of 1943 the RAF began to receive the Mustang III, with No. 122 Wing at Gravesend the first to re-equip.

A March 1944 report by the Air Fighting Development Unit compared the Mustang III against various RAF and German fighters; the conclusions concerning tactical comparison with the Bf 109G and Fw 190 were: 'In attack, the Mustang can always catch the Me 109G, except in any sort of climb (unless there is a high overtaking speed). In defence, a steep turn should be the first manoeuvre, followed, if necessary, by a dive (below 20,000 ft). A high speed climb will unfortunately not increase the range. If above 25,000 feet keep above by climbing or all-out level.

In the attack, a high speed should be maintained or regained in order to regain height initiative. An Fw 190 could not evade by diving alone. In defence a steep turn followed by a full throttle dive should increase range before regaining height and course. Dog-fighting is not altogether recommended. Do not attempt to climb away without at least 250 mph showing initially'. (AFDU Report No. 101, March 1944).

Despite the type's success and popularity with the USAAF, the RAF's fighter pilots were invariably reluctant to give-up their beloved Spitfires for the Mustang. Some ORBs and personal accounts make disparaging comments about their 'new mounts', although this usually changed after a few weeks of familiarity, whilst others recorded the event and the problems in a more matter-of-fact way. The 234 Squadron ORB for 29 September 1944 stated: 'they've come, the first batch of Mustangs, also a section of fitters etc from Air Ministry to give us the gen. F/L Conroy came to the Squadron for a few days to assist pilots in converting from Spitfires to the new type. Pilots spent all their time sitting in the Mustang cockpits getting to know the many new gadgets and instruments and also reading up Pilots Notes. The CO, Flight Commanders and deputies were able to make one 30 minute trip each.' A few days later, 4 October: 'tons of snags seem to keep turning up, but the ground crews are responding famously and coping with everything that comes along.'

Mustangs served in the fighter role with Fighter Command and 2nd TAF, and in the Armed Reconnaissance role, with increasing numbers of squadrons equipping with the type in late 1944 and early 1945. As previously mentioned, there is confusion during this period, in part the temporary allocation of units, between ADGB/Fighter Command and the 2nd TAF/AEAF in terms of squadron 'ownership'. It would seem that approximately 19 squadrons that served with ADGB/Fighter Command operated the Mustang and these are shown in the table below.

In Fighter Command service the type only lasted a year post-war, the final unit, 65 Squadron at Linton-on-Ouse, re-equipped with Hornets in May 1946.

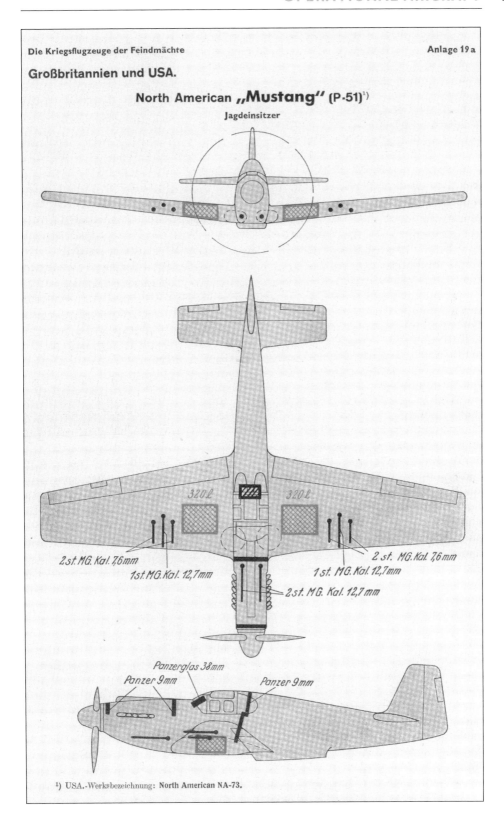

Großbritannien und USA.

North American „Mustang" (P-51)[1]

Jagdeinsitzer

2 st. MG. Kal. 7,6mm
1st. MG. Kal. 12,7mm
2 st. MG. Kal. 7,6 mm
1 st. MG. Kal. 12,7 mm
2 st. MG. Kal. 12,7 mm

Panzerglas 38mm
Panzer 9mm
Panzer 9mm

320 ℓ   320 ℓ

[1] USA.-Werksbezeichnung: North American NA-73.

North American MUSTANG
Prototype, first flight: Mustang I (AG345), 1 May 1941
Entry to service: Mustang III, 65 Sqn, Dec 1943

Squadron	Dates	Airfields
19 Sqn	Jan 1944–Mar 1946	Gravesend, Ford, Southend, Funtingdon, *Europe*, Matlask, Andrews Field, Peterhead, Acklington, Bradwell Bay, Molesworth
64 Sqn	Nov 1944–May 1946	Bradwell Bay, Bentwaters, Horsham St Faith
65 Sqn	Dec 1943–May 1946	Gravesend, Ford, Funtingdon, Ford, Southend, *Europe*, Matlask, Peterhead, Andrews Field, Bentwaters, Banff, Hethel, Spilsby, Horsham St Faith
118 Sqn	Jan 1945–Mar 1946	Bentwaters, Fairwood Common, Horsham St Faith
122 Sqn	Jan 1944–Aug 1945	Gravesend, Ford, Funtingdon, Southend, *Europe*, Matlask, Andrews Field, Peterhead, Dyce
126 Sqn	Dec 1944–Apr 1946	Bradwell Bay, Bentwaters, Hethel
129 Sqn	Mar 1944–May 1945	Heston, Llanbedr, Coolham, Ford, Brenzett, Andrews Field, Bentwaters
234 Sqn	Sep 1944–Aug 1945	North Weald, Bentwaters, Peterhead, Dyce, Hawkinge
306 Sqn	Apr 1944–Dec 1946	Coolham, Holmsley South, Ford, Brenzett, Andrews Field, Coltishall, Fairwood Common
315 Sqn	Mar 1944–Dec 1946	Heston, Llanbedr, Coolham, Holmsley South, Ford, Brenzett, Andrews Field, Coltishall, Peterhead, Fairwood Common
316 Sqn	Apr 1944–Nov 1946	Woodvale, Coltishall, West Malling, Friston, Andrews Field, Fairwood Common, Wick, Hethel
441 Sqn	May 1945–Aug 1945	Digby, Molesworth
442 Sqn	Mar 1945–Aug 1945	Hunsdon, Digby, Molesworth
611 Sqn	Mar 1945–Aug 1945	Hunsdon, Peterhead

The Cold War

Fighter Command ended the war still largely equipped with Spitfires and with an offensive rather than defensive posture, although the *Luftwaffe* had continued to make some incursions in the latter months of the war, especially at night. In terms of its post-war doctrine the Command was left with no obvious threat until the relations between East and West broke down in the late 1940s, after which the Cold War dominated the military posture for the next 50+ years. The primary role remained as it always had been – to defend the UK against air attack and to deploy fighters to other operational areas as required. The basic requirement for equipment initially comprised a mix of day and night fighters, although the all-weather aircraft gradually replaced the latter and, arguably, part of the role of the former. It was obviously going to be a jet force and although a number of piston types served into the early 1950s it was the jets, Meteors and Vampires, that soon became the backbone of the Command. In essence all that changed over the next few years was the performance of the aircraft, culminating in the supersonic Lightning, and the weapon system – the combination of radar and guns, with air-to-air missiles (AAMs) supplanting the latter. The only other significant 'change' was the suggestion that manned aircraft had not future and that surface-to-air missiles (SAMs) would dominate future air defence strategy. Fighter Command operated the Blood-hound SAM batteries that were defending the RAF's nuclear assets.

Gloster METEOR

By any standards the Gloster Meteor deserves to be classified as one of the great military aircraft; it was the first operational jet in RAF service and it was produced in large numbers, in numerous versions and was a major export success. For Fighter Command it was the main day and night fighter into the late 1950s with dozens of squadrons and hundreds of aircraft; indeed, one of the last periods when the RAF fielded an aircraft type in significant numbers. The Meteor is included in the Cold War section as it was in this period that the type was the mainstay of Fighter Command – but it did of course make its first appearance in the last year of World War Two.

Gestation of the Meteor was long and complicated and had its origins in Specification F9/40. First flight of a British jet aircraft was the E28/39 experimental aircraft (W4041) with its single small turbojet on 15 May 1941. The first actual Meteor to fly was DG206 on 5 March 1943 and production Meteor Mk. Is were given two Welland engines, which gave a max speed of around 385 mph (at sea level). It was by no means startling and reliability was, not surprisingly, a problem – but it was already recognised that development potential for pistons was limited but for jets had only just started. Standard armament was four 20 mm cannon in the nose and in July 1944 the first few aircraft were handed to 616 Squadron. Dennis Barry was one of the first of the Squadron's pilots to fly the Meteor:

> *As I taxied out to the end of the Farnborough runway in Meteor Mk I EE214/G, I ran through the drill as briefed by the Group Captain and then I positioned the aircraft ready for take-off. Throttles forward, maximum power while holding on the brakes, then brakes released and slowly accelerate down the runway. No swing, no drag, and hold the stick level until 80 mph indicated, then ease stick back and lift off the runway at 120 mph. Wheels up and climb away, retracting the flaps. The rate of climb is originally poor, 500 feet a minute, but as the power builds up the rate increases. Local flying now, the aircraft is quiet with no noise from the engines, only a 'whooshing' sound from the air passing the cockpit, like a glider. The visibility is good with only a shallow nose in front and is similar to being in an airship's observation car. Landing successfully completed, I return to my colleagues satisfied with the aircraft except for the power.*

White-painted Meteor of 616 Squadron; the Squadron was the first RAF jet unit.

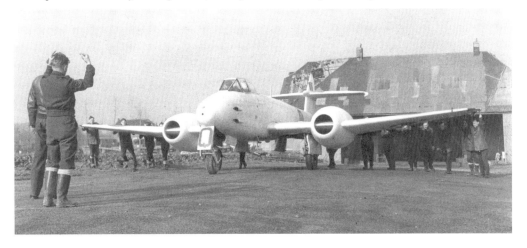

The Meteor's main contribution to operations in World War Two was in the campaign against the V-1 and pilots claimed 260 of the flying bombs between July and September 1944, with 215 of those being downed in August; the first jet 'kill' occurred on 4 August when Fg Off Dean used his wing-tip to flip-over a V-1, his guns having jammed. A further 23 were claimed in the mini V-1 campaign of March 1945. No. 616 Squadron sent a detachment to the Continent in the closing stages of the war but no jet v jet combat took place, the only targets being ground ones.

Meteor IIIs and F.3s entered service with the Command and took the type into the post-war period, where from late 1947 they gave way to the F.4 variant. This latter had the far better Derwent 5 engines and it equipped 21 squadrons in Fighter Command, becoming the first of the post-war stalwarts. The F.4 had a top speed of 585 mph at sea level – an indication of just how rapidly the jets were developing. The next variant to enter service only gave a 10 mph increase in speed but is generally considered to have been the best of the Meteors, in part because of its excellent bubble canopy and improved handling – as well as having an ejection seat. The Meteor F.8 served with 30 squadrons of Fighter Command, 10 of those being Auxiliary Air Force units; the first unit, 245 Squadron at Horsham St Faith, received F.8s in June 1950. It was an impressive force of many hundreds of aircraft but it had a limited life; 245 Squadron was also the last user, giving up its *Meatboxes* for Hunters in April 1957.

Night-fighter

The night-fighter variant was given no priority, its development being handed to Armstrong-Whitworth and the first NF.11 (WA546) not flying until 31 May 1950. Entry to service was with 29 Squadron in July 1951 when it replaced Mosquito NF.30s. The NF.11 was developed under Specification F24/48 and in essence was a lengthened airframe for two crew and nose-mounted radar, with the four 20 mm cannon being in the wings. Three other variants followed in quick succession: the NF.12 (improved radar), NF.13 (tropicalised for use in the Middle East) and NF.14 (improved avionics and a

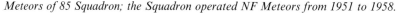

Meteors of 85 Squadron; the Squadron operated NF Meteors from 1951 to 1958.

clear-vision bubble canopy). Fighter Command used them all except the NF.13 and so was, along with squadrons in Germany, a major operator of the 556 Meteor night-fighters delivered to the RAF, the NF.11 being the commonest variant (316). The NF Meteors were reasonably effective in peace-time exercises but for Fighter Command it was a brief period as by the late 1950s most squadrons had re-equipped with Javelins or been re-roled.

A number of airworthy Meteors survive and can be seen at airshows in the UK, whilst the type is 'resident' in a large number of aviation museums.

Gloster METEOR
Prototype, first flight: DG205, 5 March 1943
Entry to service: 616 Sqn, July 1944

Squadron	Dates	Airfields
1 Sqn	Oct 1946–Jun 1958	Tangmere, Acklington, Stradishall, Waterbeach, West Raynham, Wittering
19 Sqn	Jan 1951–Jan 1957	Church Fenton
25 Sqn	Mar 1954–Apr 1959	West Malling, Tangmere, Waterbeach
29 Sqn	Jul 1951–Dec 1957	Tangmere, Acklington
33 Sqn	Sep 1957–Aug 1958	Leeming
34 Sqn	Aug 1954–Dec 1955	Tangmere
41 Sqn	Jan 1951–Jul 1955	Church Fenton, Biggin Hill
43 Sqn	Feb 1949–Sep 1954	Tangmere, Leuchars
46 Sqn	Aug 1954–Feb 1946	Odiham
54 Sqn	Apr 1952–Mar 1955	Odiham
56 Sqn	Apr 1946–Jun 1955	Bentwaters, Boxted, Acklington, Wattisham, Duxford, Thorney Island, Waterbeach
63 Sqn	Apr 1948–Jan 1957	Middle Wallop, Thorney Island, Waterbeach
64 Sqn	Dec 1950–Sep 1958	Linton-on-Ouse, Duxford
65 Sqn	Dec 1950–Feb 1957	Linton-on-Ouse, Duxford
66 Sqn	Mar 1947–Apr 1954	Duxford, Linton-on-Ouse
72 Sqn	Jul 1952–Jun 1959	North Weald, Church Fenton
74 Sqn	May 1945–Mar 1957	Colerne, Fairwood Common, Bentwaters, Horsham St Faith, Acklington
85 Sqn	Sep 1951–Nov 1958	West Malling, Church Fenton
91 Sqn	Oct 1946–Jan 1947	Duxford
92 Sqn	Jan 1947–Feb 1954	Acklington, Duxford, Linton-on-Ouse
111 Sqn	Dec 1953–Jun 1955	North Weald
124 Sqn	Aug 1945–Apr 1946	Molesworth, Bentwaters, Fairwood Common
125 Sqn	Mar 1955–Jan 1956	Stradishall
151 Sqn	Mar 1953–Oct 1955	Leuchars
152 Sqn	Jun 1954–Jul 1958	Wattisham, Stradishall
153 Sqn	Feb 1955–Jun 1958	West Malling, Waterbeach
222 Sqn	Oct 1945–Dec 1954	Molesworth, Exeter, Spilsby, Boxted, Weston Zoyland, Tangmere, Thorney Island, Leuchars
234 Sqn	Feb 1946–Sep 1946	Molesworth, Boxted
245 Sqn	Aug 1945–Apr 1957	Colerne, Fairwood Common, Bentwaters, Horsham St Faith, Stradishall
247 Sqn	Apr 1952–Jun 1955	Odiham
257 Sqn	Sep 1946–Mar 1955	Church Fenton, Acklington, Horsham St Faith, Wattisham, Wymeswold
263 Sqn	Aug 1945–Apr 1955	Manston, Acklington, Charterhall, Church Fenton, Horsham St Faith, Wattisham
264 Sqn	Nov 1951–Oct 1957	Linton-on-Ouse, Leuchars, Acklington, Middleton St George, Leeming
266 Sqn	Sep 1946–Feb 1949	Boxted, Acklington, Wattisham, Tangmere

500 Sqn	Jul 1948–Mar 1957	West Malling
504 Sqn	Oct 1949–Feb 1957	Wymeswold
600 Sqn	Mar 1950–Mar 1957	Biggin Hill
601 Sqn	Aug 1952–Mar 1957	North Weald
604 Sqn	Aug 1952–Mar 1957	North Weald
609 Sqn	Jan 1951–Mar 1957	Church Fenton
610 Sqn	Jul 1951–Mar 1957	Hooton Park
611 Sqn	May 1951–Mar 1957	Woodvale, Hooton Park
615 Sqn	Sep 1950–Mar 1957	Biggin Hill
616 Sqn	Jul 1944–Aug 1945	Culmhead, Manston, Colerne, *Europe*
	Jan 1949–Mar 1957	Finningley, Worksop

De Havilland HORNET

If it had appeared a few months earlier the Hornet may have become a significant aircraft as its long range (3,000 miles) and good all-round performance, including a max speed of around 480 mph would have made it a potent fighter in the latter stages of World War Two. Powered by two Merlins the aircraft was developed by de Havilland as a long-range fighter and was produced to Specification F12/43, the prototype (RR915) flying on 28 July 1944. It was eventually produced in two fighter variants, the F.1 and F.3, the former entering service with 64 Squadron at Horsham St Faith in February 1946. Standard armament was four 20 mm cannon but there was also provision for the fighter-bomber role with bombs or rockets under the wings. The RAF took delivery of just over 200 aircraft, with further orders cancelled with the end of the war and the run-down of strength.

Church Fenton and Horsham St Faith had two squadrons of Hornets each as the day-fighter component of their Wings and the type remained in service with the Command to March 1951, when they were replaced by Meteors. That same month saw Hornets join the Far East Air Force, with whom they saw some operational service during the anti-terrorist campaign in Malaya (Operation *Firedog*).

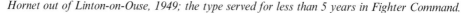

Hornet out of Linton-on-Ouse, 1949; the type served for less than 5 years in Fighter Command.

De Havilland HORNET
Prototype, first flight: RR915, 28 July 1944
Entry to service: 64 Sqn, Feb 1946

Squadron	Dates	Airfields
19 Sqn	Oct 1946–Jan 1951	Wittering, Church Fenton
41 Sqn	Jun 1948–Mar 1951	Church Fenton
64 Sqn	Feb 1946–Mar 1951	Horsham St Faith, Acklington, Linton-on-Ouse
65 Sqn	Jun 1946–Feb 1951	Horsham St Faith, Linton-on-Ouse, Acklington

De Havilland VAMPIRE

The de Havilland Vampire was the second British jet type to enter operational service, although this was just too late to see active service in World War Two. Design work, with a working name of *Spider Crab*, began in 1941 and under Specification E6/41 the design crystallised into twin-boom, this being chosen in order to limit the length of the jet pipe. Prototype Vampire LZ548 first flew, from Hatfield, in September 1943, power being provided by a single DH Goblin of 2,700 lb thrust. In May 1944 a production order was placed for 120 aircraft – to be built by English Electric at Preston as de Havilland was already committed to vital programmes such as the Mosquito. The first EE-built production Vampire F.1 (TG274), flew from Samlesbury on 20 April 1945 but it was not until the following April that the first unit, 247 Squadron at Odiham, re-equipped. The first batch of 40 aircraft had the original 2,700 lb Goblin but subsequent F.1s had a 3,100 lb version, whilst aircraft from No. 50 onwards were also given pressurised cockpits and a bubble hood. One of the major restrictions on the aircraft was that it only had a 202 gallon fuel tank – not much for a thirsty early generation jet engine! The follow-on aircraft, the F.3, had a 326-gallon tank and provision for external fuel tanks, as well as a redesigned tail. The aircraft continued to be developed and further operational marks

Vampire of 247 Squadron; the Squadron was the first to operate Vampires (from March 1946).

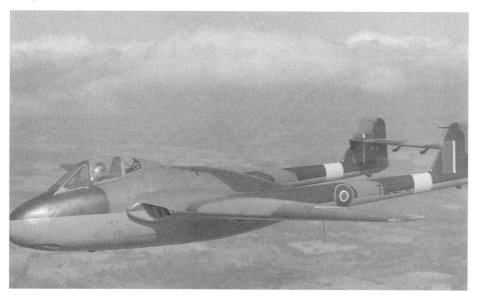

entered service – the FB.5, the first of the ground-attack variants entered service in December 1948, and the FB.9, a tropicalised version for the RAF in the Middle East and Far East, in January 1952. The only other operational variant in RAF service was the NF.10, a two-seat side-by-side night fighter that first flew in August 1949 and was aimed at the export market – the RAF having settled on the Meteor as its night fighter. The Egyptian order was subsequently barred from delivery and so the RAF took over these, and more, NF.10s.

The first NF variants joined Fighter Command in July 1951, with 25 Squadron at West Malling replacing its Mosquito NF.36s. Two further Fighter Command squadrons (25 and 151) used the NF.10 but it was a short-lived utilisation and within two years the squadrons had re-equipped with Meteors or Venom night-fighters. The day-fighter variants had a longer career, with Vampires in the Command for over 10 years, although much of this period was with the auxiliary units, the regular squadrons having re-equipped in the early 1950s. The final Fighter Command Vampire squadrons vanished with the disbandment in March 1957 of the Auxiliary Air Force.

Many museum collections house one or more Vampires and a number of airworthy examples can also be seen, mainly in the UK.

De Havilland VAMPIRE
Prototype, first flight: LZ548, September 1943
Entry to service: 247 Sqn, April 1946

Squadron	Dates	Airfields
23 Sqn	Sep 1951–Jan 1954	Coltishall, Horsham St Faith
25 Sqn	Jul 1951–Feb 1954	West Malling
54 Sqn	Oct 1946–Apr 1952	Odiham, Acklington
72 Sqn	Feb 1947–May 1953	Odiham, Acklington, North Weald
130 Sqn	Oct 1946–Jan 1947	Odiham
151 Sqn	Feb 1952–May 1953	Leuchars
247 Sqn	Mar 1946–May 1952	Chilbolton, Fairwood Common, West Malling, Odiham, Acklington
501 Sqn	Nov 1948–Feb 1957	Filton
502 Sqn	Jan 1951–Mar 1957	Aldergrove
601 Sqn	Nov 1949–Sep 1952	North Weald
602 Sqn	Jan 1951–Mar 1957	Abbotsinch, Leuchars, Renfrew
603 Sqn	May 1951–Feb 1957	Turnhouse, Leuchars
604 Sqn	Nov 1949–Aug 1952	North Weald
605 Sqn	Jul 1948–Mar 1957	Honiley
607 Sqn	Mar 1951–Mar 1957	Ouston
608 Sqn	May 1950–Feb 1957	Thornaby
612 Sqn	Jun 1951–Mar 1957	Dyce, Leuchars, Edzell
613 Sqn	Feb 1951–Mar 1957	Ringway
614 Sqn	Jul 1950–Mar 1957	Llandow

De Havilland VENOM

The Venom entered RAF service as a fighter-bomber in 1952, primarily for service in RAF Germany and it was the night fighter variant, the NF.2 that first served with Fighter Command. The NF.2 was based on a private venture (speculative and not contracted) night-fighter version that first flew in August 1950, and it was primarily aimed at the export market. The basic concept for the two-seater was the same as that of

The Venom was always an interim solution to the Command's desire for a purpose-built all-weather aircraft, which was under development as the Javelin, and although eight Fighter Command squadrons used NF Venoms it was only a four-year period, the last of the squadrons re-quipping in November 1957.

the Vampire NF.10 and it was logical that the RAF adopt the new aircraft. Despite some problems the NF.2 entered service with 23 Squadron at Coltishall in November 1953 and eventually some 90 of this version were built. Two years later (June 1955) the NF.3 joined 141 Squadron, with 129 of the improved version entering service. Standard armament was four 20 mm cannon under the nose.

The Venom was always an interim solution to the Command's desire for a purpose-built all-weather aircraft, which was under development as the Javelin, and although eight Fighter Command squadrons used NF Venoms it was only a four-year period, the last of the squadrons re-quipping in November 1957.

Like its cousin the Vampire, the Venom has survived in reasonable numbers in museums and with some airworthy aircraft.

De Havilland VENOM
Prototype, first flight: NF.2, WP227, 22 August 1950
Entry to service: 23 Squadron, November 1953

Squadron	Dates	Airfields
23 Sqn	Nov 1953–May 1957	Coltishall, Horsham St Faith
33 Sqn	Dec 1955–Jul 1957	Driffield
89 Sqn	Jan 1956–Nov 1957	Stradishall
125 Sqn	Dec 1955–May 1957	Stradishall
141 Sqn	Jun 1945–Mar 1957	Coltishall, Horsham St Faith
151 Sqn	Sep 1955–Jun 1957	Leuchars
219 Sqn	Sep 1955–Jul 1957	Driffield
253 Sqn	Apr 1955–Aug 1957	Waterbeach

North American F-86 SABRE

The Sabre established a reputation during the Korean War a an effective jet fighter, in combat with Chinese MiGs – by which time the RAF had already placed an order for the swept-wing American fighter. This was an interim measure to close a capability gap pending introduction of the Hunter and the majority of the RAF's 430 Sabres served with squadrons in Germany, with only two Fighter Command units operating the type from Linton-on-Ouse.

The prototype XP-86 flew in October 1947 and it was the F-86E variant, in production from 1950 and built by Canadair that the RAF acquired. Sabres started their career with the Wildenrath Wing in May 1953, and with 66 Squadron as the first Fighter Command user the following January. Two years later both UK squadrons had re-equipped with Hunters, but the pilots had enjoyed their brief flirtation with the Sabre.

As with most of the Cold War types the Sabre is a popular museum exhibit in the Western World and in the USA a significant number are airworthy in private collections.

F-86 Sabres of 66 Squadron at Linton-on-Ouse; the Sabre served with two squadrons in Fighter Command.

North American F-86 SABRE
Prototype, first flight: XP-86, 1 October 1947
Entry to service: 3 Sqn, May 1953

Squadron	Dates	Airfields
66 Sqn	Jan 1954–Mar 1956	Linton-on-Ouse
92 Sqn	Feb 1954–Apr 1956	Linton-on-Ouse

Supermarine SWIFT

The Swift had a 'bad reputation' and is an aircraft that is often ignored, despite its limited success as a Fighter-Recce type. Only one Fighter Command unit used the Swift, and only for thirteen months. The aircraft was the first RAF swept-wing fighter and as such was trail-blazing certain technologies, although it was ordered as an insurance against possible problems with that other swept-wing design, the Hawker Hunter. The prototype flew in August 1951 and the aircraft entered service as the F.1 with 56 Squadron at Waterbeach in February 1954. With an armament of only two Aden cannon and with limited performance, the F.1 was not an impressive fighter – and it also suffered various technical problems, which led to the loss of three of the eight aircraft with 56 Squadron! The follow-on F.2 was little better and by early 1955 the decision had been taken to phase the type out of Fighter Command. The F.3 variant did not enter service and the only 'successful' variant was the FR.5, which served with two squadrons in Germany for a few years.

Supermarine SWIFT		
Prototype, first flight: WJ960, 1 August 1951		
Entry to service: 56 Sqn, February 1954		
Squadron	*Dates*	*Airfields*
56 Sqn	Feb 1954–Mar 1955	Waterbeach

The Swift was not a success and as a fighter only served with 56 Squadron.

Hawker HUNTER

Whenever the words 'classic fighter' and 'British' are put together the Hunter comes near the top of the list, and there is no doubt that this was one of the great post-war British designs, although it did suffer problems when first introduced. The Hunter served in a number of variants and in a number of roles, with the RAF and with overseas air arms. As far as Fighter Command was concerned its heyday was in the 1950s when the Order of Battle included 15 squadrons with Hunters in the day-fighter role.

The prototypes to Specification F.3/48 were ordered in June 1948 – another of the great late 1940s designs – and the first one flew in July 1951, with entry to service of the Hunter F.1 with 43 Squadron at Leuchars in July 1954. This, like most Hunters, was

Hunters of the 43 Squadron formation team; Hunters served in the Command's squadrons from July 1954 to April 1963.

essentially a day fighter whose pilot had a gun-pack of four cannons as his means of shooting-down the enemy. The guns were a problem with the F.1 with gun-firing causing engine surge above a certain height (a problem suffered by many jet aircraft), although the problem was essentially overcome in the F.2. Variants came thick and fast; the F.4, with more fuel and improved all-round performance, entered service in June 1955 with 111 Squadron and was also to be the first variant to serve overseas with the RAF (its major usage being in RAF Germany). The F.5 came and went and then the F.6 appeared – the first of the classic Hunters and the first produced in large numbers. This Avon-powered Hunter entered service in October 1956 and within two years had re-equipped all the Fighter Command squadrons. The demise of the Hunter in the fighter role came in the early 1960s, in part with the introduction of the Lightning but also with some squadrons adopting an air support role (with the Hunter FGA.9).

The Hunter is an increasingly popular 'warbird' with private flyers and the UK in particular has a healthy population of airworthy Hunters, whilst the type is also common in museums.

Hawker HUNTER
Prototype, first flight: WB188, 20 July 1951
Entry to service: 43 Sqn, July 1954

Squadron	Dates	Airfields
1 Sqn	Sep 1955–Mar 1960	Tangmere
19 Sqn	Oct 1956–Feb 1963	Church Fenton, Leconfield
43 Sqn	Jul 1954–Jun 1961	Leuchars, (*Cyprus*)
45 Sqn	Aug 1972–Jul 1976	West Raynham, Wittering

54 Sqn	Feb 1955–Mar 1960	Odiham, Stradishall
56 Sqn	May 1955–Jan 1961	Waterbeach, Wattisham
63 Sqn	Nov 1946–Oct 1958	Waterbeach
66 Sqn	Mar 1956–Sep 1960	Linton-on-Ouse, Acklington
74 Sqn	Mar 1957–Nov 1960	Horsham St Faith, Coltishall
92 Sqn	Aug 1956–Apr 1963	Linton-on-Ouse, Middleton St George, Leconfield, (*Germany*)
111 Sqn	Jun 1955–Aug 1961	North Weald, North Luffenham, Wattisham
222 Sqn	Dec 1954–Nov 1957	Leuchars
245 Sqn	Apr 1957–Jun 1957	Stradishall
247 Sqn	May 1955–Dec 1957	Odiham
257 Sqn	Sep 1954–Mat 1957	Wattisham, Wymeswold
263 Sqn	Feb 1955–Jul 1958	Wattisham, Wymeswold

Gloster JAVELIN

The Javelin was another of the late 1940s designs that entered service in the late 1950s and was the only delta fighter to serve with the RAF. It was designed as an all-weather interceptor when wisdom said that missiles were the weapon of the future and fighters had to be able to find and destroy targets at night and in bad weather, all of which were perceived lessons of the latter part of World War Two. The Javelin was also designed for range and height to counter the new generation of Soviet bombers.

Designed to Specification F.4/48 the prototype flew on 26 November 1951, with the first production FAW.1 (XA544) getting airborne on 22 July 1954. The basis of the weapon system was a radar, operated by a navigator, and air-to-air missiles (although it was a few versions down the line before the effective Firestreak was being carried), plus four Aden cannon – a potent combination. Entry to service was with 46 Squadron at Odiham in February 1956 but within two years Fighter Command had eleven Javelin squadrons and there were others serving with the RAF overseas. A number of variants entered service, some with American radar; the FAW.2, FAW.3, FAW.4, FAW.5 and FAW.6 all being produced in limited numbers. The FAW.7 was the first to integrate the Firestreak (four missiles), and with more powerful engines and more fuel this was the

The Javelin served with eleven Fighter Command squadrons, entering service in February 1956.

best of the bunch so far, entering service in July 1958 with 33 Squadron at Leeming. With 142 aircraft built this was the most numerous variant. This was followed by the FAW.8 and with the re-manufacture of 7s into what was to some the definitive Javelin, the FAW.9. The latter entered service with 25 Squadron at Waterbeach in December 1959. Of the total of 429 Javelins most served with Fighter Command in the UK, but it was a short-lived involvement as most squadrons had re-equipped by 1962 and the final UK Javelins had gone by April 1965.

Few Javelins have survived, although a number of UK museums have examples and there is one in South Africa with the growing collection of airworthy Cold War jets, although there are no immediate plans to restore it to fly.

Gloster JAVELIN
Prototype, first flight: WD804, 26 November 1951
Entry to service: 46 Sqn, February 1956

Squadron	Dates	Airfields
23 Sqn	Mar 1957–Oct 1964	Horsham St Faith, Coltishall, Leuchars
25 Sqn	Dec 1958–Dec 1962	Waterbeach, Leuchars
33 Sqn	Jul 1958–Nov 1962	Leeming, Middleton St George
41 Sqn	Feb 1958–Dec 1963	Coltishall, Wattisham
46 Sqn	Feb 1956–Oct 1958	Odiham, Waterbeach
64 Sqn	Aug 1958–1 Apr 1965	Duxford, Waterbeach, Binbrook, (*Singapore*)
72 Sqn	Apr 1959–Jun 1961	Church Fenton, Leconfield
85 Sqn	Nov 1958–Mar 1963	Stradishall, West Malling, West Raynham
89 Sqn	Sep 1957–Nov 1958	Stradishall
141 Sqn	Feb 1957–Jan 1958	Horsham St Faith, Coltishall
151 Sqn	Jun 1957–Sep 1961	Turnhouse, Leuchars

English Electric LIGHTNING

After the Spitfire there is perhaps only one British fighter that has gained a reputation as the 'pilot dream machine' and one that thousands of enthusiasts would like to get the chance to experience – the English Electric Lightning. It was indeed an impressive machine, especially at air displays (sadly no longer to be seen unless you go to South Africa), but its operational life, and capability, was limited.

The aircraft was designed as a high-speed interceptor rather than a pure fighter; hence the emphasis on speed rather than manoeuvrability or armament. Development of what was a radical design for the late 1940s–early 1950s was complex but finally led to a first flight on 4 August 1954. The Lighting was soon demonstrating its supersonic capability, the first British fighter to achieve level-flight supersonic performance. It was not until 3 November 1959 that the first production Lightning F.1 flew, with the Central Fighter Establishment at Coltishall receiving a number of aircraft the following month and the first squadron, 74 Squadron at the same base, re-equipping from June 1960. The Tiger Squadron gave up Hunter F.6s for the new mount – and immediately doubled the maximum speed to Mach 2+, although this was a notional speed the true operational speed of the Lightning was well in excess of Mach 1. In terms of armament the concept was for an 'integrated weapon system' based on radar (Ferranti AI) and air-to-air missiles. As with most aircraft weapon systems there were problems with the radar and

A classic shot of an AAM-armed Lightning, albeit not a Figher Command squadron.

the missiles and it was some time before the planned operational capability was achieved. Indeed, the capability of the weapon system was questioned throughout much of the aircraft's life with limited radar performance and a maximum of two AAMs and Aden cannon.

By early 1961 Fighter Command had three Lightning squadrons in service, two at Wattisham and one at Coltishall. The major limitation with the aircraft was its lack of range; the engines were thirsty and the fuel limited. This is a problem that never went away. The introduction of air-to-air refuelling capability from the F.1A onwards certainly helped, as did later additions to on-board fuel with bigger tanks and conformal arrangements. The main variant to serve with Fighter Command was the F.3, with its better Avon engines and additional missile option of Red Top rather than Firestreak. This variant entered service with 74 Squadron at Leuchars in April 1964 and was followed in December 1965 by the final Lightning, the F.6. The last of 258 Lightnings, by then carrying the 'built by BAC' label, was completed in 1967, the same year that two of Fighter Command's squadrons moved overseas. The remaining squadrons played a vital role in the Cold War, providing the main response to the threat posed by Soviet long-range nuclear bombers. By the mid 1970s strength was down to two squadrons, both of which remained operational, at Binbrook, into the late 1980s. However, for the last decade of their career they were out-classed and little more than a 'manned missile', comments that will earn me a reprimand (at best) from the Lightning fraternity!

Lightings survive in a number of museums and as part of cockpit collections but the most dramatic survivors are the airworthy aircraft with Thunder City in South Africa – with the opportunity to buy a ride in this awesome fighter.

English Electric LIGHTNING
Prototype, first flight: WG760, 4 August 1954
Entry to service: 74 Sqn, June 1960

Squadron	Dates	Airfields
5 Sqn	Dec 1965–(Sep 1987)	Binbrook
11 Sqn	Apr 1967–(Apr 1988)	Leuchars, Binbrook
23 Sqn	Aug 1964–(Oct 1975)	Leuchars
29 Sqn	May 1967–(Dec 1974)	Wattisham
56 Sqn	Dec 1960–Apr 1967	Wattisham, (*Cyprus*)
74 Sqn	Jun 1960–Jun 1967	Coltishall, Leuchars, (*Singapore*)
111 Sqn	Apr 1961–(Sep 1974)	Wattisham

Bristol BLOODHOUND (SAM)

The Bloodhound Surface-to-Air Missile (SAM) has been left to last, although it was not the last 'aircraft' to enter service with Fighter Command, having pre-dated the Lightning by a couple of years. At the height of Bloodhound deployment there were ten missile sites on the eastern side of England, all positioned to defend the RAF's nuclear assets – with the main focus being cover of the Thor IRBMS.

The Bloodhound was developed in the late 1940s by the Bristol Aeroplane Co and Ferranti, with the latter providing the radar and guidance elements. These were the early days of such weapons and development was slow. The Bloodhound Mk 1 eventually entered service in December 1958, the first unit being 264 Squadron at North Coates, with four more squadrons becoming operational the following year as a defensive shield was established along the East coast. The early missile only had a range of 40 miles and its radar was of limited performance, being susceptible to jamming and having limited low level performance because of ground clutter – but it was primarily designed to engage medium to high targets. The improved Mk 2 entered service in 1964 and provided a far more effective radar and therefore overall capability; the system underwent subsequent upgrades to maintain its front-line capability and the 'faithful' Bloodhound eventually served with the RAF to 1994, nearly 30 years after Fighter Command had become Strike Command.

Bloodhound served as the RAF's main surface-to-air missile (SAM) for 40 years.

Bloodhound (SAM)
Entry to service: 264 Sqn, December 1958

Squadron	Dates	Airfields
25 Sqn	(Oct 1973–Oct 1989)	Flts at: Barkston Heath, North Coates, Wattisham, Wyton
41 Sqn	Sep 1965–(Jul 1970)	West Raynham
62 Sqn	Feb 1960–Sep 1964	Woolfox Lodge
85 Sqn	(Dec 1975–1994 ...)	Flts at: Bawdsey, North Coates, West Raynham
94 Sqn	Oct 1960–Jun 1963	Misson
112 Sqn	Nov 1964–Oct 1967	Woodhall Spa, (*Cyprus*)
141 Sqn	Apr 1959–Mar 1964	Dunholme Lodge
222 Sqn	May 1960–Jun 1964	Woodhall Spa
242 Sqn	Oct 1959–Sep 1964	Marham
247 Sqn	Jul 1960–Dec 1963	Carnaby
257 Sqn	Jul 1960–Dec 1960	Warboys
263 Sqn	Jun 1959–Jun 1963	Watton
264 Sqn	Dec 1958–Nov 1962	North Coates
266 Sqn	Dec 1959–Jun 1964	Rattlesden

Fighter Command Bloodhound missiles at 242 Squadron 'on duty' at Markham.

AOC-in-C Fighter Command

Command from:

14 Jul 1936	ACM Sir Hugh C T Dowding GCVC KCB CMG
25 Nov 1940	AM Sir W Sholto Douglas KCB MC DFC
28 Nov 1942	AM Sir Trafford Leigh Mallory KCB DSO
15 Nov 1943	AM Sir Roderic M Hill KCB MC AFC
14 May 1945	AM Sir James M Robb KBE CB DSO DFC AFC
17 Nov 1947	AM Sir William Elliott KBE CB DFC
19 Apr 1949	AM Sir Basil Embry KBE CB DSO DFC AFC
7 Apr 1953	AM Sir Dermot A Boyle KBE CB AFC
1 Jan 1956	AM Sir H L Patch CB CBE
8 Aug 1956	AM Sir Thomas Pike KCB CBE DFC
30 Jul 1959	AM Sir Hector McGregor KCB CBE DSO
8 May 1962	AM Sir Douglas Morris KCB CBE DSO DFC
3 Mar 1966	AM Sir Frederick Rosier KCB CBE DSO

Letter from ACM Dowding to Under-Secretary of State for Air 17 May 1940.

Sir,

1. I have the honour to refer to the very serious calls which have recently been made upon the Home Defence Fighter Units in an attempt to stem the German invasion on the Continent.

2. I hope and believe that our Armies may yet be victorious in France and Belgium, but we have to face the possibility that they may be defeated.

3. In this case I presume that there is no-one who will deny that England should fight on, even though the remainder of the Continent of Europe is dominated by the Germans.

4. For this purpose it is necessary to retain some minimum fighter strength in this country and I must request that the Air Council will inform me what they consider that minimum strength to be, in order that I may make my dispositions accordingly.

5. I would remind the Air Council that the last estimate of strength which they made as to the force necessary to defend this country was 52 squadrons, and my strength has now been reduced to the equivalent of 36 squadrons.

6. Once a decision has been reached as to the limit on which the Air Council and the Cabinet are prepared to stake the existence of this country, it should be made clear to the Allied Commanders on the Continent that not a single aeroplane from Fighter Command beyond that limit will be sent across the Channel, no matter how desperate the situation may become.

The impressive memorial at Kenley; most Fighter Command airfields are poorly served in respect of memorials. This one recognizes the part played by aircrew, groundcrew and WAAFS.

7. It will, of course, be remembered that the estimate of 52 squadrons was based on the assumption that the attack would come from the eastwards except in so far as the defences might be outflanked in flight. We have to face the possibility that the attacks may come from Spain or even from the north coast of France. The result is that our line is very much extended at the same time as our resources are reduced.

8. I must point out that within the last few days the equivalent of 10 squadrons have been sent to France, that the Hurricane squadrons remaining in this country are seriously depleted and that the more squadrons which are sent to France the higher will be the wastage and the more insistent the demands for reinforcement.

9. I must therefore request that as a matter of paramount importance the Air Ministry will consider and decide what level of strength is to be left to the Fighter Command for the defence of this country and will assure me that when this level has been reached, not one more fighter will be sent across the Channel however urgent and insistent the appeals for help may be.

10. I believe that, if an adequate fighter force is to be kept in this country, if the fleet remains in being and if Home Forces are suitably organised to resist invasion we should be able to carry-on the war single-handed for some time, if not indefinitely. But, if the Home Defence Force is drained away in desperate attempts to remedy the situation in France, defeat in France will involve the final, complete and irremediable defeat of this country.

Battle of Britain Squadrons

Battle of Britain – Squadron 'scorecard'

Squadron no.	Aircraft	Claims	Losses
1 Sqn	Hurricane	29	18
3 Sqn	Hurricane	1	2
17 Sqn	Hurricane	42	9
19 Sqn	Spitfire	60	7
23 Sqn	Blenheim	0	1
25 Sqn	Blenheim, Beaufighter	4	1
29 Sqn	Blenheim, Beaufighter	2	2
32 Sqn	Hurricane	48	20
41 Sqn	Spitfire	89	32
43 Sqn	Hurricane	67	25
46 Sqn	Hurricane	26	24
54 Sqn	Spitfire	52	20
56 Sqn	Hurricane	50	22
64 Sqn	Spitfire	39	13
65 Sqn	Spitfire	31	15
66 Sqn	Spitfire	53	25
72 Sqn	Spitfire	66	23
73 Sqn	Hurricane	19	17
74 Sqn	Spitfire	45	11
79 Sqn	Hurricane	25	10
85 Sqn	Hurricane	60	12
87 Sqn	Hurricane	41	11
92 Sqn	Spitfire	78	32
111 Sqn	Hurricane	51	18
141 Sqn	Defiant	3	6
145 Sqn	Hurricane	28	26
151 Sqn	Hurricane	27	17
152 Sqn	Spitfire	61	20
213 Sqn	Hurricane	83	23
219 Sqn	Blenheim, Beaufighter	0	1
222 Sqn	Spitfire	53	15
229 Sqn	Hurricane	14	12
232 Sqn	Hurricane	1	1
234 Sqn	Spitfire	69	17
235 Sqn	Blenheim	12	5
236 Sqn	Blenheim	4	6
238 Sqn	Hurricane	69	28
242 Sqn	Hurricane	69	9
245 Sqn	Hurricane	0	3
247 Sqn	Gladiator	0	0
248 Sqn	Blenheim	2	6
249 Sqn	Hurricane	72	24

253 Sqn	Hurricane	31	22
257 Sqn	Hurricane	19	17
263 Sqn	Hurricane, Whirlwind	0	0
264 Sqn	Defiant	15	10
266 Sqn	Spitfire	14	11
302 Sqn	Hurricane	25	10
303 Sqn	Hurricane	130	16
310 Sqn	Hurricane	43	11
312 Sqn	Hurricane	1	4
501 Sqn	Hurricane	100	43
504 Sqn	Hurricane	20	7
600 Sqn	Blenheim, Beaufighter	1	2
601 Sqn	Hurricane	68	16
602 Sqn	Spitfire	84	15
603 Sqn	Spitfire	67	30
604 Sqn	Blenheim, Beaufighter	1	2
605 Sqn	Hurricane	53	20
607 Sqn	Hurricane	18	15
609 Sqn	Spitfire	97	14
610 Sqn	Spitfire	58	20
611 Sqn	Spitfire	18	2
615 Sqn	Hurricane	33	13
616 Sqn	Spitfire	28	14
804 Sqn	Sea Gladiator, Martlet	0	0
808 Sqn	Fulmar	0	0
1 (Canadian) Sqn*	Hurricane	26	10

Notes
* Became 401 Sqn RCAF
1. Whilst the comparative scores of units makes interesting reading it must be borne in mind that not all units were operational throughout the period of the Battle and even amongst those that were, some spent much of the time away from the air battles of SE England.

'Churchill' gets back at the Germans; nose-art on a 17 Squadron Hurricane at Debden. The Squadron claimed 42 aircraft in the Battle of Britain.

Pilots of 41 Squadron mark-up their scoreboard.

Battle of Britain: Galland's View

In 1953 Adolf Galland, World War Two fighter ace, and *Luftwaffe* Inspector General of Fighters, compiled for the RAF's Air Historic Branch, his view of the Battle of Britain.

The Luftwaffe *had to be used in a decisive way in the Battle of Britain as a means of conducting total air war. Its size, technical equipment and the means at its disposal precluded the* Luftwaffe *from fulfilling this mission. On the other hand, in the absence of the necessary experience, the possibilities, limitations, requirements, methods and forces needed for carrying out strategic air operations were not yet known. Whatever may have been the importance of the tests of German arms in the Spanish Civil War from tactical, technical and operational points of view, they did not provide the experience that was needed nor led to the formulation of sound strategic concepts.*

One of Germany's greatest fighter pilots, Adolf Galland had gained his initial experience in the Spanish Civil War and by the outbreak of World War Two was flying Bf 109s. His flair as a fighter pilot saw him quickly promoted to command of JG26 and subsequently to the post of Inspector of Fighters. This, however, brought him into contact – and conflict – with Hermann Goering and many stormy scenes ensued. He was dismissed from this post in January 1945 and returned to combat flying leading the Me 262-equipped JV 44. The 1953 report was compiled in the light of post-war knowledge – and antipathy towards the German leadership in general and Goering in particular; however, despite this it is a useful document, the main elements of which are paraphrased and discussed in this annex.

Luftwaffe Strength

Galland makes the point that the *Luftwaffe* was less than five years old when it was 'called upon to prove its mettle in the Second World War' and that in that time the 'most powerful air force in the world at that time had been built up.' The effective strength of the *Luftwaffe* in late summer 1939 comprised 30 bomber *Gruppen* (He 111, Do 17, Ju 86) with 675 bombers, nine Ju 87 Stuka *Gruppen* with 200 aircraft, ten long-range fighter *Gruppen* with 300 Bf 110s, 13 single-engine fighter *Gruppen* with 400 Bf 109s, 21 long-range reconnaissance *Staffeln* with 104 aircraft, primarily Do 17s, and 30 close reconnaissance *Staffeln* with 200 aircraft, primarily He 126s. The majority of these were involved in the Polish campaign and the Polish Air Force was rapidly overwhelmed. Several additional *Gruppen* were formed during the first year of the war and according to German Quartermaster General records total strength had increased from less than 2,000 aircraft to around 7,000 aircraft, including over 3,000 bombers and around 2,750 fighters. German estimates gave British strength as 5,500 warplanes, but with only 3,600 of these being based in the UK and with only 200 of the 620 fighters being 'of the latest type. Thus the RAF was numerically superior to the *Luftwaffe*. However, a large proportion of the British aircraft were out of date and this enabled the *Luftwaffe* to maintain air supremacy at this stage with about 2,500 aircraft of later types.' He then comments that the balance of forces was not right – there were too few fighters, 'The reason for this is to be found in the basic conception on which the new *Luftwaffe* had been built up; it was thought of as an **attacking** force. This conformed with the strategic concept much in favour at that time: that mastery of the air should be obtained in the initial operations of a war through the destruction, on the ground, of the enemy's air power. I personally believe that Germany would not have lost the war if the production of fighters had been on the same scale in 1940 or 1941 as it was in 1944.'

To some extent this is the fighter pilot speaking – there are never enough fighters, but there is also a very valid point of air doctrine in terms of air superiority being the pre-requisite for air operations. The concept of destroying an enemy's air power 'on the ground' was a fundamentally flawed point of doctrine but one that appeared valid in the light of the Polish campaign, and indeed in the June 1941 offensive against Russia. The inherent secondary nature of the fighter implied by this doctrine was to be one of the factors limiting the effectiveness of the fighter arm during the Battle of Britain.

Fighter production in 1940 averaged only 200 aircraft a month and it was not until early 1942, as a reaction to the Allied bomber offensive against Germany, that a significant increase in rates of production began. In common with most air arms in the 1930s, the bomber was seen as the decisive weapon and most attention was paid to the development of these offensive weapons. 'The air force is a strategic, offensive weapon' and to this effect aircraft such as the Do 17 and He 111 were developed, bombers with performance superior to the contemporary He 51 and Ar 65 fighters: 'This led to a completely erroneous conception; it was believed then, and for some time afterwards, that in daylight attacks, bombers would be able to master enemy fighters and would thus not need to be escorted. In any case, fighters would not be able to accompany bombers owing to their disparity of speed.' This false premise led the RAF's bomber force into problems in late 1939 and the USAAF's B-17s to suffer heavy losses in 1942–43. The advent of high-performance fighters should have prompted changes in doctrine. 'The construction of the new Me 109 of completely revolutionary design put the problem back again in proper perspective. The sceptics asserted that the new Me 109 was not suitable for service use because of its very high take-off and landing speeds, which would give rise to insurmountable difficulties in handling it. Time has corrected these false conceptions and made one fact quite clear: the Me 109 not only possessed superior features, but it caused a revolution in fighter design throughout the world.'

The principal drawback of the single-engine fighters such as the 109 was that of operational radius, around 200 km ... 'this drawback played a decisive part in the outcome of the Battle of Britain.' With the realisation that the bombers would require fighter escort in daylight the *Luftwaffe* planners, at Goering's insistence, had to devise a twin-engined long-range fighter, the outcome being the Bf 110. The formation of such units in 1938 saw the third time when the day fighter force was required to give up a cadre of its best pilots, the previous two occasions being the expansion of the bomber force and the creation of the Stuka dive-bomber force. 'The consequences of this reduction on three separate occasions of the effective strength of fighter personnel were felt in the period between 1934 and 1939. For a long time fighter pilots were relegated to second place because they were not integrated into the operational air force. At manoeuvres, in conformity with regulations that had been drawn up governing their use, fighters were assigned the tasks of local air defence and combat for the purpose of achieving mastery in the air over front-line zones. Thus they were not included – and this was the mistake – in the operational air forces. However, the pilots of the new long-range fighters were, according to Goering, to be the elite of the fighter personnel.' Once again the fault lay in doctrine; the *Luftwaffe* had little upon which to base a strategic doctrine and thus it was constrained to operate in a more tactical sense. Whilst the Spanish and Polish experiences gave the *Luftwaffe* valuable combat experience they also provided what were to prove inappropriate lessons.

The Battle of Britain

'In order to carry out the invasion, the primary need was to obtain air superiority, and, as far as this was possible, absolute mastery of the air. Hence the task of solving the crucial problem was assigned to the air force.' The German Navy, rightly, insisted on air cover, a protective umbrella, during any invasion operation – to achieve this the *Luftwaffe* would have to destroy the RAF; three strategic missions were given to the *Luftwaffe*:

1. The blockade of Britain, in conjunction with the Navy, by air attacks on shipping and ports.
2. Softening-up for the invasion; offensive aimed at gaining air superiority.
3. Forcing Britain to surrender by waging total air war against her.

'Many voices in Germany were raised in criticism of the idea of attacking the British on their own soil. The critics maintained that not even the military occupation of the British isles would be enough to bring about the end of the war. Field Marshal Kesselring [Commander of *Luftflotte* 3], for example, headed a section of opinion that believed that an air offensive against Britain would demonstrate the limitations and weaknesses of the air force, and that it would result in our losing the most powerful instrument of political and military pressure we possessed. Hitler decided differently; once again it was principally Goering who goaded him into making his decision.' At this stage Galland was not party to the discussions of either the *Luftwaffe* hierarchy or that of the Nazi leadership; he no doubt subsequently discussed the Battle with some of those who had been part of the decision-making progress but the inclusion of hindsight perspective is inevitable, especially from such air leaders as Kesselring.

Nevertheless, it was a confident *Luftwaffe* that commenced operations against Britain; its campaigns to date – Spain, Poland and France – seemed to vindicate both its equipment and it doctrine; true, the *Luftwaffe* had greater respect for the RAF than for some of its previous opponents and there was the problem of combat radius for the single-engine fighters, but overall the planners, and the aircrew, saw few major problems.

'The second phase of the German air offensive began on 24 July, 1940, the aim being to rout the British fighter defences in combat with German fighters, and thus obtain the superiority necessary to ensure the effective employment of day bombers. To this end, German fighters were sent over the Channel on successive and intermittent sorties, first in Group strength and then by squadrons. At first the British accepted the challenge and sent up Hurricanes and Spitfires to engage the German units. The Hurricanes were out of date and their performance was far inferior to that of the Messerschmitt fighter as regards both maximum speed in level flight and rate of climb. Though the Spitfire was more manoeuvrable in turning, its maximum speed was 20–30 km per hour less. German ammunition and armament were manifestly better than those of the British. The RAF lost the greater number of fighters. But even more important than these technical drawbacks were the out-moded tactics used by the British fighters. Generally speaking, they flew in close formation of squadron strength in order to peel off immediately before making an attack. German fighters, on the other hand, flew in wide, open formations, a tactic evolved and perfected in the Spanish Civil War. About 15 days after the beginning of this phase of the Battle the British adopted the German style of flying.' The question of comparative fighter performance is one that has occupied many thousands of words and is frequently clouded by partisan viewpoints – did the rugged nature of the Hurricane make it better able to survive being hit, was the armament of the German fighters far superior, and so on. The qualitative nature of the pilots, and as Galland points out, the tactics being employed, have also to be taken into consideration. The *Luftwaffe* entered the Battle with a confident, verging on cocky, attitude and hence their morale was superb. The RAF fighter pilots were still, largely, untried and they faced what appeared to be an invincible war machine that had swept previous opponents away.

'Normally each unit made up to three sorties per day. The physical strain on pilots was very heavy; airframes and engines also suffered from these efforts. It soon became evident that Fighter Command was not deceived by the German air attacks for it did not send up its fighters on hasty missions according to the exigencies of the moment. Radar enabled the British to alert their defences in good time and to send up fighters at the right moment to intercept the German formations and to engage them when and where they chose.' The failure of the fighter tactic to draw the RAF to its destruction led to a change of tactic: 'In order to compel British fighters to fight again – the British Command had undoubtedly forbidden them to do so owing to German superiority – our fighters began to appear escorting several bombers, which attacked airfields, rail junctions and any other similar targets. The bombers were called *Lockvogel* (decoy birds) and the aim was achieved; the struggle for air supremacy resumed its rhythm.' This is the same tactic subsequently employed by the RAF, under the *Circus* operation, when offensive fighter sweeps over Occupied Europe in 1942 failed to produce any *Luftwaffe* reaction and bomber forces were employed to force a response – a tactic that met with mixed results. However, its employment by the *Luftwaffe* in 1940 was not on the same scale and was taking place at the same time as an anti-shipping campaign in English territorial waters, these latter attacks provoking a number of significant air battles. However, it was with Phase III, the direct attack on RAF airfields, that the Battle truly began. To the RAF these attacks on its airfields, and associated installations such as radar sites, were critical and many post-war commentators have concluded that if the attacks had continued then the Battle may have taken a different course. Galland, however, in his commentary puts forward a different view: 'The results obtained were very poor, for when attacks were made, practically all available British aircraft were in the air, engaged on defensive operations. Generally speaking, damage caused to the ground organisation was super-ficial. Better results would have been obtained if more small calibre bombs had been used, but the bombers were not equipped with suitable release apparatus. The British withdrew their fighter squadrons beyond London and used airfields close to the coast only for staging and emergency landings. Moreover, they had so many airfield that they had good chances of eluding attacks.' As with other parts of the Galland commentary, this smacks of post-war 'excuses' for the failure of the *Luftwaffe* campaign. Whilst it is true that the RAF had a reasonable number of airfields, the number within operating range of the combat area was limited – and all were well known to the *Luftwaffe*. RAF records show that a number of key airfields suffered significant damage, albeit repairs were rapid and the airfield, if not all of its facilities, was back in operation quite quickly; however, a concerted and continued attack on these key sites might have produced a different overall picture.

As the pace of operations increased the fighters were given four main missions:

a. Direct escort.
b. Indirect or deployed escort.
c. Free-lance patrols (*Freie Jagd*).
d. Supplementary escorts to pick up and cover returning formations and the protection of air-sea rescue services.

'Insofar as it can be said to have functioned at all, the system of escorting bombers yielded poor results. There were neither special tactical rules nor uniformity of plan; each fighter squadron carried out its missions as it thought best. Hence the quality of performance attained in these missions varied considerably. Some squadrons executed their missions in an extremely satisfactory manner, others failed miserably. It was not until late in the period of air battles that tactics were standardised.' Not surprisingly, Galland the fighter pilot was more in favour of the third type of mission, the free-lance patrol, than any of the others 'it was difficult to make them [the bomber unit commanders] understand that it is better for the German fighters to stay out of sight and thus make the enemy attack before they saw the German fighters than to remain "glued" to the formation they were escorting and thus allow the enemy to take the initiative.' This is very much the cry of the fighter pilot and was repeated by RAF and American fighter pilots when faced with similar close escort tasks that restricted their freedom of action.

The Turning Point
Goering had not been impressed with the performance of his fighter pilots in the Battle to this point and he decided on the radical move of appointing younger men to command positions to 'increase the fighting spirit and the striking power of the German fighter force. With one or two exceptions, the physical condition of the older unit commanders was not equal to the strain of modern aerial warfare.'

By early September the Battle was reaching its critical phase, Phase IV in Galland's commentary, with mass attacks against London. 'During these first large-scale attacks, Stuka squadrons were also used. They suffered heavy losses, particularly at the hands of British fighters. Goering blamed it on the fighters and declared that the standard of escort and protection was deplorable. But there was not one pilot who did not know that the fault was to be found in the technical shortcomings of the Stuka.' The bomber force usually comprised up to 500 bombers plus 200 Stukas, escorted by 500 single-engined and 200 twin-engined fighters, the attacking force forming up over the Pas de Calais before setting course for their target. German estimates that the RAF had only 200 fighters left were to prove wildly inaccurate. 'The ferocious and indomitable resistance of the British air defences, particularly RAF fighter pilots whose fighting qualities commanded the greatest admiration. Numerically very inferior at this stage of the struggle, they fought desperately and without respite, and saved their country. The organisation and the direction of the British air defences, represented by Fighter Command, showed great drive and initiative.

'It was a great advantage to the British to be able to concentrate their fighter forces in a ring around London; at this period they were not in a position effectively to protect a number of dispersed objectives simultaneously. But the *Luftwaffe* appeared to be obsessed by one idea and continued to direct its attacks against the same centre of British air defence – London. On October 20 the daylight offensive was suspended. *Luftwaffe* losses were considerable, especially bomber losses. Its war potential was weakened; but it was not exhausted as subsequent operations and later developments in the war showed.'

Galland went on to state that there were four reasons for the decision to abandon the daylight attacks:

1. Weather. The unpredictable autumn weather mitigated against large-scale daylight operations.
2. False evaluation of results. The RAF was still a potent force and German bombers and twin-engine fighters were being lost faster than they could be replaced.
3. Technical limitations of German aircraft. A number of considerations such as inadequate range of fighters and poor performance of Bf 110 and Ju 87, along with the inadequate defensive armament of the bombers.
4. Modification of the strategic plan. The German strategic shift towards the Mediterranean and Russia.

'However, there can be no doubt that the *Luftwaffe* could have continued the daylight offensive in spite of these constraints. The German Command could have given the orders for the offensive to be continued, and felt safe in doing so, if it had known the true extent of the exhaustion of the British air defences.'

The *Luftwaffe* had lost a quarter of its effective strength in personnel in the three months of its all-out offensive against Britain – but the campaign was not yet over. The final phases of the Battle of Britain were the fighter-bomber attacks and the switch to night bombing of London. In a rushed conversion programme around one third of the fighter force was equipped to carry bombs – much to the chagrin of the fighter pilots as this 'gave them a sense of inferiority.' Although they attempted to fulfil what they saw as a fruitless mission, they were soon on the receiving end of criticism from the High Command: 'The C-in-C declared with profound bitterness that the fighter arm had failed in its task of escorting bombers; he objected to the manner in which the fighter-bomber operations were carried out and added this to the fighters' previous shortcomings. The young commanders of fighter units, who were convinced that that had fulfilled their tasks during the air battles of the preceding weeks, and who had accepted severe losses without complaint, had once again to listen to grave charges being made against them.' Whilst there is a great deal of truth in what Galland says in respect of the attitude of the Nazi leadership, and Goering in particular, it most be borne in mind that in the latter part of the war he had major disagreements with the Nazi leadership.

Order of Battle
July 1936

Squadron	Airfield	Establishment	Notes
No. 11 Group (Uxbridge)			
23 Sqn	Biggin Hill	Demon	
32 Sqn	Biggin Hill	Gauntlet	
19 Sqn	Duxford	Gauntlet	
66 Sqn	Duxford	Gauntlet	
25 Sqn	Hawkinge	Fury	
604 Sqn	Hendon	Demon	
54 Sqn	Hornchurch	Gauntlet	
65 Sqn	Hornchurch	Gauntlet	
17 Sqn	Kenley	Bulldog	
111 Sqn	Northolt	Gauntlet	
56 Sqn	North Weald	Gauntlet	
1 Sqn	Tangmere	Fury	
43 Sqn	Tangmere	Fury	

Notes
1. Data based on SD161 unit location tables.
2. Three squadrons (3, 29, 41) had departed for the Abyssinian Crisis in late 1935 and were back with Fighter Command by September 1936.

Order of Battle
September 1939

Squadron	Airfield	Establishment	Notes
No. 11 Group (Uxbridge)			
32 Sqn	Biggin Hill	Hurricane	
601 Sqn	Biggin Hill	Blenheim	
3 Sqn	Croydon	Hurricane	
145 Sqn*	Croydon	Blenheim	
263 Sqn	Filton	Gladiator	
24 Sqn	Hendon	various	
248 Sqn*	Hendon	Blenheim	
54 Sqn	Hornchurch	Spitfire	
74 Sqn	Hornchurch	Spitfire	
600 Sqn	Hornchurch	Blenheim	
79 Sqn	Manston	Hurricane	
235 Sqn*	Manston	Battle	
253 Sqn	Manston	Battle	
56 Sqn	Martlesham Heath	Hurricane	
236 Sqn*	Martlesham Heath	Blenheim	
264 Sqn*	Martlesham Heath	Defiant	
25 Sqn	Northolt	Blenheim	
65 Sqn	Northolt	Spitfire	
151 Sqn	North Weald	Defiant	
604 Sqn	North Weald	Blenheim	
92 Sqn*	Tangmere	Blenheim	
501 Sqn	Tangmere	Hurricane	
605 Sqn	Tangmere	Hurricane	
Gp Pool	St Athan	Harvard, Hurricane	
No. 12 Group (Hucknall)			
17 Sqn	Debden	Hurricane	
504 Sqn	Debden	Hurricane	
29 Sqn	Debden	Blenheim	
46 Sqn	Digby	Hurricane	
229 Sqn*	Digby	Blenheim	
611 Sqn	Digby	Spitfire	
Civil Flt	Doncaster	various	
19 Sqn	Duxford	Spitfire	
66 Sqn	Duxford	Spitfire	
222 Sqn*	Duxford	Battle	
254 Sqn*	Sutton Bridge	Defiant	
266 Sqn*	Sutton Bridge	Battle	
23 Sqn	Wittering	Blenheim	
213 Sqn	Wittering	Hurricane	
610 Sqn	Wittering	Spitfire	

Squadron	Airfield	Establishment	Notes
No. 13 Group (Newcastle)			
43 Sqn	Acklington	Hurricane	
111 Sqn	Acklington	Hurricane	
152 Sqn	Acklington	Gladiator	
41 Sqn	Catterick	Spitfire	
219 Sqn*	Catterick	Blenheim	
64 Sqn	Church Fenton	Blenheim	
242 Sqn*	Church Fenton	Blenheim	
602 Sqn	Drem	Spitfire	
609 Sqn	Drem	Spitfire	
72 Sqn	Drem	Spitfire	
141 Sqn*	Grangemouth	Blenheim	
616 Sqn	Leconfield	Spitfire	
234 Sqn*	Leconfield	Spitfire	
245 Sqn*	Leconfield	Spitfire	
603 Sqn	Turnhouse	Spitfire	
Gp Pool	Aston Down	various	
No. 22 (Army Co-operation) Group (Farnborough)			
225 Sqn*	Odiham	Lysander	
614 Sqn*	Odiham	Lysander	
613 Sqn*	Odiham	Hector	
16 Sqn	Old Sarum	Lysander	
SoAC	Old Sarum	Blenheim	
Gp Pool	Old Sarum	various	

Notes
Data based on SD161 unit location tables.
* Non-operational squadron.

Order of Battle
August 1940

Squadron	Airfield	Establishment	Notes
No. 10 Group (Rudloe Manor)			
87 Sqn	Exeter	Hurricane	
213 Sqn	Exeter	Hurricane	
238 Sqn	Middle Wallop	Hurricane	
604 Sqn	Middle Wallop	Blenheim	
609 Sqn	Middle Wallop	Spitfire	
92 Sqn	Pembrey	Spitfire	
234 Sqn	St Eval	Spitfire	
152 Sqn	Warmwell	Spitfire	
No. 11 Group (Uxbridge)			
32 Sqn	Biggin Hill	Hurricane	
610 Sqn	Biggin Hill	Spitfire	
501 Sqn	Gravesend	Hurricane	
111 Sqn	Croydon	Hurricane	
17 Sqn	Debden	Hurricane	
41 Sqn	Hornchurch	Spitfire	
65 Sqn	Hornchurch	Spitfire	
74 Sqn	Hornchurch	Spitfire	
615 Sqn	Kenley	Hurricane	
64 Sqn	Kenley	Hurricane	
600 Sqn	Manston	Blenheim	
25 Sqn	Martlesham Heath	Blenheim	
85 Sqn	Martlesham Heath	Hurricane	
56 Sqn	North Weald	Hurricane	
151 Sqn	North Weald	Hurricane	
1 Sqn	Tangmere	Hurricane	
601 Sqn	Tangmere	Hurricane	
266 Sqn	Tangmere	Spitfire	
FIU	Tangmere	Blenheim	
145 Sqn	Westhampnett	Hurricane	
No. 12 Group			
23 Sqn	Collyweston	Blenheim	
66 Sqn	Coltishall	Spitfire	
242 Sqn	Coltishall	Hurricane	
29 Sqn	Digby	Blenheim	
46 Sqn	Digby	Hurricane	
611 Sqn	Digby	Spitfire	
19 Sqn	Fowlmere	Spitfire	
222 Sqn	Kirton-in-Lindsey	Spitfire	
264 Sqn	Kirton-in-Lindsey	Defiant	
229 Sqn	Wittering, Bircham Newton	Hurricane	

Squadron	Airfield	Establishment	Notes
72 Sqn	Acklington	Spitfire	
79 Sqn	Acklington	Hurricane	
245 Sqn	Aldergrove	Hurricane	
504 Sqn	Castletown	Hurricane	
808 Sqn FAA	Castletown	Fulmar	
54 Sqn	Catterick	Spitfire	
73 Sqn	Church Fenton	Hurricane	
249 Sqn	Church Fenton	Hurricane	
602 Sqn	Drem	Spitfire	
605 Sqn	Drem	Hurricane	
263 Sqn	Grangemouth	Hurricane	One Flight
616 Sqn	Leconfield	Spitfire	
219 Sqn	Leeming	Blenheim	
141 Sqn	Prestwick	Defiant	
232 Sqn	Sumburgh	Hurricane	
253 Sqn	Turnhouse	Hurricane	
603 Sqn	Turnhouse	Spitfire	
607 Sqn	Usworth	Hurricane	
3 Sqn	Wick	Hurricane	
804 Sqn FAA	Wick	Gladiator	

Order of Battle February 1941

Squadron	Airfield	Establishment	Notes
No. 9 Group (Barton Hall)			
229 Sqn	Speke	Hurricane	
312 Sqn	Speke	Hurricane	½ squadron
258 Sqn	Jurby	Hurricane	
306 Sqn	Ternhill	Hurricane	
308 Sqn	Baginton	Hurricane	
312 Sqn	Penrhos	Hurricane	½ squadron
96 Sqn	Cranage	Hurricane	
307 Sqn	Squire's Gate	Defiant	
No. 10 Group			
79 Sqn	Pembrey	Hurricane	
316 Sqn	Pembrey	Hurricane	Non-operational
501 Sqn	Filton	Hurricane	
93 Sqn	Middle Wallop	Boston	Non-operational
604 Sqn	Middle Wallop	Blenheim/Beaufighter	
238 Sqn	Chilbolton	Hurricane	
32 Sqn	Ibsley	Hurricane	
609 Sqn	Warmwell	Spitfire	
152 Sqn	Warmwell	Spitfire	
504 Sqn	Exeter	Hurricane	
263 Sqn	Exeter	Whirlwind	½ squadron
87 Sqn	Charmy Down	Hurricane	
234 Sqn	St Eval	Spitfire	
247 Sqn	St Eval	Hurricane	
263 Sqn	St Eval	Whirlwind	½ squadron
256 Sqn	Colerne	Defiant	Non-operational
No. 11 Group			
85 Sqn	Debden	Hurricane/Defiant	
17 Sqn	Martlesham Heath	Hurricane	
242 Sqn	Martlesham Heath	Hurricane	
605 Sqn	Martlesham Heath	Hurricane	½ squadron
601 Sqn	Northolt	Hurricane	
303 Sqn	Northolt	Hurricane/Spitfire	
259 Sqn	North Weald	Hurricane	
56 Sqn	North Weald	Hurricane	
64 Sqn	Southend	Spitfire II	
141 Sqn	Gravesend	Defiant	
92 Sqn	Manston	Spitfire	
91 Sqn	Hawkinge	Spitfire II	
264 Sqn	Biggin Hill	Defiant	
66 Sqn	Biggin Hill	Spitfire	

Squadron	Airfield	Establishment	Notes
74 Sqn	Biggin Hill	Spitfire	
605 Sqn	Croydon	Hurricane II	½ squadron
1 Sqn	Kenley	Hurricane	
615 Sqn	Kenley	Hurricane	
145 Sqn	Tangmere	Hurricane/Spitfire	
65 Sqn	Tangmere	Spitfire II	
219 Sqn	Tangmere	Blenheim/Beaufighter	
302 Sqn	Westhampnett	Hurricane	
610 Sqn	Westhampnett	Spitfire	
23 Sqn	Ford	Blenheim/Havoc	
No. 12 Group			
1 Sqn RCAF	Driffield	Hurricane	
616 Sqn	Kirton-in-Lindsey	Spitfire	
71 Sqn	Kirton-in-Lindsey	Hurricane	
255 Sqn	Kirton-in-Lindsey	Defiant	½ squadron
2 Sqn RCAF	Digby	Hurricane	Non-operational
46 Sqn	Digby	Hurricane	
29 Sqn	Digby	Blenheim/Beaufighter	
25 Sqn	Wittering	Blenheim/Beaufighter	
266 Sqn	Wittering	Spitfire	
151 Sqn	Wittering	Defiant	
222 Sqn	Coltishall	Spitfire	
257 Sqn	Coltishall	Hurricane	
19 Sqn	Duxford	Spitfire II	
310 Sqn	Duxford	Hurricane	
No. 13 Group			
43 Sqn	Drem	Hurricane	
603 Sqn	Drem	Spitfire II	
602 Sqn	Prestwick	Spitfire	
68 Sqn	Catterick	Blenheim	Non-operational
54 Sqn	Catterick	Spitfire	
600 Sqn	Catterick	Blenheim/Beaufighter	
245 Sqn	Aldergrove	Hurricane	
315 Sqn	Acklington	Hurricane	Non-operational
72 Sqn	Acklington	Spitfire	
No. 14 Group			
3 Sqn	Sumburgh	Hurricane	½ squadron
213 Sqn	Castletown	Hurricane	
3 Sqn	Castletown	Hurricane	½ squadron
260 Sqn	Skaebrae	Hurricane	
253 Sqn	Skaebrae	Hurricane	
111 Sqn	Dyce	Hurricane	½ squadron
111 Sqn	Montrose	Hurricane	½ squadron
232 Sqn	Elgin	Hurricane	

Order of Battle
April 1942

Squadron	Airfield	Establishment	Notes
No. 9 Group (Barton Hall)			
452 Sqn	Andreas	Spitfire	
79 Sqn	Baginton	Hurricane	
255 Sqn	High Ercall	Beaufighter	
257 Sqn	Honiley	Hurricane	
1456 Flt	Honiley	Havoc	Turbinlite
MSFU	Speke	Hurricane	
256 Sqn	Squire's Gate	Defiant	
456 Sqn	Valley	Beaufighter	
275 Sqn	Valley	Lysander/Walrus	Air-Sea Rescue
131 Sqn	Valley	Spitfire	
315 Sqn	Woodvale	Spitfire	
285 Sqn	Wrexham	Defiant	
96 Sqn	Wrexham	Defiant	
No. 10 Group (Rudloe Manor)			
312 Sqn	Angle	Spitfire	
87 Sqn	Charmy Down	Hurricane	
1454 Flt	Charmy Down	Havoc	Turbinlite
306 Sqn	Church Stanton	Spitfire	
125 Sqn	Colerne	Beaufighter	
286 Sqn	Colerne	Hurricane/Defiant	
307 Sqn	Exeter	Beaufighter	
308 Sqn	Exeter	Spitfire	
615 Sqn	Fairwood Common	Hurricane	
402 Sqn	Fairwood Common	Spitfire	
263 Sqn	Fairwood Common	Whirlwind	
267 Sqn	Harrowbeer	Lysander/Walrus	Air-Sea Rescue
302 Sqn	Harrowbeer	Spitfire	
118 Sqn	Ibsley	Spitfire	
234 Sqn	Ibsley	Spitfire	
501 Sqn	Ibsley	Spitfire	
604 Sqn	Middle Wallop	Beaufighter	
245 Sqn	Middle Wallop	Hurricane	
1458 Flt	Middle Wallop	Havoc	Turbinlite
310 Sqn	Perranporth	Spitfire	
130 Sqn	Perranporth	Spitfire	
66 Sqn	Portreath	Spitfire	
600 Sqn	Predannack	Beaufighter	
247 Sqn	Predannack	Hurricane	
1457 Flt	Predannack	Havoc	Turbinlite
1449 Flt	St Mary's	Hurricane	
175 Sqn	Warmwell	Hurricane	

Squadron	Airfield	Establishment	Notes
No. 11 Group (Uxbridge)			
72 Sqn	Biggin Hill	Spitfire	
124 Sqn	Biggin Hill	Spitfire	
418 Sqn	Bradwell Bay	Boston	
157 Sqn	Castle Camps	Mosquito	
287 Sqn	Croydon	Hurricane/Defiant	
65 Sqn	Debden	Spitfire	
111 Sqn	Debden	Spitfire	
350 Sqn	Debden	Spitfire	
FIU	Ford	Beaufighter	
401 Sqn	Gravesend	Spitfire	
91 Sqn	Hawkinge	Spitfire	
116 Sqn	Hendon	Lysander/Hurricane	
24 Sqn	Hendon	Various	Communications
1422 Flt	Heston	Havoc	Turbinlite
122 Sqn	Hornchurch	Spitfire	
313 Sqn	Hornchurch	Spitfire	
85 Sqn	Hunsdon	Havoc	
1451 Flt	Hunsdon	Havoc	Turbinlite
3 Sqn	Hunsdon	Hurricane	
485 Sqn	Kenley	Spitfire	
602 Sqn	Kenley	Spitfire	
32 Sqn	Manston	Hurricane	
174 Sqn	Manston	Hurricane	
607 Sqn	Manston	Hurricane	
23 Sqn	Manston	Havoc	One Flight
71 Sqn	Martlesham Heath	Spitfire	
340 Sqn	Merston	Spitfire	
303 Sqn	Northolt	Spitfire	
316 Sqn	Northolt	Spitfire	
317 Sqn	Northolt	Spitfire	
121 Sqn	North Weald	Spitfire	
222 Sqn	North Weald	Spitfire	
403 Sqn	North Weald	Spitfire	
457 Sqn	Redhill	Spitfire	
64 Sqn	Southend	Spitfire	
277 Sqn	Stapleford Tawney	Lysander/Walrus	Air-Sea Rescue
1 Sqn	Tangmere	Hurricane	
219 Sqn	Tangmere	Beaufighter	
23 Sqn	Tangmere	Havoc	One Flight
264 Sqn	West Malling	Defiant	
29 Sqn	West Malling	Beaufighter	
1452 Flt	West Malling	Havoc	Turbinlite
41 Sqn	Westhampnett	Spitfire	
129 Sqn	Westhampnett	Spitfire	
No. 12 Group (Watnall)			
885 Sqn FAA	Church Fenton	Hurricane	
68 Sqn	Coltishall	Beaufighter	
278 Sqn	Coltishall	Lysander/Walrus	Air-Sea Rescue
154 Sqn	Coltishall	Spitfire	One Flight
288 Sqn	Digby	Hurricane/Defiant	
409 Sqn	Digby	Beaufighter	
411 Sqn	Digby	Spitfire	
412 Sqn	Digby	Spitfire	
266 Sqn	Duxford	Typhoon	
609 Sqn	Duxford	Spitfire	
154 Sqn	Fowlmere	Spitfire	One Flight

Squadron	Airfield	Establishment	Notes
253 Sqn	Hibaldstow	Hurricane	
1459 Flt	Hibaldstow	Havoc	Turbinlite
19 Sqn	Hutton Cranswick	Spitfire	
616 Sqn	Kingcliffe	Spitfire	
133 Sqn	Kirton-in-Lindsey	Spitfire	
486 Sqn	Kirton-in-Lindsey	Hurricane	
610 Sqn	Ludham	Spitfire	
137 Sqn	Matlask	Whirlwind	
56 Sqn	Snailwell	Typhoon	
151 Sqn	Wittering	Defiant	
1453 Flt	Wittering	Havoc	Turbinlite

No. 13 Group (Newcastle)

Squadron	Airfield	Establishment	Notes
43 Sqn	Acklington	Hurricane	
141 Sqn	Acklington	Beaufighter	
1460 Flt	Acklington	Havoc	Turbinlite
406 Sqn	Ayr	Beaufighter	
134 Sqn	Ayr	Spitfire	
332 Sqn	Catterick	Spitfire	
611 Sqn	Drem	Spitfire	
410 Sqn	Drem	Defiant	
281 Sqn	Ouston	Defiant	
410 Sqn	Ouston	Defiant	One Flight
1423 Flt	Ouston	Hurricane	
289 Sqn	Turnhouse	Hurricane/Defiant	
81 Sqn	Turnhouse	Spitfire	
54 Sqn	Castletown	Spitfire	
123 Sqn	Castletown	Spitfire	
416 Sqn	Dyce	Spitfire	One Flight
416 Sqn	Montrose	Spitfire	
603 Sqn	Peterhead	Spitfire	
132 Sqn	Skaebrae	Spitfire	
331 Sqn	Skaebrae	Spitfire	
417 Sqn	Tain	Spitfire	

No. 81 Group (Worcester)
Details of this training Group are in the Aircrew Training chapter

No. 82 Group (Belfast)

Squadron	Airfield	Establishment	Notes
25 Sqn	Ballyhalbert	Beaufighter	
153 Sqn	Ballyhalbert	Beaufighter	One Flight
152 Sqn	Eglinton	Spitfire	
504 Sqn	Kirkistown	Spitfire	
153 Sqn	Limavady	Beaufighter	One Flight
74 Sqn	Long Kesh	Spitfire	
1480 Flt	Newtonards	Spitfire	

Order of Battle
April 1943

Squadron	Airfield	Establishment	Notes
No. 9 Group (Barton Hall)			
247 Sqn	High Ercall	Typhoon	
41 Sqn	High Ercall	Spitfire	
255 Sqn	Honiley	Beaufighter	
96 Sqn	Honiley	Beaufighter	
285 Sqn	Honiley	Defiant	
MSFU	Speke	Hurricane	
275 Sqn	Valley	Anson/Walrus	Air-Sea Rescue
256 Sqn	Valley	Mosquito	
456 Sqn	Valley	Mosquito	
195 Sqn	Woodvale	Typhoon	
No. 10 Group (Rudloe Manor)			
312 Sqn	Church Stanton	Spitfire	
313 Sqn	Church Stanton	Spitfire	
264 Sqn	Colerne	Mosquito	
286 Sqn	Weston-super-Mare	Defiant/Hurricane	
184 Sqn	Weston-super-Mare	Hurricane	
266 Sqn	Exeter	Typhoon	
307 Sqn	Bolt Head	Mosquito	
310 Sqn	Bolt Head	Spitfire	
125 Sqn	Fairwood Common	Beaufighter	
412 Sqn	Fairwood Common	Spitfire	
276 Sqn	Harrowbeer	Walrus/Spitfire	Air-Sea Rescue
193 Sqn	Harrowbeer	Typhoon	
129 Sqn	Ibsley	Spitfire	
504 Sqn	Ibsley	Spitfire	
616 Sqn	Ibsley	Spitfire	
406 Sqn	Middle Wallop	Beaufighter	
164 Sqn	Middle Wallop	Hurricane	
175 Sqn	Odiham	Typhoon	
174 Sqn	Odiham	Typhoon	
1449 Flt	Portreath	Hurricane	
19 Sqn	Perranporth	Spitfire	
130 Sqn	Perranporth	Spitfire	
602 Sqn	Perranporth	Spitfire	
141 Sqn	Predannack	Beaufighter	
257 Sqn	Warmwell	Typhoon	
263 Sqn	Warmwell	Whirlwind	
No. 11 Group (Uxbridge)			
1 Sqn	Biggin Hill	Typhoon	
340 Sqn	Biggin Hill	Spitfire	
611 Sqn	Biggin Hill	Spitfire	
23 Sqn	Bradwell Bay	Mosquito	

Squadron	Airfield	Establishment	Notes
157 Sqn	Bradwell Bay	Mosquito	
605 Sqn	Castle Camps	Mosquito	
287 Sqn	Croydon	Defiant/Hurricane	
418 Sqn	Ford	Mosquito	
604 Sqn	Ford	Beaufighter	
FIU	Ford	various	
277 Sqn	Gravesend	Walrus/Spitfire	Air-Sea Rescue
91 Sqn	Hawkinge	Spitfire	
303 Sqn	Heston	Spitfire	
515 Sqn	Heston	Defiant	
1422 Flt	Heston	Boston/Mosquito	
64 Sqn	Hornchurch	Spitfire	
122 Sqn	Hornchurch	Spitfire	
350 Sqn	Fairlop	Spitfire	
85 Sqn	Hunsdon	Mosquito	
3 Sqn	Hunsdon	Typhoon	
402 Sqn	Kenley	Spitfire	
403 Sqn	Kenley	Spitfire	
421 Sqn	Kenley	Spitfire	
137 Sqn	Manston	Whirlwind	
609 Sqn	Manston	Typhoon	
132 Sqn	Martlesham Heath	Spitfire	
182 Sqn	Martlesham Heath	Typhoon	
308 Sqn	Northolt	Spitfire	
315 Sqn	Northolt	Spitfire	
316 Sqn	Northolt	Spitfire	
124 Sqn	North Weald	Spitfire	
331 Sqn	North Weald	Spitfire	
332 Sqn	North Weald	Spitfire	
416 Sqn	Redhill	Spitfire	
453 Sqn	Southend	Spitfire	
129 Sqn	Tangmere	Spitfire	
486 Sqn	Tangmere	Typhoon	
485 Sqn	Merston	Spitfire	
165 Sqn	Westhampnett	Spitfire	
610 Sqn	Westhampnett	Spitfire	
29 Sqn	West Malling	Mosquito	

No. 12 Group (Watnall)

Squadron	Airfield	Establishment	Notes
183 Sqn	Church Fenton	Typhoon	
25 Sqn	Church Fenton	Mosquito	
68 Sqn	Coltishall	Beaufighter	
278 Sqn	Coltishall	Anson/Walrus	Air-Sea Rescue
56 Sqn	Coltishall	Typhoon	
118 Sqn	Coltishall	Spitfire	
288 Sqn	Digby	various	
410 Sqn	Digby	Mosquito	
411 Sqn	Digby	Spitfire	
306 Sqn	Hutton Cranswick	Spitfire	
302 Sqn	Kirton-in-Lindsey	Spitfire	
317 Sqn	Kirton-in-Lindsey	Spitfire	
167 Sqn	Ludham	Spitfire	
181 Sqn	Snailwell	Typhoon	
151 Sqn	Wittering	Mosquito	

No. 13 Group

Squadron	Airfield	Establishment	Notes
409 Sqn	Acklington	Beaufighter	
198 Sqn	Acklington	Typhoon	

Squadron	Airfield	Establishment	Notes
488 Sqn	Ayr	Beaufighter	
222 Sqn	Ayr	Spitfire	
401 Sqn	Catterick	Spitfire	
219 Sqn	Catterick	Beaufighter	
65 Sqn	Drem	Spitfire	
197 Sqn	Drem	Typhoon	
281 Sqn	Ouston	Anson/Walrus	Air-Sea Rescue
289 Sqn	Turnhouse	Defiant/Hurricane	
341 Sqn	Turnhouse	Spitfire	
No. 14 Group			
282 Sqn	Castletown	Walrus/Anson	Air-Sea Rescue
131 Sqn	Castletown	Spitfire	
245 Sqn	Peterhead	Typhoon	
66 Sqn	Skeabrae	Spitfire	
234 Sqn	Skeabrae	Spitfire	
Fighter Command units in Northern Ireland			
501 Sqn	Kirkistown	Spitfire	

No. 81 Group
Details of this training Group are included in the chapter on aircrew training.

Order of Battle
July 1944

Air Defence of Great Britain			
Squadron	*Airfield*	*Establishment*	*Notes*

No. 9 Group (Barton Hall)
The Group had taken on a training role; details in the chapter on aircrew training.

No. 10 Group (Rudloe Manor)

263 Sqn	Bolt Head	Whirlwind	
68 Sqn	Castle Camps	Mosquito	
126 Sqn	Culmhead	Spitfire	
131 Sqn	Culmhead	Spitfire	
616 Sqn	Culmhead	Spitfire	
41 Sqn	Friston	Spitfire	
610 Sqn	Friston	Spitfire	
1 Sqn	Lympne	Spitfire	
165 Sqn	Lympne	Spitfire	
276 Sqn	Portreath	Warwick	Air-Sea rescue
151 Sqn	Predannack	Mosquito	
1449 Flt	Predannack	Hurricane	
406 Sqn	Winkleigh	Beaufighter	

No. 11 Group (Uxbridge)

219 Sqn	Bradwell Bay	Mosquito	
278 Sqn	Bradwell Bay	Walrus/Spitfire	Air-Sea Rescue
229 Sqn	Coltishall	Spitfire	
96 Sqn	Ford	Mosquito	
456 Sqn	Ford	Mosquito	
350 Sqn	Friston	Spitfire	
501 Sqn	Friston	Spitfire	
64 Sqn	Harrowbeer	Spitfire	
611 Sqn	Harrowbeer	Spitfire	
418 Sqn	Holmsley South	Mosquito	
125 Sqn	Hurn	Beaufighter	
26 Sqn	Lee-on-Solent	Spitfire	
63 Sqn	Lee-on-Solent	Spitfire	
33 Sqn	Lympne	Spitfire	
74 Sqn	Lympne	Spitfire	
127 Sqn	Lympne	Spitfire	
137 Sqn	Manston	Typhoon	
605 Sqn	Manston	Mosquito	
130 Sqn	Merston	Spitfire	
303 Sqn	Merston	Spitfire	
402 Sqn	Merston	Spitfire	
234 Sqn	Predannack	Spitfire	

Air Defence of Great Britain (continued)

Squadron	Airfield	Establishment	Notes
345 Sqn	Shoreham	Spitfire	
277 Sqn	Shoreham	Walrus/Spitfire	Air-Sea Rescue
275 Sqn	Warmwell	Walrus/Spitfire	Air-Sea Rescue
274 Sqn	West Malling	Spitfire	
80 Sqn	West Malling	Spitfire	

No. 12 Group (Watnall)

307 Sqn	Church Fenton	Mosquito	
25 Sqn	Coltishall	Mosquito	
504 Sqn	Digby	Spitfire	

No. 13 Group (Inverness)

118 Sqn	Skeabrae	Spitfire	
309 Sqn	Drem	Hurricane	

No. 70 Group (Farnborough)

With the disbandment of Army Co-operation Command in May 1943, the Group was transferred to Fighter Command/Air Defence of Great Britain.

Order of Battle
July 1945

Squadron	Airfield	Establishment	Notes
No. 11 Group (Uxbridge)			
The training elements have been omitted and are included in the chapter on aircrew training.			
306 Sqn	Andrewsfield	Mustang	
309 Sqn	Andrewsfield	Mustang	
315 Sqn	Andrewsfield	Mustang	
64 Sqn	Bentwaters	Mustang	
118 Sqn	Bentwaters	Mustang	
65 Sqn	Bentwaters	Spitfire	
126 Sqn	Bentwaters	Spitfire	
25 Sqn	Castle Camps	Mosquito	
183 Sqn	Chilbolton	Spitfire	
74 Sqn	Colerne	Meteor	
329 Sqn	Harrowbeer	Spitfire	
275 Sqn	Harrowbeer	Walrus/Sea Otter	
29 Sqn	Manston	Mosquito	
310 Sqn	Manston	Spitfire	
312 Sqn	Manston	Spitfire	
313 Sqn	Manston	Spitfire	
151 Sqn	Predannack	Mosquito	
406 Sqn	Predannack	Mosquito	
No. 12 Group (Watnall)			
The training elements have been omitted and are included in the chapter on aircrew training.			
19 Sqn	Acklington	Spitfire	
26 Sqn	Chilbolton	Spitfire	
125 Sqn	Church Fenton	Beaufighter	
303 Sqn	Coltishall	Mustang	
316 Sqn	Coltishall	Mustang	
307 Sqn	Coltishall	Mosquito	
441 Sqn	Digby	Mustang	
442 Sqn	Digby	Mustang	
124 sqn	Hutton Cranswick	Spitfire	
1 Sqn	Ludham	Spitfire	
91 Sqn	Ludham	Spitfire	
No. 13 Group (Inverness)			
164 Sqn	Drem	Spitfire	
129 Sqn	Dyce	Spitfire	
165 Sqn	Dyce	Spitfire	
122 Sqn	Peterhead	Mustang	
234 Sqn	Peterhead	Mustang	
611 Sqn	Peterhead	Mustang	
603 Sqn	Skeabrae	Spitfire	

Squadron	Airfield	Establishment	Notes
No. 88 Group (Edinburgh)			
333 Sqn	Banff	Mosquito	
130 Sqn	Dyce	Spitfire	
331 Sqn	Gardemoen	Spitfire	Norway
332 Sqn	Gardemoen	Spitfire	
			128 Wing
			129 Wing
			130 Wing
			132 Wing
334 Sqn	Woodhaven	Mosquito	

Order of Battle
April 1953

Squadron	Airfield	Establishment	Notes
No. 11 Group (Hillingdon)			
Southern Sector (Box)			
501 Sqn	Filton	Vampire	
614 Sqn	Llandow	Vampire	
54 Sqn	Odiham	Meteor	
247 Sqn	Odiham	Meteor	
1 Sqn	Tangmere	Meteor	
22/29 Sqn	Tangmere	Meteor	
Metropolitan Sector (Kelvedon)			
41/253 Sqn	Biggin Hill	Meteor	
600 Sqn	Biggin Hill	Meteor	
615 Sqn	Biggin Hill	Meteor	
64 Sqn	Duxford	Meteor	
65 Sqn	Duxford	Meteor	
72 Sqn	North Weald	Meteor	
601 Sqn	North Weald	Meteor	
604 Sqn	North Weald	Meteor	
56 Sqn	Waterbeach	Meteor	
63 Sqn	Waterbeach	Meteor	
257 Sqn	Wattisham	Meteor	
263 Sqn	Wattisham	Meteor	
25 Sqn	West Malling	Vampire	
85 Sqn	West Malling	Meteor	
500 Sqn	West Malling	Meteor	
No. 12 Group (Newton)			
Northern Sector (Shipton)			
19/152 Sqn	Church Fenton	Meteor	
609 Sqn	Church Fenton	Meteor	
66 Sqn	Linton-on-Ouse	Meteor	
92 Sqn	Linton-on-Ouse	Meteor	
264 Sqn	Linton-on-Ouse	Meteor	
275 Sqn	Linton-on-Ouse	Sycamore	Search-and-Rescue
607 Sqn	Ouston	Vampire	
608 Sqn	Thornaby	Vampire	
Eastern Sector (Bawburgh)			
23 Sqn	Coltishall	Vampire	
141 Sqn	Coltishall	Meteor	
616 Sqn	Finningley	Meteor	
74/34 Sqn	Horsham St Faith	Meteor	
245 Sqn	Horsham St Faith	Meteor	

Squadron	Airfield	Establishment	Notes
613 Sqn	Ringway	Vampire	
504 Sqn	Wymeswold	Meteor	
Western Sector (Langley Lane)			
605 Sqn	Honiley	Vampire	
610 Sqn	Hooton Park	Meteor	
611 Sqn	Hooton Park	Meteor	
Caledonian Sector (Barnton Quarry)			
602 Sqn	Abbotsinch	Vampire	
502 Sqn	Aldergrove	Vampire	
612 Sqn	Dyce	Vampire	
43/17 Sqn	Leuchars	Meteor	
222 Sqn	Leuchars	Meteor	
151 Sqn	Leuchars	Vampire	
603 Sqn	Turnhouse	Vampire	

No. 81 Group (Pembrey)
Details of this training Group are in the chapter on aircrew training.

Order of Battle
January 1961

Squadron	Airfield	Establishment	Notes
FC CS	Bovingdon	Anson, Meteor	
No. 11 Group			
229 OCU	Chivenor	Hunter, Vampire	
19 Sqn	Leconfield	Hunter	
72 Sqn	Leconfield	Javelin	
228 OCU	Leeming	Meteor, Javelin, Valetta	
29 Sqn	Leuchars	Javelin	
151 Sqn	Leuchars	Javelin	
43 Sqn	Leuchars	Hunter	
	Lindholme	HQ No. 21 (ADM) Wing; Bomber Command Station	
112 Sqn	Breighton	Bloodhound	
247 Sqn	Carnaby	Bloodhound	
94 Sqn	Misson	Bloodhound	
33 Sqn	Middleton St George	Javelin	
92 Sqn	Middleton St George	Hunter	
	North Coates	HQ No. 148 (ADM) Wing	
264 Sqn	North Coates	Bloodhound	
141 Sqn	Dunholme Lodge	Bloodhound	
222 Sqn	Woodhall Spa	Bloodhound	
5 CAACU	Woodvale	Meteor, Mosquito	
No. 12 Group (Horsham St Faith)			
23 Sqn	Coltishall	Javelin	
74 Sqn	Coltishall	Lightning	
AFDS	Coltishall	various	
64 Sqn	Duxford	Javelin	
65 Sqn	Duxford	Hunter	
3/4 CAACU	Exeter	various	
Gp CF	Horsham St Faith	Anson, Meteor	
242 Sqn	Marham	Bloodhound	Bomber Command Station
	North Luffenham	HQ No. 151 (ADM) Wing; Bomber Command Station	
257 Sqn	Warboys	Bloodhound	
62 Sqn	Woolfox Lodge	Bloodhound	
SoLAW	Old Sarum	various	
1 Sqn	Stradishall	Hunter	
54 Sqn	Stradishall	Hunter	
1 GWTS	Valley	Hunter	Flying Training Command Station
25 Sqn	Waterbeach	Javelin	
46 Sqn	Waterbeach	Javelin	
41 Sqn	Wattisham	Javelin	
56 Sqn	Wattisham	Hunter	
111 Sqn	Wattisham	Hunter	

Squadron	Airfield	Establishment	Notes
	Watton	HQ No. 24 (ADM) Wing	
263 Sqn	Watton	Bloodhound	
266 Sqn	Rattlesden	Bloodhound	
85 Sqn	West Raynham	Javelin	
CFE	West Raynham	various	

Note: Data from the SD161 Location of Units.

The Javelins of 85 Squadron moved to West Raynham in September 1960 from Strandishall.

Order of Battle January 1968

Squadron	Airfield	Establishment	Notes
5 Sqn	Binbrook	Lightning	
85 Sqn	Binbrook	Canberra	
229 OCU	Chivenor	Hunter	
226 OCU	Coltishall	Lightning	
11 Sqn	Leuchars	Lightning	
23 Sqn	Leuchars	Lightning	
25 Sqn	North Coates	Bloodhound	
29 Sqn	Wattisham	Lightning	
111 Sqn	Wattisham	Lightning	
41 Sqn	West Raynham	Bloodhound	

Note: Data based on SD161 Location of Units.

85 Squadron exchanged its Javelins for Canberras and moved to Binbrook (April 19?3) to become a target facilities unit.

Claims World War Two

Air combat claims made for enemy aircraft destroyed are a contentious issue and whilst there is insufficient space here to discuss this topic it is worth explaining the RAF's official categorisations, as used during the Battle of Britain. The following details are extracted from a Fighter Command document dated November 1940.

For the early part of the Battle the RAF was using a dual system of Confirmed and Unconfirmed:

Confirmed: Enemy aircraft had to be seen on the ground or in the sea by a member of the crew or formation, or confirmed as destroyed from other sources e.g. ships, Observer Corps, etc. Or the enemy aircraft had to be seen to descend with flames issuing – it was not sufficient if only smoke was seen, alternatively, the enemy aircraft must have been seen breaking up in the air.

Unconfirmed: Enemy aircraft had to be seen to break off combat in circumstances which led pilot or crew to believe it would be a loss.

The system applied by the RAF in respect of claims changed at midnight on 13 August 1940, and from then on comprised three categories:

Cat I   – Destroyed: to cover all cases in which the enemy aircraft was positively reported to have been seen to hit the ground or sea, to break up in the air, or descend in flames, whether or not confirmation from a second source was available. This also covered enemy aircraft that landed and were captured.

Cat II   – Probably Destroyed: to be applied to those cases in which the enemy aircraft was seen to break off combat in circumstances which led to the conclusion that it must have been lost.

Cat III – Damaged: to be applied in cases in which the enemy aircraft was considered damaged when under attack, such as an undercarriage dropped or aircraft parts shot away.

Despite the official use of Cat I, II and III, records and subsequent histories have tended to simply use Destroyed, Probable and Damaged. As with all statistics there is wide variation in published figures. The tables shown are from various Fighter Command and War Office documents.

Fighter Command Claims, 1939

	Day			Night		
Month	Destroyed	Probable	Damaged	Destroyed	Probable	Damaged
Sep	0	0	0	0	0	0
Oct	10	0	0	0	0	0
Nov	4	0	0	0	0	0
Dec	2	0	0	0	0	0
Total	16	0	0	0	0	0

Note: The source table only lists aircraft destroyed by day but claims for Probable and Damaged would have been made. There were no night claims.

Fighter Command Claims, 1940

	Day			Night		
Month	Destroyed	Probable	Damaged	Destroyed	Probable	Damaged
Jan	3	0	0	0	0	0
Feb	10	0	0	0	0	0
Mar	3	0	0	0	0	0
Apr	6½	0	0	0	0	0
May	2	0	0	0	0	0
Jun	1	0	0	16	0	0
Jul	209	0	92	3	0	3
Aug	957	387	434	3	2	3
Sep	867	368	464	4	3	3
Oct	208	103	153	3	0	4
Nov	186½	62	75	2	0	3
Dec	36½	13	21	4	3	3
Total	2,489½	933	1,239	35	8	19

Fighter Command Claims, 1941

	Day			Night		
Month	Destroyed	Probable	Damaged	Destroyed	Probable	Damaged
Jan	5½	5	10	3	4	3
Feb	15½	3	14	4	2	5
Mar	20	7	24	22	7	10
Apr	28	7	28	48½	16	22
May	52	16	32	96	22	44
Jun	17	8	17	27	4	9
Jul	17	5	8	26	3	5
Aug	11	3	7	3	1	2
Sep	1	2	0	8	0	2
Oct	7	2	4	11	3	11
Nov	5	2	8	7	0	5
Dec	5	1	2	3	0	3
Total	184	61	154	258½	62	121

Fighter Command Claims, 1942

Month	Day			Night		
	Destroyed	Probable	Damaged	Destroyed	Probable	Damaged
Jan	2½	1	3	4	0	0
Feb	7	0	12	2	0	0
Mar	2	0	5	2	0	0
Apr	4	1	7	18	9½	19
May	10	4	13	14	4	6
Jun	8	3	14	23	4	13
Jul	14	0	14	32	13	21
Aug	12	2	20	21½	8	15
Sep	10	5	15	10	4	8
Oct	10	4	16	6	1	1
Nov	7	1	1	–	0	0
Dec	12	4	10	1	0	0
Total	98½	25	130	133½	43½	83

Fighter Command Claims, 1943

Month	Day			Night		
	Destroyed	Probable	Damaged	Destroyed	Probable	Damaged
Jan	21	2	12	10	0	8
Feb	11	3	9	7	2	2
Mar	22½	1	15	21½	5	2
Apr	12	3	7	6	0	2
May	12	1	4	11	1	1
Jun	11	0	3	8	1	4
Jul	7	2	0	11	0	3
Aug	5	0	2	16	4	3
Sep	2	0	1	10	1	1
Oct	9	1	2	14½	1	4
Nov	2	1	2	11	1	0
Dec	2	0	1	14	0	3
Total	116½	14	58	140	16	33

Fighter Command Claims, 1944

Month	Day			Night		
	Destroyed	Probable	Damaged	Destroyed	Probable	Damaged
Jan	0	0	1	16	3	4
Feb	5	0	1	26½	6	10
Mar	0	0	2	44	2	6
Apr	1½	0	0	33	4	4
May	5	0	0	25	5	6
Jun	1	0	0	6	2	0
Jul	0	0	0	0	0	0
Aug	0	0	0	1	0	0
Sep	0	0	0	3	2	0
Oct	2	0	1	4	0	1
Nov	0	0	0	7	1	0
Dec	0	0	0	2	0	1
Total	14½	0	5	167½	25	32

Fighter Command Claims, 1945

Month	Day			Night		
	Destroyed	Probable	Damaged	Destroyed	Probable	Damaged
Jan	0	0	0	1	0	0
Feb	0	0	0	0	0	0
Mar	0	0	0	4	0	1
Apr	0	0	0	0	0	0
May	0	0	0	0	0	0
Totals	0	0	0	5	0	1

Fighter Command Claims Summary, 1939–1945

Year	Destroyed	Probable	Damaged
1939	15	0	0
1940	3,105½	941	1,258
1941	1,213½	463	715
1942	694	293½	808
1943	927½	196	566
1944	708	59	164
1945	88	11	37
Totals	6,751½	1,963½	3,548

Note: The table includes offensive and defensive sorties.

Defensive sorties UK

Month	1939	1940	1941	1942	1943	1944	1945
Jan	–		2,350	1,994	5,711	1,121	211
Feb	–		3,339	2,396	6,484	1,510	250
Mar	–		4,995	2,134	9,090	2,251	1,006
Apr	–		8,369	4,432	10,489	2,458	178
May	–		8,575	4,605	8,397	4,542	43
Jun	–		5,713	5,654	7,458	5,793	–
Jul	–		3,506	5,457	5,049	10,356	–
Aug	–		2,375	6,385	4,444	10,622	–
Sep			1,955	4,670	4,654	1,401	–
Oct			2,790	5,447	3,153	1,261	–
Nov			2,024	3,488	2,684	884	–
Dec			1,681	3,131	1,801	421	–
Totals			47,672	49,793	69,414	42,620	1,688

Note: Summary figures for 1939 and 1940 are not available.

Definitions of Operation Types

Ａll aspects of RAF operations are littered with acronyms (abbreviations) and codenames, which are used in official records, including many of those used as source material for this book. An understanding of these codenames is essential and the following list gives those used by Fighter Command and their meanings as defined by Fighter Command. Not all were in use at the same time and not all were actually applied in the exclusive way that their definitions imply – sometimes it depended on the compiler of the record, especially with squadron Operational Record Books. *Circus, Escort, Ramrod* and *Rhubarb* are by far the commonest codenames to appear in the records.

Circus
Large-scale combined fighter and bomber operation designed with the intention of bringing the enemy fighters to action. In this type of operation powerful fighter forces are employed, and the radius of action is correspondingly limited. The comparatively small force of bombers is employed with the object of stinging the enemy fighters into action as well as doing material damage.

Cover
Fighter *Cover* implies the maintenance of air superiority in a given area for a given time in order to give freedom of action to a striking force.

Distill
Patrols against enemy minesweeping aircraft after RAF Bomber Command minelaying.

Diversion
A diversionary operation consisting of a smaller force of fighters, and possibly bombers if available, which is staged in conjunction with *Circus* operation.

Escort
The role of an *Escort* is the direct protection of the bombers. The term *Close Escort* may be introduced to indicate the formation allotted to maintain position in the immediate vicinity of the bombers.

Escort Cover
The cover of bombers and their escort from attack throughout an operation.

Feint
A small force of fighters, possibly accompanied by bombers, which approaches the enemy coast-line and withdraws before becoming engaged with enemy fighters. The purpose of

this operation is to maintain the enemy's defences at the highest possible state of preparedness.

Flower
Operations by night fighters in support of Bomber Command, in particular against enemy night fighters and night-fighter bases.

Forward Cover
The following-up of an operation and covering of the withdrawal of the bombers and their escort in the forward area.

Free Lance
The role of a *Free Lance* is to seek out and destroy enemy aircraft in an allotted area of operations.

Haunch
Offensive patrols against enemy aircraft operating from the Brest area.

Instep
Offensive fighter sweeps to intercept enemy seaplane or long-range land fighters interfering with the operations of Coastal Command aircraft in the Bay of Biscay.

Jim Crow
Shipping reconnaissance to find suitable targets for attack by fighters or fighter-bombers.

Mahmoud
Operations by night fighters against enemy night-fighters outside the radius of Bomber Command operations or on nights when Bomber Command was not operating.

Mosquito
Raids by single fighters or by a number of fighters in company up to Flight strength. (Changed to *Rhubarb* in January 1941).

Popular
Tactical reconnaissance of enemy-occupied territory to obtain information for the Army.

Ramrod
Operations in which fighters escort bombers, the primary aim of the operations being to destroy the target. These operations may be to extreme range, or provided for one reason or another with comparatively small fighter support. In such operations, owing to the limitations under which our fighters are working, the primary task is direct protection of the bombers, and general engagements with enemy fighters are not sought. If the operation in below 5,000 ft the code word should be prefixed by the word 'Low'.

Fighter Ramrod
This is a similar operation to *Ramrod* except that the fighters are escorting cannon fighters in lieu of bombers, against a selected target. Cannon attack only is employed and not bombs.

Ranger
Offensive patrols by day or night involving deep penetration of hostile territory with the object of destroying enemy bomber, reconnaissance, training and communications aircraft in rear areas, or disorganising enemy low-flying training, and of attacking enemy transport targets in rear areas.

Rear Cover
Cover the final phase of the withdrawal of the bombers and their escort to the United Kingdom.

Rhubarb
Small-scale harassing operations by day by fighters or fighter-bombers over enemy occupied territory primarily directed against enemy low-flying aircraft or ground targets.

Night Rhubarb
Similar operation by night.

Roadstead
Operations in which fighters escort bombers (including Hurricane bombers, Typhoons and Whirlwinds) in attacks on ships, whether at sea or in harbour.

Fighter Roadstead
A similar operation to a *Roadstead* except that fighters only are used without bombs.

Rodeo
Fighter offensive sweeps over enemy territory without bombers.

Serrate
Equipment for the detection of enemy AI night fighters and the operations in which *Serrate*-equipped fighters were used.

Target Cover
The establishment of air superiority over the target area a few minutes before the bombers and their escort and escort cover are due to arrive and subsequently to cover their withdrawal.

Fighter Command Battle Honours

Battle Honours

In keeping with military tradition the RAF issued Standards to its squadrons, although for a Standard to be awarded a squadron had to have been in existence for 25 years or to have 'earned the Sovereign's appreciation for especially outstanding operations.' The RAF also awarded Battle Honours and for a squadron that had a Standard, nominated Battle Honours, originally to a maximum of eight, could be displayed (emblazoned) on the Standard.

43 Squadron Standard showing a range of Battle Honours awarded whilst serving with Fighter Command.

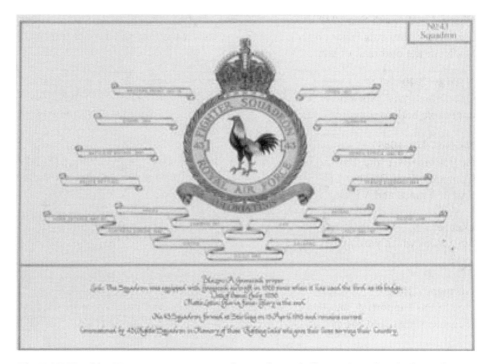

The RAF Heraldry Trust is creating a complete archive of all RAF Squadron badges, along with Battle Honour details.

There are a number of these Battle Honours that relate directly to the operations by Fighter Command. The list below includes the official title of the Battle Honour and its parameters.

Battle of Britain
Interception operations by fighter squadrons 1940 in the Battle of Britain (August to October 1940).

Home Defence 1940–1945
Interception operations after the Battle of Britain, in defence of Great Britain and Northern Ireland against enemy aircraft and flying bombs.

In addition to these two specific Battle Honours, Fighter Command squadrons were, or may have been, entitled to some of the more 'general' Honours, including:

France and Low Countries
Operations in France and Low Countries between the outbreak of war 1939–1940 and the Fall of France (3 September 1939 to 25 June 1940). Applicable both to squadrons based in France (the Air Component of the Advanced Air Striking Force) and to squadrons operating from home bases.

Dunkirk
Operations covering the evacuation of the British Expeditionary Force and the French from Dunkirk 26 May to 4 June 1940.

Channel and North Sea 1939–1945
Ship attack, anti-submarine and mining operations over the English Channel and North Sea from the outbreak of war to VE Day.

Norway 1940
Operations over Norway during the German invasion (9 April to 9 June 1940); applicable both to squadrons based in Norway and to those operating from home bases.

Biscay 1940–1945
Operations over the Bay of Biscay by aircraft of Coastal Command and Fighter Command, and Bomber Command aircraft loaned to Coastal Command, between the Fall of France and VE Day (25 June 1940 to 8 May 1945).

Dieppe
Squadrons which participated in the combined operations against Dieppe on 19 August 1942.

Normandy 1944
Operations supporting the Allied landings in Normandy and the establishment of the lodgement area, and the subsequent breakthrough (June to August 1944).

France and Germany 1944–1945
Operations over France, Belgium, Holland and Germany during the liberation of North-West Europe and the advance into the enemy's homeland, from the initiation of air action preparatory to the invasion of France to VE Day (April 1944 to 8 May 1945).

It is possible that in certain circumstances Fighter Command squadrons could have been awarded others such as **Atlantic 1939–1945** and **Biscay Ports 1940–1945**.
     The decision to award an Honour was made on the advice of the Air Historical Branch, which researched the records of the Squadron's operations and made an appropriate recommendation.

Medals

Fighter Command aircrew were eligible for the standard RAF gallantry and other medals, from the Victoria Cross to the British Empire Medal, and examples of all were indeed awarded, although there was only one Victoria Cross – won by Flt Lt E J Nicolson during the Battle of

Nicolson VC; 'During an engagement with the enemy near Southampton on 16th August, 1940 Flight Lieutenant Nicolson's aircraft was hit by four cannon shells, two of which wounded him whilst another set fire to the gravity tank. When about to abandon his aircraft owing to flames in the cockpit he sighted an enemy fighter. This he attacked and shot down, although as a result he displayed exceptional gallantry and disregard for the safety of his own life.'

A G 'Sailor' Malan was one of the Command's great fighter pilots and air leaders.

Britain (as recounted in the Operations chapter). The most frequent gallantry awards were the Distinguished Flying Cross (for officers) and the Distinguished Flying Medal (for other ranks), every one of which was well and truly earned by its recipient. A number of citations for these medals, and for the Distinguished Service Order (DSO) have been included in the Operations chapter.

A number of fighter pilots received multiple gallantry awards, including Bars for a second or even third award of the same medal. Adolph 'Sailor' Malan was one such pilot, receiving a DSO and two DFCs (DFC and Bar, usually written as DFC*) during his service with 74 Squadron. He was subsequently awarded a bar to his DSO as well as other decorations. The citations for awards were issued in an Air Ministry Bulletin (AMB) and published in the London Gazette. The citations for Malan were:

> *DFC: AMB 865 dated 9 June 1940: 'During 1940 this officer has led his flight, and on certain occasions his squadron, on 10 offensive patrols in Northern France. He has personally shot down two enemy aircraft and possibly three others. Flt Lt Malan has displayed great skill, courage and relentless determination in his attacks on the enemy'.*
>
> *Bar to DFC: AMB 1301 dated 7 August 1940: 'Since the end of May 1940 this officer has continued to lead his flight, and, on many occasions the squadron, in numerous successful engagements against the enemy. During the Dunkirk operation he shot down three enemy aircraft and assisted in destroying a further three. In June 1940 during a night attack by enemy aircraft he shot down two He 111s. His magnificent leadership, skill and courage have been largely responsible for the many successes obtained by his squadron.'*
>
> *DSO: AMB 2550 dated 19 December 1940, states: 'This officer has commanded his squadron with outstanding success over an intensive period of air operations and, by his brilliant leadership, skill and determination, has contributed largely to the successes obtained. Since early August 1940 the squadron has destroyed at least 84 enemy aircraft and damaged many more. Sqn Ldr Malan has himself destroyed at least 18 hostile aircraft and possibly another six.'*
>
> *Bar to DSO: The author has been unable to locate the details of this citation.*

Campaign Stars

RAF personnel were also entitled to Campaign Stars and there was one Clasp (a bar affixed to the ribbon of the medal) that applied to Fighter Command. This bar – 'Battle of Britain' – was worn on the 1939–1945 Star and was awarded to 'members of the crews of fighter aircraft who took part in the Battle of Britain, between 10 July and 31 October 1940.' Fighter Command personnel might also be entitled to three other Stars: the Air Crew Europe Star, the Atlantic Star and the France and Germany Star.

DFC to Sqn Ldr Barton of 85 Squadron.

German Night Attacks on Cities

Date	London		Industrial cities		Ports	
	Raids	*Tons HE*	*Raids*	*Tons HE*	*Raids*	*Tons HE*
Aug 1940	–	–	–	–	3	360
Sep 1940	22	5,359	–	–	–	–
Oct 1940	25	6,124	–	–	–	–
Nov 1940	13	2,724	4	1,038	6	1,127
Dec 1940	3	624	4	1,099	4	754
Jan 1941	2	299	1	111	4	535
Feb 1941	–	–	–	–	–	–
Mar 1941	2	233	1	122	8	1,826
Apr 1941	2	1,916	3	846	11	1,911
May 1941	1	711	3	434	8	1,746
Jun 1941	–	–	1	108	1	136
Jul 1941	–	–	–	–	1	174
Total	70		17		46	

Principal raids – by target, cities and ports 1940–1945

Target	1940	1941	1942	1943
London	62	8	–	5
Aberdeen	–	–	–	1
Bath	–	–	2	–
Belfast	–	2	–	–
Birmingham	4	6	4	–
Bristol	2	4	–	–
Canterbury	–	–	4	–
Cardiff	–	1	–	1
Chelmsford	–	–	–	3
Clydesdale	–	5	–	–
Colchester	–	–	2	–
Coventry	1	1	–	–
Cowes	–	–	1	–
Dover	–	–	1	–
Exeter	–	–	3	–
Grimsby	–	–	1	–
Hull	–	4	2	4
Ipswich	–	–	2	1
Kings Lynn	–	–	1	–
Lincoln	–	–	–	1

Principal raids – by target, cities and ports 1940–1945 (continued)

Target	1940	1941	1942	1943
Liverpool	6	5	–	–
Manchester	2	1	–	–
Middlesbrough	–	–	3	–
Newcastle	–	–	–	1
Norwich	–	–	5	4
Nottingham	–	1	–	–
Plymouth	1	7	–	4
Poole	–	–	2	–
Portland	–	–	1	–
Portsmouth	–	3	1	1
Sheffield	1	–	–	–
Southampton	4	1	2	1
Sunderland	–	–	1	2
Swansea	–	–	1	1
Weston S Mare	–	–	2	–
Weymouth	–	–	1	0
Yarmouth	–	–	–	1
York	–	–	1	

Index

Individual page references are not always included; for example, the Hurricane is referenced on most pages of the Operations chapter (to page 135) and the Spitfire for most of that chapter; indeed for all parts of this account referring to World War Two, the Spitfire is an almost page-by-page reference.

131 Sqn 186, 191, 213, 241, 242, 267, 329, 335, 335
132 Sqn 197, 267, 271, 331, 333
133 Sqn 205, 258, 267, 331
134 Sqn 210, 258, 331
136 Sqn 258
137 Sqn 70, 197, 205, 241, 242, 258, 279, 331, 333, 335
141 Sqn 16, 60, 78, 94, 149, 169–170, 191, 198, 207, 210, 262, 275, 278, 288, 301, 306, 309, 313, 324, 326, 327, 331, 332, 339, 341
145 Sqn 16, 58, 110, 242, 257, 262, 313, 323, 325, 328
151 Sqn 40, 47, 61, 130, 131, 191, 197, 198, 205, 250, 258, 275, 288, 297, 300, 301, 306, 313, 323, 325, 328, 331, 333, 335, 337, 340, 341
152 Sqn 24, 188, 189, 191, 205, 253, 267, 313, 324, 327, 331, 339
153 Sqn 275, 278, 297, 331
154 Sqn 205, 267, 330
157 Sqn 66, 175–177, 177, 197, 287, 288, 330, 333
164 Sqn 191, 258, 267, 332, 337
165 Sqn 191, 241, 242, 267, 333, 335, 337
167 Sqn 205, 267, 333
174 Sqn 191, 197, 258, 330, 332
175 Sqn 151, 191, 258, 285, 329, 332
176 Sqn 241, 242
181 Sqn 205, 285, 333
182 Sqn 258, 285, 333
183 Sqn 198, 205, 291, 333, 337
184 Sqn 191, 258, 332
186 Sqn 258, 267
193 Sqn 191, 332
195 Sqn 186, 332
197 Sqn 210, 335
198 Sqn 210, 333
213 Sqn 187, 188, 189, 191, 213, 250, 258, 313, 323, 325, 328
214 Sqn 88
219 Sqn 9, 123, 130, 185, 197, 210, 242, 262, 278, 288, 301, 313, 324, 326, 328, 330, 335, 335
222 Sqn 16, 91, 197, 198, 205, 210, 262, 267, 291, 297, 305, 309, 313, 323, 325, 328, 330, 335, 340, 341

223 Sqn 66
225 Sqn 257, 324
229 Sqn 16, 115, 117, 186, 205, 258, 313, 323, 325, 327, 335
232 Sqn 210, 211, 213, 258, 313, 326, 328
234 Sqn 16, 91, 187, 188, 189, 191, 197, 213, 242, 262, 267, 292, 294, 297, 313, 324, 325, 327, 329, 335, 335, 337
235 Sqn 313, 323
236 Sqn 313, 323
238 Sqn 188, 191, 258, 267, 313, 325, 327
239 Sqn 258
242 Sqn 115, 135, 137, 197, 201, 205, 258, 262, 267, 309, 313, 324, 325, 327, 341
243 Sqn 267
245 Sqn 16, 91, 132, 133, 134, 205, 210, 213, 254, 258, 296, 297, 305, 313, 324, 326, 328, 329, 335, 339
246 Sqn 186
247 Sqn 186, 191, 198, 198, 253, 258, 291, 297, 300, 305, 309, 313, 327, 329, 332, 339, 341
248 Sqn 175, 313, 323
249 Sqn 113–114, 117, 119, 135, 137, 188, 207, 210, 219–220, 258, 267, 299, 313, 326
253 Sqn 17–18, 21, 115, 117, 148, 198, 205, 210, 213, 219, 258, 301, 314, 323, 326, 328, 331, 339
254 Sqn 323
255 Sqn 52, 129, 130, 131, 134, 148, 186, 205, 258, 275, 278, 328, 329, 332
256 Sqn 47, 186, 191, 258, 278, 327, 329, 332
257 Sqn 74, 115, 117, 150, 153, 165, 191, 198, 205, 258, 267, 297, 305, 309, 314, 328, 329, 332, 339, 341
258 Sqn 186, 327
259 Sqn 197, 327
260 Sqn 213, 328
263 Sqn 15, 16, 91, 99–100, 125–127, 139–140, 141, 191, 198, 210, 253, 258, 278, 279, 297, 305, 309, 314, 323, 326, 327, 329, 332, 335, 339, 342